Anti-Black Prejudice in America

Its Roots in Tribalism,
Religion,
and Sexuality

ANDERS EKLOF

ISBN 978-1-7375373-1-1 (paperback)
ISBN 978-1-7375373-2-8 (hardback)
ISBN 978-1-7375373-0-4 (eBook)

Printed in the United States of America

Keynote

Playboy: Do you subscribe to the common segregationist belief that Negroes have lower standards of morality than whites?

Shelton: Yes.

Playboy: Do you also share the conviction that Negroes are endowed with larger sexual organs, greater lasting power, and more active libido than whites?

Shelton: I do.

Playboy: Do you base that belief on firsthand knowledge?

Shelton: Certainly not. But scientific texts I have read show that clearly.

Playboy: What texts?

Shelton: I can't name them offhand.

Playboy: You announced in a speech not long ago that Negroes are responsive to the phase of the moon. Just what did you mean by that?

Shelton: Our research and studies have found that there is more stirring and movement of the Negro when they have a full moon. They show an increase in the rate of crime and sex during the full moon.

(Alabama Grand Dragon of the Ku Klux Klan Robert Shelton, interviewed by *Playboy* magazine, August 1965.)

Contents

Keynote iii

Introduction 1

Part One: Tribe and Prejudice 3

    Humans as tribal beings 3

    The Peopling of the Americas 5

    The Indian Removal Act and growth of North American slavery 7

    The role of tribalism and racial prejudice in conquest and enslavement 8

    The role of instincts in forming our religions, values, and morals 9

    The evolutionary aspects of religious morality 12

    The emotions of prejudice and our attempts to cope with them 14

Part Two: Deep Historical Background 17

    The beginnings of North American slavery 17

    The growth of racial prejudice 22

    The financial value of slaves and slave labor 23

    The changing view of slavery leads to Civil War 24

    Reconstruction and the beginning of Jim Crow 28

    Lynching as a public spectacle and expression of sadistic gratification 33

    The religious aspects of lynching 42

Part Three: Deep Roots, Bitter Fruit 46

    Introduction 46

    Justifications for slavery involve picturing blacks as inherently inferior 47

    The retention of African beliefs and customs among the slaves 49

    White reactions to the customs and appearance of African slaves 51

    Interracial sexual contacts in the slave states 53

    Interracial sexual contacts in the North 59

    The morally corrosive effects of slavery 59

    The end of slavery creates fear, hatred, and the creation of Jim Crow 60

    The superior sexual power of blacks becomes official medical doctrine 62

Part Four: Sex and Sin in America 67
    Introduction 67
    The uniqueness of American prejudice against those of African ancestry 68
    The evolution of moral attitudes regarding sexual desire and activities 70
    The apostles of prudishness 73
    Prudishness becomes enshrined in law 80
    The first rumblings of liberalization begin in the 1920s 84
    Interracial and other "unnatural" sex remain taboo 87

Part Five: The Eugenics Movement. 91
    The European Origins of Eugenics 91
    Eugenics Comes to America 93
    Charles Davenport Takes Command 95
    Theory Is Put into Practice 98
    Eugenics Has a Resurgence in Europe 104
    Eugenics in the Future 108

Part Six: America Enters the Twentieth Century 110
    Introduction 110
    The trend to regret and disparage the Reconstruction era 111
    Riots and massacres of blacks 1880 - 1930 114
    America adjusts to rapid world-political and technological changes 117
    Once more, America seeks to create equality for blacks 119
    The importance of "color" in the Jim Crow era 123
    Despite Southern beliefs and wishes, racial integration begins 127

Part Seven: The '60s—Another American Revolution 130
  Introduction...130
  Chapter 1. The '60s Are Dawning: "Whole Lotta Shakin' Goin' On" 133
    America in the immediate post-WWII era 133
    The arrival of "rock and roll" 135
  Chapter 2. The Civil Rights Movement Takes Off..139
    The Supreme Court 1954 Brown vs Board of Education decision 139
    The murder of Emmett Till 140
    The Montgomery, Alabama bus boycott 144
    The Little Rock Central High School integration controversy 147
    The civil rights movement searches for new approaches 154
  Chapter 3. An Old World Order Is Shattered, and a New America Begins to Emerge 157
    The Cold War intensifies, the election of John Kennedy 157
    The Freedom Bus Rides 158
    Robert Kennedy asks for a cool-off period in the civil rights efforts 164
    Segregationists appeal to religion and anti-communism 166

James Meredith registers at "Ole Miss" 168

The spotlight falls on Alabama, and the civil rights movement stalls 172

The emergence of Malcolm X 174

Chapter 4. The Days of Hardest Trials and Greatest Victories 178

The 1963 Birmingham riots 178

George Wallace is forced to yield at the University of Alabama 181

The South responds with violence 182

The 1963 march on Washington 184

The 1963 Birmingham church bombing 187

The assassination of John Kennedy 190

The murder of Chaney, Goodman, and Schwerner 192

Reopening the 1964 murder cases 195

Chapter 5. Political Controversy and Major Legislative Victories 196

The Republican presidential election campaign of 1964 196

The 1964 Democratic National Convention in Atlantic City 197

The Gulf of Tonkin incident 201

The build-up to the Selma to Montgomery march 203

Bloody Sunday 205

Turn-around Tuesday 208

The march to Montgomery and the murder of Viola Liuzzo 210

Chapter 6. Frustration Turns Violent 213

The Watts riot of 1965 213

Martin Luther King in Chicago 215

James Meredith is shot during the March Against Fear 216

Stokely Carmichael and the push for "black power" 217

Black frustration flares up in urban riots 218

Julian Bond is elected to the Georgia legislature 221

The FBI responds to the rise of the Black Panther Party 222

Chapter 7. The Civil Rights Movement Broadens 225

The splits in society widen and deepen 225

The "Summer of Love" 226

The women's liberation movement gains momentum 229

Native American, Chicano, and Puerto Rican groups enter the fray 232

The Gay Liberation movement steps out of the closet 236

The laws against interracial intimacy and marriage are overturned 238

Atheists score a court victory 240

Martin Luther King speaks out against the Vietnam War 241

The 1967 Newark and Detroit riots 242

Martin Luther King broadens his views 245

Chapter 8. "Hell No, We Won't Go!" 247

The protests against the Vietnam war take center stage 247

The election campaigns heat up 249

Chapter 9. The Cities Explode in Riots, and the Nation Elects a Law-and-Order President............252

The cities erupt in fiery chaos when MLK is assassinated 252

The assassination of Robert Kennedy 255

The Poor People's Campaign 256

Conservative Americans flock to Richard Nixon 258

The 1968 Democratic National Convention becomes a political disaster 260

The 1968 general election becomes a blow to the civil rights movement...............................264

Divided opinions on the meaning of the 1968 elections 266

Attempts to end the war fail; young people lose faith in America..268

Chapter 10. Crash and Burn: The '60s Revolution Dies in Bitter Disillusionment 270

The Vietnam War becomes an ugly horror instead of a noble cause 270

Further left-wing radicalization of white youth...272

National guard troops shoot and kill demonstrating students..274

Nixon shows his authoritarian character 277

The Angela Davis case 278

The Attica prison uprising 282

The Pentagon Papers reveal administration lies and deceptions...283

The Watergate case, Nixon's resignation and the end of the war 285

Playboy Magazine and the moral rebellion of "the '60s" 287

Part Eight: The stubborn residue of racism in America 291

Facing our responsibility...291

Remaining racial injustice 293

Reparations: A century and a half late, trillions of dollars short?.....................................297

"Doing the right thing" 300

Index...305

Bibliography...311

Table of Figures

Figure 1 Diagram of a slave ship cargo hold (1854) 17

Figure 2 Oluale Kossola, a.k.a. Cudjo Lewis 20

Figure 3 Matilda McCrear 21

Figure 4. The lynching of Henry Smith in Paris, Texas 1893 35

Figure 5. The lynching of Thomas Shipp and Abram Smith, Marion, Indiana, 1930.........36

Figure 6. The lynching of Will Brown in Omaha, Nebraska, 1919 37

Figure 7. A crowd gathered to see Jesse Washington about to be burned, Waco, Texas, 1916. 37

Figure 8. The charred remains of Jesse Washington. (a "nigger barbecue" in Southern lingo)......38

Figure 9. Lynching victims such as Rubin Stacy were often left hanging for a long time as public
warning examples. July 19, 1935, Fort Lauderdale, Florida. 39

Figure 10. Witch trial. 43

Figure 11 The Reverend Sylvester Graham (1794 - 1851) 74

Figure 12. Dr. John Harvey Kellogg (1852 - 1943) 78

Figure 13. Anthony Comstock (1844 - 1915) 81

Figure 14 Charles Davenport 96

Figure 15 Harry Laughlin..100

Figure 16. 1916 KKK rally 113

Figure 17. KKK rallies 30,000 in Washington D.C. 1925 113

Figure 18 The aftermath of the Tulsa massacre 115

Figure 19 Walter White..125

Figure 20. W.E.B. Du Bois..126

Figure 21 Emmett "Bobo" Till at his home in Chicago 141

Figure 22 Emmett Till in his casket, with his jaw crushed, one eyeball lost, and a bullet hole in
his right temple, 1955. The corpse decayed after spending days in the Tallahatchie River......142

Figure 23 J. W. Milam (left) and Roy Bryant smiling at their trial for the murder of Emmett Till. 143

Figure 24. Damaged riverside memorial marker for Emmett Till..144

Figure 25. Rosa Parks arrested, Montgomery 1955...145

Figure 26. Anti-integration demonstration in front of the State Capitol Building in Little Rock,
Arkansas...149

Figure 27. Members of the Arkansas National Guard block the "Little Rock Nine" from entering
Little Rock Central High School, September 1957. 150

Figure 28. Elizabeth Eckford jeered and threatened by the crowd at Little Rock Central High
School, September 1957. 151

Figure 29. The Little Rock Nine escorted by members of the 101st Airborne........................151

Figure 30. School integration protest in Nashville, Tennessee, 1957 152

Figure 31. Sit-in at a Woolworth lunch counter, Greensboro, North Carolina February 1, 1960 155

Figure 32. Firebombed Greyhound bus outside Anniston, Alabama, May 14, 1961 160
Figure 33. James Meredith...169
Figure 34. Governor Ross Barnett of Mississippi at a political rally, 1962 170
Figure 35. Federal marshals arrive at Ole Miss, September 30, 1962..171
Figure 36. Burned-out cars on the campus of Ole Miss, September 30, 1962....................................172
Figure 37. George Wallace on the campaign trail...173
Figure 38. Students protest against school integration, Alabama 1963...174
Figure 39. Malcolm X speaking at a Harlem civil rights meeting, May 14, 1963. 177
Figure 40. Police dogs attacking a demonstrator in Birmingham, May 3, 1963. 179
Figure 41. Fire hoses battering young demonstrators, Birmingham, May 3, 1963.............................180
Figure 42. Governor Wallace (*left*) confronts Deputy Attorney General Katzenbach (*right*) at the
        University of Alabama at Tuscaloosa, June 11, 1963...181
Figure 43. Medgar Evers, Mississippi NAACP official, assassinated June 12, 1963 183
Figure 44. John Lewis at an SNCC meeting in April 1964. 185
Figure 45. Dr. Martin Luther King Jr., delivering his "I Have a Dream" speech,
        Washington, DC, August 28, 1963..187
Figure 46. The four girls killed in the 1963 church bombing in Birmingham...................................188
Figure 47. Damage inside the Birmingham church where the bombing victims died. 189
Figure 48. Damage to windows and cars at the 1963 Birmingham church bombing...........................189
Figure 49. Lee Harvey Oswald shot by Jack Ruby, Dallas, November 24, 1963 190
Figure 50. James Chaney, Andrew Goodman, and Michael Schwerner. 193
Figure 51. The bodies of civil rights workers Chaney, Goodman, and Schwerner were found on
        August 4, 1964. 194
Figure 52. Barry Goldwater, campaigning in the South, 1964. (Note the "Democrats for
        Goldwater" sign.)...197
Figure 53. Fanny Lou Hamer, a powerful and inspiring speaker, 1964...199
Figure 54. The USS Maddox..202
Figure 55. Bloody Sunday—the assault on demonstrators in Selma, Alabama, March 7, 1965. 206
Figure 56. Amelia Boynton, beaten unconscious at the Edmund Pettus Bridge, March 7, 1965. 207
Figure 57. "Turnaround Tuesday," Selma, March 9, 1965..209
Figure 58. The aftermath of the Watts riot, Los Angeles, August 1965. 213
Figure 59. Stokely Carmichael speaks at the University of California, Berkeley, 1966.......................218
Figure 60. SNCC member and Georgia legislator Julian Bond, 1967...222
Figure 61. Huey Newton, co-founder (with Bobby Seale) of the Black Panther Party, 1967. 223
Figure 62. The FBI to MLK "suicide letter." 224
Figure 63. Hippie gathering during the Summer of Love, San Francisco, 1967. 227
Figure 64. Gloria Steinem at the typewriter. 231
Figure 65. The Stonewall riot in New York City, June 28, 1969 238
Figure 66. Mildred and Richard Loving, 1967...239
Figure 67. The Detroit riots of July 23–24, 1967. 244
Figure 68. Buddhist monk setting himself on fire to protest the Vietnam War, 1963.......................249
Figure 69. Baltimore in flames in the wake of Martin Luther King Jr.'s assassination, April 5, 1968. 254
Figure 70. Soldiers and firefighters in the aftermath of rioting in Washington, DC, April 1968. 254
Figure 71. Burning buildings on Chicago's West Side, April 5, 1968. 255
Figure 72. The Resurrection City shantytown during the Poor People's Campaign, National
        Mall, Washington, DC, June 1968..257

Figure 73. Cleanup on the Mall after Resurrection City, June 1968.....................................258
Figure 74. The media-dubbed "police riot" at the Democratic Party convention in Chicago, 1968.........262
Figure 75. The "Battle of Michigan Avenue," Chicago, August 28, 1968...............................263
Figure 76. A crowd of hundreds of thousands at Woodstock, Bethel, New York, August 1969. 269
Figure 77. Vietnamese children fleeing from a napalm attack 271
Figure 78. Some of the victims at My Lai, March 16, 1968 271
Figure 79. Weatherman antiwar march, 1969...274
Figure 80. Ohio National Guardsmen firing at Kent State University students, May 4, 1970 275
Figure 81. Wounded student at Kent State University, where four students were shot dead 275
Figure 82. Firearm damage, Alexander Hall, Jackson State College, May 15, 1970......................276
Figure 83. Angela Davis, an advocate of communism, black power, and radical feminism, 1972. 279
Figure 84. Casualties collected following the Attica prison riot, September 1971....................282
Figure 85. Hugh Hefner and *Playboy* bunnies, 1966..289
Figure 86. Jennifer Jackson, the first black *Playboy* centerfold 289
Figure 87. Robert M. Shelton, KKK Imperial Wizard. 290

Introduction

The United States of America is a nation founded on the principle of the equal right of each person to life, liberty, and the pursuit of happiness. The brotherhood of all men is the official creed of the secular idealism that motivated the American Revolution and also of the dominant religious faith of the nation. Still, the nation has institutionalized the oppression of millions of innocent people simply because of their race. It has deprived them of their liberty, even their lives. In innumerable humiliating ways, it has blocked the path in their pursuit of happiness. Wondering about the reason, the Southern white writer, educator, and activist Lillian Smith (1897–1966) wrote in her book *Killers of the Dream*:

> How can one idea like segregation become so hypnotic a thing that it binds a whole people together, good, bad, strong, weak, ignorant and learned, sensitive, obtuse, psychotic and sane, making them one as only a common worship or a deeply shared fear can do? Why has the word taken on the terrors of taboo and the sanctity of religion?...The answer surely is worth searching for.[1]

Anti-Black Prejudice in America: Its Roots in Tribal Instinct, Religion and Sexuality is the result of such a search. It reveals that the causes of anti-black prejudice are many and varied and have some roots in innate human instincts of a tribal, religious and sexual nature. They have no supernatural origin or justification. Instead, the answer turns out to lie in the deepest recesses of our human psyche. Through the insights of psychology, we can discover our natural instincts and our true motivations, even the source and nature of our superstitions, prejudices, and religions.

Sigmund Freud (1856–1939), an Austrian physician, was taught to diagnose sickness as having a physical cause. Failing to find one in so many patients, Freud was left to conclude that there was, in fact, a nonphysical cause of the epidemic of what was often called "hysteria," and which in its most serious forms could manifest itself in severe physical and mental symptoms and disabilities. Freud theorized that the sexual drive was the most powerful motivator of almost all human ambitions and activities, and that the suppression of it and the perception of it as shameful and sinful inevitably caused serious emotional problems. The internal emotional strains arising from the strict suppression of sexual feelings produced mental disorders in many people, especially women, who were the most affected by erotophobic morality. The manifestations could rise to the level where they included severe and debilitating physical problems. His conclusion led to the revolutionary breakthrough that came to be known as psychology.

---

[1] Lillian Smith *Killers of the Dream* (New York: W. W. Norton Company, 1994) pp 79, 80

Like all pioneers in a radically new field of thought, Freud has been the subject of derision, doubt, opposition, and vilification, and not all his theories have become accepted by modern psychologists. In America, 'behaviorism" has become a widely accepted competing theory. It was pioneered by John B. Watson (1878 – 1958) in America and Ivan P. Pavlov (1849 – 1936) in Russia. It developed from experiments on the behavior of animals, establishing that responses to a stimulus can be learned by "conditioning," a form of training. Burrhus Frederic Skinner (B. F. Skinner, 1904-1990) developed the theory further with what was termed "operant conditioning" and popularized the term "behaviorism." To an extent, behaviorism turns the traditional psychology upside down. Instead of seeing innate drives as the fundamental motivators of feelings and actions, it sees those responses as learned by teachings and conditioning, and the associated feelings and physical responses as being the results.

The term "Pavlov's dogs" is often used to describe how individuals can become conditioned to respond in a predetermined manner to a particular stimulus even though the stimulus would not instinctively produce that response. Therefore, behaviorism sees habits and learned values as the dominant sources of prejudices and gives a much-reduced role to innate instincts. But the core of Freud's teachings, that the sexual drive is a natural, fundamental and in the end irrepressible side of human nature, has stood the test of time. There is no irreconcilable contradiction between the classical, Freudian psychology and the behaviorism favored by American psychologists. Just like the question of "nature or nurture," there is a part of the truth in both. Freud revels the innate, instinctive, "nature" part of the explanation whereas B.F. Skinner describes the outer forms into which our instincts have become channeled by "nurture," our learned moral and aesthetic values. Together, the two viewpoints hold the explanation for our prejudices and for the psychological problems that occur when "nature" steers us one way, and "nurture" steers us the other.

In Freud's time, the moral/emotional climate of Viennese society was such that Freud found ample support there for his theory. The culture in the United States was not much different from that of Vienna of the same era, and most of Freud's thinking would be valid if applied to bourgeoise America during that same time. Today, our perception of sexuality and our moral judgments regarding it are generally much more liberal and there is no longer the same levels of shame, guilt, and fear of divine punishment associated with it. Consequently, emotional problems brought on by suppressed sexual impulses are now far less frequent than what Freud observed in his time.

Our beliefs make us form the society in which we live, and our thoughts and feelings are our response, both instinctive and learned, to that society and our lives in it. There is no way one can separate our beliefs, thoughts, feelings and values from their historical context. Therefore, the understanding of prejudice must rely on a good knowledge of historical facts. In a whirling current of historical events, all events of which we are aware affect the overall experience of living in society. Even if they do not all seem immediately relevant, they all help determine both the contents and the emotional impact of prejudicial beliefs. Things that distract from them are also part of the history of the prejudices and affect their development.

Part One: Tribe and Prejudice

Humans as tribal beings

Humans are innately social beings. For hundreds of thousands of years, the common ancestors of all modern humans roamed the plains and mountainous forests of East Africa. They lived in social groups similar to those of our near relatives, the chimpanzees, and gorillas. For perhaps several million years further back in the distant past, we evolved in small groups of closely-knit friends and relatives: a type of society we term a tribe.

The defining feature of a small tribe is the emotional bond that exists on the individual personal level between members of the tribe. They all know one another by sight and name, and many have family relationships by blood or marriage.

In large tribes, the relationship may be more distant. Then the tribe invents metaphysical, spiritual, and mythical relationships that might refer to a common historical origin or the worship of the same god. Such a belief system has the effect of extending the sense of tribal belonging to all members. The sense of belonging fosters a strong sense of loyalty toward the tribe as a whole, not just to the members individually. The bond and the loyalty are positive features for the tribe, making it strong during adversity. The adversity might be hardship caused by capricious nature but might also be competition from other tribes.

Unfortunately, the tribal instinct also contains the tendency to see members of other tribes as "the others" who are on the outside, somehow different and alien. The tribal instinct does not produce feelings of fellowship toward members of other tribes. Instead, it usually produces mistrust and even outright hostility. While humans are social beings within the context of each tribe, each tribe as a unit is often extremely aggressive and murderous in its dealings with other tribes. To go to war and to rejoice in bloody victories over one's enemies is as natural as grieving over fallen friends and relatives. The seeming moral inconsistency of our feelings is due to the tribal instinct, and it seems inconsistent only now when we no longer live in isolated, homogeneous tribal units.

Our religious heritage still shows strong remains of tribal values, including having callous and hostile attitudes toward outsiders. For example, the Old Testament of the Bible tells the story of a confederation of tribes called the Israelites, to whom God gave the command "Thou shalt not kill." Then God commanded them to conquer other tribes and cities in the Promised Land, and to kill all their members without mercy: men, women, and children alike (Deuteronomy 2:33–34; 3:2–6; 7:2). Killing the outsiders did not fall under the ban against killing.

Holy war is a long tradition upheld in particular by members of monotheistic religions who ascribe their moral rules to the commands of a strict and jealous deity. In these cases, loyalty to the one god is a tribal bond among those who worship the same god according to the same rules. If you change the rules, then you are a heretic and deserve to die. Race or nationality are relatively recent notions among humans but have come to rival religious beliefs as tribal boundary markers.

In most tribes, it has historically been a practice to severely punish or kill members of the tribe who have "sinned" in some way against the cultural traditions of the tribe. Such sins typically include a showing of disrespect for tribal totems, taboos, or deities. The story of the Israelites is one of constant bloodshed, which the chroniclers sometimes reviled, sometimes glorified, depending on whose ox is gored—to use a biblical metaphor. Examples abound of violent intertribal rivalry and mass murder with the object of preserving the purity of the tribal faith. (See, for example, Exodus 32:27–29.)

These stories illustrate one important point: *Tribal formations in themselves tend to create a disregard for the rights and welfare of nonmembers and to produce hostility to those who deviate from the social, religious, and moral norms of the tribe. That is a natural tendency of human beings that allows negative prejudices to develop.*

It is in our nature to judge others against the values of our tribe. We develop negative and stereotypical attitudes toward members of other tribes that do not quite measure up according to these values. Those attitudes are much the result of indoctrination by elders in the tribe, but we are not completely clean slates at birth: we are genetically predisposed to be suspicious of those we see as outside our tribe, or of any member who somehow represents a threat to the cohesiveness of the tribe. This predisposition has been an evolutionary advantage that is reinforced by indoctrination. We have an innate tendency to classify people as "us" as opposed to "them" and to feel loyalty to members of our own tribe while we have little or no empathy for those of other tribes. In the competition for food, territory, and other resources, different tribes of our ancestors often came into violent conflict with each other. Intertribal warfare has always been part of human life everywhere in the world. As a result, wariness toward individuals with unfamiliar appearance increased one's probability of survival. On the other hand, humans seem to have no instinctive bar against victorious warriors taking for wives and concubines women from "enemy" tribes whose men they have slain. This practice helped reduce the destructive effects of inbreeding.

It is not surprising that history abounds with examples of the almost unbelievable cruelty of human beings toward one another. In almost every case this has been the result of an emotional dissociation between victim and perpetrator. Instincts that prevent us from killing or injuring members of our own tribe are inoperative when we deal with people we perceive to be outside our tribe and thus present a danger to us.

Our emotional dissociation from members of other tribes is usually due to some visible or imagined innate difference, or to such differences in customs and beliefs that are perceived as disrespect for one's God and hallowed traditions. The differences act as boundary markers for our tribal territories. They help us bond with our native tribe and make us unite against those on the other side of the markers.

Our modern societies have grown larger and more complex than the tightly knit groups of our nomadic hunter-gatherer ancestors. Because our instincts evolved over hundreds of thousands of generations, we still have that deeply ingrained tendency to feel and act in ways that make sense in a tribal context. Humans are a predator species; we need to kill to feed ourselves, and we have not hesitated to kill those who are our competitors in our hunt for food or territory.

Religious faiths, racism, and nationalism have extended the natural tribal boundaries to encompass large groups that still tend to exclude outsiders from the bonds of loyalty. An intense hatred of the other side usually fuels religious, racial, and nationalistic wars and manifests itself in appalling callousness and cruelty against the enemy. Enemies, savages, infidels, "those people"—all are fair game. Such tribalism manifested itself in what happened in the Western Hemisphere following the arrival there of Europeans.

The Peopling of the Americas

The general consensus among historians has traditionally been that the aboriginal population of the Americas arrived via Alaska as several waves of immigrants from Asia some time between 13,000 and 18,000 years ago, and that Europeans first set foot in the Western hemisphere when Columbus "sailed the ocean blue" in 1492.

It has since been shown conclusively that Norsemen ("Vikings") from their small settlement on Greenland preceded Columbus by almost 500 years, though their presence in North America did not become permanent.

Recent finds of stone arrowheads and tools in a rock shelter in Chiquihuite Cave in Mexico provide compelling evidence that humans arrived in the Americas much earlier than previously thought. The finds have been dated to as early as 33,000 BC, more than twice the age of the previous finds of human presence in the Western hemisphere.[2] No human remains have yet been found, therefore, no DNA evidence has been available to give a clue where those humans came from and how closely they are related to the later native American population.

No traces of Viking DNA have been found among native Americans. The brief Viking presence in North America had no measurable effect on its population, although Native American mitochondrial DNA among the Viking descendants on Iceland shows that at least one native American woman was brought to Iceland.

In contrast, when the Spanish and Portuguese arrived five hundred years later, they had an impact of calamitous proportions. Historians estimate that as many as fifty million might have perished within the subsequent century, mostly as victims of new contagious diseases. Massive epidemics of smallpox, measles, whooping cough, chicken pox, bubonic plague, typhus, diphtheria, cholera, and malaria ravaged populations that had no natural immunity. Extensive research using all modern tools, including DNA statistics among

---

[2] Ardelean, C.F., Becerra-Valdivia, L., Pedersen, M.W. *et al.* Evidence of human occupation in Mexico around the Last Glacial Maximum. *Nature* (2020). https://doi.org/10.1038/s41586-020-2509-0

surviving ethnic Native Americans and the mixture in them in present local people of European and African origins groups, have led to the grim conclusion that between eighty and ninety-five percent of the Native American population was decimated within the first one hundred and fifty years following the arrival of the Europeans. The population of Mexico was in the range of fifteen million when the Spaniards first arrived there. A century later it was one tenth of that. Within fifty years following the arrival of Columbus, the native Taino population of the island of Hispaniola was virtually extinct.[3]

Few of the invaders saw any reason to feel guilty about that. The massive death tolls in epidemics of new diseases were not inflicted intentionally by them, the argument went, but must be ascribed to the hand of God, a sign of divine approval of their conquest. Even today, most Americans refuse to apply the term genocide to the near extinction of the indigenous population caused by the arrival in the Western Hemisphere of Europeans with firearms, new pathogens, and superior technology, in the words of Pulitzer Prize winner Jared Diamond, in *Guns, Germs, and Steel*.[4]

But the conquerors themselves were not just passive observers of the horrendous mass destruction of native lives and cultures. There was clear intent behind many of the actions to expand settler land and wealth at the expense of the natives. Jeffrey Ostler, in "Genocide and American Indian History," makes the following point:

> However one resolves the question of genocide in American Indian history, it is important to recognize that European and U.S. settler colonial projects unleashed massively destructive forces on Native peoples and communities. These include violence resulting directly from settler expansion, intertribal violence (frequently aggravated by colonial intrusions), enslavement, disease, alcohol, loss of land and resources, forced removals, and assaults on tribal religion, culture, and language.[5]

In time, the indigenous populations developed some degree of resistance to the new diseases and survived, albeit in much smaller numbers. On the North American continent, a sizeable "Indian" population was present in the Southeast, on land that became the states of Alabama, Florida, Georgia, Mississippi, and Tennessee. They included the so-called "Five Civilized Tribes" of the Cherokee, Choctaw, Chickasaw, Creek, and Seminole tribes. Christian missionaries and early European settlers in the region had established friendly relations with the indigenous population, and by the early 1800s, the "civilized" tribes had adopted European customs and had integrated into the society of the growing European population of the region. They had become successful farmers who lived in permanent houses rather than tents, they had adopted the Christian faith, and had established schools where their children learned to read and write their native languages. Most also spoke English and were very deeply rooted in their native soils, where, according to

---

[3] Nathan Nunn and Nancy Qian, "*The Columbian Exchange: A History of Disease, Food, and Ideas*" (Journal of Economic Perspectives – Volume 24, no. 2 (Spring 2010):165)

[4] Jared Diamond, "*Guns, Germs and Steel; The Fates of Human Societies*" (New York: W. W. Norton & Company, 1997).

[5] [3] Jeffrey Ostler, "Genocide and American Indian History" *Oxford Research Encyclopedia of American History*", http://americanhistory.oxfordre.com/view/10.1093/acrefore/9780199329175.001.0001/acrefore-9780199329175-e-3

their tribal mythology, they had lived since the creation of the earth, and where all their ancestors were buried. They were what we today may call "ecologists," having deep respect for nature and appreciation of its beauty.

In the heat of the Southern sun, work in the fields was a hard, tedious, and unpleasant task for which the Europeans thought themselves poorly suited. Efforts to use American Natives for forced labor were generally unsuccessful. The Spanish and Portuguese conquerors of Central and South America soon decided to import massive numbers of captured Africans for use as slave labor on their sugar cane plantations on the Caribbean islands and in Central and South America. The English settlers in North America eventually decided to follow the example of the Spanish, Portuguese and other colonial powers.

In 1619, the first black slaves arrived in what was to become the United States. For the first century and a half, the number of people of African descent grew slowly in North America and was confined mainly to slave status. They were utilized as labor in growing rice and tobacco in the East Coast region, cotton and sugar cane further west and south.

The Indian Removal Act and growth of North American slavery

The invention of the cotton gin by Eli Whitney in 1794 surely escaped notice by the native population of the South at the time. But it would have grave consequences for them and eventually also for millions of people of African ancestry. The machine greatly speeded up the separation of cotton fibers from their husks. That made the picking of cotton rather than the ginning of it the bottleneck in the production of cotton destined for the weaving of cotton cloth.

The climate and soil of the South proved very favorable for the growing of this valuable crop, and it soon became obvious to adventurous European immigrants that there was a fortune to be made in cotton if one could obtain land to grow it. The land became an extremely valuable commodity, attracting large numbers of European immigrants with dreams of fortune. The quick success of cotton growing in the area spelled the end of the peaceful coexistence between immigrants and the native population. Pressure began to build to confiscate land belonging to the native tribes and establish cotton plantations owned by European immigrants, who were mostly of English and Scottish extraction.

The 1829 discovery of gold on the land belonging to the Cherokee tribe in Georgia aggravated the situation. The fate of the American Natives in the region was sealed. In 1830, the American government established the Indian Removal Act that authorized military force to evict the "Indians" from the region and allocate the land to white settlers. The massive removal effort became known as "The Trail of Tears."

During the 1830s, approximately one hundred thousand American Natives were forced from their homes, many at gunpoint, leaving their land and most of their belongings behind. Their connections to their ancient homes, deeply felt and nourished by religious beliefs, were severed. They were conducted, mostly on foot, to areas west of the Mississippi River. The conditions during the removal were harsh, and about fifteen thousand died of exhaustion, starvation, and exposure on the slow, arduous journey. But they were just Indians, and their fate did not weigh heavily on the conscience of those members of Congress who voted to create the Indian Removal Act. Nor did it concern the new inhabitants of the area, many of whom became wealthy and powerful men as owners of cotton plantations.

A few influential individuals raised their voices against the removal policy, but to no avail. Among them was Alexis de Tocqueville, the French philosopher who was in general a great admirer of the new, revolutionary nation of the United States. In his travels through the new nation, he observed some of the 1831 forced removal of Choctaw Indians in Tennessee. He commented on his observation:

> In the whole scene there was an air of ruin and destruction, something which betrayed a final and irrevocable adieu; one couldn't watch without feeling one's heart wrung. The Indians were tranquil, but sombre and taciturn. There was one who could speak English and of whom I asked why the Chactas were leaving their country. "To be free," he answered, could never get any other reason out of him. We ... watch the expulsion ... of one of the most celebrated and ancient American peoples.[6]

Another well-respected man who found the policy wrong and immoral was the poet and essayist Ralph Waldo Emerson. He was sufficiently angered to write a letter to President Martin Van Buren, protesting the removal of Cherokee Indians from Georgia. But there was too much at stake economically for humanist considerations to carry much weight in the situation. The program went forward with no delays or exceptions.

The rapid expansion of cotton plantations in the South resulted in a similarly rapid rise in the number of black slaves in the English colonies in the Western Hemisphere. The slave trade and enslavement of black Africans by Europeans was a crime against humanity of almost incomprehensible magnitude, both in the total number of victims and in duration. In its consequences for the black population of Africa and the black slaves in the Americas it exceeded in scope even the disaster to the native population of the Western Hemisphere caused by European conquest, and to which the use of African slave labor was the sequel. At the time, not many objected on moral grounds. The legal and moral rules that instinctive tribal bonds impose did not cover Native Americans and Africans. While the different European nations perpetrated these crimes against the indigenous populations of the Americas and Africa, they also fought bloody and cruel wars against each other, having little empathy for the members of enemy nations.

The role of tribalism and racial prejudice in conquest and enslavement

Muslim Arabs had been involved in the capture and enslavement of black Africans for many centuries before such activities were begun on a huge scale by the Europeans in the seventeenth through nineteenth centuries to obtain cheap labor in the European colonies in the Western Hemisphere. Neither Arabs nor

---

[6] George Wilson Pierson, *Tocqueville in America* (Johns Hopkins University Press 2715 North Charles Street, Maryland 21218-4363, 1938) Page 598

Europeans felt that they were doing anything wrong when they took captive, enslaved, and oppressed black Africans. Africans were of a different tribe and were not covered by the tribal instincts of loyalty and empathy.

Many Arabs were themselves of rather dark complexion, and in their Muslim society, there were not the same racial distinctions that developed in the European culture. Thus, many black Africans and their offspring with their Arab masters rose to high positions in Muslim society, whereas in the British colonies in North America a black slave in a cotton-growing state was almost hopelessly doomed with his or her progeny to remain powerless and subordinate to their masters simply because of their African origin.

Europeans felt justified in taking the land of the North American natives simply because they wanted it and needed it for their own advancement and enrichment. There was no moral imperative to respect the rights of the former owners. If the natives resisted, then the Europeans labeled them bloodthirsty and vicious savages, hunted them down, and killed them with no compunctions. When it was expedient to do so, the American government signed hundreds of treaties with the natives to avoid immediate hostilities but subsequently broke every single one of them, with few moral qualms.

The major colonial powers felt sure of their right to conquer and rule other nations. They quelled any native opposition with brutal force because the safety of the colonial rulers and their property was their paramount consideration. It did not make sense to them to accord the natives the same rights and respect as representatives of the ruling tribe, because it seemed self-evident that the subjugated tribes were innately inferior and unworthy of equal treatment.

Similarly, the leading Nazis undertook their effort to ethnically cleanse Europe of the Jews, not because the Nazis were uniquely evil people but because they honestly believed that the ethnic group to which they belonged was the noblest of all races; the Jews were the innately evil ones. The Nazi Germans sincerely believed that it was their sacred duty as Aryans and as patriotic members of the *Deutsche Volk* (German people) to eliminate the existential threat the Jews represented to the Aryan race. They viewed it as a difficult and unpleasant task but undertook it as a worthy and just cause, nevertheless.

Today, tribalism takes such negative and socially destructive expressions as racism, nationalism, cultural and religious bigotry, class-related antagonism, and so on. Today we often classify these phenomena as prejudices. They are all expressions of ancient instincts having to do with tribalism, but the actual contents of the prejudicial beliefs and their emotional intensity differ from case to case and from individual to individual.

The contents of prejudices are sometimes formed by circumstances that are unique to each case. That uniqueness can make them seem completely unrelated to one another, but they are typically all rooted in our ancient tribal instinct. If they also involve a related instinct, the creation of religious beliefs, then they can become even more emotional. Differences in religious beliefs have historically been a major source of hatred and murderous violence.

The role of instincts in forming our religions, values, and morals

Our most ancient and fundamental instinct is the desire to produce offspring. Most directly, this desire manifests itself as a strong longing to have a child and to see oneself in that child as he or she grows up. As the means to that end, this desire causes an individual to become drawn to another individual and to mate with that individual in a very emotional and long-lasting bond of love. The instinct is felt most urgently in particular moments as a need to experience sexual intimacy and orgasm, which is how the conception of a child occurs. These various manifestations of the instinct to produce offspring are merely different aspects of that one instinct.

Reproduction is the process that creates a family and tribe structure in the lives of humans. The family is the smallest "cell" in the structure of society, and it is among members of a family that the strongest tribal-type bonds exist. The bonds of affection and loyalty between parents and child are instinctive, as are the bonds of love between parents and the attachment between siblings. The bonds are highly emotional, and human intelligence has allowed us to conceptualize the roles that individuals play in the family structure. We understand the role of Father as a concept, quite independently of the individual who fills that role for us. The same is true of the role of Mother, and Child. We also understand the concept of Fertility, which allows the roles of Father, Mother, and Child to come into existence. Fertility is not a person whom we can look at and touch, but it is a fundamental, creative process to which we all owe our existence. Our human ancestors understood this, perhaps hundreds of thousands of years ago, and were awed by it. They paid homage to Fertility in iconic pictures and worship.

The long years required for a human child to reach maturation and self-reliance demand that the family unit remains stable and harmonious for a long time, which in turn means that the pair bonding between the father and the mother must be strong and stable. That strong, lasting pair bonding is achieved through the feeling of love. Like fertility, love is not a being who can be seen and touched. But it is a strong feeling of physical attraction, coupled with liking and admiration for the other person. When we fall in love, the feeling is quite identifiable and easily conceptualized.

Many individuals, when they "fall in love," experience feelings that are indistinguishable from those experienced by devout religious worshipers. That is particularly true in cases of so-called "limerence," a type of spellbound love that idealizes and virtually deifies the love object. It can, in extreme cases, have aspects of an obsession. It can, in fact, be an almost insurmountable obstacle to the successful establishment of an intimate relationship. Intense religiosity can also activate obsessive tendencies and produce a lack of will or ability to form intimate physical relationships with other humans. All the devotion and emotional commitment are directed toward the deity.

The concepts of Father, Mother, Child, Fertility, and Love represent the most cherished ideas of our earthly existence and humans instinctively embrace them with strong, positive emotions. We have such high regard for these concepts and feel so strongly about them that we tend to idealize them and have feelings of devotion for them. They become what Plato would call "Ideas." Devotion creates a desire to represent these concepts by physical objects such as pictures and statues, which become icons of the concepts. Before the arrivals of the monotheistic ("Abrahamic") religions, those icons were embraced with such devotion that they become gods. The polytheistic religions of antiquity all contained deities representing the icons of family life, including deities of love, sex, and fertility.

Religious beliefs have forms determined by both instincts and intellectual understanding of the world. Human factual understanding has advanced much faster in the last few millennia than has the evolution of our instincts. The increased intellectual knowledge has produced a drastic change in our religious beliefs. Multiple icons of the various idealized aspects of life in the family and tribe have merged into a single, eternal, and omnipotent male god, "the Heavenly Father." That deity does not facilitate worship of the female, loving, and sexual aspects of our lives. Despite its psychological flaws, monotheism has become the dominant form of religion in today's world, probably because it emphasizes a belief in a "personal" relationship of each individual to the deity. A very strong emotional bond develops between the deity and the worshiper, who believes that the deity takes a real, loving interest in the fate of the individual and "loves" him or her back in return for devotion and prayers.

In Christianity, there are still vestiges of polytheism, where the "Child" exists in the form of Jesus, the "Son of God," and the "Mother" is Mary, the "Holy Mother of Christ." In Catholicism, prayers and great devotion are offered to both. Catholicism also includes the veneration of a plethora of "saints," icons of various sides of human life and activities. Hybrid forms of Christian/pagan faiths such as Candomble and Santeria continue to worship traditional pagan deities in the disguise of Christian saints.

It is essential for our emotional well-being and the health of our society that we acknowledge and respect all the "religious" manifestations of our instinctive human nature. In particular, we should not let our devotion to one god turn him or her into a jealous monster who denies and denigrates any of the others and wants to punish those who show the other gods the appropriate recognition and respect. In his work *The Worship of Priapus*, the distinguished British classical scholar, patron of art and learning, and author Richard Payne Knight (1751–1824) said it well:

> There is naturally no impurity or licentiousness in the moderate and regular gratification of any natural appetite; the turpitude consisting wholly in the excess or perversion. Neither are organs of one species of enjoyment naturally to be considered a subject of shame and concealment more than any other; every refinement of modern manners on this head being derived from acquired habit, not from nature...[7]

One must, of course, qualify his statement with the general rule that the enjoyment of the natural pleasures of life must not infringe on the rights of others or cause serious harm to oneself. But we should affirm without shame or guilt our physical and emotional need for arousal, love, and intimacy. To denigrate things that we instinctively respond to with joy and pleasure is unnatural. It impoverishes our lives.

As far back as we can look in human history, religious beliefs and rituals were a central feature of all civilizations, and even in the simplest societies of tens of thousands of years ago, people carved fertility and mother figures in stone. Until our modern era, the most impressive buildings found in all civilizations were temples of worship. It is a revealing sign of our modern loss of religious sensibilities that the tallest, most impressive, and most expensive buildings in our cities are no longer churches but commercial buildings, the temples of Mammon.

---

[7] Richard P. Knight, *A Discourse on the Worship of Priapus*, part of a two-volume work also including *The Worship of the Generative Powers* (New York: Matrix House, 1966), 30.

Over the last few centuries, science has created doubts about the existence of any gods or spirits whatsoever. One can observe a steady and accelerating trend in all modern nations to become "secularized," to abandon religious beliefs and practices in favor of purely materialistic and "scientific" attitudes. In these modern societies, many individuals still experience emotions arising from ancient instincts. They describe themselves as "spiritual," that is, not believing in the deities of traditional religions but still having a fulfilling sense of awe and reverence when they contemplate the wonders and mysteries of life and the universe.

The evolutionary aspects of religious morality

Over the thousands of generations of human history, many tribes eventually became too large to make it possible to feel tight, personal bonds of family and blood relationships with everyone. Then religion became the glue that held civilizations together. In the long story of human societies, we have believed in innumerable different deities, divine families, and other supernatural beings and seldom doubted their existence. The human habit of creating religions is ubiquitous and constant, and it would not be so unless that habit has been an evolutionary advantage to us. There can be no doubt that it has become an innate, instinctive characteristic in us.

The "religious instinct" makes us respect, revere, iconize, and deify concepts that represent values and rules of evolutionary benefit to our species. They guide our behavior along paths that allow us to live peacefully with each other in a mutually beneficial manner. We are forbidden to kill or injure each other, or steal from each other, or to covet each other's possessions, or lying, which can weaken and disrupt the structures and bonds that tie our societies together. These rules have developed and survived because they have benefitted our species in the long term. Individuals who break the rules, tempted by the short term gains that can benefit them from that, are at risk of severe penalties from society. They are taught that even if they are smart or powerful enough to "get away with it" in the here and now, they will suffer even worse penalties later from an angry God. The willingness to obey the rules is, therefore, to some extent dependent on the belief in such a deity. The lack of such a belied is ranked as particularly offensive to God and worthy of the severest punishment. (In several Muslim nations today, atheism is punishable by death.) To have strict, mutually beneficial rules for how we must treat each other is quite obviously helpful in developing advanced civilizations.

All forms of human societies need to have someone in a leadership role. As tribes expanded and became towns and nations, the notion of "chief" and "king" appeared. To increase their authority to govern, the leader often claimed that his authority derived from the god that was the author of all rules. To oppose the leader was, therefore, an offense not just against him, but against the god. ("*All power is from God*," Romans 13:1,2.) His heroic deeds—and historically, it is usually a man—sometimes became legendary and became part of enduring tribal lore. Legendary tribal chiefs sometimes became so revered that they were accorded divine status in their legends. The history of religions is full of such figures; some pagan gods were once real human heroes. In the ancient world, the border between humans and gods was not always distinct. Gods could have offspring with humans (Gen 6:1–4), and many earthly kings were believed to be either the offspring of a god with a human woman, to be imbued with the spirit and authority of a god, or to be an incarnation of a god in human form. A century or so after his death, Christians proclaimed that Jesus was of the divine essence.

We find that leaders are often allowed to have multiple wives, while the ordinary citizen is expected to be monogamous. That special rule has some evolutionary benefits. An individual who attains a position as a powerful leader typically has some inherent above-average strengths. Those strengths might be intellectual as well as physical, and successful leaders have the ambition, ability, and energy to be leaders. A strong leader is a competitive advantage for a tribe or nation, and it confers an advantage to the tribe or nation if his above-average inherent strengths are propagated to as many offspring as possible. It makes evolutionary sense that he should be provided with the means to maximize the number of children, i.e., multiple wives.

In small tribes, the tribal benefits of the leader having access to more than one female is canceled by the negative consequences of extensive inbreeding. It is genetically damaging to have a tribe where a high percentage of the members are closely related. That is why many tribes have had rules that promote finding marriage partners from other tribes. Tribal warfare often resulted in the annihilation of all males in the vanquished tribe and the capturing of all females as wives or mistresses. We now judge such massacres as morally wrong, but they were, at the time, of benefit to the species.

The Old Testament gives full sanction to polygamy for kings, claiming that King Solomon had hundreds of wives. (In his case, it did not produce a numerous brood of exceptionally good and talented sons.) In Islam, every man has the right to have up to four wives as long as he can adequately provide for them all and treats them with respect. In a normal society, that is not an optimum allocation of procreative resources, given that there are very nearly as many male as female children born in any society. However, the Islamic rule was created in the very early years of Islam when constant religious warfare and geographic conquests by the faith resulted in high numbers of widows who, in order to survive, needed to be taken care of by a man. It was a rule that maximized the survival of widowed women and their present and potential future children.

Most present-day religions do not sanction polygamy even for powerful rulers. The Christian faith is strict in that regard, particularly the Roman Catholic version of it, where religious leaders are not allowed to have any wives at all. That, however, is a result of the peculiar attitude that the Christian faith has toward sexuality. The rule has no discernable direct benefit from an evolutionary standpoint. On the other hand, it tends to intensify the emotional attachment of the believer to his or her faith. Celibacy and religious devotion tend to be mutually supportive.

There is a spectrum of opinions regarding so-called "sperm banks," where sperm saved from male masturbation is frozen and stored. After thawing, it can be used to fertilize one or more females. Some sperm banks are created with a eugenic philosophy, listing relevant data about the donor, but not the name, address, or other identifying information. A woman can select a donor that appears to have above average qualities in particular areas, such as intelligence and physical attributes.

The overwhelming majority of medical ethicists and religious leaders hold strongly negative opinions about cloning humans, a process that raises a number of peculiar possibilities and philosophical and moral dilemmas. Another procedure that has long been a hotly debated issue is abortion. Those who believe that an immortal human soul is created at the moment of conception tend to see abortion at any stage in the pregnancy as the murder of an innocent child. The majority of the American public think that abortion can be justified in certain circumstances, such as in the case of a pregnancy caused by rape or incest, a severe physical malformation of the embryo, or to save the life of the mother. Those who do not believe in an immortal soul tend to consider an abortion justified also in certain other circumstances. For example, only if the mother strongly desires it, and it would have to be in the earliest stages of pregnancy, before the embryo has any mental awareness and would be viable outside the womb, and if the odds for a happy life of the child and the mother are truly dismal if the pregnancy is carried to term.

The emotions of prejudice and our attempts to cope with them

Prejudices often arise from the "us versus them" mentality created by our tribal instinct. They tend to perpetuate themselves by the mutual hostility and violence they often cause. Attitudes are hard and uncompromising, and the desire to keep the tribe "genetically pure" and undefiled by alien beliefs and customs makes having personal contacts across the tribal boundaries a traitorous offense. Physical traits that are not typical of one's tribe are ugly; to be attracted to them is perverse. Religious beliefs that contradict one's faith are offensive to the "True God" and deserve harsh penalties. Differences in religious beliefs – sometimes small disagreements between similar sects – can result in extremely violent confrontations and persecutions.

Such rigid prejudices go beyond what our instincts call for. The history of the human race is one of constant change. Mixing always takes place between different tribes, even if the first contact between them gave rise to an initial instinctive animosity. Humans are all one species, and standards of beauty are learned at a young age through cultural indoctrination in one's tribe. With later exposure to other cultures, personal preferences in that area might change. The mixing of the genetic inheritance of different races strengthens our species, and we should avoid artificial, learned, moral restrictions in that regard.

Prejudices are a common cause of unhappiness for prejudiced people. A prejudiced, bigoted, and judgmental disposition causes internal emotional tensions and conflicts. When somebody is prejudiced only toward an external tribe or group, that prejudiced person can still have a happy life—as long as the irritant of the offending group is not always there. It is possible to escape these unpleasant feelings by separating oneself from what gives offense. However, one cannot escape the awareness of oneself. The most corrosive and destructive form of prejudice involves having an image of oneself that fails to meet what one thinks is an acceptable standard. Few of us can remain emotionally healthy and happy if we see ourselves as morally weak, sinful, and worthy of punishment. If we succeed in resisting our natural urges, it is at a steep price in internal tension and stress. Or we may give in to them and suffer guilt and self-loathing as a result. Both alternatives produce fear and hatred of what has triggered the temptation.

In circumstances where prejudices exist against a particular group of people, the perception of them as "the others" can have a basis in physical appearance, beliefs, and customs. The prejudices then appear to have certain aspects of objective, undeniable truths. These undeniable differences then serve as tribal markers to ascribe to everyone in the "alien tribe" some specific other reputed characteristics. Those characteristics might not, in fact, be typical of members of that group. They are usually negative traits in the judgment of the prejudiced person and might be at least a source of ridicule. If the prejudices involve emotionally sensitive characteristics, they can trigger fear and hatred and inspire severe violence, even to the point of genocide.

Extreme sensitivity to certain issues reveals that the person is struggling internally to suppress instinctive responses to those issues. The person has succeeded in suppressing from the consciousness the instinctive but forbidden positive response to the perceived characteristics of another tribe and recognizes only the anxiety and discomfort of the inner turmoil. Such a person tends to ascribe the cause of the turmoil to other alleged characteristics of the object of prejudice, characteristics that are less emotionally jarring but still appear reasonable as support for a negative and hostile attitude. That, in psychological language, is called a "denial" response.

A related process is the "projection" response. Again, one successfully suppresses and denies forbidden feelings in oneself. In this case, however, the feelings are "projected" onto the members of the other tribe, who are thus believed to have dangerous and morally reprehensible characteristics, further intensifying one's fears and dislike of all members of that tribe.

Harvard psychologist Gordon Allport's classic study *The Nature of Prejudice* has been called "Probably the most comprehensive study of all aspects of the problem which has yet appeared." by the *Journal of Personality*.[8] Allport has illustrated the process of projection in simple words:

> There is a subtle psychological reason why Negroid characteristics favor [for those with Puritan moral convictions] an association of ideas with sex... Sex is forbidden; colored people are forbidden; the ideas begin to fuse. It is no accident that prejudiced people call tolerant people "niggerlovers." The very choice of the word suggests that they are fighting the feeling of attraction in themselves...
>
> Suppose a white woman is fascinated by the taboo against the Negro male. She is unlikely to admit, even to herself, that she finds his color and lower status attractive. She may, however, "project" her feelings, and accordingly imagine that her desire exists on the other side—that Negro males have sexually aggressive tendencies toward her. What is an inner temptation is perceived as an outer threat. Overgeneralizing her conflict, she develops an anxiety and hostility respecting the whole Negro race.[9]

The projection response is akin to the "sour grapes" response. The term comes from an old Greek fable where a fox fails to reach a bunch of grapes growing on a vine. He soothes his disappointment by convincing himself that he did not really want them anyway; they were in all certainty sour. The sour grapes response is triggered where the person wants to satisfy his or her curiosity about the tribe about which the prejudiced beliefs exist but fails in doing so. The cause of the failure might be a rejection by the members of the other tribe, perhaps for reasons of the prejudices found among that tribe. The pain of rejection discourages any further attempts and might cause resentment and strengthening of negative prejudices.

---

8   Cited on the back cover of the book (See below.)
9   Gordon W. Allport *The Nature of Prejudice* 25th anniversary edition (Addison-Wesley Publishing Company, an imprint of Pearson PLC, 1979) pp 374, 375

A fourth possible response is to recognize and admit to ourselves our real, instinctive response to the prejudicial beliefs. If we have the courage to be honest with ourselves and to defy tribal taboos, we initiate contact across tribal boundaries. The result might be the discovery that the prejudicial beliefs we held were false, or that the characteristics and customs of the other tribe were not as revolting and morally reprehensible as commonly depicted. Perhaps the beliefs and customs of our native tribe could benefit from some revision? The response eventually reduces the prevalence of prejudice and causes the gradual dissolving of tribal boundaries.

It is wise to be skeptical of simple explanations for complex situations, and this book attempts to show that American prejudices have roots that are deeper and more wide-ranging than most people realize. There are always differences among individuals with respect to the origins, content, and intensity of their prejudices. Hardly anyone, of any race, nationality, religion, or gender, is free from prejudice of some kind. They are the result of both nature and nurture, instinct and upbringing. We don't easily accept that we are prejudiced, and many Americans would probably disagree with the thesis laid out in this book to describe and explain, in particular, anti-black prejudice in America.

Part Two: Deep Historical Background

The beginnings of North American slavery

To a great extent, the racial conflict in America has its origin in the institution of slavery. To young Americans, both blacks and whites, the era of slavery is a far-off, almost mythical part of American history. Not many care to contemplate what its everyday reality was and not many fully understand the huge remaining impact it has had on the circumstances of life for today's descendants of slaves. Fewer still give a thought to the fact that there are Americans today whose lives have overlapped, timewise, with the lives of those who once served as slaves. Many former slaves survived well into the 1920s and 1930s, the decades when many still living Americans were born.

Muslim Arabs had already captured and enslaved Africans for centuries before the Spanish and the Portuguese began to employ slave labor in their colonies in the Americas. The practice was soon taken up by other European immigrants in North America and on the Caribbean islands. There were few qualms about the morality of the practice even though it involved the brutal capture and harsh oppression of millions of humans. Africa suffered immensely from the removal of so many of its young people, leading to the death of many who resisted capture, the destruction of countless families, and the starvation of older individuals who were unable to sustain themselves.

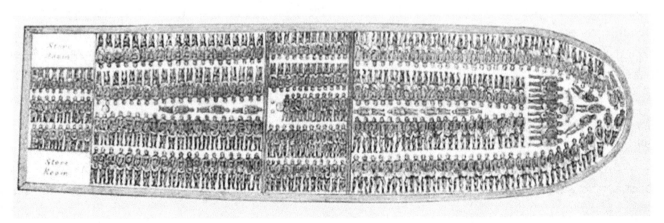

Figure 1 Diagram of a slave ship cargo hold (1854)

The transportation of the captives to the New World took place in hellish conditions. The "Middle Passage," employed sailing vessels that took three or more weeks to cross the Atlantic. The captives were chained and packed tightly, in some of the larger ships in up to three shallow "cargo decks," each too low for someone to stand up. There were no windows, no sanitary facilities, and water and some simple food were carried down to the captives by the ship's crew by lamplight. The captives were not accustomed to being out on the ocean, and many became violently seasick and screamed in terror when the ships encountered rough weather. They were naked, or mostly so, lying for weeks on the rough planks of the cargo holds, planks that were full of blood, urine, feces, and vomit. The heat and stench were horrible, and infections of wound suffered during capture or transport was common, causing additional pain. From time to time, they would be brought up on the upper, open deck in small groups to be washed off by being splashed with buckets of sea water, given food and water, and then led back down into the dark, hot, stinking cargo decks.

More than twelve million Africans were entered into this transport, but not all survived. Many died from the hellish conditions but could remain chained to others for hours or even days. Most historians estimate that as many as one and a half million died during transport and between ten and twelve million Africans were brought ashore alive in the Americas.[10] Of those, only less than 400,000 entered North America; the rest were taken to Latin America and the Caribbean.

In what was to become the United States, slavery began on a small scale, as part of the tradition of voluntary "indentured servitude." A small number of blacks arrived in Jamestown, Virginia, in late August 1619, before slavery existed there as an institution. According to the records of the event, "twenty and odd" blacks were unloaded from an English warship, the *White Lion*, in exchange for an unspecified quantity of "victuals." The English ship was authorized to operate as a privateer, a government-sanctioned pirate ship for action against Spanish or Portuguese ships in the Caribbean, where the competition was fierce between Dutch, French, British, Spanish, and Portuguese colonial interests. The *White Lion* had successfully captured a Portuguese slave ship, the San Juan Batista, bound for Vera Cruz, Mexico and had thus come into possession of the Africans. They were initially kept as indentured servants along with many Englishmen and Englishwomen who had voluntarily become indentured servants to pay for their escape from the wretched conditions in their homeland. Documentation regarding the individual Africans who arrived on the White Lion is virtually non-existent.

The first African individual to have left traces in official records was a woman who arrived together with about thirty other slaves on another British warship, the Treasurer. The Treasurer arrived at Jamestown only four days after the arrival of the White Lion. Like the White Lion, it had obtained its load of Africans from the San Juan Batista slave transport ship. By 1619, the Portuguese had already established a regular, high volume transport route for captured Africans to the Spanish, Portuguese, French, and Dutch colonies in the Caribbean and Central and South America, and piracy flourished. As far as is known, the Treasurer left only two or three of the Africans at Jamestown, and the fate of the rest is unknown.

Among those two or three was a woman who was given the name "Angela" at Jamestown, perhaps because she was captured initially in Angola. Her real African name is unknown, as is her age when she

---

[10] <u>Trans-Atlantic Slave Trade Database</u>, edited by professors David Eltis and David Richardson

arrived, or the date or cause of her death. She became a servant of a wealthy Jamestown resident, Capt. William Pierce, and was listed on his household census in 1624, 1625, and 1626 but no later. She appears there as "Angela, a Negar."

For many years, historians thought that the last surviving former slave was a man known as "Cudjo Lewis," whose African name was Oluale Kossula (or Kazoola). He had arrived in Mobile, Alabama, in 1860 on the slave smuggling ship Clotilda, 52 years after federal law had banned the importation (but not the ownership) of African slaves. "Cudjo" was captured as a teenager in what is now Benin and died in Mobile, Alabama in 1935, seventy-five years later. His story was movingly related by the black author Zora Neale Hurston in *"Barracoon: The Story of the Last "Black Cargo."* Hurston, a famous and controversial author of several books, interviewed Cudjo and wrote the book in 1928, but it was not published until 2018 – ninety years later.

More recently, research by Dr. Hannah Durkin at Newcastle University, England, has uncovered evidence of a young female who arrived on the same ship as Cudjo and survived until 1937. The girl, whose African name was Redoshi, was renamed "Sally Smith" after her owner, Mr. Washington Smith, the founder of the Bank of Selma, Alabama. According to the Selma civil rights activist Amelia Boynton, who interviewed "Sally Smith" in the early 1930s, Redoshi claimed she was twelve years of age when she was sold. The slave trader paired her with another captured African and sold the two as a "breeding couple" that would bring additional slaves into the world.

Zora Neale Hurston interviewed Sally Smith also and mentioned her to the author Langston Hughes, but apparently found the story of Cudjo more fascinating. Fortunately, photos exist of both Cudjo and Sally. Even more recently, Dr. Durkin has found records that a younger sister of Sally also arrived on Clotilda. She was only two years old when captured together with her mother and her sister Redoshi, and was given the name Matilda by the plantation owner who bought her. His last name was Creagh, but when the slaves were freed, Matilda took the last name McCrear. She died in Selma, Alabama, in 1940, the mother of fourteen children by a German-born white man whom she was forbidden by law to marry.

A grandson, Johnny Crear, witnessed violence against civil rights marchers in Selma in 1965, but did not know his grandmothers whole story until Dr. Durkin had researched it and told him about it.

Figure 2 Oluale Kossola, a.k.a. Cudjo Lewis

Figure 3 Matilda McCrear

At first, the law made no distinction between white and black indentured servants. A significant number of mixed-race children were born, however, and the ruling white masters appear to have seen this as a growing problem. People of African descent began to experience segregation and oppression. In 1662, the Virginia colony put on the books laws recognizing slavery—in contrast to indentured servitude—as a lifelong institution. The laws applied to people of African ancestry who were indentured servants—but not to whites. At first, there was not much to distinguish indentured servitude from slavery, except that the latter status was permanent. In contrast, indentured servants were often committed to service for only a fixed number of years.

The existence of mixed-race children was an obvious problem. The decision regarding them was that if the mother was a black slave, then the child would inherit her slave status. If the mother was white, then the child would be free. The rule resulted in a significant number of children being born free but inheriting many physical characteristics from their black fathers.

Before 1667, slaves could obtain their freedom by baptism and by declaring themselves to be Christian since, at that time, it was not considered proper for a Christian to hold another Christian as a slave. In 1667 the path to freedom for a slave through baptism became closed, mostly for economic reasons: a slave was valuable property. However, a significant number of free blacks already lived in the colony at that time.

The growth of racial prejudice

As the number of blacks and mixed-race offspring increased, racist prejudice began to take hold. There was a growing sense that Africans were inherently different from Europeans. Africans had obvious physical differences in skin color and hair and facial features, and their speech, customs, and habits were different. In whites, the general belief was that white men and women were superior to blacks. That conviction was reinforced by the travel reports written by British missionaries and explorers, who had begun to venture into areas of Africa that the English had previously never reached. They found the physical characteristics of the African natives frighteningly alien. Their black skin, tightly curled hair, and different facial features suggested to the Englishmen a primitive nature. The tight-laced Englishmen were particularly shocked by the shameless nakedness of the Africans and the custom of the most socially prominent men to have multiple women sexually available to them. These features of African culture suggested a lack of moral sensibility and seemed to be another indicator of a more primitive character than members of the white race. Africans were evidently a lower form of humans than Europeans. According to those who claimed to have personally encountered "wild" Africans "in their natural environment," that conclusion was indisputable.

The travel reports were written with the intent of providing income to their writers and were printed and distributed through numerous copies. They were often written to shock and titillate, and they became popular reading in many English-speaking parts of the world—not the least among the educated elite in both England and the United States. Such reports helped spread prejudicial beliefs and became instrumental in justifying slavery in the United States.

In the early eighteenth century, blacks constituted half the unfree labor force of Virginia. The white masters increasingly saw mixed-race relations among white indentured servants and black slaves as a growing problem, in part because the existence of free blacks and free mixed-race children created a practical problem in identifying escaped slaves. The belief that Africans were not fully human strengthened the conviction that interracial sexual relations were perverse and morally reprehensible—sins that endangered the post-mortal fate of one's soul. Africans were, in the opinion of many educated colonists, "lewd, lascivious and wanton people."[11] The belief in their general inferiority helped define dark skin, tightly curled black hair, and African facial features as ugly and repulsive. A Maryland law of 1681 against mixed marriages put forth the argument that such marriages were desired only by blacks, and "always to the satisfaction of their Lascivious and Lustfull desires, and to the disgrace not only of the English butt also of many other Christian nations."[12] Virginia enacted a law against mixed marriages in 1691.

African slaves began to arrive in large numbers in the 1800s when the South was taken from the Native Americans to create an extensive system of rice and cotton plantations. The plantations relied almost entirely on slave labor, which helped to create a unique culture in the slave-holding states, based on the use of African slaves as the manual labor for the system of plantations.

The new nation of the United States was founded in 1776 on the principle that all men were created equal and had the same rights to life, liberty, and the pursuit of happiness. Today it appears almost incomprehensible that the nation could at the same time hold some of its inhabitants in a harsh system of perpetual slavery, where the slaves had virtually none of those rights. As is often the case in social injustice, there was an economic incentive for this situation. Slavery, as it had developed in the preceding century, had shown itself to be profitable and convenient for the slave owners.

The financial value of slaves and slave labor

Most of the leading, wealthy, white Southern families owned slaves, and upon their backs, the economic basis of America was erected. In the states of the Deep South, one-third of all white income was derived from slavery. The economy of the entire nation was dependent on the income from slave labor. By 1840, cotton and cotton products constituted 59 percent of American exports. The web of this slave-based economy extended north to the looms of New England, and across the Atlantic to Great Britain.

Most of the economic life of the American South revolved around the system of black slavery, even for those who did not personally own slaves. Merchants, bankers, lawyers, artisans, shipping line owners, and their employees were supplying and servicing the system of growing and marketing cotton, for which the black slaves were indispensable. But the wealth generated in America by slavery was not just in what the

---

[11] Winthrop D. Jordan: *White over Black: American Attitudes toward the Negro, 1550–1812* (Chapel Hill, NC: Omohundro Institute of Early American History and Culture and the University of North Carolina Press, 116 South Boundary Street Chapel Hill, NC 27514-3808. 1968). p 32

[12] Robert J. Brugger: *Maryland, A Middle Temperament: 1634–1980* (Baltimore, MD: Johns Hopkins University Press, 1988) p 45

slaves pulled from the land but in the slaves themselves. "In 1860, slaves as an asset were worth more than all of America's manufacturing, all of the railroads, all of the productive capacity of the United States put together," the Yale historian David W. Blight has noted. "Slaves were the single largest, by far, financial asset of property in the entire American economy."

The trading of these slaves generated additional wealth. Loans were taken out for purchase, to be repaid with interest. Insurance policies were drafted against the untimely death of a slave and the loss of potential profits. Slave sales were taxed and notarized. The vending of the black body and the sundering of the black family became an economy unto themselves, estimated to have brought in tens of millions of dollars to antebellum America. In 1860 there were more millionaires per capita in the Mississippi Valley than anywhere else in the country.

There was, therefore, an economic imperative for the South, and not only for the rich elite of slave owners, that slavery must be retained as an essential part of Southern society. The economic aspects of the system blinded most Southerners to any moral and ethical aspects of it. But the answer to the paradox of slavery in this land of the free also lies in the perception that the white population had of the nature of Africans. The American form of slavery became brutal and utterly degrading not merely for economic reasons but also because the slave owners sincerely believed that blacks were inferior to whites in most respects. On an emotional as well as an intellectual level, they were perceived to be not much above animals. It seemed perfectly logical to most slave owners that they should not accord to slaves all the fundamental human rights that even the poorest of white citizens enjoyed. The slaves were simply the personal property of the plantation owner and were bought and sold like cattle. Marriage between slaves did not exist in law—no more than marriage among cattle or domestic pets would.

If an owner saw a financial need to do so, he was free to separate slave couples and their children by the sale of one or more members of the family. Female slaves were often the victims of sexual exploitation, and neither the women themselves nor their loved ones among the other slaves had a right to object to the owner availing himself of this service, even if it involved forcible rape. A failure to obey, or any other challenge to the owner's absolute authority, could result in a violent whipping. White men could even enter the homes of free blacks and rape the women without the black family having any recourse because not even free blacks could bring suit against a white man in court.

A mutually reinforcing effect was undoubtedly at work psychologically. The fact that Africans were held as slaves made it necessary for whites, as a moral rationalization, to believe that these people were a lower form of humanity. Africans were not fully human—therefore, it was reasonable that whites could employ them as slaves.

The changing view of slavery leads to Civil War

In part because of the brutal abuse legally visited upon the slaves by many owners, a majority of the population in the states where slavery was not legal believed that slavery was an evil that should be abolished nationwide. Still, Presidents George Washington, Thomas Jefferson, James Madison, James Monroe, Andrew

Jackson, Martin Van Buren, William H. Harrison, John Tyler, James K. Polk, Zachary Taylor, Andrew Johnson, and even Ulysses S. Grant were slave owners, although Van Buren and Harrison did not own slaves while serving as presidents. Thomas Jefferson owned over six hundred slaves over his lifetime, and of those, he freed only two while he was alive. He had a very ambivalent attitude in racial matters, and in 1778, he helped push through a law in the Virginia legislation that criminalized the importation of slaves into that state. As president, he signed a law in 1807 that made it illegal to import additional slaves into the United States. The law was not entirely effective, as the smuggling of slaves into the country became very profitable. Unintended consequences of the law were an increase in the price of slaves and encouragement of the breeding of slaves as a business.

Washington, Jefferson, and Franklin were all admirers of their contemporary, the leading British man of letters, Samuel Johnson. However, Johnson was not in favor of the American colonies becoming an independent nation. He once remarked acidly: "How is it that we hear the loudest yelps for liberty among the drivers of negroes?"

The opinion that slavery was an evil was expressed ever more stridently in the nation's political discourse as the years went on. Harriet Beecher Stowe's *Uncle Tom's Cabin* became an effective agent of persuasion for the abolitionist cause. It was first published in 1852, was eventually translated into many languages, and sold well internationally for more than a hundred years. It provides a very sympathetic portrayal of black slaves and a very unsympathetic description of slaveholders and white overseers. In its time, the book's depiction of the white overseer Simon Legree came to serve as the icon of absolute cruelty and evil, just as in our day, the popular culture uses the image of Hitler for that purpose.

Senator John C. Calhoun of South Carolina was an ardent leading defender of unending slavery and a staunch believer in black racial inferiority. Among leading abolitionists stood William Lloyd Garrison, a firm believer in racial equality. Together with Frederick Douglass, a former slave, Garrison became a leading voice of the abolitionist movement during the decades up to the Civil War. The two eventually quarreled, and the abolition movement lost some steam. It regained momentum with the help of the author Harriet Beecher Stove, who had shot into a leading position in the movement when her book *Uncle Tom's Cabin* became a best seller. She managed to achieve some reconciliation between Garrison and Douglass.

On March 6, 1857, the abolitionist cause was hit with a Supreme Court setback in the form of the infamous Dred Scott decision, which was to have long-lasting adverse effects. In *Dred Scott v. Sanford*, the court ruled seven to two that Scott, a slave who had been taken to a non-slave state, his wife, and their two daughters were still the property of their present master, John Sanford, and must remain under his control. In the majority opinion of the court, blacks could not be citizens of the United States and did not possess the legal standing to bring suit in a federal court.

The case and the Supreme Court decision received widespread publicity and became a focal point in the Lincoln-Douglas debates that would ultimately propel Abraham Lincoln into the presidency. The seven debates took place as part of the campaigns for the Illinois senate seat then held by Stephen Douglas.

Lincoln has achieved the reputation as one of the greatest, if not the greatest, of American presidents. He is called "the Great Emancipator" because of his 1863 emancipation proclamation, freeing the slaves of the Confederate states. However, his proclamation was mostly a propaganda ploy, perhaps to incite rebellion

ANDERS EKLOF

among the slaves in the Confederacy; he had no actual administrative control in those states. He did not at the same time free the slaves in the states that had not joined the Confederacy. His abolitionist stand was not grounded in a belief in racial equality.

In the debates, Lincoln had to defend himself against the race-baiting Douglas, who kept telling the audience that a Lincoln victory in their race would lead to racially integrated communities, with blacks enjoying rights to socialize with whites as equals, thus insinuating that racial mixing would ensue. To his surprise, Lincoln took a segregationist position that was similar to the later Supreme Court decision in the *Plessy v. Ferguson* case. (In 1896, *Plessy v. Ferguson* gave legal sanction to the "separate but equal" doctrine that became the cornerstone of Jim Crow laws that supported racial segregation in America.) Lincoln stated:

> I am not, nor ever have been, in favor of bringing about in any way the social and political equality of the white and black races … I am not nor ever have been in favor of making voters or jurors of Negroes, nor of qualifying them to hold office, nor to intermarry with white people; and I will say in addition to this that there is a physical difference between the white and black races which I believe will forever forbid the two races from living together on terms of social and political equality. And inasmuch as they cannot so live, while they do remain together there must be a position of superior and inferior, and I as much as any other man am in favor of having the superior position assigned to the white race.... I will to the very last stand by the law of this State, which forbids the marrying of white people with negroes. [13]

Lincoln was thus not a near-saintly champion of human rights. He was against slavery, but still a racist segregationist and white supremacist. Had he expressed belief in the equality of the races and racial integration, it would undoubtedly have led to a loss in the presidential election.

While campaigning as an abolitionist, and as the Union president during the Civil War, Lincoln agonized about what to do with the millions of blacks in the South once they were free. He said that his first impulse was to send them all back to Africa. Already in 1822, resettlement of former slaves had begun on a small scale in an area on the west coast of Africa, named "Liberia" to make it sound attractive to potential emigres. The private project had not had much success. In part, it was due to difficulties in raising the money for the shipping but also to the fact that many free blacks would rather remain in the United States than move to Africa, a place that had consistently been described by slavery advocates as wild, inhospitable jungle from which the slaves had once been "rescued" by being taken captive and sold into slavery in the Americas. Reason told Lincoln that shipping all freed blacks in the United States to Africa was not feasible.

"What then?" Lincoln mused. "Free them, and make them politically and socially, our equals? My own feelings will not admit this, and if mine would, we well know that those of the great mass of white people will not." [14]

---

[13] The Lincoln-Douglas Debates, 4th Debate Part I, September 18, 1858
[14] Eric Foner, *The Fiery Trial: Abraham Lincoln and American Slavery* (New York: W. W. Norton, 2010), pp. 65 – 67

The political pressure on the South to abolish slavery increased steadily in the decades leading up to the Civil War, but the South showed no inclination to bend to this pressure. Many whites in the South sincerely believed that it was their humane and moral duty to keep the black slaves under tight control by bondage because they otherwise would be ungovernable and dangerous. They were widely believed to be too lazy, stupid, and ignorant to take care of themselves without the governing hand of their white masters. Speeches in defense of slavery were just as emotional and filled with conviction as those that opposed slavery. Instead of giving in to the pressures from the Northern states to abolish slavery, the Southern states' response was to declare themselves independent from the Union and to form a new nation—the Confederate States of America—where slavery would continue. That move initiated what would be the bloodiest and most devastating war the United States has ever experienced.

Lincoln always insisted that his primary goal in the Civil War was to restore the union of the nation, not to free the slaves:

> My paramount object in this struggle is to save the Union, and is not either to save or destroy Slavery. If I could save the Union without freeing any slave, I would do it, and if I could save it by freeing all the slaves, I would do it, and if I could save it by freeing some and leaving others alone, I would also do that.[15]

Lincoln adds that his statement expressed his opinion of what his duty as president required. As for his personal preference, he stood by his wish that all men could be free.

In his Message to Congress on December 1, 1862, Lincoln presented a plan that he thought might be a way to end the war and restore the union. It described a gradual emancipation of slaves and a plan for resettling emancipated slaves in Haiti or Africa. The federal government would provide economic compensation for slaveholders for their loss of property in states that promised to completely abolish slavery by January 1, 1900. In the meantime, Lincoln proposed to allow states to be readmitted to the Union without abolishing slavery, provided that they pledged loyalty to the Union and its government.

Emboldened by Confederate battlefield victories in December, the leaders of the Confederacy rejected Lincoln's proposed gradual emancipation plan. They were determined to fight on to retain slavery in their states forever. It proved to be a tragic misjudgment.

According to the most recent and thorough analysis of documents from the war, as well as the census reports of 1860 and 1870, about three-quarters of a million combatants died in the war—mostly from disease and infected wounds. This number exceeds the combined total of American fatalities in the First and Second World Wars, the Korean War, the Vietnam War, the multiple connected wars in Afghanistan and the Middle East, and all the other minor military operations that the United States has conducted in Latin America and Africa in recent decades. To envision what this fatality count meant, one must place it in relation to the total population of the nation at the time. The free population of the United States in 1860 was about the same as the present population of the state of Texas—that is, about twenty-five million.

---

[15] Letter from Lincoln to Horace Greely, editor of the influential New York *Tribune*, Washington, August 22, 1862

The war was fought primarily on the territory of the South, and it was there that the relative number of casualties was the greatest. The white population of the South was only about 5.5 million, and of them, about every fifth man of working age died in the war. Hundreds of thousands were so gravely wounded physically and psychologically that they could not take care of themselves after the war—much less their families and property. Almost every Southern family lost at least one family member, near relative, or friend. For the South, the war was a devastating, traumatic disaster in terms of loss of life and injuries as well as economically, and it left bitter memories for generations.

Among those who sought to abolish slavery were some of the early advocates of women's rights. Suffragists Susan B. Anthony and Elizabeth Cady Stanton joined with blacks seeking voting right in 1866 to found the American Equal Rights Association (AERA). However, members of the mostly white women's rights organizations were at the same time infected with the same racist prejudices that were prevalent among men. In particular, they ascribed to the theory accepted by many in the emancipation movement that slavery had degraded the inherent character of the black race, and only by becoming free and fully assimilating into white culture could the black race "uplift" itself. At AERA's first annual meeting in 1867, Stanton made clear that she was not in favor of blacks having equal rights to whites unless the rights of women were also equal to the rights of men:

> When [Mr. Downing] puts the question to me: are you willing to have the colored man enfranchised before the women, I say no; I would not trust him with my rights; degraded, oppressed himself, he would be more despotic with the governing power than ever our Saxon rulers are... If women are still to be represented by men, then I say let only the highest type of manhood stand at the helm of State.[16]

It is noteworthy that by implication, Stanton assumes that "the best type of manhood" is represented by "Saxons." Jews, Latinos, Asians, Irishmen, and other lesser types need not apply.

Reconstruction and the beginning of Jim Crow

Following the Civil War, the question of what to do with the millions of emancipated slaves became the most urgent and vexing problem. Almost inevitably, the approach was to make the freed slaves the political and social equals of their former owners – what Lincoln once said that his "feelings would not admit." He did not live to see the emancipation become incorporated into the American Constitution. Less than a week after General Robert E. Lee's surrender at Appomattox, on April 14, Lincoln was shot by John Wilkes Booth, and his vice president, Andrew Johnson, was sworn in as the new president of the United States.

---

[16] Stanton et al., *History of Woman Suffrage, 1861 – 1876, vol. 2* (Rochester, New York: Charles Mann, 1887), pp. 214, 215.

On January 31, 1865, the House of Representatives had passed the Thirteenth Amendment, abolishing slavery nationwide. It had no immediate legal force: the amendment was not officially added to the Constitution until December 18, 1865.

The 1865 peace agreement at the end of the Civil War was remarkably lenient in the treatment of Confederate leaders and other important men in the South. President Lincoln had wanted to heal the emotional wounds of the war and prevent a complete disintegration of the political and economic structures of the vanquished states. Andrew Johnson, the new president, was a native of North Carolina and a former slave owner, and he was also unwilling to pursue punitive policies toward the Southern leaders. The intent was good, but Lincoln's assassination on April 14, 1865, was just one sign that the South was not ready to accept defeat in all its consequences.

Andrew Johnson's administration made it almost impossible for "Reconstruction" in the former Confederacy to succeed. He offered full amnesty for seditious acts to all but the highest Confederacy officials and pardoned most those a year later. They kept their freedom, what remained of their property, and voting rights. Thus, the wealthy and powerful men of the pre-war era remained the most powerful individuals after the war. When the occupying federal troops were withdrawn from the South more than a dozen years after the war, the goals of the Reconstruction, to give equal rights and opportunity to the former slaves, were soon thwarted. The white political leaders of the South retained enough power to ensure that the former slaves would remain subjugated and powerless.

Violence by white individuals and groups like the Ku Klux Klan terrorized the black population and effectively prevented black resistance. Many incidents of mob violence occurred. In May 1866, white mobs killed at least forty-eight black men and gang-raped at least five black women while looting and destroying black-owned property in Memphis, Tennessee[17]. Roiling racial violence in Louisiana reached a climax when a mob massacred one hundred and fifty blacks in Colfax, Louisiana, on April 13, 1873. The white participants in the slaughter were mostly former slaveholders, veterans of the Confederacy, and staunch segregationists. A Louisiana state court eventually exonerated all.[18]

Because the Republican Party was the party of Lincoln and the emancipation of blacks from slavery, the South became united behind the Democratic Party, a political affiliation that would remain solid for another century. The Democratic Party Congress in New Orleans, Louisiana declared in 1865:

> We hold this to be a Government of White People, made and to be perpetuated for the exclusive benefit of the White race, and... that the people of African descent cannot be considered as citizens of the United States, and that there can, in no event, nor under any circumstances, be any equality between white and other races.[19]

---

[17] Ibram X. Kendi, *STAMPED FROM THE BEGINNING, The Definitive History of Racist Ideas in America* (New York: Bold Type Books, 2016), p. 240

[18] LeeAnna Keith, *The Colfax Massacre; The untold Story of Black Power, White Terror, and the Death of Reconstruction*, New York: Oxford University Press, 2008

[19] Charles Lane: The Day Freedom Died: *The Colfax Massacre, the Supreme Court, and the Betrayal of the Reconstruction* (New York: Henry Holt and Company, 2008) p 17

The recalcitrance angered Northern politicians, who saw the fruits of their hard-won victory in the war slip away. In March 1867, Congress passed the Reconstruction Acts, abolishing the governments of the former Confederate states and reorganizing ten of the eleven states into five military districts ruled by the United States Army.

Whites in the South, already suffering greatly in the aftermath of the war, denounced granting equal rights to blacks as an unrealistic and despotic demand by naive whites in the North who had no experience of controlling large numbers of black people. The federal government's dictate, which trampled on the wishes of the populations of the South, was highly offensive. That it was going to be enforced by the same Union troops who had taken so many lives of their loved ones and friends and now occupied their lands made it even more repugnant.

The subsequent time in the South was officially named the Reconstruction. The term suggested reform and rebuilding, but in the South, it came to have the meaning of disorder and destruction, adding further suffering and humiliation for the white citizens. Many previously powerful white men had lost loved ones and valuable human property in the war and its aftermath and now faced financial ruin. The dread of what their former slaves might extract as vengeance for generations of suffering, humiliation, and brutal exploitation during slavery now added to white fear of what the future might hold.

Opportunistic adventurers from the North streamed into the South, exploiting the chaos and political power vacuum there to gain power and wealth for themselves. They became known derisively as "carpetbaggers," since they stereotypically arrived with all their earthly belongings carried in a carpetbag. The carpetbaggers' schemes often included using the newly freed blacks as their pawns. With the aid of these opportunists, some former slaves did indeed reach positions of power over their previous masters. During Reconstruction, the South sent several blacks to Washington as representatives in Congress.

The antebellum Southern economy was agricultural, with large plantations owned by a wealthy, powerful, high-status elite who viewed themselves as a sophisticated aristocracy whose superior education and supposed inherent merits gave them the right—indeed, the duty—to govern their society. Southern society was very racist and hierarchical, with a mass of poor and illiterate white citizens separated from the white elite by strict class boundaries and from blacks by customs and prejudicial beliefs. Social contacts across class boundaries were as unusual as they were in British society, and marriage outside one's social class or race was all but unthinkable.

After the war, many white Southerners placed the blame for the war and its horrendous consequences squarely on the black slaves. In combination with a fear of potential black vengeance for their suffering during slavery, that blame contributed to the buildup of resentment, fear, and hatred in the South toward the black population. In Congress, nine Southern states refused to ratify the Thirteenth Amendment to abolish slavery. With twenty-seven of the thirty-six states of the nation ratifying it, it still became the law of the land on December 6, 1865. The Fourteenth Amendment, which granted citizenship and the equal protection of the law to all persons born or naturalized in the United States, was submitted to Congress in 1866. At the time, President Andrew Johnson voiced his displeasure with the amendment by stating that the steps taken by his Secretary of State should "be considered as purely ministerial, and in no sense whatever committing the Executive to an approval or a recommendation of the amendment to the State legislatures or to the people."[20] The amendment passed despite strenuous opposition by the Southern states, and Congress ratified it on July 9, 1868.

The Fifteenth Amendment, which guaranteed the right to vote without regard to "race, color, or previous condition of servitude," was not ratified by the required majority of states until February 3, 1870. In Congress, representatives of the former Confederacy continued to argue that the Fourteenth and Fifteenth Amendments should be rescinded.

In the South, people would long remember the more than ten years of the Reconstruction as one of suffering and desperation—of trying to restore an orderly and functioning society amid coercion by the occupying Union troops to grant blacks all the rights granted to white Americans by the Constitution. In the late 1870s, the federal government tacitly admitted that Reconstruction had failed and acceded to popular pressure in the South to withdraw the widely hated Union occupying troops. The former white rulers of the South then quickly staged their own brand of reconstruction by wresting back control of the political and economic machinery of their ravaged society. They put into effect a series of laws in their states depriving all former slaves of most of their newly gained legal rights and requiring strict segregation by race in all aspects of social life. The laws came to be known as the Jim Crow laws and remained in effect in most of the South until the 1960s. They effectively nullified the Fourteenth and Fifteenth Amendments to the Constitution, which had been enacted following the Civil War to secure the civil rights of the emancipated slaves. The laws made black subordination almost as severe as when the blacks had been slaves. White terror organizations such as the Ku Klux Klan (KKK) murdered, assaulted, and intimidated blacks who sought to exercise their newly won rights.

More than a decade after the end of the war, the conditions in the South were still chaotic, desperate, and violent. Many owners of plantations were either dead, incapacitated, or bankrupt, and they could not pay their workers. Any bank accounts or cash they might have, if issued by the Confederacy, was now worthless. Even many buildings, equipment, horses, and mules required for plantation operation had ceased to exist or were now unavailable. Cotton and rice production dropped sharply, thus requiring fewer workers. Starvation and disease ravaged both the white and the black population, particularly the former slaves, who found few opportunities to obtain gainful employment as the plantation system broke down. Quite naturally, the few plantation owners who could afford to hire paid workers gave preference to white job seekers. A white person willing to pick cotton, a task at the very lowest rung of the job status ladder, was obviously in desperate straits and was more deserving of help than an ex-slave.

The plantation system was essential to the production of cotton, and to shore up the broken system, the federal government instituted a program where Northerners would be allowed to lease and run plantations that would otherwise not be able to continue operation. The former slaves could go back to working on the plantations but would be paid a salary to allow them to exist as free, independent men. For several reasons, including inexperience, incompetence, and corruption among the temporary operators of the plantations, the well-intended program was a failure. Those who benefited the least from it were the black workers who were often not given their salaries.

---

[20] President Andrew Johnson, letter to the House of Representatives, Washington, DC, June 22, 1866.

The war and its aftermath thoroughly transformed the South and coincided with the rapid industrialization of the North. At the end of the war and following the turmoil of Reconstruction, the reunited United States was no longer the nation it had been. It had gone through a violent and traumatic period that, in its practical effects on the lives of its citizens, was more transformative than the American Revolution a century earlier. The wounds and bitterness left by the Civil War and its aftermath left scars in the South for another hundred years.

While they were slaves, many blacks were whipped severely. Slaves were valuable property, however, so they were not ordinarily killed as punishment unless they were deemed to be dangerous to whites. After emancipation, the former slaves were a threat rather than the valuable assets they had been as slaves. In the chaos and desperate conditions that characterized the South following the war, violence against blacks was common, and there was not much interest in documenting it. It is thus difficult to know how many blacks were murdered during those years. The KKK and similar organizations in the South murdered thousands. An 1872 Congressional investigation found that during a span of a few weeks in 1868, more than two thousand blacks were murdered by mobs in Louisiana alone. In Texas, an incomplete survey revealed that more than a thousand were lynched between the end of the Civil War and 1882.[21]

Fear and hatred of blacks remained among many whites in the South, even after blacks had been safely eliminated from the levers of power and no longer represented a threat from a political or economic point of view. The oppression of blacks did not lessen the prejudices against them. It was still widely believed that they were dangerous and that they must be kept in submission under tight control because of their purportedly primitive nature. The former slave owners feared the black man's alleged constant sexual urge, directed especially toward white women. A horrifying boogeyman consequently appeared: the "black rapist," a brutish black man overcome with raging lust to rape white women.

Race-baiting political demagogues, sex-obsessed fundamentalist preachers, and self-proclaimed public guardians of morality evoked this image with great success. The fear of the black rapist was a central feature of the complex and twisted mix of religious fervor, anxieties, sadistic lust, and hatred that drove white Southerners to oppress, murder, and terrorize their black neighbors for a century after the Civil War. Segregation of the races became the ultimate concern—primarily to prevent sexual intimacy between people of different races. The rationalization became that granting legal equality to the black population would inevitably lead to the mixing of the races, a result that would spell the doom of the white race and its superior characteristics.

Not all white men could abide by the prohibition against interracial sex. Following the emancipation, the rape of black women by gangs of white men became a common occurrence, demonstrating that whites still had unchallengeable power over the former slaves. For the same purpose, they also murdered blacks who sought to exercise their new rights. Whites tended to envision those efforts by blacks as ambitions to reach social integration, which ultimately would lead to their access to white women. Gradually, the violence against blacks began to take the form of public lynchings. These became increasingly ritualized as they began to express more clearly the fears and suppressed sexual drives prevalent in the South.

---

[21] Walter White, *Rope and Faggot: A Biography of Judge Lynch* (Notre Dame, IN: University of Notre Dame Press, 1992), p. xii.

Lynching as a public spectacle and expression of sadistic gratification

The lynching of blacks had a complex set of motivations, purposes, and effects. Ida Wells-Barnett was one of the founders of the National Association for the Advancement of Colored People (NAACP) and an anti-lynching crusader. In 1892, she collected 728 records of lynchings in a few previous years. In her pamphlet titled *Southern Horrors: Lynch Law in All Its Phases,* she exploded the myth that the lynching of black men was the white response to the rape or attempted rape of a white woman, aimed at dissuading other black men from doing the same. She documented that only about a third of lynched black men had "ever been *charged* with rape, to say nothing of those who were innocent of the charge." Wells showed that an actual or attempted rape was usually not what motivated lynching. As we can understand today, it was the result of an obsessive urge to exorcise a threatening evil from white society.

To whites, the black man was a primitive brute, in whom there were no restraints of morality or other noble sentiments. He was a frightening, visible embodiment of animal forces that threatened not just the physical body but the very soul of every white woman. If not kept under tight control, he represented an existential threat to the white race. Lynchers felt a compelling need to demonstrate their unquestionable power over the black man, rendering him completely helpless, viciously torturing, emasculating, and mutilating him before killing him. Not a few went so far as to burn him until nothing but a grotesque, charred figure of vaguely human form remained as if they only then had demonstrated their absolute victory over the icon of raw, dangerous lust.

In 1895, Ida Wells-Barnett, after studying many cases of lynchings, hypothesized a psychological fixation on sex in relationship to lynchings, given the common practice of castration with lynchings.[22]

In 1900, the governor of South Carolina, Ben Tillman, held that civilized men had the right to "kill, kill, kill" the "creature in human form who has deflowered a white woman."[23] In a speech to the US Senate, he defended the rights of white men to do whatever was necessary to protect white women from the threat of the black rapist, and to extract the maximum penalty on the black brute themselves if that protection failed. He declared:

> "We in the South have never accepted the idea that black men have the right to govern white men, and we never will. We have never believed that he is the equal of white men, and we will never see him take out his lust on our wives and daughters without lynching him."

His attitude may seem extreme by today's standards, but it was typical of the South of his time. Thousands of black men and women were lynched, often for relatively minor crimes. Usually, the excuse was an allegation of crime of some sort, or even something as minor as a failure to submit to white authority.

---

[22] Ida Wells-Barnett, *A Red Record: A Tabulated Statistics and Alleged Causes of Lynching in the United States, 1892–1894* (Salt Lake City, UT: Project Guttenberg, 1895).

[23] John D'Emilio, Estelle B. Freedman: *Intimate Matters: A History of Sexuality in America,* First edition.) p 217

As late as 1930, Southern politicians campaigned on support for the practice of lynchings. South Carolina Senator Coleman Blease, seeking reelection, proudly stated: "Whenever the Constitution comes between me and the virtue of the white women of the South, I say to hell with the Constitution."[24]

Lynchings became public spectacles that were sometimes advertised in advance and drew large crowds of excited onlookers. They took place all across America, not just in the South. Many historians have remarked on the celebratory atmosphere surrounding the well-attended public lynchings of blacks. Many whites and others were lynched as well, but those events did not draw large audiences and lacked the festive spirit in combination with the prolonged, drawn-out torture of the victim that often took place during the lynching of a black person. An element of entertainment associated with the lynching of blacks has led some to analyze the leisure activity aspect of lynching. More accurately, perhaps, they were rituals.

By the 1890s, lynchers increasingly employed burning, torture, and dismemberment to prolong suffering and to excite a festive atmosphere among the killers and onlookers. White families brought small children to watch, newspapers sometimes printed advance notices, railroad agents sold excursion tickets to announced lynching sites, and mobs cut off black victims' fingers, toes, ears, or genitalia as souvenirs. Nor was it necessarily the handiwork of a local rabble—not infrequently, the mob was encouraged or led by people prominent in the area's political and business circles. Lynching had become a ritual of interracial social control, emotional release, and recreation rather than simply a punishment for crime.[25]

Kirk W. Fuoss, a professor at St. Lawrence University, described in a 1999 article "a great float drawn by six horses."[26] Fuoss's comparison of lynching to performing art shows is supported by an account of the lynching of Henry Smith in Paris, Texas, in 1893, where Smith was accused of raping a child, and the execution took place on a specially constructed elevated stage. Ida Wells-Barnett documented the event:

> The negro was placed upon a carnival float in mockery of a king upon his throne, and, followed by an immense crowd, was escorted through the city so that all might see the most inhuman monster known in the current history... [Then] Smith was placed upon a scaffold, six feet square and ten feet high, securely bound, within the view of all beholders.
>
> Here the victim was tortured for fifty minutes by red-hot iron brands thrust against his quivering body. Commencing at the feet the brands were placed against him inch by inch until they were thrust against the face. Then, being apparently dead, kerosene was poured upon him, cottoned hulls placed beneath him and set on fire... Curiosity seekers have carried away already all that was left of the memorable event, even to pieces of charcoal.[27]

---

24 Ibid.
25 Excerpted from a longer article in *The Reader's Companion to American History*, eds. Eric Foner and John A. Garraty (New York: Houghton Mifflin, 1991).
26 Kirk Fuoss, "Lynching Performance: Theatres of Violence," *Text and Performance Quarterly* 19, no. 1 (1999): 1–37.
27 As cited in Trudier Harris. *Exorcising Blackness: Historical and literary lynching and burning rituals.* (Bloomington: Indiana University Press, 1984).

Award-winning author and University of Virginia professor Grace Elizabeth Hale observed that the lynching of Henry Smith was "the founding event in the history of spectacle lynchings... the first blatantly public, actively promoted lynching of a southern Black by a large crowd of southern whites," with features such as "the specially chartered excursion train, the publicly sold photographs, and the widely circulated, unabashed retelling of the event by one of the lynchers."[28]

During the lynching of Henry Smith, the repeated reference to event-like themes, such as a float, carnival, and parade, indicate that the event was well organized. The "six drawn horses," the excursion train, and the float decorated in "mockery of a king" highlight the elements of festivity. The burnt remains becoming souvenirs, and the promotional materials for acquisition or purchase, are reminiscent of paraphernalia purchased at modern-day sporting events.

Figure 4. The lynching of Henry Smith in Paris, Texas 1893

Before being burned to death in Coweta County, Georgia, on April 23, 1899, Sam Hose had been stripped naked in front of a crowd of two thousand, chained to a tree, beaten, mutilated, and castrated. Kerosene-soaked wood was stacked around him and set afire to affect his slow, torturous execution. When the fire at last burned down, his charred body was cut into pieces, which were then fought over by spectators.

Some accounts of lynchings make one wonder how the participants experienced the events, which to contemporary Americans appear almost inconceivably cruel and nightmarish. As an example, one may choose the lynching of Jesse Washington in Waco, Texas, on May 15, 1916. In the 2000 book *Without Sanctuary: Lynching Photography in America*,[29] co-author James Allen explains that Washington was a mentally handicapped seventeen-year-old boy who worked on a farm, some seven miles away from the murder site. As Allen wrote, "A young white woman, Lucy Fryer, was murdered on May 8th in Robinson, Texas, and a supposed confession from this mentally handicapped young man included the admission of the murder.

---

[28] Grace Elizabeth Hale, *Making Whiteness: The Culture of Segregation in the South, 1890–1940* (New York: Pantheon Books, 1998).

[29] James Allen, Hilton Als, John Lewis, and Leon F. Litwack, *Without Sanctuary: Lynching Photography in America* (Santa Fe, NM: Twin Palms Publishers, 2000).

A May 15th trial determined that he was guilty solely based on the 'confession' and a 'presented' murder weapon after a 4-min jury deliberation."

Allen stated further:

> The boy was beaten and gagged... before preparations were already under way... Washington was beaten with shovels and bricks. Fifteen thousand men, women, and children packed the square. They climbed up poles and onto the tops of cars... Children were lifted up by their parents in the air. Washington was castrated, and his ears were cut off. A tree supported the iron chain that lifted him above the fire of boxes and sticks. Wailing, the boy attempted to climb the skillet hot chain. For this the men cut off his fingers. The executioners repeatedly lowered the boy into the flames and hoisted him out again. With each repetition, a mighty shout [from the crowd] was raised.

Figure 5. The lynching of Thomas Shipp and Abram Smith, Marion, Indiana, 1930.

Figure 6. The lynching of Will Brown in Omaha, Nebraska, 1919

Figure 7. A crowd gathered to see Jesse Washington about to be burned, Waco, Texas, 1916.

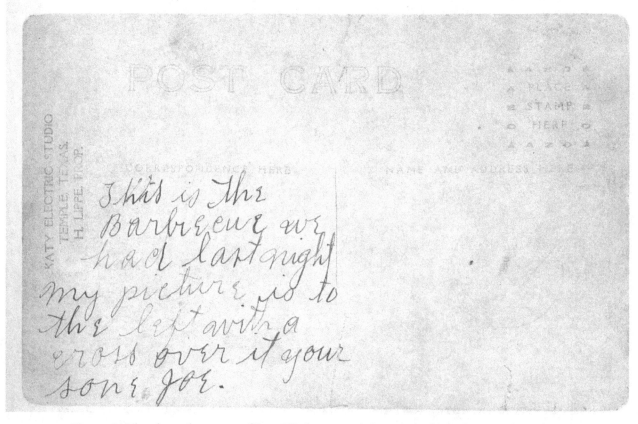

Figure 8. The charred remains of Jesse Washington. (a "nigger barbecue" in Southern lingo)

Figure 9. Lynching victims such as Rubin Stacy were often left hanging for a long
time as public warning examples. July 19, 1935, Fort Lauderdale, Florida.

Spectators took bloodcurdling photos of lynching victims, even as the often sadistic and protracted
public execution proceeded. Sometimes enterprising photographers made numerous copies of the photos
and sold them as postcards. A significant number of such photos still exist, and many show both victims
and the excited and smiling faces of the witnesses. The Pulitzer prize-winning writer and historian Leon F.
Litwack collected a large number of photos of lynching victims of both sexes, which he included in the book
Without Sanctuary: Lynching Photography in America. The pictures show not only the tortured, butchered,
hanged, and burned victims but also large crowds of witnesses, sometimes in the many thousands, including
men, women, and children, all apparently excited and pleased by what they see. At least four thousand blacks
are known to have been lynched between 1882 and 1960. Many others simply disappeared without a trace.

The book also contains many descriptions of the proceedings and comments made by white lynchers,
witnesses, and newspaper journalists. Some display a cruelty that is unfathomable to our modern sensibility,
but which a substantial majority of the devoutly religious Southern white society accepted at the time. It
is evident from both the photos and the comments quoted in the book that support for lynching was both
strong and widespread, and that many people got satisfaction out of witnessing these events. They prove

wrong the common assumptions that only crazed fanatics on the fringes of society were responsible for the lynchings and that the average citizen neither approved of nor participated in them. The photos and comments also make abundantly clear that participants and witnesses expected no legal repercussions as a result of their actions.

In his commentary on the photos, Litwack wrote:

> The photographs stretch our credulity, even numb our minds and senses to the full extent of the horror, but they must be examined if we are to understand how normal men and women could live with, participate in, and defend such atrocities, even reinterpret them so they would not see themselves or be perceived as less than civilized. The men and women who tortured, dismembered and murdered in this fashion understood very well what they were doing and thought of themselves as perfectly normal human beings... What is most disturbing about these scenes is the discovery that the perpetrators of these crimes were ordinary people, not so different from ourselves—merchants, farmers, laborers, machine operators, teachers, doctors, lawyers, policemen, students; they were family men and women, good, decent, churchgoing folk...[30]

Witness descriptions of the lynchings are horrifying for the exquisite, sadistic cruelty with which they were often carried out. *Without Sanctuary* documents many such descriptions. As an example, one may quote the description of the 1918 execution of Mary Turner, a black woman who was eight months pregnant. Her husband had been lynched, and, according to its notice of the affair, the Associated Press reported that Mary made "unwise remarks" and threatened to accuse the killers in court. The *Savannah Tribune* of May 25, 1918, reported that "the people, in their indignant mood, took exception to her remarks, as well as her attitude."

> For making such a threat, a mob of several hundred men and women decided to "teach her a lesson." After tying her ankles together, they hung her from a tree, head downward. Dousing her clothes with gasoline, they burned them from her body. While she was still alive, someone used a knife ordinarily reserved for splitting hogs to cut open the woman's abdomen. The infant fell from her womb to the ground and cried briefly, whereupon a member of this Valdosta, Georgia, crowd crushed the baby's head beneath his heel. Hundreds of bullets were then fired into Mary Turner's body, completing the work of the mob.[31]

Or one may select the report in the *Vicksburg Evening Post* about the lynching of Luther Holbert and his wife in Doddsville, Mississippi, in 1904. Luther was accused of killing his white employer. During the

---

[30] ibid, p. 34
[31] Ibid, p. 14.

search for him, a white posse killed two blacks, each of whom was mistaken for Luther Holbert. His wife was not accused of being guilty of the murder of her husband's employer but had the bad luck of being captured together with him and was thus considered an accomplice:

> When the Negroes were captured, they were tied to trees and while the funeral pyres were prepared they were forced to suffer the most fiendish tortures. The blacks were forced to hold out their hands while one finger at a time was chopped off. The fingers were distributed as souvenirs. The ears of the murderers were cut off. Holbert was beaten severely, his skull was fractured and one of his eyes, knocked out of its socket, hung by a shred from the socket... The most excruciating form of punishment consisted of the use of a large corkscrew in the hands of some of the mob. This instrument was bored into the flesh of the man and the woman, in the arms, legs and body, and then pulled out, the spirals tearing out big pieces of raw, quivering flesh every time it was withdrawn.[32]

Given that the newspapers of the day relished using sensational and gruesome language to excite their readers, one may remain somewhat skeptical about all the details of their reports. Still, lynchings were undoubtedly often conducted as much to provide entertainment for the executioners and the crowds of onlookers—sometimes numbering in the thousands—as to punish the victims. They exceeded in their cruelty and bloodlust the human killings by wild animals in the Roman Colosseum. They are particularly noteworthy for the perverse sadism and hatred with which they were conducted. In the Colosseum, it was nothing personal. In most lynchings, the torture, mutilations, castrations, and burnings were motivated by personal emotions.

Litwack, commenting on his collection of lynching photos in *Without Sanctuary*, remarked:

> What was strikingly new and different in the late nineteenth and early twentieth century was the sadism and exhibitionism that characterized white violence. The ordinary modes of execution and punishment no longer satisfied the emotional appetite of the crowd. To kill the victim was not enough; the execution became public theater, a participatory ritual of torture and death, a voyeuristic spectacle prolonged as long as possible (once for seven hours) for the benefit of the crowd. Newspapers on occasion announced in advance the time and place of a lynching, special "excursion" trains transported spectators to the scene, employers sometimes released their workers to attend, parents sent notes to school asking teachers to excuse their children, and entire families attended, the children hoisted on their parents' shoulders to miss none of the action and the accompanying festivities.[33]

---

[32] ibid, p.. 15.
[33] Ibid, pp. 13, 14

One may wonder what the underlying motivation was that would drive ordinary folks to commit such gruesome murders. In speaking of the Holocaust, the philosopher Hannah Arendt noted that the most frightening thing about evil is its ordinariness, its "banality." Evil, Arendt noted, is not usually radical, even when extreme. That observation surely applies to some degree when it comes to lynching and the willingness to espouse the tradition shown by the ordinary people in the South. In many cases, the perpetrators rationalized the killing of a black man or woman as a simple act of justice. For many, it was a necessary act that served to keep manifest the power and superiority of whites so that blacks would be kept in their place and not become "uppity" or lacking in respect for and obeisance toward whites. For some, it provided the kind of adrenaline high that others get from big game hunting or intense sports—or watching people being torn apart by lions. Humans do have a killer instinct left from our days as primitive hunters, which allows us to be excited by killing or by watching killings or violence, be it real or in movies. Nevertheless, when that killer instinct reaches such extremes as the public and sadistic torture of victims, one must look for additional, less obvious psychological drives.

The religious aspects of lynching

Jamelle Bouie, chief political correspondent for *Slate* magazine, stated it succinctly: "The lynching and torture of blacks in the Jim Crow South weren't just acts of racism. They were religious rituals."[34]

As the organization Equal Justice Initiative notes in agreement, lynchings were not only acts to demonstrate racial control and domination. They were rituals of Southern evangelicalism and the dogma that evangelicalism had at the time of purity, biblical literalism, and white supremacy.

What was the specific religious significance of the sadistic lynchings of blacks, often involving torture and castration? One cannot answer without knowledge of the "psychological profile" of the religious beliefs held by the people who perpetrated and enjoyed watching those hellish proceedings. "It is exceedingly doubtful if lynching could possibly exist under any other religion than Christianity," wrote NAACP leader Walter White in 1929. "No person who is familiar with the Bible-beating, acrobatic, fanatical preachers of hell-fire in the South, and who has seen the orgies of emotion created by them, can doubt for a moment that dangerous passions are released which contribute to emotional instability and play a part in lynching."[35]

The vast majority of black lynching victims were men. In the United States, the sadistic impulse directed toward black women was evident mostly in the violence and absolute humiliation associated with gang rape out in the open air, which the perpetrators rationalized as necessary, well-deserved punishment for some alleged misbehavior. It is psychologically significant that those men never lacked the necessary arousal to be physically able to perform their act of "civic duty."

---

[34] Jamelle Bouie, Christian Soldiers: The Lynching and Torture of Blacks in the Jim Crow South Weren't Just Acts of Racism: They Were Religious Rituals. (*Slate magazine*, February 10, 2015)

[35] Philip Dray: *At the Hands of Persons Unknown; The lynching of Black America* (New York: Random House Publishing Group) p 80

In the European witch hunts, the perceived threat came mostly from women rather than men, but otherwise, the parallel is striking. Fanatical witch hunters applied the most excruciatingly painful tortures to the naked bodies of strapped-down, helpless women to extract admissions of having committed heinous crimes in service of the Devil, even having copulated with him. If the accused were found guilty by admission under torture, or if the "Devil's mark" was found anywhere on their bodies, they were put to death in public burnings. The Devil's mark was carefully searched for and might be a dark mole or spot somewhere, perhaps hidden in the most intimate of places. Modern scholars estimate that around forty to fifty thousand women were executed as witches. (The executioners tended to favor burning, as it was known to be a most painful way to die.)

Figure 10. Witch trial.

The historian Amy Louise Wood wrote in her book *Lynching and Spectacle: Witnessing Racial Violence in America, 1890–1940*:

> Christianity was the primary lens through which most Southerners conceptualized and made sense of suffering and death of any sort. It would be inconceivable that they could inflict pain and torment on the bodies of black men without imagining that violence as a religious act, laden with Christian symbolism and significance.

The God of the white South demanded purity—embodied by the white woman. White Southerners would build the barrier with segregation. But when it was breached, lynching was the way they would mend the fence and affirm their freedom from the moral contamination, represented by blacks and black men in particular. The perceived breach was frequently sexual, defined by the myth of the black rapist, a "demon" and "beast" who set out to defile the Christian purity of white womanhood.[36]

Defenders of lynching believed their acts were a Christian duty—an act in service of God's command against racial intimacy. Wood cites a defender of lynching as saying, "It was nothing but the vengeance of an outraged God, meted out to him, through the instrumentality of the people that caused the cremation."[37]

As Professor Emeritus Donald G. Mathews of the University of North Carolina at Chapel Hill wrote in the *Journal of Southern Religion*:

> Religion permeated communal lynching because the act occurred within the context of a sacred order designed to sustain holiness. Holiness demands purity and purity was sustained in the segregated South by avoidance, margins, distances, aloofness, strict classification and racial contempt... Essential to these myths by the late 1880s was the image of the white woman whose innocence justified whatever violence white men might find "necessary" for her protection against the "black-beast-rapist.[38]

The sacred order was segregation and white supremacy, and the holiness was white female virtue.

Mathews pointed his finger at an important aspect of Southern beliefs: putting an idealized white woman on a pedestal as a symbol of purity, not unlike the Virginal Mother, a common figure in pre-Christian religions, and for Christians represented by the Virgin Mary. For a black man to desire sex with this iconized white female was sacrilegious in the extreme. The black man was a threat not just physically but also by representing and serving the forces of evil—just like a witch. The icon of the Virginal Mother must not be ravaged and polluted by the icon of sinful, raw, bestial lust.

The language employed to justify lynching, so often using the notion of the defilement of the pure, innocent white woman by a sex-crazed black brute, rings with religious fervor. The feelings of white Southerners were expressed in iconic terms: "God will burn... the Big African Brute in Hot Hell for molesting our God-like pure snowwhite angelic American Woman."[39]

Some victims of lynching were white; some were Mexicans, Jews, or Native Americans. However, those lynchings did not draw crowds of thousands of enthusiastic onlookers. Nor were those victims usually subjected to the humiliation and prolonged torture that so many black victims suffered before being hanged,

[36] Amy L. Wood, Lynching and Spectacle: Witnessing Racial Violence in America, 1890–1940 (Chapel Hill: University of North Carolina Press, 2009), p 48

[37] ibid., p. 63

[38] Donald G. Mathews: "The Southern Rite of Human Sacrifice, Part III: Sacrificing Christ/Sacrificing Black Men," *Journal of Southern Religion*, 3 (2000). http://jsreligion.org/)

[39] John D'Emilio, Estelle B. Freedman: *Intimate Matters: A History of Sexuality in America*, 3rd edition () p. 217

shot, or burned to death. Even when hanged or shot, their bodies were afterward sometimes burned to grotesque charred stumps that were put on public display. There was indisputably a ritualistic element to the lynching of blacks suggesting that blacks were symbols of something dangerous and threatening. That is why the victims were so often castrated in the ritual of lynching. Cutting off the penis of the black man was a procedure of exorcism and demonstrated victory over the demon of lust.

Part Three: Deep Roots, Bitter Fruit

Introduction

It is impossible to understand the turbulent history of American society, especially the history of its minority populations, without understanding how racial animosity, fear, prejudice, segregation, and systematic oppression of minorities have channeled its flow. From the very beginning, American Natives were stereotyped as violent savages and driven off their ancestral lands by armed force. Almost as soon as European immigrants had settled in the Americas, black Africans were captured and transported to the Americas to be used as lifelong slave labor, mostly in conditions that were extremely harsh and humiliating. While on the North American continent the American Natives were successfully removed to distant "Indian reservations" where they were no threat to white settlers, black slaves were necessarily present among their white owners. Today their descendants are the victims of most of the racial prejudice and animosity that remain among many white Americans.

Slavery allowed for the creation of a wealthy white upper class of plantation owners in the South who were wholly dependent on the labor of black slaves to sustain their wealth and privileged lifestyle. A great expansion of this society began in the early 1800s with the establishment of cotton as the dominating crop and the forced eviction of the original population of Native Americans to areas farther west, making space for vast cotton plantations. The wealthy elite that arose with the booming cotton economy came to view itself as nobility with a sophisticated and refined culture.

When one speaks of "race" in America, it is mostly in the context of relations between, on the one hand, Americans who consider themselves "white" and exclusively the descendants of European immigrants and, on the other, those who have a visible degree of African ancestry. The history of race relations in the United States shows that slavery was the most important factor in forming those relations. Slavery existed on the North American continent for more than two centuries, and where it existed, it thoroughly shaped America's culture, economics, attitudes, and popular prejudices. It helped create a stereotype of a black person that would continue to bedevil those of African ancestry long after the institution of slavery was abandoned. It is that stereotype that we need to investigate from historical, economic, and psychological perspectives.

Justifications for slavery involve picturing blacks as inherently inferior

Racial prejudices of any kind do not seem to have been common in antiquity, but some early sources available to Europeans describe black Africans as being inherently different from others, and not merely in skin color. The Arab writer and historian Leo Africanus (al-Hasan ibn Muhammad al-Wazzan al-Zaiyati, 1494–c. 1554), writing on the history of Africa, provided the most influential early description of the people of Africa. He described the African black man as living a "brutish kind of life," devoid of any religion or law and surrounded by "swarms of harlots."[40]

Jean Bodin (c. 1529–1596) was a French lawyer, economist, natural philosopher, historian, and one of the most influential political theorists of the sixteenth century. He was opposed to slavery, but after reviewing the writings of ancient authorities on the people of Africa, he concluded that a lustful disposition was characteristic of the "Ethiopian" (i.e., African) race.

Other respected authorities also contributed to the image of the African as having particularly strong erotic passions and sexual potency. The notion of blacks as being lustful and physically advantaged sexually became well established in European literature long before the first English contact with West Africa. In his influential book *White over Black: American Attitudes toward the Negro*, Winthrop Jordan summarizes the beliefs that Europeans had absorbed from numerous reputed experts on the characteristics of Africans. He concludes: "Depiction of the Negro as a lustful creature was not radically new, therefore, when Englishmen first met Negroes face to face. Seizing upon and reconfirming these long-standing and common notions about Africa, Elizabethan travelers and literati spoke very explicitly of Negroes as being especially sexual."[41]

By the early 1600s, many of the Englishmen who met the first blacks to arrive at Jamestown had thus already formed opinions of them based on rumors and statements by alleged experts. By the end of the seventeenth century, the concept of the libidinous black man had spread widely in the New World and was already well entrenched in the American psyche. These beliefs were sustained by plantation owners who used blacks as breeding stock, as well as by prominent thinkers of the period, such as Thomas Jefferson. In his *Notes on the State of Virginia*, Jefferson wrote that black men "are more ardent after their female: but love seems with them to be more eager desire, than a tender, delicate mixture of sentiment and sensation."[42]

Benjamin Rush (1745–1813) was a leading American physician and a personal friend of Jefferson's. He was an advocate of the abolition of slavery but was also strongly opposed to any mixing of the races. Curiously, Rush theorized that the blackness of black people's skin was a form of leprosy. He reasoned:

> Lepers are remarkable for having strong sexual desires. This is universal among the
> negroes, hence their uncommon fruitfulness when they are not depressed by slavery;

---

[40] Leo Africanus, *The History and Description of Africa and of the Notable Things Therein Contained* (London: Hakluyt Society, 1896).

[41] Winthrop D. Jordan, *White over Black: American Attitudes toward the Negro, 1550–1812* (Chapel Hill, NC: Omohundro Institute of Early American History and Culture and the University of North Carolina Press, Chapel Hill, NC. 1968) p. 34

[42] Quoted in Winthrop D. Jordan *The White Man's Burden, Historical Origins of Racism in the United States* (New York: Oxford University Press), p. 182

but even slavery in its worst state does not always subdue the venereal appetite, for after whole days, spent in hard labor in a hot sun in the West Indies, the black men often walk five or six miles to comply with a venereal assignation.[43]

Europeans found in the Bible other explanations for the blackness and God-ordained slave status of Africans. In the late sixteenth century, George Best, a well-traveled English adventurer, had explained the blackness as a curse from God. According to Best, Noah commanded his family to abstain from sexual intercourse while aboard the ark. Ham disobeyed the command, cleverly figuring that the first grandson of Noah born after the flood would inherit the whole world. As retribution, God willed it that Ham's wife would bear a son, named Chus, "who not only it selfe, but all his posteritie after him should bee so blacke and lothsome, that it might remain a spectacle of disobedience to all the worlde. And of this blacke and cursed Chus came all these blacke Moores which are in Africa."[44] (Chus is called Canaan in modern Bibles.)

Slave owners used the story of Noah to show that Noah had condemned blacks, identified as the descendants of Canaan, to be slaves to the descendants of his brothers Shem and Japhet forever (Gen. 9:25–27). When the American Revolution produced a formal US Constitution for how to govern the new nation, the document did not extend to slaves the same rights to "life, liberty, and the pursuit of happiness" as it promised white citizens.

One must realize that virtually all white slave masters were convinced that they were not doing anything wrong to blacks by holding them as slaves. Plantation owners felt that they had a divinely sanctioned right to exercise absolute power over their slaves. There was nothing in the Bible that spoke against slavery. As defenders of the institution of slavery liked to point out, the ancient Israelites had slaves, and Jesus made no disapproving mention of the custom.

Based on what slave masters had heard about conditions in Africa, blacks should have counted themselves lucky to escape the heathen societies of Africa. This view remained an essential component in the framework of moral justification for slavery as an institution. Even as late as the 1840s, proslavery advocates could, in all seriousness, claim that "Though they may be perpetual bondsmen, still they would emerge from darkness to light—from barbarism into civilization—from idolatry to Christianity—in short from death to life."[45]

Another Southern writer found that not only did the blacks benefit from their situation of slavery in the Americas, but they were also eager to take advantage of the opportunity. Stressing the biblical sanction of slavery, and identifying the white race with Japhet, the Native Americans with Shem, and the blacks with Canaan, he declared in inspired prose:

---

[43] Quoted in Winthrop D. Jordan, *White over Black: American Attitudes toward the Negro, 1550–1812* (Chapel Hill, NC: Omohundro Institute of Early American History and Culture and the University of North Carolina Press, 1968) p. 519.

[44] As quoted in David M. Whitford: *The Curse of Ham in the Early Modern Era: The Bible and the Justification for Slavery* (New York: Routledge, 2009), p. 106.

[45] John H. Hammond, 1845 letter to abolitionist Thomas Clarkson. Quoted by many authors, for example, Alexander Marjoribanks in his 1854 book *Travels in South and North America*, p. 330
https://books.google.se/books?id=cZ72j0YHkRIC&printsec=frontcover&dq=inauthor:%22Alexander+Marjoribanks%22&hl=sv&sa=X&ved=0ahUKEwiy4eubu7TbAhVOSZoKHfBnAhEQ6AEIPjAD#v=onepage&q&f=false

By the discovery of America, Japhet became enlarged as had been foretold 3,800 years before. He took the whole continent. He literally dwelt in the tents of Shem in Mexico and Central America. No sooner did Japhet begin to enlarge himself, and to dwell in the tents of Shem, than Canaan left his fastnesses in the wilds of Africa, where the white man's foot had never trod, and appeared on the beach to get passage to America, as if drawn thither by an impulse of his nature to fulfill his destiny of becoming Japhet's servant.[46]

An image of the black slave as dull-witted, inferior, and not fully human was necessary to justify the enslavement of blacks and to maintain a brutal and oppressive form of slavery. The same disparaging stereotype of blacks spread into much of the white American population even outside the South. Therefore, the end of slavery did not mean the end of the humiliation, exploitation, and oppression of black Americans. For another century, the belief in the inherent inferiority of black people would be the official rationalization for isolating them from white society by segregation and for denying them the same rights as whites.

The US historian Eugene D. Genovese succinctly describes the characteristics that most Europeans came to think of as typical of Africans in his massive and seminal book *Roll, Jordan, Roll: The World the Slaves Made*:

> During the seventeenth and eighteenth centuries, West African mores had shocked the Europeans. The extent of nakedness; the free use of sexual jokes, allusions, and symbols; the apparent ease with which sexual partners could sometimes be exchanged—in a word, the different standards of behavior—convinced Europeans that Africans had no standards, no morals, no restraints. Before long, Europeans were hearing lurid tales of giant penises, intercourse with apes, and assorted unspeakable (but much spoken of) transgressions against God and nature.[47]

The retention of African beliefs and customs among the slaves

The influence of African customs, values, and beliefs could be seen in many aspects of the private and familial lives of the slaves. Their masters noted, in particular, their less repressive sexual mores—mores that their owners decried but not only secretly exploited yet also promoted and encouraged by the very system of slavery. African music, with its insistent, percussive beat and excitement and the high-spirited dancing that it occasioned, became in white people's minds associated with uninhibited sexuality—a connotation that would carry over into jazz and rock and roll.

---

[46] Essay by Rev. B. M. Palmer, quoted by Stephen R. Haynes in *Noah's Curse, the Biblical Justification of American Slavery* (New York: Oxford University Press, 2002) note 87.

[47] Eugene D. Genovese, *Roll, Jordan, Roll: The World the Slaves Made* (New York: Vintage Books, 1976), p. 458.

Slaves were becoming converts to Christianity in growing numbers, but in contrast to the Spanish, French, and Portuguese in their respective American colonies, the slave owners in the English colonies were not eager to promote this conversion. Christianity might give the slaves the idea that they were, at least in the eyes of the Lord, the equals of the whites. Consequently, the slaves in what would become the United States retained for a long time the beliefs of their African ancestors. When converted to Christianity, they developed their own interpretation. In many areas, it was illegal to teach slaves to read—therefore, even the slave preachers were generally unable to read the Bible. The parts of the Bible that were most entertaining and could be remembered and retold as oral tradition—i.e., the dramatic and awesome stories of the Old Testament—became the core of the form of Christianity the slaves embraced. The situation has remained so even today among the traditional fundamentalist strains of black religiosity.

This form of Christian religion became an increasingly important factor in how the slaves saw both the world and their place in it. The biblical stories of the Old Testament became the new tribal mythology of blacks in continental North America, where the slaves particularly identified with the Hebrews enslaved in Egypt. Moses became a prototypical hero, and a messianic hope developed that a Moses would come to lead the black slaves to their freedom. Harriet Tubman (c. 1822–1913) escaped from violent, abusive slavery in Maryland and became a legendary figure by helping hundreds of other slaves flee to the North via the Underground Railroad, a chain of escape routes and hiding places arranged by the Quakers. Because of her success and daring, she became known as Black Moses. She was also a suffragette, a strong spokeswoman for women's right to vote.

The ritual of worship, which whites denounced and ridiculed as uncivilized and heathenish, also developed along distinct lines among blacks and contributed to the opinion that blacks were inherently unable to behave with restraint and dignity. The great landscape architect Frederick Law Olmsted (1822–1903), on a voyage through the antebellum South, noted that the institution of slavery had thoroughly corrupted not only the slaves but also their white masters. He expressed the theory that "power corrupts" as it pertained to the slave masters as such: "The possession of arbitrary power has always, the world over, tended irresistibly to destroy humane sensibility, magnanimity, and truth."[48]

Regarding the slaves, he noted that their lives were hard and monotonous and that on many plantations, religious rituals were almost "the only habitual recreation not purely sensual" available to the slaves, and that they participated in them "with an intensity and vehemence almost terrible to witness."[49]

Olmsted would recognize this religious fervor today if he were to visit a black Pentecostal church. The fervor of the sermon, slowly building to an intense, excitedly animated, screaming crescendo, the heavy beat of the songs of the choir, and the ecstatic trance and joyous outcries of the congregation, have always been common features of black religiosity. Notably, the form of Christianity that has made the strongest inroads in Africa in modern times has been the "charismatic" black church, which ties back to the same traditional African beliefs and traditions that helped to shape the Christianity of the slaves in the Americas.

---

[48] Frederick Law Olmsted, *A Journey in the Seaboard Slave States: With Remarks on Their Economy*, vol. 1 (London: S. Low, Son and Company, 1856), p. 115

[49] Frederick Law Olmsted, *A Journey in the Back Country: A Traveller's Observations on Cotton and Slavery*, vol. 1 (London: S. Low, Son and Company, 1860), p. 106

The influence of African beliefs has been particularly strong in Brazil and Cuba, where hybrid faiths have evolved called *Candomblé* or *Santeria* (meaning "worship of saints"), in which African pagan/voodoo gods called orishas continue to be worshiped but under the names of Christian saints. The black slaves' religious practices contributed to the belief among whites that blacks were given to outbursts of uncontrollable emotion and passion.

White reactions to the customs and appearance of African slaves

The very Victorian and bourgeois moral precepts of the newly rich plantation owners regarding white women accentuated the perceived differences between blacks and whites with regard to sexuality. Trying to embody the myth of a genteel, refined, and aristocratic society, the Southern social elite of the plantation owners developed an image of the white lady as delicate and sweet—more frightened than attracted by the crude sexual nature of men. The white woman, according to this belief, had a natural longing for childbearing and homemaking but did not have an aggressive or passionate temperament. Nor was she a strong, willful personality, so a man of low character could take advantage of her weakness. Thus, a white woman was a precious commodity that had to be zealously safeguarded. Only as a virgin could she attract a suitor with large landholdings.

The beliefs about the characteristics of the normal and respectable white woman are typified by the writings of the British surgeon William Acton (1813–1875), who made the following statement on female sexuality: "There can be no doubt that sexual feeling in the female is, in the majority of cases, in abeyance, and that it requires positive and considerable excitement to be roused at all; and even if roused, which in many instances it never can be, is very moderate compared with that of the male." After admitting that many men, "after association with the loose women of London streets," had received a false impression that women are naturally lustful, Acton reassured his readers that "married men, medical men, and married women themselves, would, if appealed to, tell a different tale, and vindicate female nature from the vile aspersions cast on it by the abandoned conduct and ungoverned lust of a few of its worst examples."[50]

Dr. Acton thus thought women lucky not to be "troubled" by sexual passion and was anxious to defend them against the "vile aspersions" cast on female nature by a few deviant "worst examples." Such language reveals that his opinions were affected by value judgments formed by Christian morality, which perhaps made it impossible for him to make an objective evaluation of his research data. To his defense, one might say that the information he gathered could have persuaded most men of his day to reach similar conclusions. Middle-class British society drilled sexual inhibitions into women so consistently, and from such a tender age, that most were perhaps frigid or frightened by sex.

Even women writers expressed similar sentiments until the 1960s. Eliza Duffey (1838–1898) was an American author, early feminist, and women's rights activist who wrote in *What Women Should Know* (1873)

---

[50] William Acton, *The Functions and Disorders of the Reproductive Organs in Childhood, Youth, Adult Age and Advanced Life, Considered in Their Physiological, Social, and Moral Relations*, 6th ed. (Philadelphia: Presley Blakiston, 1875), pp 162, 163, 164

that "the passions of men are much stronger and more easily inflamed."[51] Another female writer, Eliza Farnham, stated that "the purity of women is the everlasting barrier against which the tides of men's sensual nature surge—to be steadily beaten back, or human welfare decays in her failure."[52] Their assessments were made with the unspoken assumption that they referred to the expected readership for their books, white women of the middle and upper classes.

Travelers and literary figures of the nineteenth century often noted the emotionally stunting effect that this system of beliefs and practices had on the Southern women. One Northern visitor in 1809 found the typical Southern woman notable for a "dull, frigid insipidity, and reserve" and ascribed these traits to the fact that Southern men found their pleasure elsewhere. That, he observed, was one of the worst "curses slavery has brought on the Southern states."[53]

The unmarried Southern belle found her opportunities for exploring and expressing sexuality severely curtailed. Her contacts with young white men were tightly chaperoned; the thought of a relationship with a black man must never enter her mind. She entered marriage very ignorant of the facts of life. Even after marriage, she continued to be closely guarded and would not travel without her husband unless accompanied by a chaperone.

The 1915 film *The Birth of a Nation* by director D. W. Griffith did much to fix black stereotypes in the minds of many naive Northerners. White women were idealized as "pure" and virginal. They were supposed to be utterly ignorant about sexual matters to the extent that, as Frances Newman put it, "in Georgia a woman was not supposed to know she was a virgin until she ceased to be one."[54] Many white men joked that "until they married, they did not know that white women were capable of sexual intercourse."[55] According to Griffith, white Kentucky women would tolerate marital infidelity in their husbands as long as it was with black women. White wives joked among themselves about the lasciviousness of black women, apparently feeling that the latter were no threat to the permanence of their marriages. These dalliances thus did not have to be taken seriously and removed some of the white women's burdens in satisfying their husbands.

White Southern men, on the other hand, enjoyed far more freedom. Some had affairs with white women of ill repute or low social standing. Many more availed themselves of female slaves, who were, from a practical point of view, a more attractive choice. Slave women represented no threat to their masters, as they could claim neither rape nor seduction under false promises of marriage and had nothing to gain but much to lose from complaining, refusing, or making the affair known to the mistress of the house. Most white men took no account of the children they fathered with slave mistresses and were adept at denying their fatherhood even to themselves.

---

[51] Eliza B. Duffey, *What Women Should Know: A Woman's Book About Women* (New York: J. M. Stoddart & Co., 1873), p. 97 Reprint Arno Press, New York 1974.

[52] Eliza W. Farnham, *Woman and Her Era*, (New York: A. J. Davis & Co., 1864), p. 95

[53] John D'Emilio, Estelle B. Freedman, *Intimate Matters: A History of Sexuality in America* (Chicago: University of Chicago Press, 2012), p. 94

[54] Ibid. p.186.

[55] Ibid. p. 186

Interracial sexual contacts in the slave states

On many Southern plantations, black slaves outnumbered their white owners and their families. In daily life, most white males encountered no white females who were not part of their families, but they had the female slaves legally available to them for sexual relations. For young white males, the temptation to avail themselves of that outlet was often irresistible. An Englishman visiting South Carolina noted of the character and habits of the white colonists that "the planters are in general rich, but a set of dissipating, abandoned, and cruel people. Few even of the married ones but keep a Mulatto or a Black Girl in the house or at lodgings for certain purposes."[56]

Josiah Quincy, Jr., traveling from strait-laced Massachusetts, observed indignantly in 1773 that in South Carolina,

> The enjoyment of a negro or mulatto woman is spoken of as quite a common thing: no reluctance, delicacy or shame is made about the matter. It is far from being uncommon to see a gentleman at dinner, and his reputed offspring as slave to the master of the table. I myself saw two instances of this, and the company very facetiously would trace the lines, lineaments and features of the father and the mother in the child, and very accurately point out the more characteristic resemblance.[57]

The author Mary Boykin Chesnut (1823–1886) wrote *A Diary from Dixie*, an insightful book about the society of the South based on her diary entries during the Civil War. She remarked that "the Mulattoes one sees in every family exactly resemble the white children—and every lady tells you who is the father of all the Mulatto children in everybody's household, but those in her own she seems to think dropped from the clouds or pretends so to think."[58]

For many white Southern men, those relationships represented their introduction to physical intimacy with a woman—a fact that might help explain why black women continued to have an image of sexuality and passion. The black woman became the antithesis of the white woman—where the white woman was sweet but cool, the black woman was rough but hot; while the white woman was delicate and reserved, the black woman was physically vigorous and sexually aggressive. The white woman was to be placed on a pedestal—a romantic icon of purity and sweetness to be courted patiently and formally in the hope of eventual marriage. In contrast, the black woman was an icon of lust and sexual pleasure, always available and responsive. While the former could offer prospects of a comfortable role as a husband and a father and—in cases of arranged marriages—an increase in status and wealth, the latter provided only the immediate satisfaction of one's

---

[56] Samuel Thornely, ed., *The Journal of Nicholas Cresswell, 1774–1777* (Carlisle, Mass.: Applewood Press, 1924), p. 39.

[57] Daniel C. Littlefield, *Rice and Slaves; Ethnicity and the Slave Trade in Colonial South Carolina* (Chicago: University of Illinois Press, 1991) pp. 170, 171

[58] Quoted in Carol Bleser, ed., *Secret and Sacred: The Diaries of James Henry Hammond, a Southern Slaveholder* (New York: Oxford University Press, Inc., 1988), p. 18

urgent physical needs. Many white men found that they could worship both icons—the Madonna and the Whore—because both were symbols of what they truly needed and desired.

The situation in the American slave states might have come to resemble what it was on some of the Caribbean islands during slavery—except that there, white slave owners felt less pressured by societal norms to keep their affairs secret. To the whites who ran the sugarcane plantations, the West Indies provided a location for their businesses but did not serve as a real home—merely a temporary dwelling place whose climate presented a physical hardship. It was a dangerous and uncivilized place precisely because of the sizeable numerical advantage of the black slave population. It was not the best place for dainty British ladies. Thus, the islands had a scarcity of white women. The colonial authorities strictly enforced laws against interracial marriage, and relations between black males and white females were not tolerated, but black slave concubinage became a somewhat officially accepted aspect of life for English businessmen on these tropical islands—even for those who had their white wives and children living there with them. In these circumstances, it became so acceptable for white men to have black mistresses that having easy access to such a large number of good-looking female slaves was generally considered an employment benefit. The historian Edward Long (1734–1813) wrote indignantly of Jamaica:

> Many are the men, of every rank, quality, and degree here, who would much rather riot
> in these goatish embraces, than share the pure and lawful bliss derived from matrimonial,
> mutual love. Modesty, in this respect, has but little footing here. He who should presume
> to shew any displeasure against such a thing as simple fornication, would for his pains
> be accounted a simple blockhead; since not one in twenty can be persuaded, that there is
> either sin; or shame in cohabiting with his slave.[59]

Many men—even those who believed blacks to be inferior to whites as a race—became receptive to the charms of their bondmaids by long separation from white female company and by the inescapable whispers regarding the black woman's passion and talent for lovemaking. In the British West Indies, the Englishmen appear to have favored pure African women over mixed-race slaves. Some who sampled the delights of the black females were positively lyrical in their praises, such as the anonymous writer of "Jamaica, a Poem, in Three Parts":

> Next comes a warmer race, from sable sprung,
> to love each thought, to lust each nerve is strung;
> The Samboe dark, and the Mulattoe brown,
> the Mestize fair, and the well-limb'd Quadroon,
> and Jetty Afric, from no spurious sire,
> warm as her soil, and as her sun—on fire.
> These sooty dames, well versed in Venus' school,

---

[59] Edward Long, *The History of Jamaica* (London: T. Lowndes, 1774), p. 32

make love an art, and boast they kiss by rule.[60]

On the American continent, the white South was not all a wealthy, privileged aristocracy; it also had another side. A substantial white underclass existed who was shunned by the white elite. These whites were poor and generally illiterate and uneducated. For many of them, life was hard. They had to work their own small fields of corn and other vegetables and to tend a small number of chickens and domestic animals, thus spending a lot of time in the blazing Southern sun. As a result, they were commonly quite burned by the sun, giving rise to their epithet "rednecks."

In the South, a man's sexual exploitation of slave women did not necessarily end once he got married. Many white men were emotionally unable to end these relationships and saw no good reason to do so if they were discreet about their affairs. Although they could not publicly acknowledge these relationships, their existence continued to be a tacitly accepted reality. Some defenders of slavery, such as the novelist William Gilmore Simms, dared openly to admit that sexual exploitation of slave women was common. Simms thought it was a good thing for all involved, even for the white women, as such exploitation served as a safety valve for the lust of white men.

Sexual exploitation of female slaves was thus common in the antebellum South, but these relationships were kept hidden and not spoken of, since people in the continental colonies, even many of those who themselves engaged in such relationships, continued to think of interracial sex as something perverse and almost bestial—a breach of the divinely ordained order of nature. Since those affairs were always clandestine, it is difficult to ascertain precisely how common they were, although some would come to light after the death of a master, when the female slave and her children sometimes were manumitted (i.e., given their freedom) through a clause in the master's will. The master's family usually contested such wills, and the freedom of the manumitted slaves was often short-lived. Some states enacted laws to bar manumission altogether.

In the majority of cases, the sexual contact between white masters or overseers and slaves took the form of rape, performed habitually by the master on numerous slaves. Even if the sexual act was against the will of the female slave, it was not necessarily physically violent. As a slave, a black woman could not refuse to perform sexual services, and among the slaves, it was well known to be a part of slave life.

What may have started as a rape occasionally blossomed into a far more serious and lasting involvement, with both the master and the slave unwilling to break off the illicit relationship. It appears not to have been uncommon that slave owners had secret, long-term slave mistresses whom they never publicly acknowledged but for whom they showed much affection.[61] Governor James Henry Hammond of South Carolina, who had written more than once that "he who takes a colored mistress—with rare and extraordinary exceptions— loses caste at once," could himself not resist that temptation.[62] He bought an eighteen-year-old slave girl named Sally Johnson and her infant daughter and made Sally his mistress. When the daughter (Louisa)

---

[60] Anonymous inhabitant of Jamaica: "Jamaica, a Poem, in Three Parts" (London: William Nicoll, No. 51, Paul's Church Yard, London 1777), pp. 22, 23.

[61] Eugene D. Genovese, *Roll, Jordan, Roll: The World the Slaves Made* (New York: Vintage Books /Random House, 1976) p. 415

[62] James H. Hammond, *Governor Hammond's Letters on Southern Slavery: Addressed to Thomas Clarkson,* (Baltimore, MD: The Johns Hopkins University Library, 1845), p. 10.

reached the age of twelve, he took her as a mistress as well. He fathered at least one child by each. Unwilling to send them North to freedom, in his will, he left both mistresses and their children to his white son Harry, declaring that "slavery in the family will be their happiest earthly condition."[63]

A female slave who willingly entered a steady, intimate relationship with her owner or one of his brothers or sons could gain substantial advantages from it. The position of mistress usually offered her improved living conditions, better treatment, and greater security—she ran less risk of being sold and perhaps being separated from her children. Having children with her white master might be the first step in a multigenerational chain that would eventually lead to "passing"[64] in society and freedom for her descendants. She might also gain prestige: being selected as a mistress would be a validation of her desirability as a woman, and her status among the slaves would likely increase—perhaps in competition with other slave women. Not to be dismissed is the possibility that the woman found her white mate highly attractive both physically and as a person and thoroughly enjoyed their time together. That appears to have been the case with Thomas Jefferson and his mistress Sally Hemings[65].

Thomas Jefferson, the second president of the United States, fathered six children with his slave mistress Sally Hemings. Sally was the half-sister of Jefferson's wife, Martha (born Wayles) since they had the same father—the slave owner John Wayles. Sally's mother was Betty Hemings, one of John Wayles's slaves. Several sources claim that John Wayles fathered six children with Betty and that Sally was the youngest of these mixed-race siblings. Betty was herself the daughter of a slave owner named John Hemings and a slave named Susanna, who was of pure African ancestry. Betty was therefore given the last name Hemings, the name also given to Betty's daughter, Sally.

Sally Hemings, Jefferson's mistress, thus had a white father and a white maternal grandfather and is reported to have been quite fair-skinned. Excavations at Jefferson's residence at Monticello have revealed that Sally had her own bedroom in the house, right next to the one belonging to her owner. Jefferson did not give Sally her freedom but kept her as a slave until his death. Political enemies tried to taint Jefferson with a scandal by revealing that he had a black mistress, but Jefferson was able to credibly deny the rumor and never publicly acknowledged his relationship with Sally or his paternity of her six children.

When Jefferson died in 1826, he left only two officially acknowledged children: those he had with his white wife, Martha, who had died many years earlier. They inherited Sally and her children, who were also slaves. Since Sally was the half-sister of their mother (Martha) through their father, John Wayles, as noted above, Sally's children were their half-brothers and half-sisters through their father, Thomas. Sally's children were very light-skinned, so their physical resemblance to Jefferson's children with Martha must have been obvious. Sally and her children were soon given their freedom, but they did not receive public recognition as Jefferson's mistress and children. Four of the children were so light-skinned that they were able to "pass."

---

[63] Carol Bleser, editor: *Secret and Sacred: The Diaries of James Henry Hammond, a Southern Slaveholder* (New York: Oxford University Press, 1988) p. 19.

[64] "Passing" referred to becoming so light and otherwise appearing of European descent that one could pass oneself off as white and be absorbed into white society.

[65] Annette Gordon-Reed, *The Hemingses of Monticello: An American Family* (New York: W. W. Norton & Co., 2008)

Modern DNA testing has confirmed that a now (2018) living man named John Weeks Jefferson is the descendant of Thomas Jefferson's son by Sally Hemings, named Eston.[66]

White slave owners fathered many children with their female slaves, some of whom—like Sally Hemings—were themselves of mixed ancestry. After multi-generational occasions of having offspring with white masters, some children of slave women became so light in skin and hair color that after the end of slavery, they were able to "pass," i.e., deny their slave ancestry, and claim to be white. Like the grandchildren of Sally Hemings, they became absorbed in the white population. According to a recent DNA-based study[67], millions of today's Americans who describe themselves as white have some detectable African ancestry. Various estimates place the percentage between one and two percent overall, with a figure at the high end of the range in the population with family roots in the antebellum South. Many light-skinned Latinos consider themselves white even though their ancestry would make others classify them as black according to the old "one drop" rule. There is no uniform legal standard in the United States as to who is white.

In the white population with family roots outside the South, the incidence of African DNA is less common. Very few of those who are the descendants of the large-scale immigration from Europe between 1880 and 1920 have a detectable amount of African DNA. Those immigrants settled in parts of the United States where the black population was a tiny minority, and the racial prejudice that permeated American society soon infected them also. They left a very small DNA footprint in the American black population.

Until the early 1900s, the overwhelming majority of black Americans resided in the South, and the overwhelming majority of black Americans today are the descendants of slaves, even if they have lived for several generations outside the South. In most parts of the United States, there have until recently existed legal or customary boundaries between the races in terms of seeking a mate, and with the end of slavery, there was a sharp drop-off in the number of mixed-race children born to white fathers in the South. Still, DNA evidence indicates that today, between 75 and 90 percent of Americans who self-identify as black have some European ancestry. The figure hints at the extent of sexual exploitation of slaves that took place during slavery.

The European ancestral component remains in the black population as a heritage, even if it was introduced many generations back in the days of slavery. The majority of the children fathered by white men and slave women were too dark to pass in white society and found mates who were also dark-skinned. They remained classified as black. The African part of their genetic makeup shows great variety since Africa is the continent of greatest genetic diversity.

The high percentage of European DNA found in the black population in America did not originate in the majority of whites who lived outside the slave states, or arrived as immigrants from Europe after the Civil War. It can be traced mostly to sexual exploitation of black slave women by their white masters or members of his family. White fathers hardly ever acknowledged paternity of children born to their slaves, but ultimately, far more such children were born than white society in the past has been willing to acknowledge.

---

[66] John M. Butler, *Forensic DNA Typing: Biology, Technology, and the Genetics of STR Markers* (Burlington, MA: Elsevier Academic Press, 2005), p. 226.

[67] F. James Davis: *Who is Black? One Nation's Definition,* Tenth Anniversary Edition (University Park, PA: Pennsylvania State University Press, 1910) p. 29

Arthur W. Calhoun (1899–1975) was a professor at several American universities and the author of many books on a range of subjects. He took particular interest in social issues regarding family life and race and speculated about the reason why so many white men of the South had black slave mistresses. He concedes that "the master's right of rape" facilitated easy access to black women but points out that this right only provided the means—there also had to be a motive. In his book *A Social History of the American Family*, Calhoun ventures a theory to explain what he termed "the wholesale profligacy of the Old South":

> Close attention should be given in the light of modern psychology to the consequences upon white children of constant association with members of the other race... The more subtle effects in the realm of the unconscious will suggest themselves. White babies, for instance, commonly had negro wet nurses, and it may be wondered whether in view of the psychic importance of the suckling process there may not have been implanted in the minds of the Southern whites certain peculiar attitudes toward negro women and whether this possibility may not be a partial explanation of the sex tastes of the men of the Old South.[68]

The pioneering civil rights author Lillian Smith, who was quoted at the beginning of this book, has pointed out that the black female, well into modern times, has had a unique and psychologically important role in the raising of white children. There can be little doubt that the black wet nurse and loving baby caretaker, the "black mammy," represented a mother image to young white children in the South—one that would leave a permanent impression on their minds.

That was only one side of a conflicted image that whites had of black women. For many white Southerners, the image of the black woman has always been that of a sex object. The psychiatrist and historian Kermit Mehlinger, M. D., made an observation that seems relevant to Professor Calhoun's suggestion. Mehlinger described in vivid language the image that the white man had of the black woman:

> She was reported to be a torrid sexpot of animalistic abandon... The white man projected a schizophrenic image onto her. On the one hand, she was like a Jezebel, a passionate, hypersensous siren—easy to "make," and responding to his overtures in a completely uninhibited, receptive manner. On the other hand, she was a grinning, roly-poly Mammy, moored down to her fat bottom by the sheer weight of her ample breasts.[69]

---

[68] Arthur W. Calhoun, *A Social History of the American Family from Colonial Times to the Present* (Cleveland, OH: Arthur H. Clark Company, 1918), p. 285.

[69] Kermit Mehlinger, M. D.: "The Sexual Revolution: Disappearance of Victorian taboos has resulted in a new freedom for 'weaker sex.'" (*Ebony* magazine, August 1966), p. 58

Interracial sexual contacts in the North

Even in some Northern states, there were laws against interracial marriages. Far fewer blacks lived in the North than in the South—still, some mixed-race marriages did take place in the states that did not have institutionalized slavery. Not all whites saw these mixed-race marriages as acceptable, particularly if the man was black and the woman white. Thomas Branagan (1774–1843) was one of America's most prolific writers in the first two decades of the 1800s. He was an abolitionist but looked askance at intimate relationships between whites and blacks. After a visit to Philadelphia in 1805, he wrote:

> There are many, very many blacks who... will not be satisfied unless they get white women for wives... I have visited different parts of Africa, South America, the chief of the West India islands, and the Southern states; and I solemnly declare, I have seen more white women married to, and deluded through the arts of seduction by negroes in one year in Philadelphia, than for eight years, I was visiting the above places... There are perhaps hundreds of white women, thus fascinated by black men in this city, and there are thousands of black children by them at present, and what must it be at the future.[70]

The morally corrosive effects of slavery

The system of chattel slavery practiced in the United States inevitably led to utter moral debasement. To understand this, one only has to contemplate the two powerful incentives of greed and raw lust, both pulling in the same direction without any obstacles at all in law and with a haughty attitude of absolute power and superiority. It is all too easy to vilify those who used their privileged positions to brutally abuse, exploit, and humiliate those over whom they held such power when instead one must lay the blame on the system itself. Even such a high-minded, thoughtful, and world-wise man as Jefferson kept his mistress and their six children as slaves until his death.

The breeding of slaves like cattle became increasingly common once the demand for slaves increased in the South as King Cotton consolidated his grip on the Southern economy, while the importation of additional slaves was outlawed on January 1, 1808. The import ban was of limited effectiveness, however, since slaves were expensive, and the importation was very profitable. Smuggling of slaves continued even after it was made a capital offense in 1820. Between 1837 and 1860, seventy-four cases were brought to court in the United States, but convictions were few and usually led to only trifling sentences.[71]

Many plantation owners and male members of their families took sexual advantage of female slaves. American beauty standards usually favoured a more European look, and mulatto and "quadroon" females (discussed shortly) were particularly sought after as secret concubines. As merchandise, they, therefore,

---

[70] Thomas Branagan, *Serious Remonstrances, Addressed to the Citizens of the Northern States, and Their Representatives* (Philadelphia: Thomas T. Stiles, 1805), pp.70, 73.

[71] Hugh Thomas: *The Slave Trade: The Story of the Atlantic Slave Trade 1440–1870* (New York: Touchstone, 1999), p. 774.

brought higher prices than full-blooded blacks. Some slave owners allowed other white men to impregnate particularly good-looking slaves to obtain their offspring as a saleable commodity. Others, unwilling to keep their own children as slaves, sold the children they had themselves fathered with their slaves.

The traditions of the antebellum South lasted long enough and benefited the slave owners sufficiently to create a comfortable air of normalcy around the "peculiar institution" (as slavery was sometimes referred to) and to shape the morality of white Southerners.

During slavery, the dominant caricatures of blacks (black mammy, coon, Uncle Tom, and pickaninny), especially of "house negroes" as opposed to field-working slaves, did not portray blacks as threatening. They were depicted in a condescending but often affectionate way that one might have toward pets. They were childlike, happy, devoted to their masters, and generally harmless. Such a depiction served to make slavery morally justified. Slave owners served as quasi-parents and caretakers to the slaves, providing them with the necessities of life: food, shelter, and the order and rules required to keep them from descending into helpless chaos and barbarity. In return, the slaves performed for their owners the simple tasks for which they were particularly suited, namely the fieldwork or housework needed to keep the plantations operating profitably and comfortably. That depiction of blacks would change drastically following the end of slavery.

The end of slavery creates fear, hatred, and the creation of Jim Crow

The abolition of slavery tore apart Southern society in almost every respect. The Civil War caused a disastrous and tragic loss of life, with almost every Southern family seeing loved ones or dear friends killed or permanently disabled by the war. It destroyed the wealth and power of the previously ruling elite and set free a mass of slaves who had little if any education or skills, no experience of having to provide for themselves independently, and few employment opportunities—except, if they were lucky, continuing the work of picking cotton in slavery-like conditions on the now much-reduced plantations. Hundreds of thousands of these freed slaves succumbed to starvation and disease in the aftermath of the Civil War.[72]

The tensions and anger created by the liberation of millions of black slaves produced fear and hatred, aggravated by the beliefs about the powerful sexual nature of blacks. The fears became iconized in the form of the black rapist archetype noted earlier in the book, a sex-crazed, apelike brute who was imagined to be a constant horrifying threat to all white women. The racial polarization became total.

Whites allowed themselves to show some degree of courtesy and a friendly demeanor toward a black person in their employ without this attitude necessarily constituting a relaxation of the rules of absolute white supremacy. The interaction between the races was never allowed to reach the level of granting blacks equal rights or status to whites. Under all circumstances, blacks must show whites complete obedience, deference, and respect. Someone white must not take the side of a black person against a fellow white person—that would be an unforgivably treasonous offense against the white race.

---

[72] Jim Downs, *Sick From Freedom; African-American Illness and Suffering During the Civil War and Reconstruction* (New York: Oxford University Press, 2012)

Blacks were not allowed to sit on juries when the accused was white. If a black person accused someone white of an offense, all-white juries almost always declared the accused innocent. Instead of finding the accused white person guilty, the jurors would punish the black accuser. The accused had been found innocent, the thinking went, and therefore the accusation must have been made maliciously.

In contrast, a black person accused of an offense against a white person—or against the rules of white supremacy—seldom went unpunished. Most white Southerners considered the taking of an innocent life to be a sin—even the life of a black person—but viewed this as occasionally being justified by necessity if there was a credible accusation against a black person of having committed an offense against a white person. It was not necessary to go through a regular court procedure to establish guilt, since that might risk an acquittal or on overly lenient sentence. For many whites, the curious overriding rationale for the extra-legal procedures was to maintain respect for the law among the black citizens. In the opinion of many Southern whites, the lynching of one black offender had a net positive effect on society, since it might deter many other blacks from committing offenses.

The end of slavery produced an intensification of racial sensitivity quite beyond the creation of the black rapist image. Before the Civil War, society had a gradation in racial identification. People accepted as a reality that some people had mixed heritages in various degrees. People were officially considered mulatto if they had one supposedly purely white and one purely black parent. A quadroon, briefly mentioned earlier, was someone with one-quarter black ancestry, and an octoroon had one-eighth black ancestry—i.e., only one of the person's eight great-grandparents was black.

The membership in these classes conferred different, unofficial, location-dependent, and insecure levels of acceptance and rights, which was further complicated by the fact that if someone's mother was a slave, then that person was also a slave according to the law. In contrast, if someone's mother was white, then that person was born free, even if the father was a black slave. (The shame of having a black slave father made a mockery of the term "free.")

Once slavery was abolished, the boundaries between whites and blacks became extremely sharp. The purpose was to establish as clearly as possible the delineation between the races. Now, the definitions of racial belonging contained only two categories: white and black. The new legal rule was that if someone had even "one drop of black blood," that person was black. The "one-drop" rule was a setback for many light-skinned, mixed-race people who had previously been considered almost white and had enjoyed some of the privileges that came with whiteness. As the Jim Crow laws were created and enforced in the South, those people found themselves at the bottom of the social ladder, together with all others who were now perceived to be black, regardless of their skin color or hair texture. Blacks were allowed employment by whites in menial and household work, but other social contacts across the racial line were illegal. They had to sever the connections they once had to whites by family ties or friendship.

The superior sexual power of blacks becomes official medical doctrine

In the eighteenth through early twentieth centuries, advancements in the health sciences and anthropology did little to change existing beliefs about the sexual superiority of people of black African ethnicity. These sciences also reinforced the beliefs formed in the Victorian age about the emotional nature of respectable women. At that time, a new middle-class society developed in Europe and America characterized by a puritanical morality that strongly colored the beliefs regarding the natural chastity of women—at least white women. Respected medical authorities, rather than celibate churchmen, were now the formulators of the dogma. For almost a century following the Civil War, renowned physicians and anthropologists threw gasoline on the emotional fires of racist fears and hatred by supporting, enhancing, and lending authority to beliefs in the superiority of blacks regarding sexual organ size, desire, and performance.

The most authoritative source for information on the sexual organs of various races was Dr. Louis Jacolliot, who wrote under the pseudonym Jacobus. His book *Untrodden Fields of Anthropology* was first published in French in 1898 and was advertised as being "based on the diaries of his thirty years' practice as a French government army surgeon and physician in Asia, Oceania, America, Africa, recording his experiences, experiments, and discoveries in the sex relations and the racial practices of the arts of love in the sex life of the strange peoples of four continents."[73] In his book, he reports his observations regarding the sizes and other characteristics of the genital organs of natives of the countries in which he had worked.

Jacobus was a physician in the French army in North Africa during the 1880s and 1890s. In that capacity, he had the opportunity to examine the genital organs of many males and females in that part of the world, and to form opinions about the emotional, physical, and moral differences between people in many parts of the world in their lovemaking. Modern statisticians realize that his database was still wholly insufficient to draw reliable conclusions about the averages and deviation from averages of the genital size of different populations on earth. That is true especially because the difference in genital size between individuals within a given population will be far greater than any difference in average size among different populations. Nevertheless, the opinions Jacobus expressed conformed to the widespread beliefs among his contemporaries—beliefs that still exist in our own time and provide no small amount of material for black comedians as well as for sex-obsessed white racists.

Jacobus claimed that "in no branch of the human race are the male organs more developed than in the African Negro... In fact, with the exception of the Arab, who runs him very close in this respect, the Sudanese Negro possesses the largest genital organ of all the races of mankind."[74]

According to Jacobus, the physical dimensions of the African genitals aid in achieving an unequaled potency:

> In order to spend [ejaculate] the black requires a very prolonged rubbing and the receptacle is large and well lubricated. A Negro is therefore able to make the act of coition last a

[73] Jacobus (Louis Jacolliot), *Untrodden Fields of Anthropology* (New York: Falstaff Press, 1937)
[74] Ibid., Volume II. –"Africa," p. 64.

long time before he spends and can even, if he likes, keep back the supreme moment by modulating his thrust. He can thus accomplish amorous exploits which would knock up [out] a European... The Negro takes a much longer time before he spends than the white man does. I should estimate that he is, on an average, quite three times as long in finishing a copulation as the white man is; and I am not exaggerating.[75]

Jacobus believed that the black female was the natural match for her man. He wrote:

The Negress requires a "man stallion" to make her feel the proper physiological sensations, and she seldom finds him except in the male of her own race[76]... To obtain the sensation of voluptuousness... the Negress requires a slow copulation which only the black man, with his huge penis, can give her. It is certain that a well-fed, circumcised Negro can perform on a woman nearly the whole night and only spend five or six times.[77]

A leading British surgeon of the time, Dr. Charles White, also spoke with authority and frankness about human anatomy. After carefully examining many skeletons, corpses, and living bodies of whites and blacks, Dr. White concluded that the black race was characterized by, among other things, a larger penis. The doctor was so impressed with the penises of black men that he kept a preserved specimen in his personal collection of anatomical curiosities.

Since Nature had generously endowed her to be a match for her man, the black woman might, as a side benefit, have less pain and difficulty in childbirth. Dr. White found this to be true and added that she also has larger breasts and nipples than her white counterparts.

In keeping with its staid and proper Victorian style, *Encyclopaedia Britannica* was circumspect in describing the sexual characteristics of blacks. The classic 1911 edition, however, included the theory that although black children often showed some potential for intellectual progress, the "arrest and even deterioration in mental development is no doubt largely due to the fact that after puberty sexual matters take the first place in the negro's life and thoughts."[78]

The pioneering British physician and sexologist Havelock Ellis reported in 1913 that:

I am informed that the sexual power of Negroes and slower ejaculation are the cause of the favor with which they are viewed by some white women of strong sexual passions in America and by many prostitutes. At one time there was a special house in New York City to which white women resorted for these "buck lovers." The women came heavily veiled and would inspect the penises of the men before making the selection.[79]

---

[75] As quoted in Vern L. Bullough, Bonnie Bullough, *Human Sexuality: An Encyclopedia* (New York: Routledge, 2013) p. 509
[76] Ibid.
[77] Ibid.
[78] Robert McC. Adams, Neil J. Smelser, and Donald J. Treiman, eds., *Behavioral and Social Science Research Part 1* (Washington, DC: National Academy Press, 1982), p. 86.
[79] David M. Friedman, *A Mind of Its Own: A Cultural History of the Penis* (New York: The Free Press, 2001), p. 119.

The French author Remy de Gourmont stated that "one knows that a cat's tongue is rough; so is the tongue and all other mucous surfaces of Negroes. This roughness of surface notably augments the genital pleasure as men who have known Negro women testify."[80]

Robert Wilson Shufeldt (1850–1934) was a highly respected American surgeon and ethnographer who had strong views on racial matters. In his book *America's Greatest Problem: The Negro*, he quoted a fellow medical doctor, William Lee Howard, as follows:

> Nature has endowed him [the Negro] with several ethnic characteristics which must be recognized as ineffaceable by man... especially the large but flexible sex organ which adapts itself to the peculiar sex organs of the female and her demands... These ethnic traits call for a large sexual area in the cortex of the Negro brain which soon after puberty works night and day... The chief, the controlling primal instinct in the African is the sexual.[81]

Contemporary scientific evidence gives support for neither Howard's belief in certain "ineffaceable ethnic characteristics" of the black man, a connection between penis size and the size of an associated area in the cortex of the brain, nor Ellis's theory about a correlation between pigmentation and sexual potency and passion.

In the book *Roll, Jordan, Roll* mentioned earlier, Genovese expressed the significant insight that "the titillating and violence-provoking theory of the superpotency of [the] superpenis, while whispered about for several centuries, did not become an obsession in the South until after emancipation, when it served the purposes of racial segregationists."[82] It helped maintain a fear of black men in general as potential rapists and also became part of the fascination with the black man in the abstract as an icon of sexual potency and lust.

The prevalence of the belief in the large size of black genitals plus a continued high level of public interest in the subject have motivated many studies even in modern days. Some of these studies are of questionable origins. As a result, an internet search of "penis size and race" yields a multitude of links serving up a veritable smorgasbord of worldwide statistical data, from which one can pick to find support for whatever one believes. However, most studies have failed to find any significant racial differences, nor have they verified that hand or foot size can be a reliable indicator of penis size. General conclusions are that the average erect penis is about five and a half inches in length with individual differences within ethnic groups being much greater than the difference in average between groups. A representative data set is available at penissizes.org/average-penis-size-ethnicity-race-and-country. It shows data from forty different studies.

---

[80] J. A. Rogers, *Sex and Race*, Volume III: *Why White and Black Mix In Spite of Opposition* (St. Petersburg, FL: Helga M. Rogers,), p. 150.

[81] Robert Wilson Shufeldt, *America's Greatest Problem: The Negro* (Philadelphia: Davis, 1915) p. 99.

[82] Eugene D. Genovese, Roll, Jordan, Roll: The World the Slaves Made (New York: Vintage Books, 1976), p. 462

The highly respected British Journal of Urology International (BJUI) presented a summary of the results of twenty different studies, including a total of 15,521 men.[83]. Its general conclusions were summarized this way:

> It is not possible from the present meta-analysis to draw any conclusions about any differences in penile size across different races... The greatest proportion of the participants in the present meta-analysis were Caucasoids. There was only one study of 320 men in Negroids and two studies of 445 men in Mongoloids. There are no indications of differences in racial variability in our present study; e.g., the study from Nigeria was not a positive outlier. The question of racial variability can only be resolved by the measurements with large enough population being made by practitioners following the same method with other variables that may influence penis size (such as height) being kept constant. Future studies should also ensure they accurately report the race of their participants and conduct inter-rater reliability.

Even some modern-day, self-proclaimed authorities on the matter of racial differences maintain beliefs about the superior size of black genitals. Some, like Robert Shelton of the KKK, quoted at the opening of this book, can claim neither credible academic knowledge nor firsthand life experience to lend authority to their opinions. J. Philippe Rushton, a professor of psychology at the University of Western Ontario, is not as easy to dismiss without further comment. In his 1994 book *Race, Evolution, and Behavior: A Life History Perspective*, Rushton describes the human species as having three major racial divisions—Mongoloids, Caucasoids, and Negroids—whom he claims represent different stages of evolutionary progression covering a broad range of physical and mental characteristics. In Rushton's view, Negroids are the least advanced and Mongoloids the most advanced, with Caucasoids falling somewhere in between—but, of course, a lot closer to the Mongoloids.[84]

Rushton's theory is that mental sophistication has a natural inverse correlation with genital size. He explains this idea by claiming that for as long as two hundred thousand years, the Negroid race has evolved via a different strategy for survival and propagation than that used by Mongoloids and Caucasoids. The strategy evolved because, according to Rushton, the environment and climate in Asia and Europe require for one's survival more ingenuity, inventiveness, and hard work than in Africa. They demand a longer maturation period among infants and thus more parental effort, which discourages the production of large broods of children. For those reasons, Rushton claims, Africans are free to produce numerous offspring and have evolved to be physically more capable of doing so.

In his book, he cites numerous well-respected sources for his data, using facts and figures extracted from hundreds of studies, both historical and modern, and he attempts to draw on anthropological data and evolutionary theory to buttress his arguments. As a scholarly effort, it is massive, broad, and packed

---

[83] BJUI Volume 115, Issue 6 (June 2015), pp 987-986; https://onlinelibrary.wiley.com/doi/full/10.1111/bju.13010

[84] Philippe J. Rushton, *Race, Evolution and Behavior: A Life History Perspective* (Port Huron, MI: Charles Darwin Research Institute, 1994). Rushton is the author of many articles and six books.

with real, true, and interesting data. As such, it has received positive reviews by some respected scientists such as Harvard biologist E. O. Wilson and American psychologist and writer Linda Gottfredson, professor emeritus of educational psychology at the University of Delaware and co-director of the Delaware-Johns Hopkins Project for the Study of Intelligence and Society.

However, his conclusions have been dismissed by the great majority of reputable anthropologists, psychologists, and social scientists. C. Loring Brace, Professor Emeritus at the University of Michigan's Department of Anthropology and Curator Emeritus at the University's Museum of Anthropological Archaeology, expressed well the consensus of the many critics of Rushton's book. Brace, like most critics of Rushton's work, focused on its tone of biased advocacy. In his 1996 review of Rushton's book he states:

> *Race, Evolution, and Behavior* is an amalgamation of bad biology and inexcusable anthropology. It is not science but advocacy, and advocacy for the promotion of "racialism."

In some parts of the book, Rushton's reasoning is uncomfortably similar to the racist arguments put forth by the Nazis. He has appeared at conferences for racist organizations and written articles for numerous publications associated with them, for example, the monthly magazine *American Renaissance*. It is the mouthpiece of the New Century Foundation, an organization founded by Jared Taylor, a well-known racist and white supremacist. The organization is designated a "white nationalist hate group" by the Southern Poverty Law Center. Unfortunately, humans tend to stubbornly believe what they have told if they "feel it" to be true. Rushton's arguments find resonance in many minds.

Part Four: Sex and Sin in America

Introduction

It is not easy for people today to envision the mindset of people living in America one hundred years ago when moral attitudes were quite different from those of today. Far less formed by religious fundamentalism and Victorian prudishness than were their forefathers a century ago, they find it hard to believe that there was a time when religious beliefs not only tolerated but inspired the castration and burning to death of a black man because he was accused of having approached a white woman.

To many readers, the preceding chapter, "Deep Roots, Bitter Fruit," might seem to exaggerate the extent of sexual factors in the prejudices held by white Americans against persons of African descent. Their significance becomes manifest when one considers the attitude and beliefs that prevailed in American society with regard to sex in the era when anti-black prejudice reached a peak. The history of anti-black prejudice in America does not make sense until that dimension of the situation is visible.

"Eugenics," the need to maintain the "purity" of the white race, has been the rationale employed by most of the strident and violent defenders of racial segregation and white dominance. For many of them, the tribal instinct has undoubtedly been a significant part of their motivations to keep the white race "undefiled" by "black" genes. But the issue goes much deeper. It has a moral foundation built upon religious notions, and it affected the entire American society, well beyond any notions of race per se. It was a morality shaped by the Christian faith, which had evolved to associate sexual desire with sin and the Devil.

To acquaint younger readers with the contextual situation of that past, the following explores the attitudes that made American racial prejudice particularly obsessive and emotional. Contrary to the traditional understanding, it was a moral framework created predominantly by concerns other than about "racial purity." It included a great deal of concern about one's social standing in this life as well as the fate of one's soul in the afterlife. Obsessive concern about sex and a belief in its sinfulness and shamefulness permeated the entire value system of American society in the late 1800s through the first half of the 1900s. That aspect of the problem will now be investigated.

The uniqueness of American prejudice against those of African ancestry

In the history of the United States, many ethnic groups have suffered from segregation and discrimination, perhaps none more so than the original inhabitants of the land. Native Americans were killed in large numbers when they tried to defend their lands and culture, but *they were not viciously tortured in well-attended public lynchings.* For generations, Irish and Italian immigrants experienced contempt and social isolation from Americans who were of British extraction, and Chinese laborers found only menial jobs available to them. Latin-Americans have until recently been treated as second-class citizens. *But those ethnic groups have not been targeted with the same obsessive fear and hatred as has been the hallmark of anti-black feelings.* They have not been the victims of well-advertised, sadistic, long, drawn-out public executions attended by thousands of white spectators, watching with awed fascination as the victims were tortured, emasculated, and burned to death until their charred remains were barely recognized as being human.

Why the difference? The reason had a lot to do with a common belief among both blacks and whites in America: Compared to whites, blacks were both physically stronger, more passionate, and less morally inhibited in their sexuality. One might have thought that it made them attractive mates for many whites. Instead, the obsessively prudish morality instilled by devoutly held religious faith inevitably made blacks the targets of particularly fearful prejudice. Attempts to ignore and suppress our instinctive drives are seldom effective. If we continually forbid ourselves to do what our instincts bid us do, unhealthy emotional distress is often the result.[85]

Attempts to suppress strong natural urges because they are deemed "sinful" merely breeds guilt and pain. Guilt and pain are unpleasant states of mind and generate fear and hatred of what is causing them. The inevitable failure to eliminate the natural urges can at best lead to a stand-off: We suppress the conscious awareness of their true nature and disguise them as feelings that are morally more acceptable, perhaps even required according to the value system that our faith and traditions have inculcated in us.

Hatred can stem from many sources. It can, for example, be fired by a desire for vengeance for past grief and suffering inflicted by the hated group. That cannot be the motivating factor for white hateful prejudice against blacks. Black Americans are the ones who have, for centuries, been the victims of white cruelty and oppression, not the other way around.

Hatred can also be based on jealousy, where the jealousy might be about power, wealth, or public esteem and adulation. In this regard also, it would make sense for blacks to hate whites rather than the other way around. Whites have traditionally enjoyed most privileges and advantages.

Jealousy is also often associated with unrequited love, and on that score, whites seem to have little reason for hating blacks. American culture has always relentlessly promoted light skin, straight, preferably blond hair, and European type facial features as the ideal for beauty. Popular media, including advertising, magazines, television, and the movie industry, have drummed those entirely arbitrary standards into much

---

[85] "Unexpressed emotions will never die. They are buried alive and will come forth later in uglier ways." The saying is by many attributed to Sigmund Freud, but a search of his complete works fails to locate it. (https://www.holybooks.com/sigmund-freud-the-complete-works/)

of the black as well as the white population. Reliable statistics are not available, but it is probably more common for blacks to be charmed by the looks of whites than the other way around.

A third common reason for hatred is fear, a belief that the hated person or group represents an immediate, grave danger to some aspect of the security and welfare of oneself or one's group. Fear is indeed at the bottom of white anti-black hatred, but that fear has complicated reasons, not all of which are acknowledged and understood by those who have them. The appearance of a particularly frightening and sexually threatening stereotype, the "black rapist" was a direct result of the imagined sexual power of blacks. As imagined by Robert Shelton, the Alabama head of the Ku Klux Klan, he was out there on nights with a full moon, lurking in the dark shadows, mad with desire, and driven by uncontrollable lust to seek to ravage white women.

The female counterpart, the "Jezebel" stereotype, was less frightening. Women are less physically aggressive and powerful than men, and men could defend themselves against any unwanted approaches. Furthermore, men were not perceived as being as naturally modest, "pure," and in need of protection of their "honor" as women. Even if they succumbed to the temptation of an "unnatural" affair, white men were not so irredeemably tainted as white women by the sexual experience with a member of the black race.

There was some factual basis for the reputation that blacks had for a more liberal sexual morality. That morality was ascribed by whites to an innate nature of blacks but was, instead, the product of long cultural traditions in combination with subsequent generations of slavery conditions. It derived from both the more liberal traditions that existed in the African societies, from which the blacks had been involuntarily brought to America, and from the conditions of slavery, where the slave masters unconcernedly undermined black family bonds. Marriage was not legally binding between slaves, and black families were sometimes broken up by the sale of individual members. Black women were exploited sexually by their white owners, sometimes in the form of rape or secret concubinage. At other times, the exploitation took the form of the use as breeding stock, where the slave owners selected the mating partners and demanded that they have children. After the emancipation, the oppressed conditions in which most former slaves continued to live did not encourage the extremely prudish attitudes that prevailed in the white society.

The belief that blacks were naturally promiscuous was sustained by the continued exploitation of black women by white men. For many Southern men, their first sexual experience was with a young black girl, and some white men sustained relationships with a secret mistress for years, keeping the woman dependent on him by providing support of various kinds to make her life easier. The black woman usually also had a black lover or husband, who was her "regular man." Sometimes the black man, unable to provide for her and her children – one or more of whom might be with the white man – was disrespected by her because he could not deny the white man access to her, and her white sometimes lover could provide better. It would have been remarkable if black society had instantly copied the mores and behavior of middle-class Victorian white America.

In their book *Intimate Matters: A History of Sexuality in America*, John D'Emilio and Estelle Freedman illustrate the customs and attitudes that prevailed in the Jim Crow era South:

> Except among the small black elite, female chastity before marriage was not prized. The
> pregnancy that might occur from premarital experimentation did not carry a stigma, and

women who had given birth out of wedlock did not find their opportunities for wedlock compromised. While nuclear families predominated in black rural communities, many of them evolved out of what began as simple cohabitation, with a legal marriage following after a time.[86]

Part Two of this book touched on the subject of religious feelings motivating the fear and hatred of blacks. The material there is by itself too superficial to be entirely convincing. Giving a full account of the origin and psychological problems of Christian sexual morality is not feasible in this book. It is too complex and too broad a subject in psychology, history, geography, and time. For those who would like to know more about the origins of the very restrictive Christian morality, the book *The Divine Tragedy: The Vengeance of the Forsaken Gods*[87] provides a penetrating look at the history of religious beliefs as an evolutionary-psychological phenomenon, a part of the instinctive nature of the human mentality. It shows how certain religious beliefs create internal emotional conflicts that the devout believer constantly experiences as anxiety, guilt, and sadomasochistic impulses. They can give rise to bizarrely prudish attitudes as well as obsessive fears of all that tempts one into "sin." A "sin" is more than an offense against a human; it is disobedience of God. It amounts to a breaking of a taboo, a rule given by a fearsome deity, and the offense may result in receiving the most horrifying punishment: Eternal extreme torture in a burning hell. It is, therefore, imperative that sources of temptation are removed or rendered impotent.

The evolution of moral attitudes regarding sexual desire and activities

Until the early 1700s, devoutly religious Christians who were obsessed with sexuality were mostly celibate priests and monks. For some of them, it reached the level where they would pursue alleged witches with a sadistic fury, driven by their belief that sex was of the Devil. However, for the average person in the sixteenth through early eighteenth centuries, lust did not have the dire connotations it would later have. During the era of slavery, sexual exploitation of female slaves by their owners was common. It was seldom carried on openly and was denied by the white men if at all plausible, but there is little evidence that it was a cause of shame and guilt and fear of eternal damnation in those who engaged in it. During the slavery era, the situation in some parts of the South threatened to go the way of the British and French Caribbean colonies, where the sexual exploitation of slaves had reportedly reached debauched levels, and a significant proportion of children of slave women were obviously of mixed heritage.[88],[89]

---

[86] John D'Emilio and Estelle Freedman, *Intimate Matters: A History of Sexuality in America,* (New York, Harper & Row, Publishers, 1988), p. 187.
[87] Eklof, Anders: *The Divine Tragedy: The Vengeance of the Forsaken Gods* (Norrisville, NC: Lulu Publishing, not yet published.)
[88] Edward Long, *The History of Jamaica* (London: T. Lowndes, 1774), p. 32.
[89] Anonymous, *Jamaica, a Poem, in Three Parts* (London: William Nicoll, 1777), pp.22,23.

In the eighteenth century, religiosity increased in the American population, and it took a very guilt-ridden, sadomasochistic flavor. As concern about miscegenation increased, so did the indignation of the guardians of morality about the sexual habits of slave owners. Apprehension over a perceived general decline in morality grew into a wave of religious fervor known as the Great Awakening, which swept over the colonies in 1740–41. Fire-and-brimstone preachers attracted huge crowds everywhere and whipped weeping congregations into an ecstasy of panic as they held forth on the agonies that God was going to visit upon them shortly and forever after. Similar waves of religious fervor have since swept the nation from time to time, and the style of preaching—coupled with ecstatic and uncontrollable outbursts of pent-up emotional energy among the listeners, sometimes to the point of fainting—has been a standard feature of fundamentalist denominations ever since. The first (and a later second) Great Awakening helped religion remain the most powerful daily influence on the thoughts, emotions, and behaviors of Americans in most segments of the population.

Prodded by religious leaders, legislative bodies occasionally broke the silence of decency on the subject and censured some of their fellow members and slave owners. A South Carolina grand jury in 1743 issued a public condemnation of "the too common practice of criminal conversation with Negro and other slave wenches in this province, as an enormity and an evil of general ill-consequence."[90] The proclamation was given little heed.

In the 1700s, the Puritan colonists in the North were arguably more devout than the typical Southerner. As the population density increased, roads improved, and sea-lanes saw increased traffic, the improving communications might have aided the upsurge in religiosity nationwide in the American colonies. The Puritan minister Jonathan Edwards (1703–58) has been called the most influential American of his time and was the most important fervent prophet of Puritan faith and morals. He saw no moral conflict between, on the one hand, him owning slaves and defending slavery on the base of Biblical text, and, on the other, preaching the "golden rule," commanding everyone to treat others a one wants to be treated by them.

The following extract from his sermon "Sinners in the Hands of an Angry God" illustrates the character of the Puritan self-image and the sadomasochistic flavor of their fears:

> The God that holds you over the pit of Hell, much as one holds a spider or some loathsome insect over a fire, abhors you, and is dreadfully provoked: His wrath towards you burns like fire; He looks upon you as worthy of nothing else but to be cast into the fire; He is of purer eyes than to bear to have you in his sight: You are ten thousand times more abominable in his eyes than the most hateful venomous serpent is in yours....And it would be a wonder if some that are now present should not be in Hell in a very short time, even before this year is out. And it would be no wonder if some persons, that now sit here in some seats of this meeting house in health, quiet and secure, should be there before tomorrow morning.[91]

---

[90] Daniel C. Littlefield, *Rice and Slaves; Ethnicity and the Slave Trade in Colonial South Carolina* (Chicago: University of Illinois Press, 1991), p.170
[91] Tracey D. Lawrence, ed., *The Greatest Sermons Ever Preached* (New York: Harper Collins, 2005), pp. 104, 110

Some were chastened and made repentant by such vitriolic vituperation. Others were not, but the level of anxiety about the subject of sex increased noticeably. An ancient belief was revived, clearly through religious influence, in the early eighteenth century. The theory held that the loss of semen causes a loss of virility. The mechanism thought to be involved was a "rarefication" of vital spirit in the blood to create semen. The more semen a man ejaculated, the more vital fluid he lost from his blood.

The newly established authority of science buttressed opinions based on little more than religion-derived moral precepts and irrational fears. Many highly educated and respected physicians joined the clergy and other vociferous anti-vice crusaders in a campaign to alert the public to the perils of immoral thought and behavior. The *Boston Medical and Surgical Journal* reported that the loss of semen associated with masturbation or sexual intercourse could significantly weaken a man's vitality. Men must minimize such loss because "sturdy manhood… loses its energy and bends under the too frequent expenditure of this important secretion."[92] No one mentioned that semen, once it is produced, plays no part at all in the metabolism of its owner and is produced, in fact, for the sole purpose of being—unavoidably—"expended."

The most influential of the new theorists was the Swiss physician S. A. Tissot (1728–1797), who in the 1750s formulated the theory of "degeneracy," an all-encompassing term for a plethora of frightful consequences of sexual activity and dirty thoughts. He published numerous books on the subject of the allegedly devastating effects of masturbation on both the mind and the body. According to his theory, the loss of semen (and, for women, what was thought to be the female counterpart) entirely weakened and debilitated people's physical and mental faculties, making them susceptible to all kinds of disease and enfeeblement. An English-language translation of Tissot's *Treatise on the Diseases Produced by Onanism* appeared in London in 1776, and an American edition was printed in New York in 1832.[93] (Onanism is another word for masturbation.) Tissot's theories received widespread acceptance on both sides of the Atlantic.

It is remarkable how an entire civilization, including its most intelligent and learned men, can become persuaded by such patently false hogwash and come under its influence for generations, even centuries. The worst example is the belief in the satanic powers of witches, where eminent scholars for hundreds of years produced thoroughly reasoned and impressively learned treatises on the causes, methods, and effects of the evil acts perpetrated by witches; it coincided with the belief, supported by Bible quotations, that "lust in women is insatiable." It is no coincidence that the obsessive erotophobia[94] of the Victorian age developed as the witch hysteria faded, and that subsequently, the frequency of sadistic lynchings of black men increased just as the teachings of Tissot and others of his persuasion began to lose popular support. Nor is it a coincidence that all such mentally unsound obsessions and acts have since almost disappeared under the influence of secular science and the liberalization of sexual attitudes at the expense of fundamentalist religion. There is, unfortunately, an inherent trait of fundamentalist, monotheistic religion that it almost unavoidably leads to suppression of a natural reverence for sexual matters and causes it to be replaced by fear and disgust. The Christian God is "a jealous God" (Exodus 20:5), who tolerates no reverence for other

---

[92] *The Boston Medical and Surgical Journal* 12. (1835), p. 96

[93] Samuel Auguste David Tissot, *A Treatise on the Diseases Produced by Onanism* (English version first published by Collins and Hannay, New York, 1832).

[94] Erotophobia = revulsion and fear experienced by sights or thoughts of sexual matters.

gods. To be a "good Christian," it is necessary to demonize the deities of physical beauty, sex, and fertility, for which we instinctively feel reverence.

The full flowering of the irrational dogmas of Tissot and his followers would come in the fertile soil of American Puritan sex anxieties. In the nineteenth century, American society, like the societies of much of Europe, became obsessed with prudery. Any symbol of sexuality was hidden or obscured. Sex was something one must not speak of—or even think of too much—because it would lead to grievous sin. Having sexual fantasies produced fear, shame, and guilt. The 1800s saw the rise of the urban middle class, in which people's social status was closely tied to their perceived propriety and respectability, which could easily be lost by scandals involving sexual immorality or by having a reputation for holding nonconformist beliefs. The urban middle class, which was alienated from both the rich and powerful industrial magnates and from the poverty-stricken industrial worker, came to bristle like a demographic hedgehog with prickles of Victorian bigotry, fastidiousness, and prudishness. Blacks, Jews, Irish, Italians, Chinese, Indians, Mexicans, or other ethnic, racial, or religious minorities and the poor "white trash" were frozen out. Respectable people shunned social interaction with these outsiders.

The term "Victorian age" derives from the name of the British Queen Victoria, whose reign (1837–1901) coincided with the peak of widespread sexual anxieties and guilt. It is, however, wrong to ascribe to Queen Victoria the origin of the contemporary prevailing attitudes. She was the product, not the source of them, and they were present before she was even born (1819) and remained strong, particularly in the United States, long after her death in 1901.

Among the middle class, Puritan obsession with sexual morality reached an absurd intensity. The overriding issue, to which all others became subordinate, was the control of the demon of sexual urges.

The apostles of prudishness

In the first half of the nineteenth century, a new fundamentalist revival known as of the Second Great Awakening swept the country. In it, the erotophobia always present in the conservative Christian faith was fanned to a hysterical pitch by churchmen, lay moral vigilantes, and even scientists of the era.

Benjamin Rush (the friend of Thomas Jefferson's mentioned earlier) became the first American physician to expound on Tissot's degeneracy theories. Rush proclaimed that there really was only one disease, which could take many outward forms. The underlying disease, according to Rush, was a pathologically excited or irritable state of mind or a physical body part. To avoid such a condition, Rush prescribed proper diet, moderate exercise, and minimization of sexual activity. The two former items, although they were good and necessary in themselves, were especially valuable as a means to accomplish the third. It was necessary to avoid such food and drink as might cause lustful thoughts and passions, which in turn could lead to unnecessary loss of semen. Exercise would have the side benefit of distracting one from sexual temptations.

Rush found an avid disciple in the most influential—and one of the most obviously obsessed—crusaders against sexual passion: the Reverend Sylvester Graham, for whose vegetarian followers the graham cracker was later invented. With Graham, avoidance of sexual passion became the central feature of a strict regimen of health. His movement, infused with Puritan erotophobia and moral judgments, would today qualify as a weird cult, but in the middle of the nineteenth century, it was resonant with the emotional climate of the times.

Figure 11 The Reverend Sylvester Graham (1794 - 1851)

Graham's first thirty years of life gave no indication that his future would be bright. A dissolute drifter, he seemed destined for obscurity. In a sudden change of heart, he foreswore alcohol and found direction and purpose in his life in the temperance movement. Also becoming concerned with a proper diet, he espoused vegetarianism and abstinence from coffee, tea, and spicy foods, which he thought would stimulate sexual passion. To remain healthy, Graham thought, one had to minimize sexual activity and suppress sexual desire—and eat generous helpings of bread made from whole wheat. The flour produced according to Graham's directions became known as graham flour. He also trained as an evangelist and became an ordained minister at age thirty-four. The training helped him become an impassioned and charismatic speaker who could stir his listeners as effectively as any revival preacher.

Graham was a prominent figure in the new witch hunt that swept across America, where pornography, prostitution, masturbation, homosexuality, and even plain old fornication were the most wicked evils that threatened Christians. His most significant contribution to the prudishness of his time was a book called *A*

Lecture to Young Men, which became a model for innumerable pamphlets and books that were bestsellers in the late nineteenth and early twentieth centuries.[95] These writings purported to contain scientific information on the sexual organs and the terrifying consequences of their excessive or inappropriate use.

The worst abuse of the genital organs, according to Graham's dogma, was masturbation. It was particularly damaging to both body and mind and could lead to a chronic state of unrelieved lust, attended by bodily degeneration, causing more "irritability" of the senses and thus more lust, and so on. The downward spiral could ultimately end in insanity and even death. The following extract from his book provides a good sample of a Grahamite fire-and-brimstone sermon. The subject is his favorite: the consequences of the "solitary vice" or "self-abuse": masturbation. After listing epilepsy and paralysis, he states:

> Apoplexy is also a legitimate, and not infrequent effect of these causes, which increases with terrible efficacy the fearfulness of the general anarchy of the system, and sometimes, forecloses the whole, by sudden death, even in the very act of venereal indulgence; and thrusts the filthy transgressor with all his abominable pollutions upon him, uncovered, into the presence of God, where perhaps the only utterance which will greet his ear, will be—"He that is filthy, let him be filthy still!"[96]
>
> Sometimes, general mental decay continues with the continued abuses, till the wretched transgressor sinks into miserable fatuity, and finally becomes a confirmed and degraded idiot, whose deeply sunken and vacant, glossy eye, and livid, shrivelled countenance, and ulcerous, toothless gums, and the foetid breath, and feeble, broken voice, and emaciated and dwarfish and crooked body, and almost hairless head—covered, perhaps, with suppurating blisters and running sores—denote a premature old age! A blighted body—and a ruined soul!—and he drags out the remnant of his loathsome existence, in exclusive devotion to his horridly abominable sensuality... Even when he attempts to pray to the omniscient and holy God, these filthy harpies of his imagination will often flit between his soul and heaven, and shake pollution on him from their horrid wings![97]

Saving the best parts for the finale, Graham goes into the gruesome effects that the ghastly vice has on the abused organs themselves:

> The genital organs, themselves, often suffer in the most extreme degree. Their peculiar susceptibilities and sensibilities become morbidly excessive,—an undue quantity of blood is received and retained in them,—the secretion of the parts becoming unhealthy and excessive, and extremely irritating and debilitating,—tending always to turgescence,

---

95 Sylvester Graham, *A Lecture to Young Men* (Providence, RI: Weeden and Cory, 1834); facsimile reprint edition: Arno Press, New York, 1974.

96 Sylvester Graham, A Lecture to Young Men on Chastity, 4th ed, (Boston, MA: George W. Light, 1938), p. 119

97 Ibid.pp. 121, 122

inflammation, and change of structure. Heat and burning of the parts—shocking enlargement of the spermatic cords—swelling—inflammation—intense sensibility—excruciating pain—induration—scirrhus and ulceration of the testicles, are among the terrible evils which result from venereal excess. In other cases, a general withering, and impotence and decay of the parts commences and continues on, till almost every vestige of the insignia, and all the power of virility are gone. But before this shocking result of continued outrage has taken place, the extremely debilitated, and excessively irritable parts, sympathizing with all the disturbances of the brain and alimentary canal; and in fact, with those of every part of the system, become excited on every slight occasion, and the involuntary emission of crude and watery, and sometimes bloody semen occurs; and in many instances, a continual gonorrhea, or constant dribbling of thin purulent matter from the penis, is experienced.[98]

Addressing himself to youth specifically, he struck a chord sure to send shivers of horror down the spine of his readers. Masturbation would cause pimples, perhaps permanent, and so severe as to be fatal:

Pimples of a livid hue, come out upon the forehead and about the nose, and sometimes over the whole face,—and even ulcerous sores, in some cases, break out upon the head, breast, back, and thighs; and these sometimes enlarge into permanent fistulas, of a cancerous character, and continue, perhaps for years, to discharge great quantities of foetid, loathsome pus; and not unfrequently terminate in death...[99]

In this environment of extreme sexual inhibitions, the horrible consequences of masturbation seemed to capture the attention of all zealous moralists. Among these was Ellen Harmon White, the founder of the Seventh Day Adventist Church. Inspired by a revelation from God, White wrote *An Appeal to Mothers: The Great Cause of the Physical, Mental and Moral Ruin of Many of the Children of Our Time*, her great cause being none other than that of masturbation.[100]

Although she was less idolized than the white Southern woman archetype and had more freedom to socialize and be involved with issues outside her immediate family concerns, a Northern nineteenth-century middle-class woman was still captive to an extremely repressive moral code that denied her the expression of sexual passion. The unmarried, middle-class woman was understandably pitied. She had few opportunities to find employment that would allow her an independent existence in anything but poverty. She generally had to live with her family until marriage, and anyone courting her would be subject to intense scrutiny and questioning by her parents to make sure of his social status and honorable intentions. Premarital sex, if discovered by vigilant parents or relatives, was hushed up as a shameful family secret under the provision

[98] Ibid, pp. 125, 126
[99] Ibid, p. 112
[100] Ellen G. White *An Appeal to Women: The Great Cause of the Physical, Mental, and Moral Ruin of the Children of our Time* (Battle Creek, MI: Steam Press, 1864)

that the couple would get married as soon as possible. If a pregnancy resulted, but marriage did not, both parties risked being branded for life as a fallen woman and a scoundrel, respectively. Both labels could have disastrous results for the future in terms of marriage and career prospects.

Working-class white women in the North and poor white women on small farms in the South and Appalachia lived lives of harsh material deprivation and hardship but generally had more experience and less anxiety about sex. In consequence, they were generally viewed with a mixture of fascination and contempt by those higher up on the rungs of society. Such women occupied a position somewhere between "good" white women—the modest, virginal women of the Southern planter class or the Northern middle or upper classes—and black women, who neither in the South nor in the North could aspire to an image of anything but a loose woman who was at the mercy of her ungovernable passions. In the North, many young middle-class men came to rely on white working-class women or white prostitutes for their first sexual experience, just as many young Southern men before the Civil War were almost formally initiated into adulthood through intercourse with a female slave and in later eras used their still superior status to gain access to black females by force or material or economic "help."

As the issue of the abolition of slavery loomed ever larger and became more vexing, people felt widespread apprehension about the consequences of abolition. The unease helped spark a new wave of religious revival, as mentioned earlier, known as the second Great Awakening of the early nineteenth century. Religious devotion became particularly fervent in the South and has remained so into modern days: not without justification are the Deep South and the South-West called the Bible Belt. In *Killers of the Dream*, mentioned earlier, Lillian Smith gave powerful witness to the steamy atmosphere of fundamentalist religion in the South of the 1920s and earlier and to the marvelous intoxication of fear, guilt, and titillation that rose in the congregations as the preachers elaborated on the congregation's shameful sins and forbidden pleasures, and how these were sure to extract the most horrible price in divine retribution.

The new tide of sexual anxiety that accompanied the intensification of religious fervor manifested itself in the extremely restrictive mores of the middle class and also infected scientists with its paranoia. Moralizing tracts about the dangers of sex masqueraded as medical advice and health-care programs. The intensity of the hysteria increased in the middle of the nineteenth century when abolition became the most burning issue in American politics.

The anxiety was stoked and exploited by self-appointed health experts like Sylvester Graham and by bona fide medical doctors like John Kellogg, by flamboyant preachers like the Reverend John Todd, and by slick merchandisers like James Caleb Jackson. Jackson was a disciple of Graham's and was the proprietor of a popular health resort in Dansville, New York, called Our Home on the Hillside. The resort became famous for its program of water baths, massages, special diets, and exercises, combined with nature trips and wholesome entertainment. The resort also hosted regular lectures on the threat to health posed by alcohol, tobacco, and sex. The dangers of sex were expounded on in two books for sale at the resort: *Hints on the Reproductive Organs* and *The Sexual Organism and Its Healthy Management*.[101] Although the books harped

---

[101] James Caleb Jackson, *Hints on the Reproductive Organs* and *The Sexual Organism and Its Healthy Management* (Boston, MA: B. Leverett Emerson, 1862)

on the dire health consequences of the use of these organs, one might imagine that in the moral climate of the day, the reading of these books contributed in no small measure to the enjoyment of a stay at the resort.

Jackson also invented the first cold breakfast cereal, which he prepared from graham flour. It was sufficiently bland to fit into a diet designed not to inflame sexual desire and was sold by a company associated with the resort.

The most famous cereal designed to help suppress these dangerous passions was invented by John Kellogg. Kellogg worked at the Western Health Reform Institute in Battle Creek, Michigan, a health-care facility associated with the Seventh Day Adventist Church. He was a surgeon of considerable reputation and became the leading health expert at the institute, which he later renamed the Medical and Surgical Sanitarium, popularly known as the Battle Creek Sanitarium. Kellogg became interested in the health benefits of various diets, and it was in this context that he developed the cornflake that to this day bears his name.

Figure 12. Dr. John Harvey Kellogg (1852 - 1943)

Kellogg had a morbid fear of sex. Although he married a nursing student at the sanitarium, the couple never had sexual relations, and he spent his honeymoon writing *Plain Facts for Old and Young Embracing the*

Natural History and Hygiene of Organic Life, the main thesis of which can be summed up in a quote from the book: "The reproductive act is the most exhausting of all vital acts. Its effect on the undeveloped person is to retard growth, weaken the constitution, and dwarf the intellect."[102]

Kellogg also wrote the two large works *Ladies' Guide in Health and Disease: Girlhood, Maidenhood, Wifehood, Motherhood* and *Man the Masterpiece, or Plain Truths Told about Boyhood, Youth, and Manhood*. Both were printed in many editions between the early 1880s and the early 1900s. In both books, parents were warned about the terrible effects of masturbation and were told to keep a sharp eye out for any signs that their children might be indulging in this horrible vice. Kellogg enumerated thirty-nine such signs that should elicit suspicion, signs that range from lassitude to round shoulders, a capricious appetite, pimples, biting of nails, and other sundry habits and idiosyncrasies that one observes in most teenagers.

For persistent cases, Kellogg advised drastic remedies. In small male children, the pain of circumcision without anesthetics would have a "salutary effect upon the mind, especially if it be connected with the idea of punishment." For older children, he recommended a different procedure:

> [W]e have become acquainted with a method of treatment of this disorder which is applicable in refractory cases, and we have employed it with entire satisfaction. It consists in the application of one or more silver sutures in such a way as to prevent erection. The prepuce, or foreskin, is drawn forward over the glans, and the needle to which the wire is attached is passed through from one side to the other. After drawing the wire through, the ends are twisted together, and cut off close. It is now impossible for an erection to occur, and the slight irritation thus produced acts as a most powerful means of overcoming the disposition to resort to the practice.

For young girls, he instead prescribed the application of pure carbolic acid to the clitoris.[103]

The circumcision of newborn males became common in America—not for religious or health reasons but because doctors believed that it reduced the risk that the boys would fall into the destructive habit of masturbation. Nowadays, we recognize that circumcision does not affect this habit.

John Todd and other revivalist preachers thrived on the rising tide of sexual vice that followed urbanization and the immigration of large numbers of single, poor, and uneducated women. Pornography and prostitution provided juicy subjects for fiery sermons, but the number-one target of the church was "licentiousness," a code word for a multitude of sexual sins and a word vague enough in its meaning to cover most of the secret guilt felt by excited congregations. A minister with a flair for imagery warned his upstate New York flock that this "loathsome monster—licentiousness—crawls, tracking the earth with his fetid slime and poisoning the atmosphere with his syphilitic breath."[104]

---

[102] John H. Kellogg, M. D. *Plain Facts for Old and Young Embracing the Natural History and Hygiene of Organic Life* (Burlington, Iowa: I. F. Segner, 1887) p. 119

[103] Ibid. pp. 295, 296

[104] John D'Emilio and Estelle B. Freedman, *Intimate Matters; A History of Sexuality in America*, 3rd ed. (Chicago, Ill: University of Chicago Press,, 2012), p. 143.

Popular periodicals devoted much space to articles on the sorry state of morality in contemporary society. One of the most passionate anti-vice crusaders of the early 1800s was John R. McDowall, a Princeton divinity student who briefly produced a pamphlet named *McDowall's Journal*. According to an alarming report in *McDowall's Journal* in 1833, ten thousand harlots prowled the streets of New York City, waiting to corrupt innocent young boys.[105]

Prudishness becomes enshrined in law

Homosexuality also began to be vilified in the strongest terms in the nineteenth century. Homosexuality was viewed not as a sexual orientation, as it is in today's terms, but as individual occurrences of sinful sexual activities. Homosexual intercourse was grouped with heterosexual sodomy, oral sex, and masturbation under the heading of onanism—a spilling of seed without the purpose of procreation—after Onan, who aroused the wrath of God for "spilling his seed" on the ground rather than impregnating his dead brother's wife (Genesis 38:9). In the latter half of the century, however, medical texts began to speak of homosexuality as a specific character trait, classifying it as a disease or at least a manifestation of some mental or bodily defect. Religious moralists went on the attack with great fervor and distinguished homosexuality from onanism by labeling it sodomy, a sin so heinous that in divine punishment for the act, God had wiped out the entire cities of Sodom and Gomorrah in a rain of fire and brimstone (Genesis 19:24). Many considered it almost bizarre that two women would be sexually attracted to each other. Medical and legal authorities believed lesbianism to be so rare and so harmless that it was not made illegal, just considered shameful.

Erotophobia became reflected in myriad laws and regulations, to a considerable degree because of the determined efforts of Anthony Comstock (1844–1915). As shown by a diary from his years as a young man, he was constantly tormented by guilt over his own moral weakness, as he frequently sank into an unmentionable shameful sin that one can easily deduce to have been masturbation. He blamed his relentless sexual arousal on the devil and prayed avidly to God for strength to resist—and, failing at that, for forgiveness and mercy.

At a young age, Comstock began his campaign to fight the production and distribution of erotic-themed items. In 1868, at age twenty-four, he managed to get two New York booksellers arrested for selling pornographic material. The legal basis for the arrest was a law passed in Albany after pressure from the local Young Men's Christian Association (YMCA), which in its campaign against vice wanted to eliminate obscene literature. The YMCA was duly impressed with the piety and zeal of this young crusader against erotica and threw its considerable resources and prestige behind him.

Comstock quickly outgrew the confines of the YMCA. He tirelessly and successfully lobbied state and federal legislatures to clamp down on pornography. In 1873, Congress, preoccupied with Reconstruction, passed without debate the so-called Comstock Act. The anti-obscenity law was strengthened in the 1880s

---

[105] Steven Minz, *Moralists & Modernizers: America's Pre-Civil War Reformers* (Baltimore, MD: Johns Hopkins University Press, 1995), p. 68.

and 1890s, and Comstock appointed himself as an unpaid postal inspector to enforce the Comstock Act's prohibition against using the postal service to distribute obscene material. Under the label of "obscene material," Comstock included not only pornographic writings and pictures but also information about birth control and products or advertisement for products used for birth control or abortion purposes.

In 1873, Comstock founded the New York Society for the Suppression of Vice, which spawned similar and associated organizations nationwide, usually financed by prominent businessmen and other upstanding citizens. Eventually, almost all the states added "little Comstock acts" to their bodies of laws. A veritable army of anti-vice warriors joined Comstock's crusade, but there was no doubt who the true anti-obscenity champion was. In the year 1875 alone, Comstock scored forty-seven arrests and the imposition of more than nine thousand different fines. In a public report, he wrote:

Figure 13. Anthony Comstock (1844 - 1915)

These I have seized and destroyed: Obscene photographs, stereoscopic and other pictures, more than one hundred and eighty-two thousand; obscene books and pamphlets, more than five tons; obscene letter-press in sheets, more than two tons; sheets of impure songs, catalogues, handbills, etc., more than twenty-one thousand; obscene microscopic watch and knife charms, and finger rings, more than five thousand; obscene negative plates for printing photographs and stereoscopic views, about six hundred and twenty-five; obscene woodcut engravings, obscene lithographic stones destroyed, three hundred and fifty; stereotype plates for printing obscene books, more than five tons; obscene transparent playing cards, nearly six thousand; obscene and immoral rubber articles, over thirty thousand; lead molds for manufacturing rubber goods, twelve sets, or more than seven hundred pounds; newspapers seized, about four thousand six hundred; letters from all parts of the country ordering these goods, about fifteen thousand; names of dealers in account-books seized, about six thousand; lists of names in the hands of dealers, that are sold as merchandise to forward circulars or catalogues to, independent of letters and accountbooks seized, more than seven thousand; arrest of dealers since Oct. 9, 1871, more than fifty.[106]

These statistics do not mention the human victims of Comstock's relentless drive to stamp out obscenity. He employed the same tactics of intimidation, character assassination, and hysteria-mongering against those who disagreed with him as Joseph McCarthy would later use in the 1950s to persecute suspected and actual communists. Several people committed suicide after having been jailed and stamped as vile and depraved by Comstock—who, because of his stridency and fanaticism, did not himself escape suspicions of sexual perversity. Ida Craddock, one of Comstock's suicide victims, published a public letter before taking her own life in which she called for an investigation of his activities:

Perhaps it may be that in my death more than in my life, the American people may be shocked into investigating the dreadful state of affairs which permits that unctuous sexual hypocrite, Anthony Comstock, to wax fat and arrogant, and to trample upon the liberties of the people, invading, in my own case, both my right to freedom of religion and to freedom of the press.[107]

In his book *Frauds Exposed: Or How the People Are Deceived and Robbed, and Youth Corrupted*, Comstock makes revealing claims about the effect of obscene material:

The effect of this cursed business on our youth and society, no pen can describe. It breeds lust. Lust defiles the body, debauches the imagination, corrupts the mind, deadens the will, destroys the memory, sears the conscience, hardens the heart, and damns the soul. It unnerves the arm and steals away the elastic step. It robs the soul of many virtues, and imprints upon the mind of the youth, visions that throughout life curses a man or

---

[106] As quoted in *Medical Times, A Weekly Journal od Medical and Surgical Science,* 3 (August 16, 1873).
[107] John D'Emilio and Estelle B. Freedman, Intimate Matters: A History of Sexuality in America (New York: Harper and Rowe, 1988), p. 161.

woman. Like a panorama, the imagination seems to keep this hated thing before the mind, until it wears its way deeper and deeper, plunging the victim into practices that he loathes.[108]

Taking into account Comstock's youthful diaries, it seems obvious that his almost desperate attempts to eradicate all public mention or depiction of sexual themes were motivated by lifelong pain, guilt, and terror as his own imagination "kept this hated thing" before his mind, "seared his conscience," and "plunged" him "into practices that he loathed." Possibly he could identify with the spider or some loathsome insect that Jonathan Edwards compared his congregation to and feared being cast by God into the eternal fire.

In the early 1900s, the insights of Sigmund Freud began to have an impact on the thinking of those in the medical profession. Slowly, the stamp of scientific authority was withdrawn from at least the most absurd of the teachings about the physical and mental dangers of sex. Most medical professionals acknowledged that sexual urges in both men and women were normal and healthy. Psychiatrists discovered that the denial of one's sexual urges, not the satisfaction of them, was the more common cause of mental disturbance.

The stuffy and difficult books written by and for psychologists could not compete for public attention with the lurid sermons written by men like Sylvester Graham, and the general population was not well-informed about the newfangled theories of psychology. But a fresh breeze was blowing in American society. The old demon of sex was losing some of its dreadfulness in the light of the new dawn.

The movement to give voting rights to women drew increased attention to gender issues generally, including the sensitive issues of sexuality. Freud had made waves with his assertion that the sex drive was a dominating instinct in humans. Biologists began to shock their Victorian society with studies and publications that explored human sexuality.

A contemporary to Freud, the British physician Havelock Ellis, became the preeminent authority on human physical sexuality and was the first to popularize the term "homosexual." Ellis argued that homosexuality was a "congenital physiological abnormality," not a choice, and should be decriminalized. In his *Studies in the Psychology of Sex* (1897), Ellis argued that more liberal sexual attitudes need to be included as an item on the agenda of all progressive activists: "The question of sex – with the racial questions that rest on it – stands before the coming generations as the chief problem for solution." Echoing Freud, Ellis stated: "In this particular field the evil of ignorance is magnified by our efforts to suppress that which never can be suppressed, though in the effort of suppression it may become perverted."

Prurient fantasy has been fertile soil for the prejudices that white Americans have nourished toward people of African ancestry. When sexuality became an acceptable topic of study for psychologists and medical scientists, "experts" of dubious distinction realized the commercial potential of publications that titillated readers while playing on their fears and fascinations. An issue that continued to fascinate was differences between races.

---

[108] Quoted in Heywood Broun and Margaret Leech, Anthony Comstock, Roundsman of the Lord (New York: Literary Guild of America, 1927): pp. 80–81.

The large size and potency of the black man's penis was old news; now some enterprising publications drew curious readers with allegations that there was a difference between white women and black ones in the size and shape of the clitoris. According to one such allegedly scientific study, the clitoris of "Aryan American women" was "imprisoned" and demurely hidden behind its hood. In contrast, the clitoris of the black woman was "free" and prominently exhibited due to its larger size. The size of the clitoris was alleged to correlate to the strength of the woman's sexual desire and enjoyment of the sexual act.[109] The depiction of black women as promiscuous and sexually aggressive had new support from the purportedly scientific findings of its explanation: The large clitoris.

At the time, even Havelock Ellis regarded "modesty" in a woman as a most important factor in her sexual attractiveness. The supposedly scientific data about the large size of the clitoris of the black female and her consequent voluptuousness confirmed for many their conviction that black women were not respectable and worthy of serious relationships and marriage.

Homosexuality, previously a taboo subject, hidden by silence, was beginning to be recognized by psychologists and many medical men as a common phenomenon in both men and women. It was a subject that the new "sexologists" eagerly sought to inform the public about. Homosexuals of both genders were soon pictured as lascivious sex fiends.

The first rumblings of liberalization begin in the 1920s

In the 1920s, Puritan morality was no longer universally accepted even in white middle-class society, especially not in the urban areas of the North. After a long struggle, women had obtained the right to vote. Evermore rebellious voices were being raised, not only by advocating "free love" and the justification of sexual relations by sincere love rather than by marriage but also by claiming that women had the same right and desire as men to obtain pleasure within such relations. Not surprisingly, these opinions were often voiced by women—many of whom had found their self-confidence and outspokenness in the abolitionist movement and had turned toward women's issues following the Civil War.

At first, these rebels attracted few open followers, but their messages were not without effect. Women began to object to their subservient role in society in general. Demands for more rights related to sexuality and procreation followed the call for the right to vote. The achievements of the antislavery and women's rights activist Susan B. Anthony (1820–1906), Planned Parenthood founder Margaret Sanger (1883–1966), and many other pioneering women were tremendously important, changing not only the lives of women but also affecting the very fabric of American culture.

Biology was increasingly taught in high schools, replacing the millennia-old books of the Bible as an explanation of the world. Outcries of rage met science's challenges to the stories of the Bible. Fundamentalists denounced Darwin's theory of evolution as ridiculous and scandalously vile and heretical; many states

---

[109] Ibram X. Kendi, *STAMPED FROM THE BEGINNING; The Definitive Ideas of Racism in America* (New York: Bold Type Books, 2017), pp. 280, 281.

outlawed the teaching of evolution in school. In the famous Scopes Monkey Trial of 1925 (formally *The State of Tennessee v. John Thomas Scopes*), a high school teacher named John Scopes was convicted of breaking a Tennessee law against such teachings and lost his job.

The white conservative establishment gathered its forces in reaction to the revision of traditional beliefs and liberalization of morals. In the 1920s, as noted earlier, the KKK staged a massive comeback that would reach a membership in the millions. The Klan now turned its rage against not only blacks but also against Jews and Catholics. In the South and rural areas across the country, racial fears and religious fundamentalism remained strong; blacks were frequently lynched to beat down any attempt on their part to achieve equal status with whites. Antiblack sentiments were part of a spectrum of anxieties and hatreds stemming from a feeling that society was being dangerously corrupted and led astray by all the modern changes in technology, music, and social mores—all of which were the result of disrespect and disobedience of the strict ascetic commands of old-time religion.

The KKK and religious organizations mobilized a range of social and political movements. They launched highly emotional religious and legislative campaigns against prostitution and the imagined "white slavery" rings that purportedly kidnapped young white women and forced them into prostitution. Everywhere voices were raised to warn against the horrors of venereal disease, and the South passed additional Jim Crow segregation laws to strengthen barriers between the races that would be impenetrable by initiatives from the black side. (In their position of unchallengeable power, white men continued to find ways to breach the wall and with impunity assault black women.[110])

In the sometimes-hysterical fervor of these miscellaneous movements, sectarian differences inevitably arose: moralists could severely censure those who were too explicit in their statement of facts about sexually transmitted diseases. Even a member of the American Medical Association described the subject of venereal disease as so "attendant with filth" that it would be to "besmirch ourselves by discussing it in public" and in 1906, when the *Ladies Home Journal* published a series of articles about venereal disease, it lost seventy-five thousand outraged subscribers.[111] A roar of indignation met suggestions that sex education should be introduced in public schools to make young people aware of the risk of disease.

The economic problems of the 1930s diverted some attention away from the issues of race and sexual morality. They also put a damper on the optimism and exuberance that had caused many people to embrace the freedom and expressiveness of the Jazz Age of the 1920s. During the Depression, life became somber, if not downright grim, so the outrage of the moralists was not as frequently aroused. The strong leadership for social justice that President Roosevelt exerted provided further discouragement for racial violence, such that in the 1930s, the frequency of lynchings declined. Klan membership also dwindled rapidly, but even in 1930, an estimated seventy-five thousand whites attended public lynchings of black people.

The outbreak of World War II continued to provide an emotional diversion from the problem of racial tensions. Several cultural factors reinforced and made permanent the more liberal attitudes toward sex that first came into the open in the 1920s. Among those factors were increasing urbanization, the availability of

---

[110] John Dollard, Caste and Class in a Southern Town (New York: Routledge, 1937), p. 139.
[111] John D'Emilio, Estelle B. Freedman: *Intimate Matters: A History of Sexuality in America*, 2nd ed. (Chicago, IL: University of Chicago Press), p. 207.

the car for many young and unmarried wage earners, the widespread acceptance and popularity of jazz music and associated dance fads, and the romantic themes promoted by the movies of the time. A large increase in the number of older teens who attended coeducational high schools led to the new practice of casual dating, which made it more difficult for parents to exert control over the behavior of their children. For the average young white American, music, commercial entertainment, and socializing with the opposite sex became much more the focus of life than ever before.

For blacks, the cultural changes included big changes in the population patterns and increased access to comparatively well-paying jobs. A wave of migration of blacks from the rural South to the industrial jobs of Northern cities substantially increased the daily contacts between blacks and whites there and created a unique "hip" black urban culture—with a style of music, slang vocabulary, and overt sexuality that many young whites admired and imitated.

Even so, sex was still not a subject fit for public discussion in polite society. The new medium of television portrayed an America that was peculiarly sanitized, having no poor people or blacks. TV programs showed no scenes of adult interracial socialization because that would have been too suggestive of interracial sex. Wanton violence, cruelty, and homicide did not have the same restrictions: the mass deaths of American Indians, Germans, Japanese, and gangsters were among the most popular scenes for the entertainment of the viewing public. Those scenes were also, in a sense, sanitized: blood was usually not visible in all this violence.

The popularity of violent TV shows and movies, pitching heroes with whom we might identify as "our side" against hordes of villains, enemy soldiers, or alien creatures, illustrates how the tribal instinct makes us insensitive to, and actually makes us enjoy seeing, the suffering of those with whom we feel no bonds of familial or tribal loyalty. Killing the enemy is not a crime but a heroic act, and the more, the merrier. This factor has always been a part of the motivation for vicious, callous violence; one should not overlook this factor when investigating lynchings and other manifestations of hatred against blacks in America.

Although interracial sex was unmentionable in public, it continued to flourish on the surreptitious and usually episodic level in larger communities (where gossip was not as ever-present a threat as it could be in small towns) as well as on the commercial level of urban prostitution. Many white men continued to seek the favors of black women—whose image in the mind of most whites was still one of uninhibited and intense sexuality. Those who sought out black prostitutes were often seeking something more than a quick release. For example, during the Harlem Renaissance of the 1920s and '30s, many whites frequented the nightclubs of Harlem to listen to jazz and watch "exotic girls" dance. Many were also looking to find a black prostitute. Their emotional experience was one of romantic, sexual excitement, whether or not they ended the evening with the embrace of one of those "nature girls."

In the 1940s and '50s, most of the nightclubs closed or became dangerously seedy, but white men continued to make pilgrimages into Harlem to find sexual experiences they were unable to find elsewhere. Young Malcolm X, at the time a streetwise and observant hustler in Harlem, plied his trade at the popular after-hours places. He discovered that white women—as well as white men—also flocked to Harlem in search of novel, exotic, and extraordinary sex. Malcolm X said that "these Harlem places crawled with white people. These whites were just mad for Negro 'atmosphere,' especially some of the places which had what you might call Negro soul... Both white men and women, it seemed, would get almost mesmerized by Negroes."[112]

The end of World War II meant the return to civilian life for hundreds of thousands of young unmarried men. They produced the baby-boomer generation that would come of age in the late 1950s and the 1960s and set in motion the most turbulent peacetime social revolution that America had ever seen. Their parents had not received much, if any, sex education in school, and people still had very little public knowledge about sex.

In his landmark 1953 report on female sexuality, Alfred Kinsey presented statistical evidence that shed more light on the sexual attitudes prevailing in the late 1800s. According to Kinsey, married couples of the generation born in the late 1800s were often not aware that orgasm was possible for a white female, and fully a third of the women in that age group usually remained clothed during intercourse. Kinsey reported a steady increase in awareness of and sensitivity to the sexual needs of women among the respondents born in later decades.

Kinsey also showed the strong correlation that existed between a devout Christian or Jewish faith and sexual restraints and inhibitions. Women who characterized themselves as "devout" had far less premarital and homosexual experience and were much less likely to masturbate or to be able to reach orgasm than those who labeled themselves "inactive" in religious matters.

When the two volumes of the Kinsey Report on human sexuality were published, they took a swipe at Freud and questioned the whole idea of sublimation of the sex drive into intellectual expressions. Kinsey stated, "The assumption that there can be such sublimation of erotic impulse as to allow an appreciable number of males to get along for considerable periods of time without sexual activity is not yet substantiated by specific data."[113]

Kinsey and his associates conducted the interviews that yielded the data over a period of several years. They included a few subjects from nonwhite races, but in the published data, Kinsey limited his data compilation to information from 5,300 white males and 5,940 white females. For those more than eleven thousand subjects, he presented and analyzed massive amounts of data on such wide-ranging subjects as masturbation, homosexual experiences, and sex with animals but, curiously, made no mention of interracial sexual experiences. Many of the subjects must have had such experiences—certainly more than the number of people who were having sex with animals. Statistics on interracial sex would have been very important for sociologists.

Interracial and other "unnatural" sex remain taboo

In his report on male sexuality, Kinsey stated that between five and ten percent of males were homosexuals or were aroused by thoughts or pictures of nude men. Male homosexual acts were not just

[112] Alex Haley, *The Autobiography of Malcolm X*, (New York: Ballantine Books, Random House Publishing Group, 2015) pp. 108, 109.

[113] Alfred C. Kinsey et al., *Sexual Behavior in the Human Male* (Bloomington, IN: Indiana University Press, 1948), p. 217.

sinful in the doctrine of the Church; they were illegal in all states. As early as 1779, the state of Virginia instituted a law that punished homosexual acts by castration. Until well into the 1960s, the FBI and other law enforcement agencies diligently tried to identify and arrest gay men, especially those employed by the government. Incarceration for many years could be the result of a conviction. Many thousands lost their jobs and were often ostracized socially if they were even suspected of homosexual tendencies. Not until 1962 did a state (Illinois) remove homosexuality from the category of illegal acts. Most other states were slow to follow. Several Southern states labeled "sodomy" a criminal offense until 2003.

"Fornication" and "adultery," both referring to sexual activity outside of marriage, were criminal offenses in most places. So were "unnatural" sexual acts such as anal and oral sex, theoretically even for married couples. (The medieval Church had made it a part of Christian teaching that all sexual acts that could not result in pregnancy were inherently sinful. Sex must be engaged in only for the purpose of procreation.)

By the year 1800, most states in the union had enacted laws barring interracial marriages. Some of those laws forbade marriages of whites to all non-whites, but the majority applied only to marriages between whites and blacks. There was a prevailing attitude in most of the country that blacks constituted a special category. Sexual relations with a black person, especially through marriage, was a sign of perverse lasciviousness. If such marriages became common, it would present an existential threat to the white race. Such liaisons were, therefore, particularly morally detestable and ought to be outlawed. Especially strong barriers to prevent sexual contacts with blacks were justified.

Following the emancipation and the Reconstruction era, racial segregation of blacks became strictly enforced in most of the United States, particularly in the states of the former Confederacy, where blacks constituted a large percentage of the population.

In 1871, during the height of the Reconstruction, Representative Andrew King of Missouri proposed that Congress introduce a nationwide ban on interracial marriages, but Congress, dominated by northern states that had forced the former slave states to end slavery, refused to enact such a law. However, the "anti-miscegenation laws" already in the books in many states were left standing.

In the South, in particular, a black man having sexual access to white women remained a totally unacceptable idea. It produced outrage and revulsion when it became known that the first black heavyweight boxing champion, Jack Johnson, had married first one white woman, Etta Duryea, and then another, Lucille Cameron. In 1913, Representative Seaborn Roddenberry of Georgia spoke in Congress:

> No brutality, no infamy, no degradation in all the years of southern slavery, possessed such villainous character and such atrocious qualities as the provision of the laws of Illinois, Massachusetts, and other states which allow the marriage of the Negro, Jack Johnson, to a woman of Caucasian strain. Gentleman, I offer this resolution... that the States of the Union may have an opportunity to ratify it... Intermarriage between whites and blacks is repulsive and averse to every sentiment of pure American spirit. It is abhorrent and repugnant to the very principles of Saxon government. It is subversive of social peace. It is destructive of moral supremacy, and ultimately this slavery of white women to black beasts will bring this nation a conflict as fatal as ever reddened the soil of Virginia or

crimsoned the mountain paths of Pennsylvania... Let us uproot and exterminate now this debasing, ultra-demoralizing, un-American and inhuman leprosy.[114]

Roddenberry's proposal of a nationwide ban on marriages between whites and blacks did not get enacted into federal law but found many sympathetic listeners. Political representatives proposed such bans in nineteen states that did not already have them. Singled out by Rep. Roddenberry as an offender of all decency, Massachusetts, in response, enacted a law that did not allow marriages in that state of people who were legally barred from marrying in their home states. It mirrored later legal efforts to prevent same-sex marriages.

In the South, the civil rights movement began to stir in the early 1950s, and it caused a flare-up of white fear and hatred there. The idea of abandoning strict segregation raised the frightening specter of racial mingling and the alleged damage that it would cause to the white race. It seems obvious, however, that the fear of the black rapist stereotype did not stem predominantly from any risk of possible damage to the white race from racial mixing. White feelings on the subject would have changed little if white women had access to the Pill and avoided pregnancy in every case of interracial liaisons. What created the strongest feelings of rage and revulsion was the mere thought of a pure, white virgin forced to have rough, bestial sex with a hugely endowed black man. It was declared to be the most traumatic and horrifying experience a young woman could have and could be expected to leave her damaged for life, if not in body, at least in her soul. The prevention of sex between black men and white women—not the maintenance of what people believed to be white racial purity—was the true overriding goal of maintaining segregation.

In a 1956 interview with *Look* magazine in which Roy Bryant and his half-brother J. W. Milam admitted to having killed Emmett Till (discussed earlier in this book), the two men described the whole series of events that occurred during the murder. Bryant and Milam took Till to the edge of the Tallahatchie River in their truck, where they ordered him to take all his clothes off; they then asked him whether he had ever had a sexual experience with a white woman. When Till defiantly affirmed that he had, Milam, in a rage, pistol-whipped him and then shot him in the head. Milam explained his action in this way:

> As long as I live and can do anything about it, niggers are gonna stay in their place. Niggers ain't gonna vote where I live. If they did, they'd control the government. They ain't gonna go to school with my kids. And when a nigger gets close to mentioning sex with a white woman, he's tired o' livin'. I'm likely to kill him.[115]

When Milam pulled the trigger to blow Emmet's brains out with a .45 caliber bullet, he did not contemplate any of the potential and allegedly tragic consequences of Till's experience, such as a mixed-race child being born to the couple. It was just the thought that Till had experienced sex with a white woman that triggered the instinctive, murderous rage.

---

[114] *Congressional Record*, 62d. Congr., 3d. Sess., December 11, 1912, pp. 502–503

[115] William Bradford Huie, "The Shocking Story of Approved Killing in Mississippi," (*LOOK* magazine, January 24, 1956), pp. 46 - 49

When the Supreme Court decided in 1954 that the South must racially integrate its schools, white Southerners almost in unison denounced the decision as being motivated by some sinister and morally repugnant scheme to allow black men access to white women. For example, when Walter C. Givhan, an Alabama state senator and state chairman of the White Citizens' Council, was asked about the decision, he responded, "What is the real purpose of this? To open the bedroom doors of our white women to Negro men."[116]

---

[116] State Senator Walter C. Givhan in a speech at Linden, Alabama, December 1954. (http://www.thenewblackmagazine.com/view.aspx?index=902)

Part Five: The Eugenics Movement.

The book *War Against the Weak* by Edwin Black is a devastating account of the American eugenics programs of the early 1900s aimed at "improving the breed" of the American population. The following relies to a great extent on its narrative and factual information.[117]

The European Origins of Eugenics

"Eugenics" is a term coined by the nineteenth-century British scientist Sir Francis Galton. It joins the Greek words for "well" and "born." The term is associated with the idea of breeding for desirable qualities - not just plants and livestock, as had long been practiced, but humans. Galton can be considered the father of the racial theories of the twentieth century and the first prominent advocate of social policies, formulated into laws, aimed at enhancing the "quality" of humankind.

In British society, in particular, the industrial revolution had produced stark contrasts between rich and poor, between the educated and the ignorant, between the stately homes, elegant dress, and refined manners of the upper class and the primitive living quarters, worn rags and crude language of the workers.

The very class-conscious British society of the Victorian era took it as a given that lower-class correlated well with low intelligence and a tendency toward criminality and social irresponsibility. It was statistically plain that the lower classes produced the majority of the wards of society, i.e., those who did not contribute to the wealth of society as a whole but constituted an ever-increasing economic load on it. Jails, "madhouses," hospitals, and charity homes housed a growing population of those who seemed to be incorrigible criminals or afflicted with incurable physical and mental handicaps. Leading authorities at the time discerned an alarming trend: The people of the lower classes propagated themselves much more rapidly than those at the upper rungs of the social ladder.

It seemed not only morally right but economically necessary to reverse present population trends, which in the long run would bring unimaginable misfortune on the nation. Imperial Britons, accustomed

---

[117] Edwin Black, *War Against the Weak: Eugenics and America's Campaign to Create A Master Race* (New York: Thunder's Mouth Press, an imprint of Avalon Publishing Group, 2004).

to seeing themselves as a people superior to the rest of the world, envisioned with horror a future England dominated by the impoverished dregs of society.

The trend could only be reversed by suppressing the propagation of "inferior" people and encouraging the smart, ambitious elites of society to have more children. It was a simple principle, but almost impossibly difficult to implement. Apart from practical difficulties, there was something morally repugnant about interfering with the processes of procreation. In the latter half of the nineteenth century, sexuality was a taboo subject, and religious convictions strongly condemned any attempt to prevent conception or terminate a pregnancy.

However, the religiously based moral concerns soon had to struggle with modern ideas founded on science. In the 1850s, Herbert Spencer, an influential British philosopher, published *Social Statics*. ("Statistics," in modern vocabulary.) In it, he maintained that human beings and society were subject to the laws of Nature, not the will of God, and that the laws of nature were amoral, favoring the strong over the weak. It was Spencer who first coined the term "survival of the fittest." Spencer believed that charity was un-natural and damaging to society, as it allowed those less "fit" to survive and propagate. In the end, Spencer argued, it would be both moral and beneficial to humanity if it eliminated the less "fit."

Charles Darwin contributed to the growth of national and racial prejudices in the scientific establishment when, in 1859, he published his famous book The Origin of Species. In it, he proposed that physical traits were subject to gradual change under the influence of the environment. If Darwin was right, and the human race was in a gradual evolutionary process, population groups isolated from each other in different climates would eventually have different characteristics. These differences included external characteristics such as skin color, but also mental ones. That was not merely plausible; it seemed downright irrefutable.

Now there was a scientific explanation for the observable differences between people of different nationalities and races! There was no longer any reason to doubt the existence of national traits. To the British, and indeed to most people in the colonizing European nations, it seemed apparent that different races were on different levels in terms of their intellectual and organizational capacity. There was no longer a mystery how that could be so: Evolution explained it.

Spencer, in 1863, wrote a book named *Principles of Biology*, in which he suggested that some sort of "physiological units" carried the inherited characteristics that resided in the egg/ovary and sperm/pollen of sexually reproductive species. However, how the inheritance process worked in quantitative terms was still not established.

Enter Gregor Mendel, an obscure Czech monk who had conducted extensive experimentation on plants to amass mathematical statistics on how traits were inherited. Mendel found that there were simple rules to express the probability of the appearance of heritable traits in a new generation of plants when the two parent plants did not both possess these traits. Mendel's discoveries at first did not attract much attention, but this changed when Sir Francis Galton became aware of them. Galton was a cousin of Charles Darwin and the man who discovered that no two fingerprints seemed to be alike. His discovery became a powerful tool for the conviction of criminals who had left their prints on a crime scene.

Galton turned his inquisitive eyes toward other personal traits, and soon discerned patterns that conformed to the inheritance statistics discovered by Mendel. Galton was more interested in exceptional talents and gifts than in the "unfit," and in 1869 published a book entitled *Hereditary Genius*. In it, he suggested that the human race could be improved by judicious marriage patterns, pairing people of exceptional talent and beauty. In this way, society could intentionally create a superior race of people. By using intelligence and knowledge of how inheritance worked, human beings could now hasten the progress of evolution.

In 1883, Galton published *Inquiries into Human Faculty and Development*, where he first used the term "eugenics" for intentionally breeding humans in order to produce superior offspring. The idea of breeding superior offspring has been called "positive eugenics," as opposed to the more Spencerian idea of eliminating the "unfit," which has been called "negative eugenics." Spencer and Galton were thinking in terms of improvements within their British society. However, the idea of "eugenics" proved tremendously seductive when extended to its logical conclusion, which was the improvement of humanity as a whole.

Spencer, Galton, and others who would follow to theorize and advocate along eugenic lines were in the main highly respected and well-intentioned people, sincerely convinced of the importance and moral righteousness of intervening in the evolutionary process. The goal was positive and desirable: to produce highly gifted men to advance and rule humankind and to reduce, if not eliminate, suffering due to disease, crime, and inherited physical and mental handicaps. They had lifted their gaze, as it were, from the suffering of countless sick, disabled, and impoverished individuals. They saw humanity in its entirety as an organism, one afflicted with a multitude of inherited defects and weaknesses that could now be cured. From this perspective, eugenics seemed a genuinely noble cause. It seemed so also to a growing number of medical experts, social philosophers, criminologists, and many others who began to take an interest in it.

Notions of the inherent superiority of members of the educated and wealthy class were amplified along "racial" lines when the mechanized industrial nations of Europe easily subjugated and exploited parts of the globe where people still lived in simple agrarian societies. It seemed so self-evident to the colonial masters that they were smarter, harder working, more "responsible," and more organizationally talented than their subjects. The difference was presumably due to inherent characteristics. Usually, the physical characteristics of the subjugated people were also considered less attractive, and those of the colonial masters idealized. Such prejudices acted to discourage intermixing, and the British, in particular, set up strong social barriers between themselves and their colonial servants.

Eugenics Comes to America

The United States was itself the product of colonization, and after gaining independence, retained an internal "transplanted colony" in the form of a large population of African slaves. Also, the mainly West European-derived population of American settlers conducted a century-long struggle against the indigenous Americans, ending in the near extinction of the latter and their forced relocation to "reservations." Other ethnic groups confronting the English-speaking citizens of the United States were Mexicans and immigrants from China, India, Japan, and other Asian countries. Especially concerning the descendants of Africans, white Americans developed intensely negative prejudices and fears. Those prejudices were held by almost all, often in a highly emotional and obsessive manner, and did not initially have any backing by objective science. However, the new "science" of eugenics appeared to lend credence and moral acceptability to the prejudices and the social barriers that existed in the United States between different ethnic and racial groups. "Jim Crow" laws already criminalized intimacy and marriage between blacks and whites in the majority of the states. In many states, these and similar laws covered not only blacks but native Americans, Mexicans, and Asians as well. In these circumstances, it was hardly surprising that the pseudo-science of eugenics found a particularly receptive establishment in the United States.

The idea of eugenics became a powerful notion in America for about half a century, from the late 1800s up to World War II. That period coincided with the heyday of sexually highly repressive "Victorian" morality, and together, the two deeply affected the relations between blacks and whites in the nation.

Victorian morality was anchored in the very devout, fundamentalist Christian religion that saturated American society. Its extreme prudishness gave rise to emotion-based racial prejudice against blacks, who were believed to be predominantly sexual, immoral beings. In its time, Victorian morality was highly compatible with the worldview of the majority of Americans. It contained two of the major roots of American racial prejudice: deep religiosity and sexual anxieties.

Eugenics, on the other hand, was never to the same extent a movement that caught the fancy of the masses. It was a set of theories with a much more intellectual content than religion-based morality, and its spectacular but relatively brief success involved mostly intellectuals and leading characters in the worlds of politics, health care, and the criminal justice system. However, eugenic theory included the belief that racial mixing was detrimental to the white race; therefore, it came to be embraced also by many who, for such reasons, were opposed to racial mixing. Whether guided by intellectual conviction or pure irrational emotion, those supporters of the cause of eugenics manifested the third major root of those prejudices: the tribal instinct. Many obsessed racists insisted on racial segregation and white supremacy, mainly out of a desire to defend the white race against threats to its purity, economic/political power, and survival. Many others opposed racial mixing for the reason that they found interracial sexual contacts morally abhorrent regardless of whether any offspring was, or could be, the result. They embraced the eugenics theories as a satisfactory justification for their feelings.

In an era that could see bewildering mixtures of seemingly incompatible radical ideas shared within any particular advocacy group, the idealistic goal of improving the human race appealed to activists of all stripes. Its clarion call inspired feminist author Victoria Woodhull, a staunch and outspoken early champion of women's rights and racial equality, an advocate of birth control but an avid opponent of abortion. In 1891, Woodhull wrote: "The best minds of to-day have accepted the fact that if superior people are desired, they must be bred; and if imbeciles, criminals, paupers and [the] otherwise unfit are undesirable citizens they must not be bred."[118]

---

[118] Victoria C. Woodhull, *The rapid multiplication of the unfit* (The Women's Anthropological Society of America, 1891)

Birth control pioneer and activist Margaret Sanger also strongly emphasized eugenic principles. In her book *The Pivot of Civilization*, she wrote:

> The emergency problem of segregation and sterilization must be faced immediately. Every feeble-minded girl or woman of the hereditary type, especially of the moron class, should be segregated during the reproductive period. Otherwise, she is almost certain to bear imbecile children, who in turn are just as certain to breed other defectives. The male defectives are no less dangerous. Segregation carried out for one or two generations would give us only partial control of the problem. Moreover, when we realize that each feeble-minded person is a potential source of an endless progeny of defects, we prefer the policy of immediate sterilization, of making sure that parenthood is absolutely prohibited to the feeble-minded.[119]

Racist segregationists like Madison Grant and Lothrop Stoddard, who would become leading figures in the movement, were excited by the veneer of scientific justification for their convictions that eugenics provided. Eminent men of science and academia like Alexander Graham Bell and Stanford University president David Starr Jordan championed it. Super-wealthy philanthropists like Andrew Carnegie and John D. Rockefeller financed the efforts. Innumerable dedicated civil servants in state and federal government offices saw eugenics as the most practical means to combat crime, poverty, disease, and virtually all inherited physical and mental defects. Those age-old curses on humanity could be lifted thanks to this new revolutionary science if society only had the will and courage to take it to practical implementation.

Charles Davenport Takes Command

The man who would for decades be the leading figure of the eugenics movement, not only in the United States but the world, was American zoologist Charles Davenport. Davenport believed firmly in the inherent natural differences between the human races. He was sure that within each race, the traits of each individual were mostly inherited, with the agent of transmission being "protoplasm," a structural component of the cells. Thus intelligence, talent, ambition, honesty, courage, and steadfastness were as much a question of the presence of these qualities in the parents as were hair and eye color and other physical characteristics. In the same way, slothfulness, "feeblemindedness," criminality, immorality, and poor health were inherited characteristics. Indeed, almost all negative individual traits were, to a high degree, "Mendelian" factors. They existed in all races, with each race exhibiting positive and negative characteristics to varying and specific degrees. In Davenport's opinion, the "Nordic race," i.e., Germans, Anglo Saxons, and people from Scandinavia, were the cream of the crop among humans.

---

[119] Margaret Sanger, The Pivot of Civilization (Whitefish, MT: Kessinger Publishing, LLC, 2010)

Early in his career, Davenport became fascinated with Galton and his theories of positive eugenics. These theories relied heavily on the inheritance rules discovered by Gregor Mendel. Davenport approached the newly formed Carnegie Institute and applied for funds to establish a Biological Experiment Station at Cold Spring Harbor on Long Island. The work he proposed to conduct would be, in Davenport's words, "analytical and experimental study of ... race change," and to "investigate ... the method of Evolution."

The trustees of the Carnegie Institution were impressed and inspired by Davenports plans, qualifications, and dedication to the task. They agreed to fund him.

Davenport soon found a well-established organization with good connections to the government already interested in the type of research he planned to do. In 1903, the U.S. Secretary of Agriculture had requested that an agency be created to bring Mendelian knowledge into the efforts to improve both livestock and plant seed. Thus, an organization named the American Breeders Association (ABA) was created. Now the efforts would gradually expand to a spectacular and noble end: Nothing less than the improvement of humankind.

Figure 14 Charles Davenport

The first annual meeting of the ABA took place in St. Louis in December 1903. It elected Davenport to its permanent five-man oversight committee. The ABA had already established two organizational sections, one on animals, the other on plants. Davenport took the initiative in creating a third working unit, the Eugenics Committee. Its initial task was to establish an extensive database of the blood of various segments of the population. Analysis of the blood was expected to provide correlation with individual traits, family histories, and racial backgrounds. The resolution that created the Eugenics Committee gave a clear indication of where this database was supposed to lead American society: The goal was to "emphasize the value of superior blood and the menace to society of inferior blood." Davenport later told an ABA audience: "Society must protect itself; as it claims the right to deprive the murderer of his life, so also it may annihilate the hideous serpent of hopelessly vicious protoplasm."

In a report to the committee, Davenport expressed moral indignation at "such mongrelization as is proceeding on a vast scale in this country... Shall we not rather take the steps... to dry up the springs that feed a torrent of defective and degenerate protoplasm?" Such "drying up" could be easily affected: "By segregation during the reproductive period or even by sterilization." In Davenport's estimation, it would entail long term imprisonment or sterilization of as many as two million citizens. However, the future beneficial effects of this "drying up of inferior protoplasm" would justify the cost and effort.

Davenport's laboratories, established in 1904 as a part of the Carnegie Institution, was named the Station for Experimental Evolution. Everything was first class, as befitted such a glamorous member of the prestigious institution. Recruitment of top talents began, as did the establishment of a vast library with books and periodicals of relevance to eugenics. Still, the laboratory got off to a slow start. Not until 1909 was it ready to translate its theoretical and lab work into concrete proposals for legal and social initiatives.

When the ABA held its annual meeting in 1909, it had already expanded its Eugenics Committee staff and bureaucracy. It had created subcommittees on various human defects, such as criminality, insanity, "feeblemindedness," "hereditary pauperism," and "race mongrelization." Davenport persuaded the ABA to give the committee the status of a full organizational section and to begin collecting detailed family histories from vast numbers of citizens.

Alexander Graham Bell was a strong supporter of Davenport's ideas and had worked with him to generate a questionnaire suited for the purpose. Bell used his personal influence to circulate the forms to high schools and colleges, and the ABA as an organization distributed 5,000 copies. The forms asked specific questions about health status and congenital defects in the families of the respondents. The intent was to identify the families in which "inferior protoplasm" was present, even if, as Mendel would predict, it did not manifest itself in every individual. Such information was necessary if the "torrent of defective protoplasm" was to be dried up.

The sending out of a few thousand questionnaires was little more than a gesture, yielding results that would undoubtedly be of academic interest, but hardly sufficient to create an effective practical eugenics program for the entire nation. For Davenport, nothing less would suffice. Indeed, it was a kind of task that should be undertaken throughout the world if Mankind were to free itself forever from the scourges of poverty, crime, and disease.

The scope of the work was daunting. To tackle it, Davenport needed a bigger organization and a much more exhaustive database. The solution was to establish a national "Eugenics Record Office," with a goal to register the genetic background of every American, complete with a family history of health and race. It was a monumental task, but Davenport thought he knew where to get a good start in the collection of details about defective protoplasm among American families. "They lay hidden," he explained, "in records of our numerous charity organizations, our 42 institutions for the feebleminded, our 115 schools and homes of the deaf and blind, our 350 hospitals for the insane, our 1,200 refuge homes, our 1,300 prisons, our 1,500 hospitals, and our 2,500 almshouses. Our great insurance companies and our college gymnasiums have tens of thousands of records of the characters of human bloodlines."

ABA president Willet Hays believed that Davenport's aims were of supreme importance. He suggested in an article in American Breeders Magazine that every human being in the world should at birth be given a unique, eleven-digit number by which one could trace his or her ancestry. As he or she grew up, the number would enable the Eugenics Committee to keep detailed records of the physical and mental traits of the person. With this multi-generational database, Hayes proposed to give each person a "genetic rating," showing the quality of the person in terms of inheritable traits. "Eugenic problems are much the same throughout as the problems of plant breeding and animal improvement... May we not hope to... lop off the defective classes below, and also increase the number of the efficient at the top?"

Davenport's plans for the Eugenics Record Office showed the need for substantial additional funds. But funding turned out not to be a problem. In addition to access to money from the Carnegie Institution for his work, Davenport was able to tap into the enormous wealth and philanthropic interests of the widow of railroad and banking mogul E. M. Harriman.

Even assuming that a complete eugenic database of all Americans could be compiled, there would naturally be many practical problems encountered in making use of it. Positive eugenics had to battle the unfortunate predilection of even superior people to fall in love, which often led to sub-optimal pairing for producing offspring. It would be politically impossible to pass the needed legislation to compel the social elite to let reason, not irrational emotion, guide them in this respect.

Negative eugenics seemed to offer more promise: To a considerable extent, the poor, the criminal, the insane, and the disabled were already incarcerated or otherwise under the control of state or charitable institutions. The medical establishment and the penal authorities expressed great interest in the promise of eugenics. Were not many insane asylums, hospitals, and prisons in practice already involved in eugenics, preventing defective protoplasm from spreading?

As the ERO went into operation, Davenport reported to Mary Harriman that one of its first goals would be "the segregation of imbeciles during the reproductive period." He described steps he had taken to initiate the program: "This office has addressed to the Secretary of State of each state a request for a list of officials charged with the care of imbeciles, insane, criminals, and paupers, so as to be in a position to move at once... as soon as funds for a campaign are available. I feel sure that many states can be induced to contribute funds for the study of the bloodlines that furnish their defective and delinquent classes..."

Theory Is Put into Practice

By his personality, Davenport was a scientist rather than an in-the-field activist of the sort needed to get the eugenics program implemented all across the nation. For this position, he hired the energetic, ambitious, and idealistic Harry Laughlin.

Laughlin was a man with far-reaching dreams of a future world order, where the entire world would be under a single government. This world would be dominated by the best human stock, drawn, naturally, from the eugenically highest quality nations. Pruning the American stock utilizing eugenic practices was an exciting prospect, the first opportunity Laughlin had found to work toward the practical realization of his dream.

The present system of prisons and institutions was demonstrably inadequate for eugenic purposes. Too many individuals with harmful protoplasm were allowed to live free lives in a society where they married and had children: There were clear indications that the general quality of the American population was sinking. In part, this lowering was due to the rapid influx of immigrants from various parts of the world. Erecting barriers against immigration of persons of lesser eugenic value became a critical plank in the overall program of eugenics. In response to eugenic pressures, the Congress passed the Immigration Acts of 1917, 1921, and 1924, which sharply reduced immigration from Asian and East European countries, while not substantially restricting immigration from Britain, Ireland, Scandinavian countries, and Germany. The 1924 Act contained the Asian Exclusion Act, which limited immigration to persons eligible for naturalization. It made it almost impossible for East Asians and South Asians to immigrate. It also imposed severe restrictions on immigration from African and Middle Eastern countries.

Where undesirable bloodlines were already present in the population, the preferred means of terminating them was, in the view of most eugenicists, incarceration or compulsory sterilization of millions of these carriers of harmful inheritances. Davenport estimated that ten percent of the American population was eugenically so defective that it had to be kept from procreating. In eugenics circles, this became referred to as "the submerged tenth."

It seemed the movement was starting to take off. Eugenics was a subject more and more discussed in the medical, legal, and penological communities. It was a subject of great interest in most intellectual circles, including among politicians. The Carnegie Institution gave another ten million dollars to Davenport's efforts, Mrs. Harriman increased her contributions, and the Rockefeller Foundation became involved, adding both cash, human resources, and its prestige to the work.

In May 1911, the ABA's eugenic section adopted the following resolution: "Resolved: that the chair appoint a committee commissioned to study and report on the best practical means for cutting off the defective germ-plasm of the American population." Harry Laughlin, the secretary of the new commission, was able to attract a stellar advisory board, including a future Nobel Prize winner for medicine and highly renowned economists, statisticians, psychiatrists, and other men of learning and public stature.

Figure 15 Harry Laughlin

Soon the promising start was hobbled by legal issues. The advisory panel identified many legal problems with the planned campaign of mass incarceration and sterilization. Sterilization of already incarcerated criminals could be considered a second punishment, or as a cruel and unusual punishment. However, in the opinion of Louis Marshall, the committee's principal legal advisor, this objection might not arise if the original sentencing judge ordered the eugenic sterilization. If criminals with long sentences could shorten them somewhat by submitting to voluntary sterilization as a condition for early release, there would be no legal problem. But Marshall warned that to extend the sterilization program beyond criminal offenders would probably run into constitutional difficulties. Ominously he added: "I fear that the public is not as yet prepared to deal with this problem."

Because of the unpreparedness of the American public, the ABA decided not to pursue, for the moment, additional methods proposed by Laughlin for improving the American breed. These methods, outlined in an eighteen point program, included new, more restrictive marriage laws and euthanasia for the insane and severely handicapped.

Laughlin was not alone in contemplating euthanasia for eugenic purposes. Paul Popenoe, the leading figure in California's eugenic movement and co-author of the popular textbook *Applied Eugenics*, held that execution was the most rational way of dealing with the feebleminded. He wrote: "From a historical point of view, the first method which presents itself is execution... Its value in keeping up the standard of the race should not be underestimated." In his widely read book, *The Passing of the Great Race,*" Madison Grant, president of the Eugenics Research Association and the American Eugenics Society, wrote: "Mistaken regard for what are believed to be divine laws and a sentimental belief in the sanctity of human life tend to prevent both the elimination of defective infants and the sterilization of such adults as are themselves of no value to the community. The laws of Nature require the obliteration of the unfit, and human life is valuable only when it is of use to the community or race."

While there were, at least for now, some constitutional difficulties along the way, Laughlin envisioned that more eugenic progress might be possible in other nations. The last of Laughlin's eighteen points was named "International Cooperation." In this point, he proposed that the Eugenics Record Office would investigate "the possible application of the sterilization of defectives in foreign countries, ..."

There had already been sterilizations undertaken in the United States for eugenic purposes, without legal sanction. In the mid-1890s, Kansas physician F. Hoyt Pilcher surgically sterilized fifty-eight children, considered feebleminded. When it became public knowledge, Kansans broadly condemned it and demanded that the practice be stopped. The board of the Kansas Home of the Feebleminded decided to halt the sterilizations but defended it against its critics.

Indiana Reformatory at Jefferson employed castration of male inmates to "cure" them of masturbation. The doctor, Harry Clay Sharp, became a believer in eugenics after reading an 1899 article in the Journal of the American Medical Association (JAMA) by Chicago physician Albert Ochsner. In the article, Ochsner advocated compulsory vasectomy (a much less drastic operation than castration, but not useful to "cure" masturbation) for prison inmates "to eliminate all habitual criminals from the possibility of having children." He recommended the operation as a eugenic measure to reduce the number of "born criminals" as well as "chronic inebriates, imbeciles, perverts, and paupers."

After reading the article, Dr. Sharp performed a vasectomy on scores of inmates at the Reformatory. In a 1902 article in the New York Medical Journal, he extolled the procedure as a tool for human betterment. "We make choice of the best rams for our sheep... and keep the best dogs. How careful then should we be in begetting of children!" Widespread use of sterilization was a necessary and rational means, Sharp said, of "eradicating from our midst a most dangerous and hurtful class... Radical methods are necessary."

Involuntary sterilization was on uncertain grounds from a constitutional point of view. It was necessary to clarify the legality of the operation, and Sharp urged his fellow doctors to lobby for new laws. At the same time, he asked doctors at every state institution to "render every male sterile who passes through its portals, whether it be an almshouse, insane asylum, institute for the feeble-minded, reformatory or prison."

Sharp himself was not about to shirk what he saw as his moral duty. By 1904, he had performed 176 vasectomies. By 1906, the number had risen to 206, and the lobbying to explicitly legalize the procedure for eugenic reasons scored its first success in Indiana. Three more states followed in 1909: Washington, Connecticut, and California. The trend was unmistakable, but Davenport and his followers remained frustrated by the slow pace of progress. So far, only a few hundred defective persons had been sterilized, far too few to have a significant impact.

Nor was there good news from other nations. Indeed, the eugenics movement had become an American effort predominantly. Eugenicists in the United States and Europe all felt the need to regroup and coordinate their work, to bolster their scientific foundations, and to raise the public awareness of the dire long term consequences of present population trends. An international eugenics conference met in London in July 1912.

The First International Congress on Eugenics brought together some four hundred delegates, with participants from the United States and several European countries. Major Leonard Darwin, the son of Charles Darwin, was appointed president of the conference. Several vice presidents were also appointed, among them Davenport and Alexander Graham Bell. Among many luminaries in attendance were Winston Churchill, at the time Britain's First Lord of the Admiralty. Churchill was concerned about a purported sharp increase in the number of the mentally deficient in Britain and saw eugenics as the most promising approach to reverse the trend.

American delegates dominated the proceedings of the five-day conference. Attendees hailed as revolutionary the work by Davenport via the ERO and the ABA. A prominent British eugenicist declared that Davenport was a man "to whom all of us in this country are immensely indebted, for his work has far outstripped anything of ours." Though the conference did not achieve much of immediate concrete value, it did raise the profile and status of eugenics in the scientific community worldwide. The American medical community was enthusiastic. The Journal of the American Medical Association headlined: "The International Eugenics Congress, An Event of Great Importance to the History of Evolution, Has Taken Place."

Increasingly, courses in eugenic theory were available at America's most prestigious universities: Harvard, Princeton, Yale, New York University, The University of Chicago, Stanford, Northwestern University, The University of California at Berkley, and scores of others. The subject found its way into the majority of high school textbooks.

The success of eugenics in America among the intellectual elite was perhaps due to the pervasiveness of racial prejudices in a nation containing such a variety of ethnic groups, and where the intellectual elite was still of predominantly Anglo Saxon stock. Race was an issue that most Americans were aware of in their daily lives. For many generations, they had accepted as a plain, observable fact that a hierarchy of races existed, where "white" people of European ancestry represented the most refined and advanced form of humans, with other races ranking below them in degrees roughly corresponding to the darkness of their skin. Racial prejudice of a purely instinctive, emotional, irrational nature permeated American society, reaching a climax in the Victorian era. Eugenic theories now gave them some intellectual rationalization and respectability.

By the 1930s, the enthusiasm about eugenics had begun to wane in the United States. Concrete programs to further eugenic goals remained confined to areas under the direct control of the intellectual elite, such as the medical and penological fields. Laws prohibiting marriage between blacks and whites had existed for more than two centuries. They had been on the books of all Southern and many other states since the end of Reconstruction, but the public was not in favor of creating further restrictions on marriage. Despite ultimately tens of thousands of sterilizations performed for eugenic reasons in the nation, there was never a public acceptance of sterilization of millions to improve the breed. A groundswell of radical eugenic fervor failed to materialize among the masses.

On other fronts, there was more success. By 1950, a prohibition of interracial marriage and intimacy existed in thirty-one of the forty-eight states. Marriage between a white person and a Negro ("an infamous crime" according to the North Carolina statute) could in several states result in a ten-year prison term. In states that did not have legal prohibitions, a popular opinion prevailed that "race-mixing" was perverse, morally repugnant, and harmful to society. It had such a stigma attached to it that it was statistically not a significant problem.

The general population of America had a sense that interfering in the natural process of fertility and birth was wrong, a grave sin. That belief was based on fundamentalist Biblical interpretation. Prophylactics such as condoms were not allowed, and Church doctrine equated abortion at any stage of the pregnancy with murder. Male masturbation was also a sin since it "wasted" male seed.

There was, as is the case with much religion-based morality, a great deal of ignorance of natural facts, illogic, and hypocrisy attending those rules. Sexually mature women deliver one (or more) eggs each month, and in the overwhelming majority of the cases, that egg is "wasted" by not being fertilized. Perhaps because no sexual intercourse took place (a "virtuous" reason), or the sperm was blocked by a condom (a "sinful" reason). Sexually mature men continuously produce sperm that they must regularly ejaculate, either through intercourse with a favorably inclined woman (a "permissible" manner if the woman is his wife), or in the sleep (possibly caused by the Devil, in which case the man was an innocent victim), or by masturbation (a "sinful" manner).

Such religion-based prohibitions against interfering with fertility were not always strong enough to withstand the pressures of racist fears and eugenic theory. Ironically, it was the South, where the fundamentalist churches were particularly strong, that took the lead in incorporating contraceptive advice and devices in a state-financed public health service. The reason was the perceived threat of a high birth rate among the region's black population.

Cold statistical evidence showed clearly that for a long time, the fertility rate of the Southern black population had been less than that of the white population on a similar economic level. Still, white fear of losing control over blacks by becoming outnumbered kept alive the desire to limit black fertility. The Birth Control Federation of America proposed a "Negro Project," whose stated purpose was to restrain black reproduction. According to the program's advocates, "the mass of Negroes... particularly in the South, still breed carelessly and disastrously." Cleverly, the sentence was a quote from none other than W. E. B. DuBois, in his day the best-known black advocate of racial equality and justice.[120] White doctors frequently sterilized black women who were under medical care for some reason unrelated to childbirth or fertility, sometimes without the consent or understanding of the patient. Many states enacted laws to compel sterilization for a variety of eugenic reasons—reasons that, in practice, seemed to apply mainly to blacks.[121]

---

[120] W. E. B. DuBois, *Black Folk and Birth Control*, (New York: *Birth Control Review*, 16, No. 6, June 1932), p. 166
[121] Quoted in D'Emilio and Freedman, *Intimate Matters*, 247, 248, 315.

Eugenics Has a Resurgence in Europe

The eugenicists were frustrated but not ready to give up. Throughout the 1920s, Americans were at the forefront of worldwide eugenics agitation, theorizing, and data collection. Books by American eugenicists were the most authoritative textbooks of the movement. They were avidly studied and referred to by their colleagues in other countries and bolstered the racist prejudices of many ordinary citizens, even those who, according to eugenic theory, might be judged defective themselves. Some time after his release from a prison in Germany, an inmate wrote letters to two American authors on eugenic subjects, Madison Grant and Leon Whitney, expressing his admiration for their work. He had studied their writings avidly during his incarceration. He especially thanked Madison Grant for writing the book *The Passing of the Great Race*, which he declared was "his Bible." The letters bore his signature: Adolf Hitler.

Grant had indeed formulated the creed that the young German would make his own, and subsequently that of the Nazi state: "The laws of Nature require the obliteration of the unfit, and human life is valuable only when it is of use to the community or race."

During the 1920s and '30s, German eugenicists achieved prominence and eventually eclipsed their American predecessors. When Hitler rose to power, American eugenicists were awed and not a little envious of the progress that could be made under a fascist dictatorship where the long term good of the nation was given priority over the short term wellbeing of carriers of harmful inheritance. They fretted over the comparatively slow progress in America, as typified by the experience of the state of Virginia. Virginia had passed a sterilization act in 1924, but eugenicists in the state were disappointed by the minimal application of the act. A crucial case in favor of eugenic sterilization under the Virginia law reached the U.S. Supreme Court in 1927. In the case of Buck v. Bell, the court decided with only one dissenting vote that Carrie Buck had received due process of law and that her sterilization was lawful. Writing the opinion for the majority, Justice Oliver Wendell Holmes stated:

"It is better for the world if instead of waiting to execute degenerate offspring for crime or let them starve for their imbecility, society can prevent those who are manifestly unfit from continuing their kind. The principle that sustains compulsory vaccination is broad enough to cover cutting the Fallopian tubes."

Even such an unequivocally positive decision by the Supreme Court failed to accelerate the pace of sterilizations. In 1934, the superintendent of Virginia's Western State Hospital, Joseph deJarnette, complained in the Richmond Times-Dispatch that "the Germans are beating us at our own game."

However, cooperation across the Atlantic was good. Money from American philanthropic foundations, mainly the Rockefeller Foundation, continued to flow to German eugenicists and racial researchers. In December 1929, the Rockefeller Foundation began a five-year subsidy of a German "anthropological survey." The survey was undisguisedly eugenic in purpose and directed toward German Jews. The survey was conducted under the leadership of the German anthropologist Eugen Fischer, who would become a close collaborator with Davenport, and eventually became a prominent figure in the Nazi campaign against the Jews. A lively correspondence between German and American eugenicists continued even after the outbreak of WW II in June 1939. It would be more than two more years until America was in a war against the Nazis, who by then had already proceeded with euthanasia of mentally retarded individuals and some with incurable, inheritable diseases.

Davenport always had hope that eugenics would become a policy of nations around the globe. In 1929, when the American movement was losing steam and was becoming eclipsed by its German counterpart, Davenport sought to recapture the initiative by mass mailing a missive to eugenics organizations and government officials around the world. In his capacity of president of the International Federation of Eugenic Organizations (IFEO), he wrote:

"The committee on race crossing of the Federation is seeking to plot the lines, or areas, where race crossing between dissimilar, more or less pure races is now occurring or has been occurring during the last two generations. The committee would appreciate very much your assistance. We would be glad to have a statement from you as to the location in your country or the principal regions of such race crossing, the races involved (e.g. European and negro, European and Amerindian, Chinese, Malay, North European and Mediterranean) together with the number of generations during which hybridization has been going on on a significant scale."

Responses streamed in from most European countries, from numerous countries in Asia, Africa, South America, even from remote areas like Fiji, Tahiti, and the Azores. The data indicated that race hybridization was a vast, global problem. But Davenport's data gained him little or nothing in terms of practical results. The Germans kept forging ahead of him, aided by a totalitarian regime with a firm commitment to eugenic goals but little concern for individual civil liberties. One of the leading German authorities on heredity and eugenics, Ernst Rüdin, would soon replace Davenport as the president of the IFEO, and Davenport asked Eugen Fischer to assume the chairmanship of the Committee on Race Crossing.

The Nazis paid due tribute to the American pioneers of eugenics. They admitted that they had gained immensely from their studies of American Jim Crow laws and laws that eugenicists had managed to enact regarding segregation, incarceration, and sterilization of undesirables. In response, American eugenicists were not shy in praising the achievements of their German brothers in the faith. American medical and eugenics journals frequently carried English translations of German articles and reviews of German books. In December 1930, Eugenical News contained a long article by Rüdin, where he made the standard case for eugenics in elegantly simple terms. Rüdin wrote:

"Humanity demands that we take care of all that are diseased - of the hereditarily diseased too - according to our best knowledge and power; it demands that we try to cure them from their personal illnesses. But there is no cure for the hereditary dispositions themselves. In its own interest, consequently, and with due respect to the laws of nature, humanity must not go so far as to permit a human being to transmit his diseased hereditary disposition to his offspring. In other words: Humanity itself calls out for an energetic halt of the propagation of the bearer of diseased hereditary dispositions."

Rüdin contributed to the writing of the first Nazi eugenic law, decreed on July 14, 1933. The law made sterilization compulsory for persons with any of nine categories of hereditary defects. The German government announced that 400,000 Germans were immediately subject to the requirement. Davenport's organizations obtained copies of the statute and provided a verbatim translation in the next issue of Eugenical News. In an accompanying commentary, Davenport could not keep from claiming some of the credit:

> "Doubtless the legislative and court history of the experimental sterilization laws in 27 states of the American union provided the experience, which Germany used in writing her new national sterilization statute. To one versed in the history of eugenical sterilization in America, the text of the German statute reads almost like the 'American model sterilization law.'"

Outside Germany, public revulsion rose over the brutal methods of the Nazi regime. Generally, the American scientific community viewed with distaste the ruckus over what should be rational, unemotional subjects, and tried to stay above the political fray. However, the public outcry made some American financiers and politicians more hesitant to support eugenic programs openly. The Carnegie Institution, while not ending its support for Davenport, also supported rival researchers who had become uncomfortable with the value judgments that were the essence of eugenics. Those researchers veered off in a more purely scientific direction by research on what they termed "genetics" rather than eugenics. For public relations reasons, the Carnegie Institution began to refer to the Eugenics Research Office as the "Genetics Research Office" or simply the "Research Office."

The Rockefeller Foundation found itself under attack by many Jewish and civil rights groups for its continuing funding of German race research and the anti-Jewish propaganda that was associated with it. It continued the funding while trying to explain and defend it as being going strictly to scientific, not political projects. Nevertheless, the Rockefeller Foundation also began funding research that was not under the control of the eugenics organizations and used the term "genetics," which now began to carve out its own niche in the academic community. Like eugenicists, genetic researchers were trying to discover the mechanism of heredity but were careful not to draw any conclusions in terms of social engineering.

Ardent eugenicists, like Davenport, Laughlin, and others, never faltered in their admiration for the Nazi eugenic and racial policies. In 1934, after spending six months in Germany to study Nazi eugenics programs, W. W. Peters wrote a long article in the American Journal of Public Health praising German efforts. In the article, Peters recommended similar programs for America and other countries: "This particular program which Germany has launched merits the attention of all public health workers in other countries."

Germany's eugenic and racial policies were indeed the cause of much excitement among American eugenicists. A speech by German Interior Minister Wilhelm Frick was roundly criticized by the New York Times as evidence of racial and religious oppression but was printed in full in English translation in the Eugenical News in an issue wholly devoted to German eugenics. The issue was full of praise for the Nazi sterilization campaign and Hitler. It predicted that Nazi-style eugenics policies would soon be implemented across Europe. "This State Cause," Eugenical News proclaimed, "does not only concern Germany but all

European people. But may we be the first to thank this one man, Adolf Hitler, and to follow him on the way toward a biological salvation of humanity."

The American business community, like the scientific community, saw the political issues surrounding Germany's eugenic and racial programs as mostly irrelevant, an unfortunate distraction and hindrance. Despite the political problems, German-American trade flourished. IBM, in particular, made huge profits from its contracts with the German government.

IBM had developed a system in 1927 - '28 for a research project on the population of blacks, whites, and mulattos in Jamaica. The system was developed especially for Davenports Eugenics Record Office and was technically a marvel of its time. Compared to previous methods, the computerized system was a big step forward in efficiency for recording, storing, retrieving, and correlating all sorts of data on individuals, including data on their family trees, their physical and mental traits, and their addresses.

During Germany's Nazi regime, IBM, under the leadership of its president, Thomas Watson, adapted it to serve the vastly greater database considered by the German authorities. The Nazi regime was one of the first large organizations to make use of IBM punch cards. In 1934, IBM assigned its German subsidiary in Berlin to manufacture the machines and cards needed to introduce modern efficiency into the data collecting and processing. The opening of a huge new facility, built for the purpose, was accomplished with glamorous pomp and circumstance. Numerous Nazi party officials were in attendance, and swastika flags and Storm Trooper honor guards ringed the subsidiary's manager, Willi Heidinger, and the personal representative of IBM president Thomas Watson, who was at his side. Heidinger spoke emotionally about the great good that would be accomplished with the help of the IBM system. He compared Germany to the human body:

"The physician examines the human body and determines whether... all organs are working to the benefit of the entire organism. We [IBM]... dissect, cell by cell, the German cultural body... These characteristics are grouped like the organs of our cultural body, and they will be calculated and determined with the help of our tabulating machine.

"We are proud that we may assist in... a task that provides our nation's Physician [Adolf Hitler] with the material he needs for his examinations. Our Physician can then determine whether the calculated values are in harmony with the health of our people. It also means that if such is not the case, our Physician can take corrective procedures to correct the sick circumstances... We have the deepest trust in our Physician and will follow his instructions in blind faith, because we know that he will lead our people to a great future. Hail to our German people and der Führer!"

When given a verbatim translation of the speech, Watson cabled Heidinger a congratulatory telegram for a job well done, and sentiments well expressed.

The IBM system was eagerly put into operation by the SS Race Office and greatly facilitated the identification and apprehension of persons of Jewish ancestry in the Third Reich.

After 1935, Germany's Nazi government had increasingly tense and frosty relations with Roosevelt's the United States, and most of the American press hammered Nazi ideology and policies as cruel and immoral.

There was considerable popular antipathy in the United States for anything that smacked of heavy-handed government compulsion, and eugenics tended to involve just that sort of thing – or did at any rate in Germany. Still, under the radar of the public media, eugenic sterilizations of institutionalized individuals continued in many states, especially California, and American eugenicists remained eager to expand the program. They maintained good contacts with their German counterparts, some of which had risen to prominent positions in Hitler's anti-Jewish crusade. Harry Laughlin received an honorary degree from the University of Heidelberg for his pioneering eugenic work, and throughout the 1930s, numerous Americans visited German academic and eugenic institutions, even eugenic courts, and unfailingly came back home full of admiration.

The greatest paradox in American society has always been the declaration that "all men are created equal," when in almost every aspect of life in America, the laws, traditions, and popular beliefs have violated this tenet for all racial minorities, particularly blacks. The public's growing distaste for Hitler and his racial purification attempts in no way lessened the oppression and violence experienced by Americans of African descent. Blacks were lynched, beaten, shot, and threatened, often on the flimsiest of pretexts. Public accommodations remained strictly segregated all across the former Confederacy and not a few other states, and laws against intermarriage were rigidly enforced. Blacks received segregated, substandard education and health care, and could not obtain jobs that provided status and good income. When America entered WW II, it was with a strictly segregated military, where no white man would be subjected to the indignity of having to take orders from a black man. Black units were assigned support duty, such as cooking, cleaning up, and performing tasks that involved hard and sometimes dangerous manual labor.

In 1945, the worldwide reaction of horror at the revelation of Hitler's brutal extermination camps dealt a severe blow to the whole field of eugenics. Theories of racial superiority and social systems that segregated and oppressed people based on race lost all respectability and credibility in most of the nations on earth. But America, while claiming to be the champion of individual liberty and equality, continued such policies. Even as American judges condemned Nazi racist policies and oppression at the Nuremberg Trials, Jim Crow laws, which had been the models of Nazi legislation, remained in effect in America. After the Nuremberg trials, some 20,000 Americans were sterilized for eugenic reasons by state and federal programs on Indian reservations and in U.S. territories such as Puerto Rico. In many states, almost insurmountable barriers remained for blacks to participate in the democratic process. Not until 1967 did the Supreme Court strike down laws that made it illegal for a black person to marry a white person, and even then, such laws remained on the books of several states. In 2000, Alabama, the last holdout, repealed its miscegenation laws.

Eugenics in the Future

Racism and racial prejudice of the most virulent sort permeated American society in the first half of the 20th century and well into the second half, certainly no less than it permeated Germany. American culture was for centuries deeply imbued with the same racist ideas that drove the Nazis to their horrifying excesses. Most of the leading American eugenicists agreed that the white race was superior and must be protected from the corrosive effects of racial mixing. Individuals with inferior genes must be prevented from infecting others with their inheritable defects. Well respected and famous Americans played an essential part in the creation of the eugenic theories and coldly efficient machinery used to "weed out" alien blood in the Third Reich. Strict segregation, sterilization, and in many cases, euthanasia were the necessary remedies.

What if the horrors of Nazi eugenic practices had never occurred or become known to the world? Until the end of World War II, eugenics had a mostly positive image. We cannot blithely assume that the danger of misguided idealism has dissipated forever. Genetic research has made astonishing progress, and our scientific knowledge is growing at an exponential rate, raising many new and troubling ethical questions at a rate that exceeds our ability to reach wise and well-contemplated answers. In 1953, James Watson and Francis Crick told the world that the hereditary material within the cell is a double helix-shaped aggregation of just four different, simple compounds, repeated over and over in various sequences. Since then, the sequences of these compounds have been mapped for humans as well as for many simpler organisms. This "Human Genome" holds the information about all our individual inheritable traits. With astounding rapidity, scientists are discovering the functions of the various pieces of genetic material, and they have identified some of the genes that produce some inherited diseases. Cures for previously incurable conditions are presently being affected by manipulation of genetic material.

In 1978, the first "test-tube baby" was born. Today, "in vitro fertilization" is commonplace, and is often the choice of couples who are unsuccessful at producing a normal conception. At the same time, abortion of unwanted pregnancies takes place at a rate of millions per year, worldwide. Many of these are for eugenic reasons, as medical experts are now able to detect abnormalities in the fetus at very early stages of pregnancy.

Without a doubt, we will soon be able to identify the genetic basis for intelligence and other mental and physical characteristics. We will be able to produce, almost at will, offspring with what we deem to be desirable characteristics. We will indeed be able to create a "super race." Numerous animals have now been "cloned," which means that they are created artificially from the genetic material of another animal of the same type, and have identical genetic makeup, like an identical twin. In 2019, Chinese scientists claimed to have cloned thirty human embryos to be used as sources of stem cells, but many countries have introduced legislation to make human cloning illegal. However, the technology to produce a genetically identical copy of someone exists now, and there can be little doubt that the day is near when somebody does it, whether it is illegal or not. Large numbers of individuals are interested in having themselves (or a dead or dying loved one) cloned, and some are willing to pay millions of dollars for it. Somebody will want to go down in history as the medical pioneer to achieve this unparalleled feat, whether it will be in ignominy or glory.

The means to mass-produce human beings with specific, desirable characteristics will be at hand, certainly within the lifetime of most of our young children. What use will they make of it?

Part Six: America Enters the Twentieth Century

Introduction

Throughout the late nineteenth and the twentieth century, American society went through large, rapid changes that affected every segment of the American population. They included transformative domestic and world political events, rapid technological advances, and better, science-focused education, and they changed how people perceived the realities of life. That, in turn, affected the intellectual and emotional content of their prejudices.

The circumstances of life differed in different parts of the nation. Of most importance to the nature of anti-black prejudices was, of course, the South, where most of the black population lived. The Civil War left the entire region broken, suffering, and sharply divided along racial lines. The subsequent Reconstruction era did nothing to ease the bitter resentment that many Southern whites felt against the "Yankee" North that had brutally and bloodily crushed the peaceful, prosperous society of the pre-war South and left a chaos where the former slaves, once extremely valuable property and essential for the operation of the plantations, were now a burden and a danger.

However, many factors worked toward healing the cracks in the Union that occurred with the Civil War. The South began to industrialize, and there was a significant migration of corporate managerial personnel, technocrats, scientists, and other well-educated people to the South. Nationwide restaurant, hotel, grocery, and department store chains became integral parts of the economy. The major highway system and the automobile enabled the American population to travel more and to see and familiarize themselves with different parts of the country. After WWII, the nationwide coverage of the three major TV networks (ABC, CBS, and NBC) brought the same national and world news to all parts of the country, strengthening the feeling of national unity.

The American military had a strong presence in the South, where many major Army, Air Force, and Navy bases were located. During World Wars I and II and the Korean War, and as the nation felt the threat of the Cold War and potential nuclear war, the South developed a more national rather than regional outlook. Fighting for their country in faraway lands, military personnel became accustomed to thinking in national rather than local terms. The frequent relocation of military personnel within the United States also helped erase their sense of narrowly defined geographical rootedness.

Deep political polarization developed again between the South and the rest of the country when the Jim Crow laws of the South came under attack by the black civil rights movement and its white supporters. It produced a flare-up of racial animosity and violence across the South. However, the majority of the population of the South had no desire to secede from the Union once more. The Cold War and the space program to send a man to the moon were welding America together more strongly than ever. While the Vietnam War produced violent political protests and disorder, that polarization was along age rather than domestic geographic or racial lines. During the Vietnam War, many white soldiers found themselves abandoning their old prejudices, becoming supporters of the black struggle for equality, and establishing deep friendships across racial lines.

The trend to regret and disparage the Reconstruction era

Reconstruction failed and left bitterness and angry feelings on all sides. Authors of the period were beginning to portray the Reconstruction era as a tragic mistake. Works such as *Reconstruction and the Constitution 1866–1876*, by John W. Burgess (1902), and *Essays on the Civil War and Reconstruction*, by William A. Dunning (1904)[122], set the course of academic coverage of the period. These books by respected historians depicted blacks as members of "a race of men which has never of itself succeeded in subjecting passion to reason, has never therefore, created any civilization of any kind."[123] Granting voting rights to such men had been a grave mistake, "a monstrous thing," which was guaranteed to make a failure out of a democratic society. Nostalgic Southerners, but also most educated people in the rest of the country, began to think of the Reconstruction era as a sad and disgraceful period of American history, one that "accomplished not one useful result, and left behind it, not one pleasant memory."[124] In his 1929 national bestseller *The Tragic Era: The Revolution after Lincoln*, historian Claude G. Bowers (1878–1958) wrote that the upstanding Christian Southerners "literally were put to the torture" by "emissaries of hate," who had stirred up the black population to an unjustified hatred of their former masters and had even inspired "lustful assaults" by black men on white women.[125]

It was undeniably a time of great suffering, grief, corruption, and political turmoil in the South. The goal set by the victorious North of elevating the newly freed slaves to equality with the white population in all respects was far from achieved. But most white Americans did not blame that failure on the refusal by Southern whites to recognize the legal and social equality of blacks. Because of prevailing fears, prejudices, and economic desperation, most white Southerners resisted with all means at their disposal, including

---

[122] William Archibald Dunning, *Essays on the Civil War and Reconstruction: And Related Topics* (ChiZine Publications, 2018)

[123] John William Burgess, *Reconstruction and the Constitution, 1866–1876* (New York: C. Scribner's Sons, 1902), p. 133

[124] Winfred B. Moore, Joseph F. Tripp, *Looking South: Chapters in the Story of an American Region* (Westport, CT: Greenwood Press, 1989), p. 11

[125] Claude G. Bowers, *The Tragic Era: The Revolution after Lincoln* (Boston: Houghton Mifflin, 1929), pp. vi, 199, 308.

terrorism and murder, the granting of equal rights to all citizens. They became obsessed with establishing an oppressive society where blacks were almost as subordinate, poor, and powerless as they had been under slavery.

The failure of blacks to elevate their living conditions and educational level to levels comparative to white Southerners was explained as the result of their inherent inability to do so. That alleged inability became the excuse and rationale for depriving them of the means to do so. A highly prejudiced and erroneous view of the slavery and Reconstruction eras remained the official teachings of American history books until the 1960s, which saw the reactivation of the unfinished business of reconstruction.[126]

As noted earlier, the movie director D. W. Griffith exploited this myth with *The Birth of a Nation*, which in 1915 created a sensation with its dramatic depiction of the Civil War and its aftermath. The movie canonized in vivid pictures all the worst stereotypes of the "primitive" Negro. Much less jaded and cynical than today's audiences, the viewers of this movie came away frightened and aghast at the crudeness of black people. They were moved to tears as one of the white heroines committed suicide rather than become a victim of a sex-crazed black rapist (who was played in the movie by a white actor in blackface). Their hearts swelled with exhilaration as the KKK rode to the rescue of the main female character of the movie, who was besieged by a whole band of raging blacks. Most of those watching the movie were of the understanding that if the blacks caught her, she would be brutally raped by them all.

The movie not only depicted blacks in the worst possible light (except for the loyal, happy prewar slaves) but also vilified carpetbaggers and their protectors—the Northern politicians and soldiers. That depiction provoked anger and protest in many Northern cities, but in a stroke of PR genius, the author of the book on which the picture was based, a North Carolina minister named Thomas Dixon, arranged for a special showing of the film in the White House. President Woodrow Wilson declared himself very moved. The film was, he was quoted as saying, "like writing history with lightning... my only regret is that it is all so terribly true."[127]

By glorifying the Klan as the defender of morality, civilization, and the white race, the movie contributed to the sudden reemergence of the Klan in 1915. For the next decade, the KKK grew rapidly into a formidable force for political intimidation and violent terrorism, and anti-black sentiments reached a peak. The KKK, which had faded in influence in the 1870s, once more became a powerful political force in the 1920s. In 1925, the group had an estimated membership of four million nationwide. In the South, the KKK may have counted among its members a majority of adult males in the white population. In 1925, the group staged a march in Washington that brought thirty thousand of its members into the street in Klan robes. The period saw a rash of lynchings and nighttime KKK rallies where hate-spewing, racist speakers riled their crowds to a frenzy in the light of huge, flaming crosses.

---

[126] Eric Foner, *Reconstruction; America's Unfinished revolution 1863 – 1877* (New York: Harper and Row, 1988)

[127] The Wilson statement first appeared in the New York Post on March 4, 1915, and has been widely circulated. President Wilson later denied having said it.

Figure 16. 1916 KKK rally

Figure 17. KKK rallies 30,000 in Washington D.C. 1925

Riots and massacres of blacks 1880 - 1930

Between the end of the Reconstruction and the beginning of the Great Depression in 1929, thousands of individual blacks were lynched by white mobs, often after having been accused of some crime with little or no proof. Also, riots and massacres occurred in the South as the white population consolidated its destruction of the hated system of Reconstruction. By violence and intimidation, the white population wrested back full control of the political and economic life of the region.

Even as America went through profound societal and technological changes, racial issues remained important. Especially in the South, contempt, fear, and hatred of blacks remained obsessive in many whites. The 1890s saw a crescendo of lynchings. Lynchings and mob rampages against black Americans were not confined to the South.

Among the worst were a series of outbreaks that occurred in St. Louis and East St. Louis in the summer of 1917, which left as many as two hundred and fifty blacks dead. Six thousand were left homeless, and the costs of material damages were estimated at close to eight million in 2020 dollars.

It was rare that white participants in massacres of blacks were taken to court and convicted of serious crimes, including murder. In contrast, when blacks killed whites in major racial confrontations, "justice" was meted out swiftly and severely. For example, in the August 23, 1917 riot in Houston, Texas, (also referred to as the Camp Logan Mutiny) one hundred and fifty-six black soldiers of the Third Battalion of the Twenty-fourth U.S. Infantry Regiment became involved in a violent confrontation with white Houston police after reported police harassment of black citizens. In the melee, eleven civilians, five policemen, and four soldiers were killed. The soldiers were accused of mutiny and tried at three court-martials: nineteen received death sentences, and forty-one sentences of life imprisonment.

Following the end of World War I in November 1918, black soldiers returning from service in Europe became targets of attacks by whites. Some black veterans incautiously described how well and respectfully they had been treated in Europe. Some bragged about having experienced sex with French women, or even having killed a German enemy, - a white person! Rumors along those lines, if they reached the white population in the South, spread like wildfire. Some of the worst riots in American history until the 1960s took place in the South in response to white fears of blacks becoming "uppity" and losing respect for whites.

In a letter to a newspaper editor, a white reader warned:

> The Negro returned soldier who is full of the "equal rights" treatment he got in Europe during the past months will do exceedingly well to remember that for every one of him there are about a thousand white returned soldiers who were completely fed up on the same equal rights stuff over there, and they are not going to stand for one moment any internal rot started by any yellow-faced coon who has the hellish idea that he is as good as a white man or a white woman.[128].

---

[128] Paul Ortiz *Emancipation Betrayed: The Hidden History of black organizing and White Violence in Florida from Reconstruction to the Bloody Election of 1920.* (Berkley, CA 2005), p. 162

The rash of race riots crested in the summer of 1919, called "the Red Summer," during which more than three dozen cities all across the nation were scenes of bloody violence by white mobs against blacks. The cities struck by violent race riots included Memphis, TN, Philadelphia, PA, Washington, D.C., New Orleans, LA, Chicago, IL, New York, NY, Omaha, NE, and Baltimore, MD.

Race riots continued for several years after Red Summer, reaching catastrophic proportions in some black communities. In November 1920, the Ocoee Massacre in Florida transformed Ocoee into a "sundown town" for forty years, allowing no blacks to remain within city limits after sundown.

The Tulsa, Oklahoma race riot on May 31 – June 1, 1921, has been called "the single worst incident of racial violence in American history."[129] Before the riot, the city's black Greenwood section was a prosperous, thriving community. White resentment of black success bubbled over when a black man was accused of assaulting a white woman. A huge white mob flooded into Greenwood, burning and looting black homes and businesses and killing black residents.

Figure 18 The aftermath of the Tulsa massacre

The riot destroyed more than 35 city blocks and resulted in scores, possibly hundreds, of deaths. More than eight hundred people were hospitalized, and thousands were left homeless. At the time, the costs of material damages were estimated to be about 1.5 million dollars in real estate and 750,000 in personal property, a total of about thirty-two million in 2019 dollars. The event was hushed down by local historians

---

[129] Oklahoma Historical Society: the article is named Tulsa Race Massacre.
Available at https://www.okhistory.org/publications/enc/entry.php?entry=TU013

and has until recently been a largely forgotten part of U.S. history. Few Americans who saw the 2019 HBO drama "Watchmen" had ever before heard of the incident.

A notorious case was the Rosewood massacre in Florida in January 1923. The town of Rosewood on the west coast of Florida was a small, black community that was completely burned to the ground by a white mob, looking for a black man who had allegedly attacked a white woman in the nearby town of Sumner. Officially, the death toll was six blacks and two whites, but black eyewitnesses claim a count of at least 100. The town remained wholly abandoned and has ceased to exist. The incident was largely forgotten until 1982, when a report about it was published in the *St. Petersburg Times*, containing eyewitness accounts by still living survivors. It was the subject of the movie *Rosewood* in 1997.

Racial tensions simmered across the nation, in part because of the migration of millions of blacks from the South into cities in the North. The influx of large numbers of blacks caused alarm and apprehension in areas that were previously virtually all-white. The apprehension was not always just a racial matter. Though they were mostly race-motivated, the riots were part of a broader spectrum of anxieties and disturbances that frequently involved labor disputes and political agitation. Communist activists fought to organize workers into labor unions while at the same time allying themselves with black civil rights advocates.

Imported with European immigrants, there were strong antisemitic prejudices firmly entrenched in American society, and anti-Semitic and anti-black racial prejudices became entwined in a manner that would persist well into the 1960s. They were further cemented through the belief that communism was a Jewish conspiracy to achieve a worldwide Jewish control over the economies of all nations. It was a common belief that in the service of that end, communists sought to weaken the moral fiber of Christian nations by spreading the evil doctrine of atheism. Jews and their stooges, white communists, were exploiting black desires for equal rights to create chaos and dissent in white society, weakening the resistance to the communist message. They were using blacks as tools to achieve their ends, just as carpetbaggers did during Reconstruction. As part of their exploitation of blacks, they encouraged racial mixing, a measure that would weaken the resolve and ability of America to resist communism.

Conservative, religious Americans thus firmly believed in a menacing constellation of forces, seeking the destruction of all American democratic freedoms, morality, religious faith, and white ethnic purity. Those beliefs infected J. Edgar Hoover as he began his career in the FBI and later motivated him to doggedly seek proof of a communist influence on Martin Luther King and the black civil rights movement of the 1960s.

Blacks were still murdered in the South in large numbers in the 1940s and '50s, but now in a more clandestine manner. Once public sentiment turned against the practice of public lynchings, victims were murdered "at the hands of persons unknown."[130] The killers struck at night with few witnesses and left their victims hanging from trees or light poles, where they would be found the next day. Eventually, when the murderers ran the risk of being held to legal account for their actions, they hid the corpses where they would not be discovered. Law officers in the South were often themselves complicit in these killings, and it was virtually unheard of that the murder of a black person by the KKK or like-minded whites would result in an arrest.

---

[130] Philip Dray: *At the Hands of Persons Unknown: The Lynching of Black America.* (New York: Random House, 2002) p. ix.

For decades, liberal members of the US Congress attempted to make lynching illegal and punishable as murder, but congressmen from the South were able to block them. Not until 1946 was a federal court able to return a guilty verdict against a white man who had committed a race-motivated murder. The case was against Tom Crews, a white policeman in Suwannee County in Florida. In September 1945, Crews arrested Sam McFadden, a black Army veteran, for being "disrespectful." McFadden apparently resisted arrest, whereupon Crews forced McFadden, at gunpoint, to jump into the Suwannee river. McFadden could not swim, something Crews was probably aware of. Consequently, McFadden drowned.

A local court failed to press charges against Crews, but a federal investigation into the case began. Murder was a state crime in which the federal authority had no jurisdiction, but the investigators charged Crews with violating McFadden's civil rights, a federal offense. Crews was convicted in a federal court and received a sentence of one year in jail and a $1,000 fine.

As the first conviction in a race-motivated murder, it was important in a symbolic sense, but unfortunately, it was not effective as a precedence-setting case. Not long after the conviction of Crews in Florida, a very grisly lynching occurred in Georgia, known as the lynching at Moore's Ford. Two black married couples were murdered by a group of fifteen to twenty white men, who fired an estimated total of sixty times into them after tying them to trees. The victims were ripped apart by a hail of pistol slugs and shotgun pellets. One of the women was seven months pregnant, and after she was shot multiple times, someone cut the fetus out of her body with a knife.[131] None of the perpetrators was ever brought to court. Out of fear of retaliation, no one in the local community was willing to accuse anyone of participating in the slaughter. It became yet another one of a lynchings "at the hands of persons unknown." No federal charges could be brought in the case, but it received national publicity and was a factor in President Truman's issuing of Executive Order 9808, *Establishing the President's Committee on Civil Rights.*

Public sentiment slowly turned against the custom of lynching, especially outside the South, just as it had turned a hundred years earlier against slavery. Lynching as a big public spectacle of barbaric cruelty gradually became rarer after the 1920s, even though it continued to occur well into the 1930s.

The term "lynching" has recently fallen out of favor; killings by private men or organizations are now labeled simply "murder." When a racial or another discriminatory motive is behind a murder, the added label "hate crime" is now applied, and such a murder draws a heavier penalty than a killing that is motivated by other factors.

America adjusts to rapid world-political and technological changes

At the end of the nineteenth century, white America felt that the "racial question" had been settled. The Indian Wars of the late 1800 had driven Native Americans off the lands needed by European immigrants for mineral and oil exploration, forestry, farming, and cattle ranching. The nagging moral issue of slavery in

---

[131] Anthony S. Pitch, *The Last Lynching: How a Gruesome Mass Murder Rocked a Small Georgia Town* (New York, NY: Skyhorse Publishing, 2016)

"the land of the free" had been eliminated, and blacks seemed to pose little threat since they were everywhere kept out of white social circles. Jim Crow ruled the South with an iron fist, and most whites perceived discrimination and segregation as solutions, not problems. Occasional racial disturbances did not appear to indicate that anything was wrong with how American society was organized; instead, they were further proof that white society had to keep tight reins on the black population.

The oppression, violence, and injustices suffered by blacks were not of much concern for the average white American. Most of the black population still lived in rural areas of the South, with a smaller but growing number concentrated in clearly delimited black ghettos of big cities in the North. Elsewhere, "out of sight, out of mind," described the situation. Therefore, white America was able to focus on other things besides black-white race relations.

There were wars to draw some of the attention away from domestic problems – the Spanish-American War, the First and Second World War, and the Korean War, plus dozens of smaller-scale American interventions in Latin America. There were also plenty of domestic issues that were both exciting and worrying. The post-Civil War era saw rapid industrialization and urbanization of America. There was a steady stream of exciting scientific and technological progress that brought the electrification and the electric light bulb, automobiles, air travel, movies, telephones, and radios to the masses.

The discovery of oil in Pennsylvania in the mid-1800s was followed by finding additional deposits in the Appalachian Basin and the Mid-Continent states. Vast oilfields were discovered in Texas in the 1930s and changed the image of that state from one of cowboys and vast herds of cattle to one of oil "gushers" and fabulously rich "oil barons." Abundant coal, oil, and steel produced cheap energy, fuel, and raw material to propel the American auto industry to a world-leading position. These changes were life-changing for many Americans and helped create worldwide recognition of America as a land of the future, where opportunities were unlimited for anyone with the talent and ambition to succeed. The big city with its skyscrapers, the movies about the Wild West, and the jazz music became the image that America projected outward, a glamorous, rich world to which people everywhere dreamed of emigrating.

Immigration from North-Western Europe was not a problem, but the growth of the population with Asian, East-European, and Catholic backgrounds worried many Americans. They thought of their nation as "Anglo-Saxon" by ethnicity and devoutly Protestant Christian in its faith. In the view of many, those very characteristics were responsible for the admirable ethos as well as the intellectual and material success of America. Therefore, to preserve those traits in America, it was necessary to maintain a majority of pure, white Anglo-Saxons in control of the nation. Not just blacks but all other alien races must remain minorities and not be allowed to dilute and contaminate the superior core stock of the American population.

A law from 1882, the Chinese Exclusion Act, already barred entry by Chinese laborers. The Immigration Act of 1917 extended the bar to the Asia-Pacific zone, which included South-East Asia, India, and the Muslim nations of the Near East. Inspired by the eugenics movement, it listed characteristics of persons anywhere who would be denied entry, including (in alphabetical order): alcoholics, anarchists, contract laborers, criminals, convicts, epileptics, feebleminded persons, idiots, illiterates, imbeciles, insane persons, paupers, persons afflicted with contagious disease, persons being mentally or physically defective, persons with constitutional psychopathic inferiority, political radicals, polygamists, prostitutes, and vagrants.

In 1921, new laws were adopted to further restrict immigration based on country of origin. A significant motivation for the limits set on immigration from Eastern Europe was the perceived danger of the large number of Jews who sought to escape from the oppression and discrimination they experienced in Poland and Russia. In 1924, the law was tightened even further. Not until 1965 did Congress enact sweeping changes to those laws to do away with national quotas.

Labor relations and labor organizations also began to be hot political topics. In the post-Civil War South, the textile industry created "mill towns" where a particular company controlled the entire economy of the town. It meant that workers were captives of the company, having little power to influence wages and working conditions. The same situation existed further north in coal mining communities. (The song "*Thirteen Tons*" by Merle Travis says it well: "You load sixteen tons, what do you get? Another day older and deeper in debt. Saint Peter, don't you call me, 'cause I can't go - I owe my soul to the company store.")

Populist and socialist ideology achieved some cooperation across racial lines based on shared economic interests. In the industrial North and Mid-West, communist calls for the solidarity of all workers of the world helped build the unionization of industrial workers. The booming auto industry was fertile soil for union organizers, laying the foundation for an American middle class that would come to enjoy a living standard for workers unprecedented in history.

The labor movement was forcefully opposed by major corporations and, in most cases, by the political establishment, often with the use of massive mobilization of law enforcement personnel and mass arrests. Labor disputes motivated many bloody riots in the early 1900s. In some cases, they took on a racial cast because company officials hired black, poorly paid workers to break strikes by white union members.

In the South, the entrenched elite was staunchly anti-union, seeing unions as a communist plot against profitable business. Politicians depicted unions as threats to the freedom of both enterprise and individual workers. They used the label "right-to-work" for new laws that made unionizing and labor strikes difficult since, by law, workers had the right to cross strike picket lines and go to work if they were not union members. Corporate management used the argument that unionization of workers could even be a back door to racial integration, since the labor movement was influenced by the godless, mongrelization-favoring communist, accepting blacks into unions. To control the tensions that began to build along class and wealth lines, Southern business leaders used the racial hierarchy to break up the unity of workers. Even the poorest whites could be sure that they were not on the bottom of the social hierarchy. They were superior to blacks and had to take advantage of the rights that it gave them. At the end of World War I, returning white soldiers were able to cause the firing of black workers to get their jobs.

Once more, America seeks to create equality for blacks

In the middle of the twentieth century, the world went through a transformative struggle that eventually forced the major colonial powers to retreat from their holdings in Africa, Asia, and the Caribbean. In this process, the ideology of communism played a significant role. Its utopian, racism-free, anti-colonialist ideology appealed to the impoverished, powerless masses of the independence-seeking populations, and its military and organizational support for groups that opposed the colonial rulers gave credence to its claim of being on the side of the native peoples.

Communist propaganda used the issue of inequalities and oppression in America very effectively to depict what they claimed that a capitalist economy looks like. In the 1930s, the Roosevelt administration took some modest initiatives to begin to reduce the discrimination suffered by blacks, but the most ambitious project to address the issue was a study funded in 1938 by the Carnegie Corporation of New York. The Carnegie Corporation was established in 1911 by the wealthy Andrew Carnegie as a philanthropic organization "to promote the advancement and diffusion of knowledge and understanding."

The leadership of the study project was awarded to the Swedish Nobel-laureate economist Gunnar Myrdal. His task was to investigate and analyze all aspects of American race relations. The choice of Myrdal was the result of his credentials as an internationally respected expert on socio-economic conditions who, from the perspective of a neutral observer with no vested interest in the outcome of his study, could present a thorough, unbiased view of the effects of racism in America.

To be sure that he could produce an authoritative work of lasting value, Myrdal assembled a stellar team of some of the most renowned and respected academics in America in the fields of history, economics, and sociology. The study was perhaps a bigger project than he initially envisioned. It would take six years to complete. Myrdal hoped that it could become the reference point for practical, political, and economic programs to come to grips with the problem.

The result of the study was a report named *An American Dilemma: The Negro Problem and Modern Democracy*.[132] It would become the most exhaustive and wide-ranging study ever of the issue. It contains about 1,500 pages of text in tiny font size, divided into forty-five chapters, six appendices, and other parts. It contains massive amounts of tables, figures, hundreds of literature references, and so many footnotes that they are collected toward the end of the book in over two hundred and fifty pages of text.

In *An American Dilemma*, Myrdal concentrated on the economic and pragmatic aspects of race relations in the United States. The book includes comments about lynchings that show his understanding of the psychological and religious factors that drove so many people to participate in and be spectators at lynchings:

> The danger of Negroes' desire to rape white women has acquired a special and strategic position in the defense of the lynching practice. Actually, only 23 percent of the victims were accused of raping or attempting to rape. There is much reason to believe that this figure has been inflated by the fact that a mob which makes the accusation of rape is secure against any further investigation; by the broad Southern definition of rape to include all sex relations between Negro men and white women; and by the psychopathic fears of white women in their contacts with Negro men. The causes of lynching must, therefore, be sought outside the Southern rationalization of "protecting white womanhood."

---

[132] Myrdal et al., *An American Dilemma*, (New York: Harper and Brothers Publishers, 1944)

This does not mean that sex, in a subtler sense, is not a background factor in lynching. The South has an obsession with sex that helps make this region quite irrational in dealing with Negroes generally. In a special sense, too, as William Archer, Thomas P. Bailey, and Sir Harry Johnston early pointed out, lynching is a way of punishing Negroes for the white Southerner's own guilt feelings in violating Negro women, or for presumed Negro sexual superiority. The dullness and insecurity of rural Southern life, as well as the eminence of emotional puritanical religion, also create an emphasis upon sex in the South that especially affects adolescent, unmarried, and climacteric women, who are inclined to give significance to innocent incidents.[133] The atmosphere around lynching is astonishing like that of the tragic phenomenon of "witch hunting" which disgraced early Protestantism in so many countries. The sadistic elements in most lynchings also point to a close relation between lynching and thwarted sexual urges.[134]

The report was published in 1944, the last year of World War II. The nation was preoccupied with fighting in the largest and bloodiest war in human history, and not in a mood to do self-critical introspection. Despite its first-rate qualities in both substance and language, the book had little impact beyond a narrow elite of academics and social activists. For the moment, the political establishment was not concerned with understanding and solving the problems of racial prejudice and its consequences. Furthermore, the conclusions and recommendations of the Myrdal report met angry opposition by conservative critics who were afraid that abandonment of racial segregation would have irreparable, disastrous consequences for the American white majority, its culture, and its way of life. Others found the content offensive and damaging to the image of America. The report, the impressive result of many man-years of work by the most knowledgeable experts in the nation, was buried by silence.

However, the end of World War II laid bare the horrors committed by men and women serving an ideology of racism. The world was appalled by pictures of staples of dead, emaciated, naked bodies ready for annihilation in industrial-scale cremation ovens; individuals who were deemed inferior and undesirable and met their death simply because they were of a supposedly inferior "race." In the eyes of the world, racism suddenly became an ideology that was utterly morally bankrupt and must not exist in a just, democratic society.

At the beginning of the Truman administration, the massive document *An American Dilemma* had already been successfully disparaged by conservative American critics as a "radical leftist" and "socialist" work that slandered America and gave a voice to its enemies. However, President Truman was aware of the international political cost of the well-publicized social injustices in the nation. On September 19, 1946, in a meeting with NAACP leaders, he was presented with graphic evidence of the lynching of African American veterans who had returned after serving in World War II. Heedful of the advice by his foreign policy experts

---

[133] At the time when "An American Dilemma" was written, climacteric women, i.e., women past their menstruating age, were generally expected to have ceased sexual activity in their marriages. Since they could no longer procreate, sexual activity was considered unjustified and morally wrong according to Christian beliefs.

[134] Myrdal et al., *An American Dilemma*, (New York: Harper and Brothers Publishers, 1944) 561–62.

that racial discrimination in America provided rich fodder for communist propaganda, he issued Executive Order 9808, *Establishing the President's Committee on Civil Rights*. It ordered the formation of a high-level government committee to study the issue of racial injustice. In October 1947, the Committee on Civil Rights presented its findings in a report titled *To Secure These Rights*. (A title probably calculated to sound more positive and America-promoting than *An American Dilemma*.) It warned that in advancing American interests in the struggle against the communist world, "Our domestic civil rights shortcomings are a serious obstacle."

Like Myrdal's *An American Dilemma* the report identified deep, systemic problems throughout American society. They existed in almost every aspect of life – education, employment, entertainment, voting, military service, religious services, and social interactions. It eloquently states the creed by which America likes to be perceived:

> This concept of equality which is so vital a part of the American heritage knows no kinship with notions of human uniformity or regimentation. We abhor the totalitarian arrogance which makes one man say that he will respect another man as his equal only if he has "my race, my religion, my political views, my social position." In our land men are equal, but they are free to be different. From these very differences among our people has come the great human and national strength of America.
>
> Thus, the aspirations and achievements of each member of our society are to be limited only by the skills and energies he brings to the opportunities equally offered to all Americans. We can tolerate no restrictions upon the individual which depend upon irrelevant factors such as his race, his color, his religion or the social position to which he is born.[135]

The report was not well received: a Gallup poll revealed that only six percent of America's white population felt that securing equal rights by blacks was an urgent matter. A far larger percentage of whites, particularly in the South, were opposed to any such programs altogether. Since blacks contributed only a minuscule percentage of votes or financial support for political campaigns, there was very little public pressure on elected officials to cater to black desires. Despite the less than enthusiastic reception the report received by the established powers – including a total disavowal by politicians in the South – it encouraged activists in the black civil rights movement.

Truman did not let himself be immediately stymied by negative public reaction. On February 2, 1948, he submitted to Congress a proposed legislative program to take federal action to correct some of the existing injustices. Congress, dominated by conservatives, simply refused to act on the proposal. Incensed, Truman, on July 26, took the bold step of issuing executive order 9981 to abolish discrimination "on the basis of race, color, religion or national origin" in the United States Armed Forces. It led to the desegregation of the national military.

---

[135] Available at https://www.trumanlibrary.gov/library/to-secure-these-rights (Page 4)

The U.S. military was traditionally segregated, with blacks serving in all-black noncombat divisions and being assigned jobs as cooks, drivers, and stevedores. An exception was the establishment of an all-black fighter pilot and bombardier group, which became known as "The Tuskegee Airmen," and served with distinction. In 1948, however, Executive Order 9981 removed racial restrictions on the location and capacity in which a member of the military could serve. Truman used the method of an executive order to affect it. He knew that if the issue were submitted to Congress for debate and legislation, it would not have passed. Members of Congress, especially those from the South, repeatedly tried to have it rescinded or overruled by law, but their efforts failed.

In practice, not much happened as a result of the order until the situation in the Korean War became desperate. When that war began in 1950, US armed forces were still segregated along racial lines. Faced with heavy losses and manpower shortages in its white combat units, the army began accepting black replacements into the previously all-white units. The army high command kept its collective fingers crossed since this experiment was generally considered risky for morale among the troops, but the black soldiers performed well. They showed that integrated combat units could perform under fire. As a result, on July 26, 1951, the U.S. Army formally announced its plans to desegregate in all respects. For the remainder of the Korean War, and in future conflicts, the U.S. national armed forces played a major role in providing equal opportunity for blacks.

The full integration of all national forces was accomplished on paper on October 30, 1954, but not all individual states followed the federal lead. The U.S. Constitution allows each state to have its own military force, somewhat confusingly named the state National Guard. State National Guards are usually under the command of their respective state governors. They are intended as a rapidly responding armed force for quelling local disturbances and providing a variety of services during all types of emergencies. Guard members are volunteer citizen soldiers who maintain a civilian life in addition to their military roles. In the South, the state National Guards continued to be white-only forces. The states' rights doctrine continued to be used as the legal basis of segregation.

The importance of "color" in the Jim Crow era

During the slavery era, light-skinned slaves often had a somewhat higher status than the dark-skinned ones. They were usually "house slaves," not field workers. Not many slave owners admitted to having a familial relationship with them, but it was at least tacitly admitted that they were of mixed race. A few of their owners/fathers, through a clause in their wills, went as far as to "manumit" their children, i.e., free them rather than to arrange for their sale or transfer as an inheritance to a family member.

Neither as slaves nor after emancipation were free blacks accorded the same rights and respect as whites. However, many of them assumed, like most whites, that a mixed parentage had resulted in some improvement in their innate characteristics. Being of mixed race produced in many blacks an essentially racist sense of superiority over the purely African population. That fuzzy color line persisted to some degree among black Americans long after emancipation and could be detected throughout the Jim Crow era.[136] Light skin conferred more status, more respect, and more opportunities in a professional and business sense, and, in rare cases, allowed the addition of more "white blood." For a black person, even one of very light skin color, to marry a white person was illegal in most states, and even where it was legal, most white Americans saw it as a scandal. Some blacks also found it offensive, a sign of rejection by the black individual of his or her own race.

Though it entailed a risk of being killed by racist whites, it was still usually a positive factor in the career of an ambitious and talented black man to marry a woman from a respected white family. It was rare for a successful, light-skinned black man or woman to seek a mate with African-type features and dark skin. However, the gradual "whitening" of the American black population produced by those attitudes was not always by choice. Rape by white men of "black" women of all shades of beige, brown, and black remained a common thing even after emancipation.

Following the Civil War, black institutions of higher learning sprang up, registering black teacher and student applicants with the best academic credentials. More often than not, that meant graduates from integrated schools in the North, a high percentage of whom were of mixed race and had light skin color but were still classed as black by the American society. Black churches, social clubs, and civic organizations were eager to attract well-known and respected members of the black population in order to enhance their own status, influence, and financial well-being. Again, those with lighter skin were more likely than those of darker color to already have a respected status in a society still wholly dominated by whites. As a result, the majority of the leading men in the black population of the early and mid-twentieth century were of mixed race, not a few so light that they could be taken for whites. Walter White joined the National Association for the Advancement of Colored People (NAACP) in 1918 as an investigator. Because he looked like he was "pure" white, he was able to attend meetings with white segregationists incognito in the South. He served as the executive secretary of the organization from 1931 to 1955.

---

[136] Ibram X. Kendi, *STAMPED FROM THE BEGINNING, The Definitive History of Racist Ideas in America* (New York: Bold Type Books, 2017), pp. 243, 244.

Figure 19 Walter White

There were early mixed-race advocates of equal rights like Frederick Douglas and Booker T. Washington, and many outstanding scientists like Charles R. Drew, the medical researcher who invented the blood bank for blood transfusions, and George W. Carver, an agricultural scientist who invented peanut butter. Outstanding men and women in all forms of art were drawn to New York to create "the Harlem Renaissance" of the 1920s and 1930s. Still, most of the prominent individuals in black America illustrated that "color," in the sense of the lightness of one's skin, continued to affect the opportunities for social and economic advancement. One factor in the choice of Rosa Parks to initiate the Montgomery bus boycott in 1955 likely was that she had medium-brown skin and somewhat European facial features. She "looked more respectable" than the stereotypical Southern black woman.

Perhaps the most influential intellectuals and civil rights advocates of the first half of the twentieth century was William Edward Burghardt Du Bois, known simply as W.E.B. Du Bois. He was an American historian, sociologist, civil rights activist, and acclaimed author. He was born in 1868 in Great Barrington, Massachusetts, to a mother of German stock and a French-Haitian father. He had an illustrious academic career, graduating from the University of Berlin, Germany, and then Harvard, where he was the first man with known African heritage to earn a doctorate. In 1909, together with Ida B. Wells and a handful of other prominent black, Jewish and white civil rights activist, he founded the National Association for the Advancement of Colored People (NAACP).

Figure 20. W.E.B. Du Bois

In its day (1903), W.E.B. Du Bois's most famous work, *The Souls of Black Folk*, was hailed by almost all critics as the most enlightened and penetrating study ever of America's black population.[137] The black intellectual William H. Ferris (1874 – 1941) called *The Souls of Black Folk* 'the political Bible of the negro race.' Fifty years after its publication, its main theme inspired the word "soul" for the characteristically black popular music rooted in blues and gospel, and the "Black is Beautiful" credo. In the more than one hundred years since its publication, the book has attained an almost legendary status in the black community. It powerfully argues that blacks are no mere beasts without deep intellect or keen emotional sensitivity. Du Bois asserted that blacks have a different but equally advanced and valuable character as whites, "a certain spiritual joyousness; a sensuous, tropical love of life, in vivid contrast to the cool and cautious New England reason."

Undeniably, most blacks of the days of Du Bois lived lives of poverty, ignorance, and immorality born of hopelessness and despair, which caused whites to perceive blacks as inherently inferior. Du Bois saw their plight as an inevitable consequence of their history as slaves and the oppression and discrimination they had suffered since emancipation. Despite his avowed anti-racism, Du Bois thus maintained a belief in an inherent difference between the races. He still called for assimilation and integration of blacks into the mainstream American population and culture – while carrying with them some of the best features of their own culture. While retaining some of the traditional prejudices, he gave a prescription for the best and most feasible solution to "An American Dilemma."

---

[137] W.E.B. Du Bois, *The Souls of Black Folk* (New York: The New American Library, 1969)

It is not racist to believe – as some racist blacks, as well as whites, would hold it to be– that mixing with whites and assimilating into mainstream society will help blacks to "elevate" themselves. It does not presuppose that blacks are inherently incapable of "elevating" themselves on their own. One can assume that they have the same potential as whites for succeeding in all areas of life, educationally, professionally, and economically, and still see integration in its fullest meaning as advantageous for the black population – as well as for all other ethnic groups. What blacks lack is not equal potential, but equal opportunity.

Even today, racist beliefs and values still support de facto discrimination in many sides of black life, sometimes subtle but sometimes stark, even when there is no objective basis for discrimination. For example, European-based definitions of physical beauty are deeply ingrained in the American public, across all ethnic groups, social levels, and ages. Even among blacks, the prevailing standards of beauty have always been European-like facial features, light skin and eyes, and "good," i.e., straight hair. In 1940 – '41, American psychologists Mamie Clark and Kenneth Clark conducted a famous study with black children that inquired into their preference among choices of dolls. A clear majority of the children chose dolls with European features, skin color, and blonde hair over dolls that looked more African. The indoctrination of children begins early, and once a set of values has been implanted, it often resists changing.

Malcolm X, thinking back on his youth and his first "conk" hair straightening session, identified it as his "first really big step toward self-degradation: when I endured all of that pain, literally burning my flesh to have it look like a white man's hair."

Historical statistics show that many mixed-race, light-skinned blacks have had better success in life simply because of their light skin. It caused others to give them more respect and opportunity than would have been given a dark-skinned person. That is racist, but it has been an unfortunate reality in American society for a hundred and fifty years. Among both blacks and whites, there will probably always be some who nostalgically or out of tribal instinct want to keep their race "pure," but there is no scientific evidence that "purity" confers an advantage. On the contrary: a wider genetic heritage has health advantages.

Not all blacks would choose white mates if they had a completely open choice, but a sufficient number would do so to make the "racial" categorization meaningless in a few generations. Among young white Americans, racial prejudice is fading so rapidly that there would be no lack of responsive white mates at least to start the process. It would be a self-reinforcing process: the more blurred the color line becomes, the less important it also becomes. That is a good thing socially.

Despite Southern beliefs and wishes, racial integration begins

For a century after the emancipation of the slaves, many white Southerners had a romanticized image of the old South as a peaceful, God-fearing, refined civilization. Legends of the bravery and prowess of the Confederate troops were kept alive by many statues and monuments and by naming buildings and streets in honor of the famed Confederate military leaders. The cherished family lore of almost every Southern family was replete with proudly patriotic war tales and stories of the horrific suffering during the Civil War and Reconstruction at the hands of the Yankees.

In the South, people preferred not to use the term "Civil War." They instead called it the War between the States or even the War of Northern Aggression. They did not describe it as a war to free the slaves but as a war to uphold the constitutional principle of "states' rights." Those terminologies were important for psychological reasons. They framed the war as being about true democratic principles and the freedom from despotic government that the US Constitution promised. That perspective cast the Confederacy as the valiant defender of the rights of individual states to legislate according to the will of the people of those states. (Whites generally assumed that "the people" meant "the white people.") In the view of the South, that right was sacrosanct and still existed, no matter what the federal government said and no matter what the outcome of the war had been.

In the aftermath of World War II, the Western world began to see racial separation and a race-based hierarchy in society as morally unacceptable. A few holdouts against this trend were notable—mainly the apartheid regime in South Africa and the parts of the United States where slavery had remained institutionalized less than a century earlier. However, in those nations, black citizens' struggles to achieve the same rights as their white compatriots began to draw the increased attention of the rest of the world. Most nations strongly condemned the continuing oppression and violence of the black minority, and it became an embarrassment for the United States, which—somewhat ironically—liked to portray itself as the champion of liberty and equality for all and the defender of democracy in the free world. The federal government of the United States realized that the segregation and oppression suffered by its black population continued to be a huge propaganda issue to be exploited by the communists. That bolstered its support for the lawsuit that would change the course of race relations in the United States.

Under the surface—and not yet much noticed by the average white Southerner—organized black rebellion was beginning to take shape. In 1952, the NAACP filed a lawsuit, *Brown v. Board of Education of Topeka, Kansas*, in which the group argued that separate schools for white and black children constituted an unequal educational opportunity for black children and was therefore unconstitutional. This lawsuit is widely considered the opening shot of the modern civil rights movement in America.

The case was first argued in court in December 1952 and then argued again on appeal in the Supreme Court a year later. A federal government brief to the court urged it to take into consideration more than domestic constitutional law. Secretary of State Dean Acheson stated in the government brief:

> "The United States is under constant attack in the foreign press, over the foreign radio, and in such international bodies as the United Nations because of various practices of discrimination against minority groups in this country.... [T]he continuance of racial discrimination in the United States remains a source of constant embarrassment to this Government in the day-to-day conduct of its foreign relations; and it jeopardizes the effective maintenance of our moral leadership of the free and democratic nations of the world."[138]

---

[138] US Government brief to the Supreme Court, filed by Attorney General James P. McGranery in December 1952, urging the court to make the decision that was announced seventeen months later.

In May 1954, the Supreme Court made its historically momentous decision: school segregation based on race was indeed unconstitutional. The decision was breathtaking in its implications and sent shock waves through not just the South but the entire nation. A shell fired on Fort Sumter had been the start of the Civil War. The decision by the Supreme Court set in motion an avalanche of change that would—at least on paper—guarantee the freedom promised by the Emancipation Proclamation and for which a horrific war had been fought.

The racial integration of the U.S. military demanded by Truman's Executive Order 9981 in 1948 was a significant step forward, both in real, practical terms, and as a symbolic marker of official government policy. Just six years later, the highest court in the land had taken side against school segregation in a ruling applicable nationwide. It showed that the federal government was willing to take effective action in support of black demands for non-discrimination.

The federal government's increasing pressure on the Southern states to dismantle racial segregation met determined resistance by virtually the entire white population of the region. The pressure set off a serious and violent confrontation involving the rights of America's black citizens and stirred deep passions on both sides. The promise of racial equality had been reneged on by the American government for almost a century. Now, a new era was to begin.

Part Seven: The '60s—Another American Revolution

Introduction

The decade of the 1960s was a significant turning point in American history, but Americans tend to have very divergent opinions on the nature and significance of that period in history. Describing the 1960s in a way that most people of that day would agree with is difficult precisely because that era was experienced so differently by people from different geographical areas and by those of different ages at the time, and their social, ideological, religious, and ethnic backgrounds. Sharply divergent views on the 1960s still exist today, even among historians and others who are knowledgeable about it. One of the few things that all can agree on is this: the era was not in any way normal.

It was a turbulent time of unprecedented youthful rebellion, social upheaval, violence, anarchy, reaction, effervescent love, burning hate, boundless idealism, unbridled optimism, and desperate fears. Most young Americans experienced the '60s as a uniquely positive and joyful time—a time of loud and exuberant rock and roll, of freedom and idealism, and of fast and flashy cars. It was the beginning of women's liberation and a new sexual openness. Those who spent their formative years in that tumultuous epoch could not escape being affected by it. Many were at that stage of their lives: in 1960, more than a third of all Americans were under the age of eighteen.

At the time, most members of older generations saw the sixties as an era of a deplorable breakdown of law and order and the abandonment of traditional morals—a troubled and tense time when America was beleaguered by external, as well as internal threats. Some perceived it primarily as a time when a distant, overreaching, and corrupt federal government was forcing individual states to adopt new and repugnant rules on how people must live.

In his bestselling book, *Boom! Voices of the Sixties*, Tom Brokaw provides an insight into how many middle-class white Americans experienced the '60s. Brokaw was born in Webster, South Dakota, in 1940. His was a middle-class family in a small Midwestern town, and in his formative years, he lived what one might call a sheltered life, typical of that environment. There were no racial tensions or highly emotional prejudices, no abject poverty, no sharp political antagonisms, and no civil disorders. It was a calm, law-abiding, moderately conservative environment with wholesome American values and a traditional outlook.

As an adult, his professional career as a newsman took off and made him the anchor and managing editor of *NBC Nightly News* for twenty-two years from 1982 to 2004. In his career, he became thoroughly familiar with the tumultuous events of the 1960s—yet his book reveals that he remained a product of his early environment altogether. Brokaw found himself a somewhat puzzled outsider who observed and reported on chaotic and violent events. His ability to do so calmly, credibly, and professionally allowed him to reach the pinnacle of his profession. But in his book, he shows himself to be limited by his background when it comes to perceiving the full context and meaning of the era. Growing up in small-town South Dakota, he seems to have been unaware of the magnitude and significance of the social and attitudinal changes occurring in the 1950s and early 1960s from the civil rights movement, rock and roll, and the liberalization of sexual mores. He describes himself this way:

> I fit the prototype of the typical young white male of the time. I had been a crew-cut apostle of the Boy Scouts, reciting the Pledge of Allegiance to the flag, attending Sunday school and church, drinking too much beer in college but never smoking dope; marijuana in the Fifties and early Sixties was the stuff of jazz musicians and hoodlums in faraway places.
>
> Before I married the love of my life, my high school classmate Meredith, we had never spent a night together. In those days, parked cars and curfews were the defining limits of courtship.[139]

Tom Brokaw perceived the tumult of the 1960s as a sudden, shocking, and bewildering breakdown of social order and traditional morality. It brought political assassinations, massive demonstrations, urban riots, and racial strife to a nation that he was brought up to see as the paragon of democracy, justice, and opportunity for all. The circumstances of his upbringing had prevented him from seeing the continued hardships of discrimination, exploitation, poverty, and humiliation that the majority of America's black population faced. His background as a Sunday school-attending Boy Scout in a conservative Mid-Western small town left him untouched as a teenager by the fervor of the rock and roll music, the pathos and passion of the civil rights movement, and the faith-challenging new morality of the sexual revolution.

He defines the '60s era as beginning in 1963 with the assassination of John F. Kennedy and ending in 1974 with the resignation of Richard Nixon. Those were events of top significance to grown-ups of the time (and thus to news anchors), but they were not central to the life experience of the youth. The true essence and meaning of the '60s was a rebellion of the youth. The '60s were about the alternative values and rebellious actions of that segment of the population, but they were not shared and experienced by Tom Brokaw, who equated jazz musicians with "hoodlums in faraway places" and could in no way understand and

---

[139] Tom Brokaw, *Boom! Voices of the Sixties* (New York: Random House, 2007). Page 5.

empathize with the passions and excesses that he witnessed. It is not surprising that he ends the introductory section of his book with:

> I also believe that on many of the important levels, the meaning of that amazing decade
> is still emerging, and for the rest of my days, when my mind wanders back to the Sixties,
> I will probably think: Boom!—What was that all about?[140]

Not everyone was able to keep this kind of objective reporter's eye on what was going on. Many others of Brokaw's generation were swept up in the maelstrom of social change and could not avoid taking sides in the many-sided struggles. Ultimately, many came to feel the anger, disappointment, and frustrations of an unfinished—and in many respects, failed—social revolution. The late 1960s became characterized by outraged antiwar protest marches, violent political demonstrations, and large-scale urban riots.

In the late 1960s, once disillusionment began to set in, the era also saw the proliferation of communes of young drug-dazed hippies who danced to Indian music in the sunshine with flowers in their hair. With religious-like fervor, they urged other young people to reject and withdraw from a corrupt and violent society and to follow them—to "make love, not war." For many young whites, it became a time of LSD, psychedelic art, hedonistic partying, and sexual promiscuity ahead of an anticipated apocalypse. The experiences of those young people differed drastically from those of Brokaw. For some of them, the '60s ended with the gigantic finale of the Woodstock musical "happening" in the summer of 1969, followed by the numbing shock of the Ohio National Guard's killing of four students at Kent State University the next year. Others experienced the passionate struggle of the 1960s as continuing without pause or relief until the final withdrawal of American troops from Vietnam in 1975.

---

[140] Brokaw, *Boom! Voices of the Sixties*. Page XXI.

Chapter 1. The '60s Are Dawning: "Whole Lotta Shakin' Goin' On"

America in the immediate post-WWII era

The '60s, like any other historical era, are inseparable from the context of events and circumstances that preceded the era. Therefore, to get a real feeling for what that tumultuous era was like, one must know something about this context—which was not just provincially American but involved truly earthshaking historical events on a global scale. It was not a bolt of lightning from a blue sky. Storm clouds had been gathering for a long time.

The seeds of the 1960s were sown in the late 1940s and early 1950s, and the aftershocks of the cultural earthquake of the '60s continued through the 1970s. In a broad sense, what we call the '60s did not start on January 1, 1960, and end on December 31, 1969. As a social and cultural phenomenon, one could argue that they began with the 1954 Supreme Court decision that school segregation based on race was unconstitutional. The court decision had little immediate consequences for black citizens but would prove to be a watershed in the legal history of the nation. One might also argue that the wrenching transformative seizures of American society that characterized the '60s had an inseparable continuum all the way to the inglorious conclusion of the Vietnam War in 1975.

Unquestionably, the era left the landscape of American society forever changed. The changes were so broad and significant that every aspect of society felt the overall cumulative effect. Not all of them specifically concerned the relations between blacks and whites in the nation, but they all provided a context that must be taken into account when studying that issue. For example, in the mid to late 1960s, the Vietnam War played a decisive role in the loss of support among white youth for the black civil rights struggle. Earlier, young and idealistic white college students had entered the South in large numbers to support that movement and were instrumental in focusing media and political attention on it. White victims of segregationist violence created widespread publicity, and publicity was the lifeblood of the movement. Before 1964, a young white man faced little risk of being drafted and put in harm's way in a war that he opposed. Once opposition to the war became the dominant issue from both a moral and a personal safety standpoint for these young whites, the black civil rights movement drew far fewer white activist supporters. As a result, it lost much of its momentum.

The forces at play in the 1950s and 1960s were not limited to what was happening within the borders of the United States. In 1945, the defeat of Germany and Japan in the largest and bloodiest war in human history had not produced peace. It had instead divided the world into two main, and fiercely antagonistic, political blocs. The communist bloc, led by the Soviet Union, made clear its intent to convert the entire world into a communist system. Most of the rest of the world, led by the United States, made it equally clear that any attempt to achieve this goal by military force would be resisted by all available means—including nuclear weapons. The attention of most Americans was drawn to that international issue—not to domestic conditions.

In 1938, Congress had formed the House Un-American Activities Committee (HUAC). In its hunt for supposedly dangerous subversives of all kinds, it was empowered to use means normally associated with oppressive police states. During the Eisenhower administration, America became obsessed with the fear of communism. Communist spying and subversive activities allegedly infected the very core of America and were finding sympathizers and collaborators in all corners of society, particularly in the liberal and leftist-leaning sectors of the political and entertainment establishments. The fear of communist infiltration into American society reached a peak in the early 1950s with the actions of the grandstanding Senator Joseph McCarthy of Wisconsin. McCarthy and the head of the FBI, J. Edgar Hoover, conducted veritable witch hunts in their zeal to root out all communist sympathizers from important and influential positions in society.

Many lives and careers in the entertainment and media fields were ruined by unproven allegations of treasonous attitudes and activities and by the blacklisting of artists. "Blacklisting" in Hollywood referred to a list of names of artists with known or suspected ties to or sympathies with communist organizations. A person whose name, rightly or wrongly, was included on that list found it almost impossible to have the name removed or to keep or obtain employment as an artist. He or she was under surveillance by the FBI and might be called to testify against others in the hearings of the HUAC. The blacklist was first created in 1947 and came to an end in the 1960s. The HUAC remained in existence until 1975.

McCarthy himself went down in spectacular fashion in 1954 during the televised Army-McCarthy congressional hearings in the summer of that year. His ruthless methods were revealed to be psychotic and fanatical. He lost his influence and was censured by the Senate in December. But the search for communist agents and their ties to leftist organizations in the United States continued apace in a less public manner through covert activities by the FBI and the Central Intelligence Agency (CIA). One of the most important targets for the domestic surveillance was the black civil rights movement. The suspected influence of communist agents on leaders of that movement led to covert attempts by the FBI and other government agencies to sabotage and otherwise limit the movement's agenda.

Despite the looming threat of communism and the Soviet Union, the majority of the white population of the United States felt mostly patriotic pride and confidence. They had good reasons to do so. Domestic natural resources were plentiful—especially coal and oil. While other industrial nations were crippled, bankrupted, and left in physical ruins by the ravages of war, American factories and transportation systems remained untouched. Indeed, they had benefited hugely from the demands of wartime production, paid for by unprecedented government spending and reaching a productivity unequaled elsewhere in the world. Factories, modernized and made efficient by the demands of the war, now churned out consumer goods in astounding volumes and of great diversity, and the affluence of the majority population was generally beyond even the dreams of those in most other nations. An increasing percentage of American families now owned cars—most of them far more powerful and luxurious than what people in other countries could afford. Electric cooking ranges, dishwashing machines, and other novel modern conveniences made America the envy of most of the rest of the world. Americans reveled in the conviction that their nation was the richest, most powerful, and best nation on earth—indeed in all history.

The lifestyle of the average American changed drastically over the two decades following World War II, and not merely by the sudden plenitude of consumer goods. From having lived predominantly on farms and in small villages and towns, Americans were now drawn to the larger cities and their suburbs, enticed by the availability of well-paying industrial and office jobs. The middle class was expanding, and its income was increasing. However, in many ways, the living circumstances of the middle class were incompatible with the traditional American values of individual uniqueness and freedom.

Many of the new suburban areas had eerily similar looks that betrayed central planning and cookie-cutter mass production. Planned communities such as the several ones named Levittown after the builder William Levitt and his company were cost-effective and offered plenty of conveniences but had a dreary sameness to all the houses. The ideals of the perfect family life were celebrated in popular TV shows of the day, such as *Father Knows Best*, *The Adventures of Ozzie and Harriet*, and *Leave It to Beaver*, all depicting comfortable, happy, all-white families undisturbed by tragic or life-changing events.

The sameness of the living conditions of most suburban middle-class families offered few opportunities to realize the very American desire to express one's unique individuality. To fit in and be socially accepted, one must not appear to be odd and radical in one's beliefs or lifestyle. The husband was the breadwinner, and the wife cooked and cleaned and took care of the children. They all attended church together—and, as Martin Luther King Jr. observed, "the most segregated hour of Christian America is eleven o'clock on Sunday morning"[141] Optimally, the husband belonged to some civic organization, which customarily was also racially exclusive.

Middle-class life in the early 1950s was particularly frustrating for teenagers. They were bored by its gray sameness, its day-to-day predictability, and its very Victorian, prudish, and strict rules for meeting members of the opposite sex. But a change of truly landslide proportions was about to occur. The triggers were cars and rock and roll.

The arrival of "rock and roll"

In the 1950s, teenagers–particularly white ones–were becoming an important part of the American economy. With the increasing wealth of the middle class, fashionable–and expensive–shoes, clothing, and accessories became mandatory for teenagers of both sexes who felt the pressure to keep up with trends and fads and stay "cool." For many young men, after finishing high school and landing their first paying job, buying a car was a high priority.

The ability to drive a car was essential in America, where public transportation was not widely available, and the freedom and convenience offered by car ownership were highly valued. It was common for boys to obtain a driver's license at age sixteen, and in rural parts of the country, some drove cars without having a license.

---

[141] Martin Luther King, Jr. in an appearance on NBC's *Meet the Press* on April 17, 1960.

One of the new features of cars in the 1950s were built-in radios. Only AM monophonic transmissions existed, but that provided sufficient sound quality for the car radios of the day. Most American radio stations transmitted pop tunes and country and western music, and some played light jazz and big band dance music. This rather bland musical menu was also available as 78 rpm records. These 78s could be played a limited number of times before the sound became full of hiss and distortion. It was not a musical menu or medium that could satisfy the insatiable musical appetite of bored teenagers for very long.

In some of the larger cities, most of which had significant black populations, there were radio stations that catered to that audience. Transmissions by radio stations of the time, operating in the 535 to 1,705 kHz band, could carry much farther at night than in the daytime. Stations in Saint Louis, Nashville, Chicago, New York, and other major cities were heard over wide areas at night. Teenagers were cruising the streets and highways listening to the wild new music they had discovered on the car radio. Blues and hot jazz—music traditionally favored by blacks—now began to reach a growing audience of white teenagers.

A style that also incorporated some country and western influences turned out to be easily digested by those whites who found the raw blues music a bit too primitive and "black" sounding and modern jazz too sophisticated. Songs by early rock and roll stars such as Fats Domino had a heavy, engaging rhythm and catchy, easily remembered words and melodies. This style of early rock and roll, having some characteristics of the more familiar pop and country music, caught on big among teenagers across the country. The breakthrough of rock and roll music thus came via car radio. It was then exploited commercially via records and movies like the 1955 movie *Blackboard Jungle*, which introduced the first international rock and roll megahit, Bill Haley's "Rock Around the Clock." It is a prime example of rockabilly, the rock and roll sound that owes a lot to hillbilly—i.e., country—music.

The new music also benefited from advancements in recording technology. In the 1950s, the arrival of low-cost vinyl 45 and 33⅓ rpm records helped spread the music that many teens had discovered on car radios, and the buyers were primarily teenagers. Teenagers wanted to hear their favorite songs many times—often several times a day—and the new vinyl records, in combination with record players using very lightweight diamond-tipped needles, allowed the records to be played a far greater number of times than what had been the case with 78s. Compared to the old 78s, the new 45 rpm vinyl records were smaller, lighter, and cheaper. They also had better sound quality. The larger 33⅓ rpm records could contain many songs on each side. Soon all the teenager-oriented music was available only on vinyl.

Recording companies were worried that the stars of this new music were almost all black. That was expected to limit the white customer base for rock and roll records, and especially to encounter resistance from disapproving parents of this teenage fan base. Talent scouts were on the lookout for white singers who could perform in a style similar to that of black artists. The breakthrough occurred when Sam Phillips of the small record company Sun Records in Nashville found Elvis Presley, a white Mississippi truck driver who liked the music he heard on black-oriented radio stations. Elvis had learned to sing those songs, but he had his own unique style that set him apart from the black singers, and that quickly made him a superstar. Elvis had the looks, sound, and provocative body movements that drove white teenage girls to ecstasy and made young white boys want to be and look like him.

The sales of Elvis records boomed, and his success brought many other white singers onto the bandwagon. Carl Perkins, Gene Vincent, Buddy Holly, Jerry Lee Lewis, the Everly Brothers, Ricky Nelson, and many others became teenage idols in the 1950s. White artists tended to straddle the border between traditional pop music and rock and roll as performed by black artists. The term "rock and roll" had been coined in 1951 by Alan Freed, a popular white disc jockey at WJW in Cleveland, Ohio. Freed became the most effective promoter of the new music and favored the sound of black performers. The rumored sexual connotations of the term "rock and roll" undoubtedly contributed to its quick adoption by its young fans: the music often had sexual innuendos in its lyrics and a rhythm that seemed to throb with sexual arousal. The term became widely applied to the music. As the music's popularity soared, the term became somewhat of a sales gimmick. All performers in a broad spectrum of styles wanted their music to have that label. Radio and records—and also eventually television—caught on to the popularity of rock and roll, helping to spread the music into every corner of the nation. Rock and roll–themed movies also helped propel the new teenage idols into superstar status.

At public performances by these immensely popular teenage idols, many female fans were transported into frenzied, screaming, crying ecstasy. The level of excitement occasionally reached a point where they fainted. The quality of their idols' performances was seldom such that it could explain this extreme reaction. The behavior seemed to be a motivation in itself, where the musical concert facilitated and provided an excuse to scream out suppressed feelings and frustrations. The happiness experienced in these moments of ecstasy was genuine and appeared not unlike that experienced during Pentecostal church services.

The availability of cars, whether equipped with a radio or not, opened up exciting possibilities for teenagers in the 1950s. They could meet members of the opposite sex in unsupervised privacy. Drive-in movies became all the rage, as they offered a dark place where seeing a movie was sometimes less of a priority than engaging in hot romance in the back seat. Teenagers, spurred on by the suggestive lyrics, emotional vocals, and heavy rhythms of rock and roll, took advantage of the new opportunities. Movies were also quick to discover the new teenage affluence, freedom, and rebellious attitude. In 1953, Marlon Brando's *The Wild One* exploited the desire to revolt against a narrow-minded authority structure, and in 1955, James Dean's *Rebel Without a Cause* presented a sensitive teenage role model who was tormented by feelings of being rootless, bored, aimless, misunderstood, and lonely. That seemed to catch the romantic teenage spirit of the time.

The risk of contracting a sexually transmitted disease was not yet high in the 1950s, but girls were frightened of the possibility of becoming pregnant. That restraint on behavior lifted when "The Pill" became available in 1960. The Pill is an oral contraceptive that, when taken regularly, is about 99.7 percent effective in preventing pregnancy during a one-year time span, even with frequent sexual intercourse. All the ingredients of the cultural revolution of the '60s were then falling into place.

The wild new music expressed the jubilant spirit of rebelliousness and ebullient youthful energy that came to power the civil rights movement and the sexual revolution during the teenage heydays of the "baby boomers." It met the same shocked and contemptuous reception by the older generation as had jazz music thirty years earlier, and for the same fundamental reasons. Many whites of the older generation thought of it as "Negro music." (In so-called polite company, it was sometimes referred to as "race music.") It was deemed crude, uncouth, and blatantly sexually suggestive. Church and civic leaders condemned it in the strongest terms, and parents were exhorted to forbid their children to listen to it or to buy records of that type.

The rejection of this music by parents and other authority figures merely made it even more attractive to young people. The tight-laced sexual morality of the older generation, which was the primary reason for their rejection of rock and roll, was, in turn, rejected by the young, rebellious teenagers. The sexual revolution, both symbolized by and enabled by The Pill, got underway. The Pill became officially available as a contraceptive in 1960, and its use soon became widespread despite vociferous opposition by most church denominations. Now that they were less fearful of unwanted pregnancy, many young couples explored sexuality, not to procreate but to express their love and to experience great excitement and physical pleasure.

The new youth culture of the United States became a fortuitous and unique confluence of three rebellious and liberating movements that would truly transform the nation. Jazz had helped break down some of the racial barriers in the 1920s and '30s; in the 1950s and '60s, rock and roll did the same thing but on a much greater scale. The tsunami of the rock and roll revolution joined the groundswell of the liberalization of sexual attitudes and the rising tide of the civil rights movement in an irresistible flood that included the feminist movement and the gay rights movement to become the chaotic cultural upheaval of the 1960s. These trends were all so successful because they coincided with, supported, and reinforced one another. Without this synergy, none of them would have been as far-reaching, broad, deep, and consequential as the combination of all three was. But the ground was laid, and the seeds sown, in the 1950s. By 1959, America was already a very different place than it had been ten or even five years earlier. A new dynamic was present—a heedless willingness to challenge tradition that augured very well for America's future. The dam of stultifying Victorian morality and fearful racial prejudice was breaking.

Chapter 2. The Civil Rights Movement Takes Off

The Supreme Court 1954 Brown vs Board of Education decision

Although jazz music had a significant white audience since the 1920s, most of white America remained separated from black society and culture well into the 1950s. Outside the South, white families paid little attention to racial matters. The racial polarization of society seemed so traditional and static that it had attained the air of normalcy.

In the middle and late 1950s, however, rock and roll music made blacks more visible and acceptable within the world of young whites, many of whom had favorite black artists. For the vast majority of whites, even among most young rock and roll fans, interracial dating was still very much a taboo—but in the urban North, an increasing number of adventuresome individuals let curiosity overcome fear. Maintaining strict social separation of the races seemed less of an imperative when sex was no longer such a highly charged issue.

Inspired by what they heard in music by black artists, many young whites thought it cool to adopt "jive talk" and slang expressions coined by blacks and to know and even count as a friend a black person. The tight walls of racial separation began to crumble. The notion that blacks deserved equal rights seemed increasingly reasonable. In many parts of the North and West, the black population was small, and schools were already mostly integrated. Thus, the Supreme Court decision in 1954 that all schools had to desegregate did not cause the same shock and resentment there as it did in the South.

That decision was sensational and far-reaching, but the South did not comply. Southern legislators and governors understood that allowing the ruling to take effect in their states against the will of the state's population would set a dangerous precedent. A flurry of consultations and legislation followed, aimed at defending the principle of states' rights—the alleged rights the states had under the US Constitution to establish their own laws. On January 24, 1956, the governors of Georgia, Mississippi, North Carolina, South Carolina, and Virginia agreed to use their executive powers to block the integration of schools in their states. February and March saw legislative action completed. The state legislature of Alabama overwhelmingly passed a nullification resolution that declared the Supreme Court's school desegregation decision to be "null, void and of no effect" in Alabama. The state of Virginia passed a resolution that the Supreme Court's decision was an illegal encroachment on states' rights. The Mississippi state legislature agreed, calling the decision invalid in their state. Senator Harry Byrd of Virginia called for "massive resistance" to all federal demands for desegregation. Members of the congressional delegations from the Southern states composed a document known as the Southern Manifesto, in which they declared their strong opposition to school desegregation. Nineteen senators and eighty-two members of the House of Representatives signed it, including the unanimous entire congressional delegations from the former Confederate states of Alabama, Arkansas, Georgia, Louisiana, Mississippi, and South Carolina.

Through various legal actions, the states of the old Confederacy began a coordinated delaying tactic that they hoped could keep segregation in effect until further Supreme Court cases could be brought that might side with the South regarding states' rights under the US Constitution. Mississippi was quick to respond. On September 16, 1954, Mississippi passed an amendment to its state constitution in which it abolished all public schools; for white students, the state helped establish private, segregated schools. Blacks had to create, fund, staff, and maintain the facilities for black children. To ensure that those schools were kept segregated, the state passed a law on April 5, 1955, penalizing white students by jail and fines if they attended black schools. For the time being, the conservative Eisenhower administration seemed content to take a wait-and-see attitude on the matter.

Not long thereafter, a citizens' association was formed in Mississippi, named White Citizens' Councils (WCC). It quickly acquired members all over the South. By 1956, it claimed almost one hundred and fifty thousand members in Mississippi and Alabama. It vowed to use all legal means to oppose integration. Many of the members were also members of the KKK, and the WCC came to stand for, not entirely jokingly, the "White Collar Clan." It became virtually mandatory for anyone with political or business ambitions in the Deep South to be a member of the WCC. Leading businessmen and state and local politicians in the South were members, which in some states gave the organization a dominating influence in state legislatures. The Councils played a decisive role in the 1959 election of staunch segregationist Ross Barnett to the Mississippi governor's office.

The WCC gained power and momentum in Mississippi in 1956 when the Mississippi legislature formed the State Sovereignty Commission, which organized a covert network that kept surveillance of black and white individuals with known ties to black civil rights organizations. Like the FBI, it employed paid informants to provide information about organizations and individuals under surveillance. Information was used to plan moves in opposition to black attempts to obtain equal rights. The WCC always claimed to be against the use of violence but regularly leaked the information gathered by the State Sovereignty Commission to the KKK. From 1960 to 1964, the commission funded the WCC with $190,000 of state funds.[142] In 1964, the Sov-Com passed on information regarding civil rights workers James Chaney, Michael Schwerner, and Andrew Goodman to the conspirators in their murders during Freedom Summer.[143]

The 1954 Supreme Court decision raised the consciousness among many whites outside the South of the issue of racial segregation and its oppressive effect on black citizens. The issue received a lot more publicity in 1955 with the murder of Emmet Till in Mississippi.

The murder of Emmett Till

The race-motivated killing of a black man in the South usually did not create headlines. But because of the age of the victim and the brutality of the crime, the murder of fourteen-year-old Emmett Till drew attention nationwide. The story was also followed closely by news organizations in many other countries.

---

[142] Maryanne Vollers, Ghosts of Mississippi: The Murder of Medgar Evers, the Trials of Byron de la Beckwith, and the Haunting of the New South (New York, Little, Brown 1995.)
[143] Irons, Jenny. *Reconstituting Whiteness: the Mississippi State Sovereignty Commission.* (Nashville: Vanderbilt University, 2010)

Figure 21 Emmett "Bobo" Till at his home in Chicago

Emmett Till was on a visit from his home in Chicago to relatives in Mississippi. He and some friends went to the grocery store owned by one of the accused killers, Roy Bryant, where Emmett was said to have been disrespectful toward the store owner's wife. In later recanted testimony, she claimed that Emmett had made some sexually suggestive comments to her. She told her husband, who became furious and contacted his friend J. W. Milam to discuss what to do. The two men agreed that Emmett had to be "taught a lesson."

The two men found Emmett at his grandfather's house and abducted him. They pistol-whipped him and beat him so viciously that they crushed his jaw and caused one of his eyes to come out of its socket. One of the men then shot Emmett in the head and threw him in the Tallahatchie River. His body was tied to a heavy fan from a cotton gin to make sure it would remain hidden.

After three days, however, a man fishing in the river discovered the body, which was pulled ashore and placed in a local mortuary. There could be no doubt that the body was the victim of deliberate homicide. Roy Bryant and J. W. Milam were quickly identified as suspects in the murder.

In court, it should have been an open-and-shut case. The evidence against the accused killers was overwhelming, and no other person was ever suspected of having committed the murder. Still, the white defendants were declared innocent. Widely distributed pictures of the defendants confidently smiling in the courtroom during the trial illustrated the sham and travesty of the proceedings.

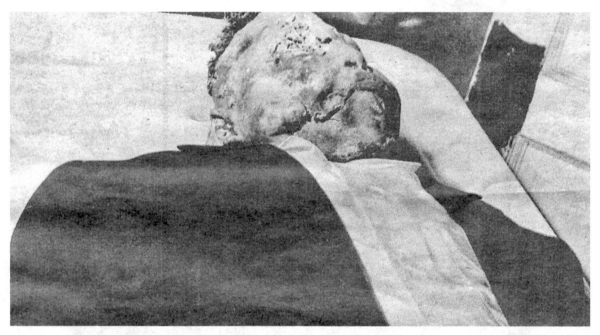

Figure 22 Emmett Till in his casket, with his jaw crushed, one eyeball lost, and a bullet hole in his right temple, 1955. The corpse decayed after spending days in the Tallahatchie River.

The killing of Emmett Till involved no sexual humiliation besides the demand that Emmet remove his clothes before he was pistol-whipped and shot. But sadistic torture was always feared in connection with lynchings. A conversation arranged in 2003 by PBS in connection with its series *The American Experience* featured four distinguished American historians talking about the murder of Emmett Till in 1955. The conversation was transcribed and made available as an article, "Sex and Race in 1955 Mississippi."[144]

The moderator asked, "Mamie Till Mobley describes looking at her son's body and feeling relief that the killers hadn't mutilated his genitals. Why was she afraid they might?" Jane Dailey responded:

> Mamie Mobley was afraid that her son's killers had mutilated his genitals because it was very common for lynchers to do exactly that. At the height of the Southern lynching craze (which peaked in 1892), naked black men were castrated by white men in full view of white women and children. In Atlanta in April 1899, for instance, Sam Hose was

---

[144] http://www.pbs.org/wgbh/americanexperience/features/emmett-sex-and-race/

burned before a crowd of thousands for killing his employer and allegedly raping the white man's wife. Before setting him alight, his executioners cut off his fingers, ears, and genitals, and skinned his face.[145]

The press coverage of the trial of Emmett's killers tarnished the image of the United States on the international stage, not only because of the murder itself but also because of the blatant miscarriage of justice during the trial that followed. The courtroom was segregated, and black visitors and reporters were ordered to give the seats closest to the bench and jury to whites. It was obvious that the all-white jury contained local citizens who had ingrained attitudes about the proper place of blacks in society. They were unlikely to risk imperiling their personal ties in the community by finding their white neighbors guilty of murder. Jurors were allowed to drink beer while on duty, and many spectators in the courtroom wore handguns in plain sight in their belt holsters—perhaps not-so-subtle reminders to the jurors that they had better return the "right" verdict.

Protected against further prosecution by the double jeopardy clause of the Fifth Amendment to the US Constitution, the two accused men later admitted in a Look magazine interview to having committed the murder. The trial and the magazine article kept the issue of racial injustice alive in the minds of many fair-minded and concerned white citizens. Together, they contributed significantly to the gradual change in attitudes that occurred in American society in the 1950s concerning race and civil rights. It was becoming increasingly difficult to be oblivious and unconcerned about such a prominent issue.

Figure 23 J. W. Milam (left) and Roy Bryant smiling at their trial for the murder of Emmett Till.

---

[145] Ibid.

In the South, the issue remained a top priority for the white population, but only on the side of protecting the status quo. Many years after the event, when a memorial sign was placed where Emmett Till's body had been taken out of the river, the marker was repeatedly damaged and defaced.

Figure 24. Damaged riverside memorial marker for Emmett Till.

The Montgomery, Alabama bus boycott

The next big news item to involve black demands for equal rights was the Montgomery bus boycott in 1955–56, which elevated to national prominence Dr. Martin Luther King Jr. and the tactics of nonviolent protest. The boycott began in December 1955 when Dr. King was not yet twenty-six, but his leadership qualities were already unmistakable. The yearlong boycott was a strong signal that blacks were finally able to organize as a group. The group had considerable economic clout and showed that in the end, the color that would win was the green of a dollar bill.

American schoolbooks portray the Montgomery bus boycott as a heartwarming story about a humble seamstress, Rosa Parks, who was tired after a long day's work and was sitting in a bus seat that was denied to her because of her race. When she was arrested for it, she was able to enlist the support of other good people, and together they were able to change the unfair customs of their community by boycotting the bus company. A happy ending, and a victory for good over evil!

In reality, the boycott was no spur-of-the-moment event. It had long been planned, and it met a violent response. The NAACP had been searching for a suitable "victim" and had looked at and rejected several candidates before finding Parks. The first choice by the planners of the boycott was a fifteen-year-old girl named Claudette Colvin, who had been arrested for refusing to give up her seat to a white person, as Rosa Parks later would be. But young Claudette turned out to be pregnant. That made her a poor choice to be a standard-bearer for her race in this critical case, where the image of black people was very much a factor to consider.

Almost a year later, Rosa Parks was the perfect choice. She was an educated, well-spoken woman with a humble, grandmotherly air about her. However, she was also a longtime NAACP worker who was very familiar with the laws, customs, and tactics of segregationists. She had dealt with some very brutal cases, including a gang rape of a young woman on her way home from church. Her skin was not so dark as to invoke negative stereotypes, nor was she particularly good-looking. Being physically very attractive could have had adverse effects in a situation where most people considered interracial attraction perverse and upsetting. The planners of the boycott knew very well that hot, irrational emotions would govern the white reaction. It was best to avoid unnecessary provocation of any sort—especially anything that could hint at the danger of interracial intimacy.

The bus boycott lasted about a year before it achieved complete victory. In that time, the homes of Dr. King and an NAACP worker were bombed, eighty-nine blacks were arrested, and many more were threatened and intimidated.

By that time, the legal case of bus segregation had reached the Supreme Court, where, on November 13, 1956, the Alabama segregation law was, as expected, unanimously found to be unconstitutional. The Montgomery authorities refused to recognize the US Supreme Court decision as binding, and the president of the Alabama Public Service Commission, C. C. Owen, declared that segregation must be maintained "to keep down violence and bloodshed." He was supported by Luther Ingalls, who was the chairman of the racist Central Alabama Citizens Council and who predicted that "any attempt to enforce this decision will inevitably lead to riot and bloodshed."[146]

Figure 25. Rosa Parks arrested, Montgomery 1955.

---

[146] http://www.pdst.ie/sites/default/files/Montgomery%20Bus%20Boycott%2C%201956.pdf, p. 32, "Ominous Rumblings."

Federal marshals were then ordered in on December 20, 1956, to enforce the desegregation order. The federal intervention demonstrated that there would be no turning back, but the segregationists continued to show their disapproval. Once the Montgomery bus system was successfully integrated, a wave of bombings of black homes, churches, and other properties occurred. A predawn volley of six bombings on January 10, 1957, heavily damaged four black churches in Montgomery. The homes of two of the local leaders of the boycott, Rev. Ralph Abernathy and Rev. Robert Graetz, were also targeted. Fortunately, the attacks resulted in no deaths or serious injuries. To deflect moderate whites' criticism of their methods, segregationists pointed out that no one had been identified as being responsible for the bombings and that the perpetrators may have been either blacks or communists who were out to make white segregationists look bad. Following the bombings, a few buses were shot at, forcing the bus company to suspend the bus service for a while. Eventually, the violence died down, and bus service resumed, now integrated.

For the moment, the Montgomery bus boycott may have looked to some like only a small local victory—but as a precedent, the boycott was extremely important. It demonstrated that blacks had the right to demand service by public transportation, just as they had the right to attend public schools. The Supreme Court decision, although it specifically applied to Alabama, would be found valid in any other state where a similar case was brought. Nevertheless, the South stubbornly resisted abiding by the ruling. Like the public schools in other states throughout the South, local bus service remained segregated as a result of the states' rights theory. The federal government, fearing that taking further court action would trigger widespread violence across the South, did not do so for the time being.

Once it became ever more apparent that the civil rights movement had momentum, and that the system of segregation in the South was under serious challenge, the South began to seethe with resentment against what many viewed as the unconstitutional federal encroachment against the Southern states' rights. In the South, the system of segregation was more than a tradition: it was the manifestation of an entire worldview. The system was based on deeply held convictions about fundamental racial differences between blacks and whites and was securely anchored in state law. These state laws ignored the Fourteenth and Fifteenth Amendments to the US Constitution, which, as noted earlier, were enacted during the Reconstruction era following the Civil War. The amendments had met bitter opposition by white Southerners when they were first proposed, but the US government forced them on the states of the former Confederacy as a condition for their readmission into the United States. They guaranteed, respectively, equal protection under the law and the right to vote, regardless of a person's race.

In 1956, five Southern governors launched a coordinated effort to find ways to avoid enforcing the Supreme Court school desegregation decision. Southern legislators now called for the rejection of the Fourteenth and Fifteenth Amendments in their states. On February 28, 1957, the Georgia state Senate voted to declare the amendments null and void in that state. On April 18, 1957, Florida followed suit by declaring the Supreme Court desegregation decision null and void there. In 1959, in response to black voter registration efforts, Alabama passed laws designed to limit such registration. The Southern states continued to argue that the US Constitution allowed the individual states to enact laws that superseded federal law in those areas.

The idea that blacks and whites would mingle socially on equal terms was highly offensive and frightening to most whites because it would make it more likely that they would then also mingle more intimately. The 1944 study *An American Dilemma* mentioned earlier concluded that the ultimate purpose of racial segregation was very clearly and unambiguously to prevent intimacy across racial lines. The content of the report caused a brief stir when it was published, but politicians were eager to let it be ignored and forgotten. To conservatives, the report was merely further proof that morally deficient liberals, Jews, black radicals, and communists were beginning to have a dangerous influence on American society.

Black activists, for their part, saw with increasing anger how public schools remained segregated throughout the South despite the 1954 Supreme Court decision that the racial segregation of public schools was unconstitutional. They decided that it was time to test the power of federal law over state law. It was essential to demolish the Southern states' argument that the US Constitution granted them states' rights to maintain segregation if the majority of the population in the states wanted to do so. If the states' rights argument could be sunk, then the ruling by the Supreme Court must prevail, and the federal government would have no choice but to enforce those rulings everywhere.

Activists did have a few minor successes in achieving school integration but no great breakthrough. Widespread local refusals to desegregate did not provoke federal intervention to enforce the Supreme Court order. The beginning of the school year saw unsuccessful attempts to integrate schools in Texarkana, Texas, and Clay, Kentucky. There was, on the other hand, a successful and violence-free integration of schools in Louisville, Kentucky, and in September 1956, twelve black students, protected by Tennessee National Guard troops, were enrolled in a previously all-white high school in Clinton, Tennessee. The troops had to use tear gas to quell rioting by white mobs, but the situation simmered down. The events did not make headline news across the country, but segregationists saw them as beginning cracks in the walls of segregation. In response, Louisiana enacted a law, Act 579, which banned racially integrated social and athletic events:

> All persons, firms and corporations are prohibited from sponsoring, arranging, participating in, or permitting on premises under their control any dancing, social functions, entertainments, athletic training, games, sports or contests and other such activities involving personal and social contacts, in which the participants or contestants are members of the white and negro races. Acts 1956, No. 579, § 1.

The Little Rock Central High School integration controversy

The case that drew both national and international attention was the riot at Little Rock, Arkansas, in 1957, where, with the help of the NAACP, nine black students were registered to attend the previously all-white Central High School in Little Rock, Arkansas, for the 1957–58 school year.

Arkansas Governor Orville Faubus was himself not as hardline a racist as many other Southern politicians, but he was alarmed at the prospect of his state becoming a showcase for school integration. As the governor of the state, he might then look like a traitor to the Southern cause. On September 2, the day before the school year started, he ordered the Arkansas National Guard to surround the school and prevent the nine students from entering the next day. The rationalization and justification were, as usual, states' rights and the need to maintain public order. In a televised speech, Faubus claimed that he had received reports that white supremacists from all over the state were planning to come to Little Rock to create trouble if the students were allowed into the school. The students must be prevented from entering or "blood would run in the streets," the Arkansas governor ominously predicted.[147]

The blockade by the Arkansas National Guard held for a few weeks. The black students could not attend school. But on Friday, September 20, the NAACP obtained a court injunction that prevented Faubus from using the National Guard for this purpose. Faubus announced that he would comply with the court order and withdraw his National Guard but expressed the hope that the black students would have the good sense to stay away from the school "until integration could occur without violence."[148] He did not offer any opinion on when that might be. Meanwhile, massive public demonstrations made it abundantly clear that the overwhelming majority of white Southerners were strongly opposed to the integration of schools.

On Monday, September 23, the nine young students gathered as a group and set off toward Central High. A mob had already gathered outside the school, jeering and screaming threats and beating some black reporters who had come to cover the event. When the word spread that the nine were now inside the school, the crowd nearly rioted. By 11:30 a.m., police on the scene felt that they could no longer control the situation and that the crowd might storm the school and forcibly remove the black students, perhaps seriously injuring them in the process. The students were then smuggled out through a back door, but the mob did not disperse even after being told that the students were no longer in the school. Chief editor Harry Ashmore of the *Arkansas Gazette* received words from reporters at the scene that the situation was getting out of control. Calling from Washington, US Deputy Attorney General William Rogers asked Ashmore about the situation and received the reply, "the police have been routed; the mob is in the street, and we're close to a reign of terror."[149]

Only six days earlier, President Eisenhower had said that he could not imagine a set of circumstances "that would ever induce me to send federal troops into... any area to enforce the orders of a federal court."[150] He was being closely informed about the growing problem in Little Rock, and realized the seriousness of the situation. He seemed to have no alternative but to intervene with federal military force.

The U.S. Constitution allows the federal government to "federalize" any particular state National Guard at any time, even for use only within its own state. It is then under the command of the commander in chief of the United States (i.e., the president), who can counter any order the particular state governor has issued. Eisenhower used his constitutional power to place the Arkansas National Guard under federal command and ordered it to redeploy around the school but to ensure, rather than to block, the school attendance of

---

[147] http://www.watson.org/~lisa/blackhistory/school-integration/lilrock/faubus.html

[148] http://www.watson.org/~lisa/blackhistory/school-integration/lilrock/9enter.html

[149] Elizabeth Jacoway, *Turn Away Thy Son: Little Rock, the Crisis That Shocked the Nation* (New York: Free Press, a Division of Simon and Shuster, 2007) p. 173.

[150] Ibid., p. 174

the nine black students. That entailed considerable risk, given the feelings Southern segregationists harbored toward the federal government.

On the one hand, the use of a federalized state National Guard to maintain order had the advantage that it would be citizens of that state who were maintaining order, not federal forces from the North. To many Southerners, the introduction of such a force would look like a renewed occupation by Yankee troops that only eighty years earlier had left the South after having devastated the region and had compounded the injury and offense by forcing the inhabitants to accept their former slaves as their equals. There were still some Southerners alive who remembered that traumatic era. They had impressed on their children a general distrust of the federal government and a fear of what legal equality for blacks would do to society.

On the other hand, many members of the all-white Arkansas National Guard would obey a federal order to assist in the integration of schools in Arkansas only with great reluctance. Just three weeks earlier, their democratically elected governor had ordered them to do what most of them considered right and necessary, and what was the will of their fellow Arkansans. Now a distant federal government of questionable legitimacy was telling them to do just the opposite.

Figure 26. Anti-integration demonstration in front of the State Capitol Building in Little Rock, Arkansas

A situation could easily develop where they would have to injure or even kill their fellow white Arkansans to enable black students to violate all local law and tradition. But to underscore that they must follow their new orders, that failure to obey federal orders is a very serious federal offense, and that failure to do so would have severe personal consequences, Eisenhower also sent to Little Rock a sizable contingent of federal soldiers from the elite 101st Airborne Division of the army, known as the Screaming Eagles. The 101st was an integrated military force, but to minimize the provocation, all the soldiers sent to Little Rock were white.

It was still a very dicey situation. The news networks flocked to Little Rock, contributing to the tension and inflamed feelings through radio and TV broadcasts.

Several days of serious rioting followed, but the federalized Arkansas National Guard did not mutiny but helped restore order. Once the nine black students were able to attend class, they were each day escorted by the personal protection of several soldiers from the 101st Airborne, not by soldiers from the Arkansas National Guard.

Figure 27. Members of the Arkansas National Guard block the "Little Rock Nine" from entering Little Rock Central High School, September 1957.

Figure 28. Elizabeth Eckford jeered and threatened by the crowd at
Little Rock Central High School, September 1957.

Figure 29. The Little Rock Nine escorted by members of the 101st Airborne.

The sense of moral outrage, beleaguerment, and desperation among Southern whites over the federal determination to enforce school integration was given a boost on October 4, 1957. The Soviet Union launched the first Earth-orbiting satellite, *Sputnik 1*. It was a complete surprise and caused a sensation worldwide. The "Red Scare," the almost hysterical fear of communism, held America in its grip, no more so than in the South, where the strongly religious population tended to see the atheistic ideology of communism as inspired by the devil. It was an article of faith among segregationists that communists had infiltrated and had started to subvert the American government, and that the Soviet Union was supporting the civil rights movement. It was frightening to realize that the godless communist dictatorship of America's deadly enemy now had the capability to send into orbit satellites that might very well be armed with nuclear bombs, which could be dropped from space on the United States at any time. Across the South, people demonstrated angrily against what they felt was unconstitutional and un-American federal demands to abandon segregation.

Figure 30. School integration protest in Nashville, Tennessee, 1957

In Figure 31 above, note the small paper held by the man in front, which reads "Conquer and Breed. White Folks!... Negro Rape... Get Negroes out of White Schools Today." The reference at the bottom of the large placard (2 Peter 2:1–2) reads: "But there were false prophets also among the people, even as there shall be false teachers among you, who secretly shall bring in damnable heresies, even denying that the Lord has bought them, and bring upon themselves swift destruction. And many shall follow their evil ways; by reason of whom the way of truth shall be evil spoken of."

But widespread protests failed to stop the process. Helmeted federal troops with bayonets affixed to their rifles accompanied the nine students as they entered the school building.

Throughout the school year, the nine black students were jeered, harassed, and bullied by white students, but they persevered. One was expelled in February 1958 for verbally retaliating against a white bully by calling her "white trash," but the remaining eight finished the school year. In May, Ernest Green, the oldest of the nine, became the first black graduate of Little Rock Central High School. The 101st Airborne had been gradually withdrawn from Little Rock during the school year, but 125 federalized Arkansas National Guardsmen maintained order during the graduation ceremonies.

The first graduation of a black student at Central High was not by any means the end of the story in Little Rock. Governor Faubus had a package of laws passed in 1958 by the Arkansas legislature that gave him the power to close down public schools in any part of the state. The laws came too late to prevent the graduation of Ernest Green, but the school was shut down for the 1958–59 school year.

The families of the Little Rock Nine continued to live under enormous pressure. Some family members lost their jobs, and others moved away from Little Rock; only five of the nine students remained. During the school year 1958 – 1959, they were able to continue their high school education by taking correspondence courses through the University of Arkansas, a high-profile white school that the governor was unwilling to shut down. Finally, in the summer of 1959, a federal court declared that the act that Governor Faubus had used to shut down Arkansas public schools was unconstitutional. The five students still in Little Rock were able to attend school again and to graduate from Little Rock Central High School.

The rulings by federal courts created much anger in the South. The response all across the region was not to comply with the rulings but to follow the example set by Mississippi by shutting down many public schools and creating a system of private schools that could legally maintain segregation. Large numbers of white parents decided to pull their children out of public schools rather than have them exposed to black children. This private, segregated school system experienced rapid growth, while the funding and quality of black schools declined. The Florida legislature voted to shut down any school that was integrated by reliance on federal troops. To prevent integration, Governor J. Lindsay Almond of Virginia shut down one school in Front Royal, two in Charlottesville, and six in Norfolk.

The all-white private schools became the bulwark of staunch opposition to integration. Local and state politics became dominated by the openly racist, segregationist White Citizens' Councils (WCC), which shared many members with the more secretive KKK. The WCC controlled not only the schools but also the courts and the police forces. The South felt it must maintain a completely united front against federal demands for desegregation.

But the hopes and feelings of the black population could not be suppressed, and the events of the previous few years had shown that the winds of change and progress had begun to stir. The 1954 school desegregation order, the 1956 Montgomery bus boycott, and the events in Little Rock showed that the federal government and the Supreme Court were supportive of black demands and that by organizing, demonstrating nonviolently, and persisting, the black population could make progress toward equal civil rights and integration.

The civil rights movement searches for new approaches

Not all black civil rights activists embraced nonviolence as a fundamental philosophy that they had to adhere to in all circumstances. Armed resistance against KKK terrorism had also proved effective in some cases. In a 1957 case that drew considerable attention, a group of armed blacks under the leadership of a man named Robert F. Williams had successfully driven back an attack by Klansmen on the home of an NAACP member in Monroe, North Carolina.

A couple of years later, in 1959, several white men were arrested in Monroe for sexually assaulting black women but were acquitted in court. An arrest of white men on such grounds was very unusual, but the verdict was no great surprise. White men accused of assaulting black women almost always escaped punishment. Incensed by the verdict, Robert Williams declared in an interview with United Press International reporters that he would "meet violence with violence"[151] as a policy. This statement created quite a stir, and the *New York Times* quoted Williams on its front page. The *Carolina Times* called it "the biggest civil rights story of 1959."

For his advocacy of violence in self-defense, Williams was for a time suspended from the NAACP by its national chairman, Roy Wilkins. However, the NAACP national convention later passed a resolution that said, "We do not deny, but reaffirm the right of individual and collective self-defense against unlawful assaults."[152] Although Martin Luther King Jr. at first objected to this statement, it reflected the feelings of many blacks, both within and beyond the ranks of the NAACP. The statement sent a notice to white America that black civil rights activists' patience and forbearance had limits. It was a statement that the federal government had to take at face value while it formulated its policy for enforcing the decisions of the Supreme Court.

However, the nonviolent tactics soon proved successful. At 4:30 p.m. on February 1, 1960, four black students from North Carolina State Agricultural and Technical University sat down at the whites-only lunch counter at the Woolworth store in Greensboro and asked to be served. They were not served, and they had to leave when the store closed for the day. There was no violence, but for the moment, no progress, either.

A much larger group of students arrived the next day and were also refused service. The story became news, and thus the sit-in movement was born. The movement gave rise to a new militant organization called the Student Nonviolent Coordinating Committee, or SNCC (pronounced "snick"). The movement quickly spread and grew. On February 13, 1960, a sit-in began at a lunch counter in Nashville, Tennessee, and then expanded to other lunch counters across the city. It became a massive and protracted operation, during which more than one hundred and fifty blacks were arrested. On May 10, 1960, the movement achieved victory when six downtown stores began serving blacks at their lunch counters for the first time.

---

[151] Robert F. Williams, *Negroes with Guns* (Detroit, MI: Wayne State University Press, 1998), p. XXIV
[152] 50th Convention of the NAACP, New York City, July 19, 1959

Figure 31. Sit-in at a Woolworth lunch counter, Greensboro, North Carolina February 1, 1960

During World War II, General Eisenhower had been the top Allied commander in Europe. At that time, blacks did not serve in combat roles. Since that time, however, Eisenhower had surely noted that in Korea, black soldiers had fought, bled, and died honorably side by side with their white brothers-in-arms. His military background had probably played a role in his decision to send federal soldiers to Little Rock in 1957 to enforce the desegregation order issued by the Supreme Court. To Eisenhower, it must have seemed hard to justify that blacks, who had fought valiantly for their country in war, were not allowed to buy a cup of coffee at a lunch counter in the South. He issued a statement in support of the sit-in movement, saying that he was "deeply sympathetic with the efforts of any group to enjoy the rights of equality that they are guaranteed by the Constitution."[153]

The lunch counter sit-in movement was successful in highlighting in the national news media the injustices and humiliations suffered by blacks under segregation. In areas outside the South, white America—particularly the younger generation—was waking up from obliviousness and neglect to become seriously concerned about equal rights and opportunities that were supposedly guaranteed by the US Constitution. Political pressure began to mount to do something about the situation in the South, and some whites from

---

[153] N.Y. Times, March 17, 1960, p. 16, col. 1.

the North and Midwest went south to participate in black demonstrations. They were bitterly denounced in the South as communist agitators and moral degenerates.

Nonviolence came to be the official tactic of the black civil rights movement, espoused in particular by its most influential leader, Martin Luther King Jr. Its success was undeniable, but many black leaders would admit later that they had adopted nonviolence as a tactic only because it appeared to be effective. Sometimes it achieved immediate results once white opposition crumbled from a lack of hard commitment. Where the opposition was more determined and violent, the opposition increased white sympathy and political support for the movement outside the South.[154]

***

As late as the mid-1960s, murder motivated by racial prejudice was still a threat to all members and supporters of the black civil rights movement. Between 1961 and 1965, twenty-one murders of civil rights activists were recorded in the South, without a single person being convicted of these crimes in local courts.

---

[154] A bullet-item timeline of the 1954 – 1968 civil rights movement is available at https://en.wikipedia.org/wiki/ Timeline_of_the_civil_rights_movement

Chapter 3. An Old World Order Is Shattered, and a New America Begins to Emerge

The Cold War intensifies, the election of John Kennedy

As the decade of the 1960s began, the whole world was becoming ever more unpredictable, chaotic, and perilous. The threat posed by communism was growing steadily greater, and most adult Americans were well aware of the danger. America's European allies were preparing to withdraw from their colonies everywhere, which made them appear to be weakened by the fear of communism. They were becoming too dependent on American military power to be of much help in resisting worldwide communist aggression.

Soviet technological prowess had been demonstrated with the launch of the Sputnik satellites, and on May 1, 1960, an American U2 spy plane was shot down by a Soviet anti-aircraft missile. The wreckage was left sufficiently intact that Soviet engineers and scientists could derive secret and very important information about the advanced technology used in its construction. The American CIA and the Defence Department had been convinced that the U2 plane was flying at too high an altitude to be reached by Soviet missiles. The shoot-down of the U2 added to the fear that the Soviet Union was ahead of the United States in rocket technology. It further stoked American fears of the Soviet Union and communism, and therefore also added fuel to the fire of anti-integration sentiments in the South, where many were convinced that the civil rights movement was an evil scheme by the communists to weaken American society.

The burden of leadership of the free world rested increasingly on the shoulders of the United States. It was a burden that was beginning to exact a heavy price in both material and spiritual resources. To stand up to the challenge, America needed a strong, confident, and inspiring leader—and the country found one in John Fitzgerald Kennedy.

John F. Kennedy was young, charismatic, and energetic, and he had a charming, beautiful wife. Together, they captured the hearts of not only the American people but most of the Western world as well. The newly available communications medium of television was seemingly tailor-made for them, and the couple enjoyed huge celebrity status. Following his election as president in 1960, Kennedy struck a defiant and inspiring note in his inaugural speech:

> Let every nation know, whether it wishes us well or ill, that we shall pay any price, bear
> any burden, meet any hardship, support any friend, oppose any foe, in order to assure
> the survival and the success of liberty.[155]

The threat from the Soviet Union loomed ever larger. On April 12, 1961, the Soviet cosmonaut Yuri Gagarin completed a full orbit around Earth aboard the *Vostok* spacecraft. It became a sensation almost

---

[155] John F. Kennedy Presidential Library and Museum,
https://www.jfklibrary.org/Research/Research-Aids/Ready-Reference/JFK-Quotations/Inaugural-Address.aspx

on the level of the launch of *Sputnik 1* in 1957. Gagarin's orbital flight showed that the Soviet Union was still ahead of the United States in terms of technology. In response, on May 25, 1961, Kennedy delivered a special message to Congress on "urgent national needs." To justify a massive increase in the budget for the National Aeronautics and Space Administration (NASA), he announced a breathtaking goal: that "this nation should commit itself to achieving the goal, before the decade is out, of landing a man on the moon and returning him safely to the earth."[156]

The announcement astonished the public, both in the United States and abroad. Going to the moon had been a dream of humankind for countless generations, but it had seemed an impossible task—now the president promised it would be a reality within a decade! The prospect took the edge off Gagarin's achievement, and on May 5, 1961, a mere two weeks after Gagarin's orbit, US Navy Commander Alan B. Shepard Jr. achieved enough altitude aboard an American rocket-launched capsule for the launch to qualify as a spaceflight. He did not orbit Earth, but the achievement was sufficient to demonstrate that America was beginning to catch up with the Soviet Union. For the time being, Kennedy could again turn his attention to domestic issues.

The South remained a barrel of gunpowder, where racial tensions constantly threatened to ignite violence and trigger another confrontation between segregationist state governors and the federal administration. For a while, the bullying tactics of the WCC and its unofficial affiliate, the KKK, sufficed to maintain the status quo. Black demands for equal rights were ignored—or silenced violently if they became too insistent.

During reporting on the 1960 election campaign, most political observers believed that if elected president, John F. Kennedy would be even more favorably disposed toward black demands for equal rights than the conservative Eisenhower. It seemed likely that blacks, frustrated by the lack of further progress on the integration of schools and other public facilities in the South, would then become bolder and more aggressive in pushing for these rights. The South braced itself for what could be expected, but whites expressed strong support for the defiant stands taken by their elected local politicians. The broad consensus was that segregation must be maintained and that the South had not yet lost that battle. For whites, the stakes seemed too high to permit any compromise on this issue.

The Freedom Bus Rides

Soon another front opened in the civil rights struggle. Several federal court judgments had already declared all segregated seating in interstate travel to be unconstitutional, but the relevant federal agencies had not enforced those decisions. Blacks had failed to achieve integration of the Greyhound and Trailways bus companies in the South. A group of thirteen activists, both black and white, male and female, decided to try to rectify this situation by riding buses together from Washington, DC, through the segregated South to New Orleans. The activities were mostly planned and organized by the Congress of Racial Equality

---

[156] Address Before a Joint Session of Congress, 25 May 1961.

(CORE), but SNCC also played an important role. The first two buses, one Greyhound and one Trailways, left Washington on May 4, 1961, and were scheduled to arrive in New Orleans on May 17.

Nothing very dramatic occurred as the buses passed through Virginia and North Carolina, but as the news of the buses spread throughout the South, segregationists began to plan their response. In Alabama, following the Montgomery bus boycott, all bus services within the state of Alabama were already desegregated by law, so the Freedom Riders could not be arrested there—but they could be shown that they were not safe. An initial attack on the riders would be made in Anniston, Alabama, once they had passed the Georgia–Alabama state line. If that did not stop them, then a final assault would be made in Birmingham, where Public Safety Commissioner Bull Connor told the local KKK leadership that those who attacked the buses would have fifteen minutes before any police would become involved.

On May 14, 1961, an angry mob of whites attacked the first of the two buses (the Greyhound) outside Anniston and forced it to stop on the highway. The mob firebombed the bus and attempted to hold the doors shut to burn the riders to death. Accounts of the event differ, but the mob appears to have retreated and made escape possible from the bus either because its fuel tank exploded or because an undercover state investigator in the crowd brandished a revolver and ordered the mob to back off.

Members of the mob attacked and beat the passengers as they rushed from the burning bus. By this time, the state highway patrol had arrived, and only their warning shots in the air prevented the riders from being lynched. Several of the riders were injured, and many of them were taken to the local hospital, where another threatening mob began to gather outside. At 2:00 a.m., black civil rights activists in private vehicles were able to rush the hospitalized riders away to safety.

An hour after the firebombing of the Greyhound bus, the Trailways bus arrived in Anniston. A group of eight Klansmen immediately boarded the bus and began assaulting the Freedom Riders, leaving most of them injured, but the Klansmen made no attempt to set that bus on fire or otherwise kill the riders.

The firebombing had destroyed the Greyhound bus, but the Freedom Riders, despite their injuries and threats of further violence, decided to continue the journey on the Trailways bus. When the bus pulled into the Birmingham bus station, a large crowd, armed with baseball bats and iron pipes, was waiting for them. When they exited the bus, the riders were subjected to vicious beatings, leaving some with lifelong injuries. The attackers focused their hatred particularly on the white Freedom Riders, whom they saw as treasonous communist agitators and morally degenerate race mixers. One white Freedom Rider, James Peck, already injured by a beating in Anniston, received so many blows to the head that he required fifty-three stitches. Bleeding profusely, he was at first refused service at one hospital but was taken in at a second one.

Figure 32. Firebombed Greyhound bus outside Anniston, Alabama, May 14, 1961

The violence failed to deter the Freedom Riders, but some were unable to continue because of their injuries. Diane Nash, a leader of SNCC, believed that if the violence were to succeed in stopping the Freedom Riders, then the segregationists would become encouraged, which would then persuade them to rely even more on violence and terror as a means to resist blacks' attempts to secure equal rights and integration. That could be a serious blow to the movement because it might scare off many whites who sympathized with the movement but had no personal stake in it. At some point, the segregationist violence might result in retaliatory or defensive violence by blacks, which could also reduce the willingness of whites to participate. Nash's appeal for more volunteers succeeded, with people from across the eastern United States arriving in Birmingham to board the bus for the continued journey to Montgomery.

Astounded, shaken, and angered by the stubbornness of the Freedom Riders, the KKK once more mobilized its forces. The bus carrying the riders was scheduled to leave Birmingham for Montgomery on May 19, 1961, so a mob armed with iron pipes and baseball bats began gathering at the bus terminal in Montgomery. Others were reportedly waiting along the highway from Birmingham to attack the bus as it came by. An angry screaming crowd surrounded the bus at the Birmingham bus terminal. Frightened, the Greyhound company bus driver refused to leave Birmingham.

By now the federal administration was well aware of the situation. It pressured the Greyhound company to find a driver willing to drive the bus. The US Attorney General's office managed to extract a promise from Governor John Patterson of Alabama to use whatever force was necessary to protect the bus from violent mobs and snipers along the road to Montgomery. On May 20, 1961, the bus finally left Birmingham and proceeded at ninety miles an hour, escorted by a contingent of the Alabama State Highway Patrol.

The highway patrol vehicles left the bus once it reached the Montgomery city limits. The US Attorney General's office had not thought it necessary to reach an agreement also with the Montgomery City police to take over responsibility from the state highway patrol authorities once the bus entered the city. The all-white city police were not inclined to volunteer their services, and the bus was left unprotected.

At the bus station on South Court Street, the scene at the Birmingham bus station was repeated. A white mob was waiting, armed with baseball bats and iron pipes. Again, the local police did not intervene as the riders exited the bus and were met with a hail of blows. White riders were singled out for particularly vicious pummeling. The mob also attacked reporters and news photographers and smashed their equipment. A US Justice Department official, on the scene to try to control and report on the situation, was beaten unconscious and left lying in the street.

Many riders suffered serious injuries. Ambulances refused to take them to the hospital, but local blacks were able to rescue some of the injured and transport them to where they could get medical service. Once all the Freedom Riders had left the bus terminal, the mob dispersed, reveling in having beaten up its opponents and gloating over its perceived triumph. For the third time, the hated Yankee integrationists had been severely beaten, with the police making no attempt to stop the violence. Now the "niggers" and "niggerlovers" must have had enough and must have realized that the South was not going to yield. Ever.

The next evening, May 21, 1961, more than fifteen hundred people, both black and white, gathered at the First Baptist Church of Rev. Ralph Abernathy in Montgomery to honor the Freedom Riders. It was a gathering of most of the leading figures of the civil rights movement. Among the speakers were Dr. Martin Luther King Jr., Rev. Fred Shuttlesworth, and James Farmer of CORE. Word of the meeting had spread to Montgomery's white citizens, and more than three thousand angry whites now surrounded the church. Although the crowd grew increasingly menacing, neither the Montgomery police nor the state police took action. A small force from the US Marshals Service managed to keep the crowd from attacking the church and perhaps firebombing it, while the leaders inside the church made a telephone call directly to the president, appealing for immediate federal protection. President Kennedy then called the Alabama governor and threatened intervention by federal troops if local law enforcement proved unwilling or unable to keep order.

The situation at the church could have become extremely violent at any moment, but an intervention by federal troops to protect blacks would have created an incendiary situation—even more so than in Little Rock a few years earlier. The emotions in the South around the issue of states' rights had become very intense, and the distrust and hatred of the federal government now ran very deep. Federal intervention would have only increased the impulse by racists to rebel and to organize more violent and fanatical opposition to integration.

Faced with the probably dire consequences of federal military intervention, Governor Patterson had little choice but to promise the president that the Alabama National Guard would immediately be deployed to keep a lid on the situation. In the early morning of May 22, 1961, the National Guard arrived, secured the area, and convinced the white mob to disperse. That averted serious bloodshed for the moment, but it did not solve the problem. Neither side in the conflict was in the mood to compromise or give up. Black Southerners were now much better organized, united, motivated, and confident of ultimate victory than they had been at Little Rock a few years earlier. The leaders who had gathered in the church were determined that the Freedom Rides would continue.

The bonding effect of jointly experienced dangerous events is well-known. These experiences also instill pride and self-confidence, and among the participants in the Freedom Rides, the spirit of solidarity was strong, and the level of motivation high. For many black participants, it was a giddy and joyous feeling to be openly defying the white segregationist power structure, even if their defiance did not produce immediate victory. The conviction that they were the equals of whites sank in, replacing fears and poor self-images.

The next day, May 22, 1961, in response to appeals from SNCC and CORE, enough additional Freedom Rider volunteers arrived in Montgomery to replace those who were still in the hospital and to add to the total number of riders. This leg of the journey would lead from Montgomery, Alabama, to Jackson, Mississippi. During the night and morning, the Kennedy administration had worked out a deal with the governors of Alabama and Mississippi. In exchange for having the state police and National Guards of both states protecting the riders from mob violence, the Jackson police would be allowed to arrest the riders as they exited the bus—the charges against them being that they had violated the segregation laws of Mississippi. For the moment, the federal government would not challenge the validity or constitutionality of those laws.

The first bus, escorted by highway patrol and National Guard vehicles, traveled to Jackson without any problems. Once the bus arrived in Jackson, all the riders were immediately arrested and put in jail. The second busload of riders from Montgomery encountered the same fate.

The strategy of the Freedom Riders now became to fill the jails. There was no shortage of volunteers, and it did not take long to fill enough buses to cause the jails in Jackson and Hinds counties in Mississippi to become overcrowded. But the strategy was not successful. The Mississippi state authorities transferred the overflow to the large and notorious Parchman Farm (the Mississippi State Penitentiary), where many experienced harsh and abusive treatment. Freedom Riders continued to arrive for a while, and at one time, more than three hundred of them were incarcerated at Parchman Farm. Now, the Freedom Rides had for all practical purposes run their course. For the time being, they had not succeeded in overturning the local segregation laws of any state.

Adding to the Freedom Riders' disappointment, the Kennedy administration had taken an unexpectedly low profile during the crisis. There was still no federal enforcement of bus desegregation court decisions. The chief law enforcement member in the land, Attorney General Robert Kennedy, was quoted as saying that he did "not feel that the Department of Justice [could] side with one group or the other in disputes over Constitutional rights." Such disputes were up to the courts to resolve, Kennedy seemed to be saying. While this may have been correct per se, the fact remained that the 1955 ruling by the Interstate Commerce

Commission (ICC) in *Sara Keys v. Carolina Coach Company* had already declared that bus segregation in interstate travel violated the US Constitution.

Sarah Keys was a black woman, a private in the United States Army, and on August 2, 1952, she was wearing her military uniform as she boarded a bus to return from Fort Dix to her home in North Carolina. She found a seat in the front part of the bus. When the bus entered North Carolina and made a stop at Roanoke Rapids, the bus driver told her to move to the back, as required by North Carolina law. When she refused, the bus driver told all the passengers that they had to switch to another bus. Another, empty bus was at hand, and the passengers began boarding that bus, but Keys was refused entry. She was instead arrested for alleged disorderly conduct and spent thirteen hours in jail.

With the help of the NAACP, Keys sued the Carolina Coach Company. It took three years of court procedures before a decision was made in favor of Keys by the ICC. The decision was issued on November 7, 1955, just six days before Rosa Parks was arrested for refusing to give up her seat on a bus in Montgomery, Alabama. The decision applied to all buses for interstate travel and could have been used to strike down, nationwide, the segregation laws that were challenged by the Freedom Riders. However, the responsible enforcement agency was the Interstate Commerce Commission, which was chaired by a Southerner, J. Monroe Johnson of South Carolina, and the ICC had shown no interest in enforcing the ruling.

The Freedom Riders had put the federal government in a difficult position. Doing nothing to enforce Supreme Court decisions would mark the government as powerless and itself tainted by racism; it might also lead to a more violent policy by the ever more powerful black civil rights organizations and their growing numbers of white sympathizers. Acting too forcefully would further intensify most Southern whites' already very emotional resistance to black demands for integration, which to these whites simply meant moral collapse and race mixing. The firmness of the final goal had to be accompanied by respect, understanding, and patience on the part of the federal government.

Besides the purely political and legal issue of which states' rights could be read into the Constitution, the possibility existed that bloody riots and genocidal, antiblack rampages by white mobs would break out across the entire South if federal troops clashed with armed segregationists. Many whites felt that a new era of Yankee-imposed Reconstruction was looming. The old Confederate battle flag, the ultimate symbol of rebellion against dictates by the federal government, was brought back to public display with increasing frequency throughout the South. The "Stars and Bars" flag was waved at KKK meetings and marches and quickly attained almost religious significance. It came to symbolize much more than just a belief in white racial superiority; it was also a sign of respect and admiration for romanticized Southern ancestors who had fought so well and so valiantly for what many Southerners still considered a noble cause—namely, to protect and uphold the same freedoms, moral values, and hallowed traditions of which segregationists imagined themselves to be the preservers. In the view of the segregationists, it was preposterous to claim that the Constitution gave equal rights to blacks. Slavery had continued for nearly a century after the document was written! The Constitution was written by and for whites and was intended to protect the individual freedom of whites. The Constitution itself counted blacks as only three-fifths of a person; how could the federal government now demand that they be treated as equal to whites?

In the view of many Southerners, America had veered away from the constitutional promise that each man was free to follow his own way of life, liberty, and the pursuit of happiness. The federal government had become intolerably dictatorial and oppressive. Notions obtained from Jews, Catholics, communists, and amoral liberals were destroying the pure and noble ideals of the founders of the Constitution. It did not take long before the rebel flag became the symbol of states' rights and was flying from the flagpoles of state capitol buildings across the South.

Some rabble-rousing Southern politicians even promised that "the South will rise again," neglecting to remind their listeners of the unfortunate consequences of what had happened the first time the South rose in rebellion. From a practical point of view, a real military confrontation between federal troops and Southern state forces would, of course, be entirely out of the question. Southern politicians knew that very well, and hardly any of them seriously wanted or even dreamed of such a confrontation. But that did not keep them from hinting at it being a possibility. Not that long ago, in 1948, Senator Strom Thurmond had said: "There's not enough troops in the army to force the southern people to break down segregation and admit the nigger race into our theaters, into our swimming pools, into our homes and into our churches."[157] [158]There were enough deluded fanatics among the KKK and the WCC that one could not ignore the risk of widespread and bloody riots, terrorism, and guerrilla-type operations. President Kennedy and members of his administration were keenly aware of that risk.

Robert Kennedy asks for a cool-off period in the civil rights efforts

The Freedom Rides generated much worldwide publicity and condemnation of the United States. The national embarrassment was undeniable, and following the Mississippi jailing of the Freedom Riders, on May 29, 1961, the brother of President Kennedy, Attorney General Robert Kennedy, sent a petition to the ICC asking it to enforce the ruling in the *Sara Keys v. Carolina Coach Company* case. Addressing himself to the leaders of the civil rights organizations, he called for a cooling-off period to calm things down. He criticized the rides for being unpatriotic and for calling international attention to the nation's internal problems

As could be predicted, the Southern Christian Leadership Conference (SCLC), CORE, and SNCC leaders rejected Kennedy's request for a cooling-off period. James Farmer, the head of CORE, responded by saying, "We have been cooling off for 350 years, and if we cooled off any more, we'd be in a deep freeze."[159]

---

[157] Strom Thurmond speech in the run-up to his 1948 campaign for the presidency on the ticket of the States' Rights Democratic Party, also known as the "Dixiecrats."

[158] Thurmond had himself broken the "anti-miscegenation laws" of Georgia by impregnating his family's then fifteen-year-old black maid, Carrie Butler. It is not known when their relationship began. Their secret daughter, Essie Mae, was born on October 12, 1925. Many years later, Thurmond first met his daughter and acknowledged her. He began to secretly support her financially.
See http://www.nbcnews.com/id/3842554/ns/us_news-life/t/sex-race-american-south/#.XezHb_x7nAQ

[159] Response to Kennedy's request for a cooling-off period, made while the situation at First Baptist Church of Rev. Ralph Abernathy in Montgomery was reaching a crisis stage. (See http://todayinclh.com/?event=memo-to-ag-robert-kennedy-theres-been-a-cooling-off-period-for-95-years)

The enforcement of desegregation orders was by no means uniform, and the organizers of the rides could not yet declare victory. During the summer of 1961, more Freedom Riders crisscrossed the South, producing nothing but hundreds of additional arrests—three hundred in Jackson, Mississippi, alone. In some instances, the Freedom Riders encountered violence and stubborn white opposition, but the national media no longer paid much attention to them. The federal government still hesitated to intervene with force, fearing that doing so would merely aggravate the tensions.

The riders were relatively successful in desegregating various facilities along their travel routes, such as restaurants and hotels. Large restaurant and hotel chains ordered their affiliates in the South to offer no resistance, fearing boycotts of their businesses nationwide if they refused to serve black customers in the South. Employees who would not abide by this order were either fired, or they left voluntarily.

The director of the FBI, J. Edgar Hoover, was convinced that communists were exploiting the nascent black civil rights movement to create dissent and disorder in American society. He ordered the movement's most prominent leader, Dr. Martin Luther King Jr., placed under secret FBI surveillance with the aim of discovering ties that he might have with known communists. The FBI did not find any, but Hoover still maintained the surveillance, hoping to discover evidence of personal misconduct that could then be used to blackmail and pressure Dr. King.

Hoover's suspicions of communist influence in the civil rights movement did have some reasonable grounds. The American Communist Party—officially the Communist Party USA (CPUSA)—had long been supportive of the efforts of black Americans to achieve equal rights with whites. This support had become very visible with the party's involvement in the sensationalized trials of the "Scottsboro Boys" in the 1930s. The case involved nine young black men accused of raping two white women on board a train between Chattanooga, Tennessee, and Memphis on March 31, 1931. They and four young whites, two men and two women, were "hoboing" on the train, i.e., riding without tickets by jumping aboard boxcars or other freight cars. It was a common thing in Depression-era America that young people were traveling around in that manner, seeking employment. The two women claimed that they had been raped by twelve black men with pistols and knives. The nine black men who became known as "the Scottsboro Boys" were arrested and put in jail in Scottsboro, Alabama. They escaped lynching only because the Alabama governor, Benjamin M. Miller, ordered National Guard troops to surround and secure the jail.

The NAACP did not rush to the defense of the nine, fearing that its own support and the safety of its members would be endangered if there were any guilty verdicts in the case, an almost certain prospect, given the nature of the accusations. Instead, the Communist Party moved aggressively to provide competent legal counsel for the accused, seeing its involvement as a great recruiting tool among southern blacks and northern liberals.

All nine were quickly found guilty by a lower Alabama court, but the defense did not give up. The accused were kept in jail while a long, drawn-out series of trials followed that were extensively covered by the news media. Five years later, in 1936, discussions began about the possibility of a compromise settlement in the case. In the eyes of many observers, the case had become one of *The White People of Alabama v. The Rest of the World.*[160] In July of 1937, following more than six years of abuse and threats in jail with the prospect of a death sentence in front of them, four of the nine had their charges dropped. To all unbiased observers, it was apparent that the charges of rape against all the Scottsboro nine were completely fabricated, and it was expected that the remaining five also would have the charges against them dropped. That did not happen. None of them was executed but remained in jail for many years before they were pardoned or, in one case, escaped.

In the South, the setting aside of the first guilty verdict against all nine had stirred a great deal of anger, and the involvement by the Communist Party had caused an identification of the party with all kinds of morally abhorrent causes—not the least of them being the mixing of the races.

Racism was pervasive throughout American society, and blacks were not the only targets. Anti-Semitism had also reached high levels. Discrimination against Jews was widespread. The KKK and similar racist organizations noted that lawyers associated with civil rights organizations contained a disproportionately large number of Jews, many of whom were known for their leftist political leanings. The distrust and dislike of Jews fed the common and long-held notion that communism was a Jewish plot to achieve world domination. This belief was one of the foundational tenets of Nazi Germany's beliefs but was also widely shared by racist Southerners. When white Southerners called for unflagging resistance to the black civil rights movement, the call did not reflect only fear of the alleged disastrous effects of racial mingling and miscegenation. It was also motivated by the conviction that America and everything it stood for were threatened by communism and its attendant horrors, among which were a loss of freedom, a destruction of religion and God-fearing morality, a consequent weakening of society by mixing of the races—and ultimately, a takeover of a weakened and morally corrupted America by the Soviet Union.

Segregationists appeal to religion and anti-communism

The racial oppression and segregation in the South was by far the most troublesome domestic issue of the late '50s and early '60s. The South, comprising roughly the states of the old Confederacy, was the most conservative, least educated, poorest, and most religiously fundamentalist part of the nation. Its social system of segregation and its violent racial oppression were becoming an international embarrassment to America.

President Kennedy was sympathetic to the civil rights movement in principle, but he was also keenly aware of the tremendous emotional volatility of the issue. As a moderately liberal Northerner, and as the first Catholic to be elected president, he knew that his popularity was never high in the South, which was staunchly fundamentalist Protestant and conservative. He hesitated to take strong action on the issue because he knew it would further inflame the already violent and passionate situation in the South.

As the decade of the 1960s began, Kennedy had to face severe international challenges. The growing strength of the Soviet Union and the seemingly inexorable advance of communism in Asia, Africa, and Latin

---

[160] Douglas O. Linder, The Trials of "The Scottsboro Boys": An Account
http://famous-trials.com/scottsboroboys/1531-home

America put a strain on US economic and military resources. The Cuban missile crisis of 1962 brought the world to the brink of a nuclear war that could have been devastating for all of humankind.

The nation continued to be beset by sharp internal divisions stemming from the tense civil rights situation in the South. The overthrow of racial segregation in the South was the most substantial domestic issue of the early 1960s, as divisive as the social upheavals in the late '60s and early '70s concerning the Vietnam War. Racial segregation was undoubtedly the most complex problem psychologically, making it particularly difficult to deal with and resolve rationally.

One of the angles of the problem was mostly political and ideological—the fear of communism. This fear had risen to a fever pitch in the nation during the 1950s, much due to the witch-hunting Senator Joseph McCarthy. The Cuban missile crisis seemed to justify the fear, as the American public suddenly realized that the nation was in the crosshairs of an array of huge, nuclear-capable ballistic missiles installed in Cuba by the Soviet Union.

Southern religiosity played a large and not fully acknowledged role in the resistance to integration simply because Southern religion was both strong and very Victorian in its attitude toward sexuality—and interracial sexual acts were considered utterly morally depraved. They were abominable in the eyes of God because they were assumed to be acts of pure lasciviousness and unbridled, perverse lust. The fundamentalist moralists and theologians viewed sexual lust as the preeminent tool of Satan to lead astray those of weak faith or character.

The strongest revulsion felt by segregationists at the prospect of integration was triggered by the idea of white women having sex with black men. The traditional attitudes and values of white Southern men relative to white women were typical of adherents of puritanical, fundamentalist religion—not much different from that of fundamentalist Muslim men: women are "protected" by societal rules that isolate them from danger and temptation. They are, on the one hand, romanticized—imagined as pure and (ideally) lacking in sexual desire in their virginal state—yet, on the other hand, often treated as property and servants once they enter marriage. Women who lost their virginity before marriage were considered fallen and tainted. To have experienced sex with a black man was unforgivable.

Thoroughly infused with both anti-communist fervor and sexual anxieties, Southern fundamentalist dogma included the firm belief that communists, Jews, Catholics, the United Nations, and other international organizations were the tools of Satan. These organizations, segregationists believed, were using the struggle by American blacks to bring down the United States, which was the bastion of faith, democracy, and moral righteousness in the world. In the view of fervent fundamentalists, the white youths from the North who were streaming into the South to demonstrate and march with blacks were godless communist agitators with despicably loose sexual mores who were there to encourage Southern blacks to seek white sexual partners.

J. H. "Dick" Melton (1922–1995), one of the most prominent and strident spokesmen for white religious organizations such as the Baptist Bible Fellowship, expressed well their extreme views. In his book *A Biblical Baptist Systematic Theology: Ecclesiology* (volume 1), Melton wrote:

> Integration is Satan's master plan. When he gets all the governments of the world integrated into the United Nations, all the races integrated into one mongrel race in which

each individual race has lost its identity, and all the religious bodies integrated into one ecclesiastical dictatorship, the anti-Christ will take over this integrated monster. Then, only the Second Coming of the Lord will save the remnant that refuses to integrate.[161]

Such were the dire consequences of giving in to black demands for equal rights! Satan would make sure that race mixing and religious apostasy would be the result. Only those who refused to integrate were going to be saved at the End of Days.

While the efforts to desegregate bus transportation were not very successful, by August 1961, the sit-in movement had attracted more than seventy thousand participants and had generated more than three thousand arrests. The movement received extensive news coverage. Sit-in demonstrations continued in the South for several years, even after the passage in 1964 of the Civil Rights Act that made segregated lunch counters illegal. A few participants were injured by white mobs and by police while being arrested, but on the whole, it was a spectacular example of the effectiveness of nonviolent demonstrations.

Despite the wishes of the Kennedy administration, in 1962, black civil rights organizations such as the SCLC, the NAACP, SNCC, CORE, and others did not let up in their efforts to achieve integration in the South. The integration of schools and universities was a high priority, as was the registration of black voters. The private, often church-organized private schools were a difficult target. They began to multiply and fill with white children once public schools became integrated. Many previously all-white public schools thus became depopulated and were now closed, while other public schools became all-black and overcrowded places. Being private, the all-white schools were not subject to the school desegregation order of 1954. State universities were subject to the desegregation order, though local pressure in the Southern states had so far prevented the admission of blacks.

James Meredith registers at "Ole Miss"

In early 1961, James Meredith, a black man born in Mississippi in 1933, applied for admission to the University of Mississippi, affectionately known as Ole Miss. The university had an all-white student body, and Meredith was refused admission despite being an air force veteran who, after returning to civilian life, had attended the all-black Jackson State University for two years. On May 31, with the help of the NAACP, Meredith filed suit in the US District Court for the Southern District of Mississippi, alleging that the university had illegally rejected him merely on the basis of his race.

The suit went through many hearings and eventually reached the Supreme Court, which ruled in Meredith's favor. On September 13, 1962, university officials were given a court order to register Meredith. The court order further intensified the feelings of anger in Mississippi against the federal government. The governor of Mississippi, Ross Barnett, then injected himself into the controversy and made an impassioned,

---

[161] As quoted in Jeffrey D. Lavoie, *Segregation and the Baptist Bible Fellowship* (Cambridge Station, CA, Academica Press, 2013), p. 57

widely televised speech that came close to calling for rebellion, where he painted the issue as one of life or death for the white race. He declared:

> I speak to you now in the moment of our greatest crisis since the War between the States... We must either submit to the unlawful dictates of the Federal Government or stand up like men and tell them no. The day of reckoning has been delayed as long as possible. It is now upon us. This is the day, and this is the hour... I have said in every county in Mississippi that no school in our state will be integrated while I am your governor. I repeat to you tonight: no school in our state will be integrated while I am your governor. There is no case in history where the Caucasian race has survived social integration.

We will not drink from the cup of genocide.[162]

Figure 33. James Meredith

To obtain legal grounds for his stand, Barnett obtained new and rapidly enacted state legislation that denied admission to any state school to any person "who has a crime of moral turpitude against him."

---

[162] John F. Kennedy Presidential Library and Museum Historical resources
http://microsites.jfklibrary.org/olemiss/controversy/doc2.html

Meredith had earlier been accused and convicted of false voter registration in Jackson County, which was sufficient to bar him from admission.

Further court action ensued, with Governor Barnett being threatened with arrest and jail and heavy fines for disobeying a court order. He was ultimately forced to yield and let Meredith attend Ole Miss. But the situation on the ground looked ominous. To ensure Meredith's safety, Attorney General Robert Kennedy ordered five hundred federal marshals to accompany Meredith as he was registering at the school. On September 29, 1962, the tensions were running so high that President Kennedy issued a proclamation ordering all who attempted to block or disrupt the registration of Meredith at Ole Miss to "cease and desist therefrom and to disperse and retire peaceably forthwith." His proclamation included references to his authority as president to use the federalized state militia and federal military force to suppress any opposition.

Figure 34. Governor Ross Barnett of Mississippi at a political rally, 1962

Governor Barnett promised to maintain order on the campus and ordered the state highway patrol forces to achieve it. But in the evening of September 29, 1962, these forces were withdrawn, and a riot immediately broke out. The president had no choice but to send in the federalized Mississippi National Guard, accompanied by a considerable force of federal marshals. The presence of federal troops created more anger and did not immediately stop the rioting. Jeering crowds assaulted federal soldiers with rocks, bricks, and small-arms fire. Two people were killed by gunshot wounds, numerous cars were set on fire, and some university property was damaged.

On October 1, 1962, once troops had established control of the campus, Meredith was formally enrolled in the University of Mississippi. Fortunately, after Meredith's enrollment, the situation at Ole Miss calmed down. Like the Little Rock Nine five years earlier, Meredith suffered continuous harassment and abuse from the white students. He was still able to graduate on August 18, 1963, earning a degree in political science.

Figure 35. Federal marshals arrive at Ole Miss, September 30, 1962.

Figure 36. Burned-out cars on the campus of Ole Miss, September 30, 1962.

Later in October of 1962, the attention of both the nation and the world was riveted by the Cuban missile crisis, and the civil rights issue faded for a while from newspaper front pages and television screens. Once the acute Cuban crisis was over, the Kennedy administration could again pay much-needed attention to the still deteriorating racial situation in the South; 1962 was an election year for many political offices, albeit not for president.

The spotlight falls on Alabama, and the civil rights movement stalls

In Alabama, as in many other states, the office of governor was at stake. Several colorful characters contended, among them Bull Connor, the temperamental, hardline segregationist who held the office of Birmingham public safety commissioner. Among his competition were the alcoholic, relatively moderate former governor Jim "Peace in the Valley" Folsom and the "Fighting Judge," George Wallace, a former Alabama Golden Gloves boxing champion.

Figure 37. George Wallace on the campaign trail

Wallace was cocky, loud, and pugnacious but not truly a through and through racist. But having lost the previous governor's election in 1958 to outspoken segregationist Patterson, he vowed, "No other son-of-a-bitch will ever out-nigger me again."[163] Running a strong states' rights campaign, Wallace won the November election. His victory did not bode well for the civil rights struggle.

---

[163] Dan T. Carter, *The Politics of Rage; George Wallace, the Origins of the New Conservatism, and the Transformation of American Politics,* (New York: Simon and Schuster, 1995) p. 96.

Figure 38. Students protest against school integration, Alabama 1963

The emergence of Malcolm X

For many years, an organization calling itself the Nation of Islam (NOI), headquartered in Chicago, had preached that blacks were the true children of God while whites were the spawn of the devil. The leader of the NOI was a man calling himself Elijah Muhammad, born in 1897 in Sandersville, Georgia, as Elijah Robert Poole. As its name suggests, the Nation of Islam embraced a form of Islam, but one that differed in many ways from the nonracially oriented orthodox Islam. The American media referred to the organization as the Black Muslims. It was thus as Black Muslims that they became known to the American public, even though the group did not refer to themselves by that name. Many members of the NOI disowned their last names—which they said were signs of their subordination to whites—and replaced them with an X, symbolizing that they no longer knew the names of their black ancestors.

Most members of this movement believed that Elijah Muhammad was a great prophet—a true spokesman for God—and that his commands must be obeyed. The demands he placed on his disciples were strict. One must not smoke, drink alcohol, or take any form of drugs. No criminal activity or sexual misconduct was tolerated, and one must always speak to and treat fellow Muslims with courtesy and respect. Black women must be modest and chaste until marriage, and they must then be strong and faithful supporters and helpmates to their husbands.

The task of the highest priority for all NOI members was to inform all black Americans of their true, superior nature and to pull them out of the despair, hopelessness, and immoral lifestyle that they had fallen into as the result of the oppression and exploitation by whites. To extricate the black race in America from its destructive environment, black Americans should stick together and become self-sufficient in every way, eventually creating their own nation in some part of the southern United States that would be set aside. It was from the South that the vast majority of the black population could trace their American ancestry, and it was where most of them still lived. Outside the South, the black population was concentrated in big cities spread across the nation, but most had fairly recently arrived from the South. A factor in their focus on the South was that black nationalists were looking for arable land, which was not available in the urban centers of the North and Midwest, where blacks had come in search of work. Blacks in the South were overwhelmingly farmers and had long been able to provide much of their food. Black Muslims hoped to be able to supply virtually all their own food to avoid being dependent on white society in such an important respect.

The apostles of the organization were remarkably successful in reforming all kinds of hardened criminals, drug addicts, and derelicts. They found converts among the most down-and-out people in the streets and the inmates of the toughest prisons. One such person was Malcolm Little. After converting to the faith of the NOI while he was in prison, he changed his name to Malcolm X.

Malcolm X was a remarkable man. *The Autobiography of Malcolm X*, a book written by Alex Haley as the result of many, many hours of interviewing Malcolm, makes for riveting, revealing, and profoundly educational reading.[164]

Malcolm was born on May 19, 1925, in Omaha, Nebraska. His father Earl Little, a Baptist minister, and his wife Louise were adherents of the philosophy of Marcus Garvey, a flamboyant businessman and civil rights activist who believed that America's blacks could achieve freedom only by separating themselves from the white power structure and becoming self-sufficient and self-governing. For this, Malcolm's family was continually harassed and threatened by the Ku Klux Klan, and their home was set on fire and burned to the ground. Fortunately, no one was killed. In what turned out to be an unsuccessful attempt to escape the continuing threats, they moved first to Milwaukee, Wisconsin, and then to Lansing, Michigan.

When Malcolm was six years of age, his father was found dead on the tracks of a streetcar line, his body virtually cut in half. His wife was convinced he had been killed by the racists who continued to harass the family, and she never overcame the shock. In 1937 she was committed to a mental institution where she remained for twenty-six years.

Now in effect an orphan, Malcolm was sent to a juvenile detention home in Mason, Michigan. He was able to attend Mason High School, where he was one of only a few black children. He excelled academically but dropped out of school at age fifteen and moved to live with his older half-sister Ella in Boston. In Boston, he soon got himself in trouble, involving himself in various criminal activities. In 1946, aged twenty-one, he was arrested for larceny and sentenced to ten years in jail. There, he was exposed to the teaching of Elijah Muhammad and the Nation of Islam, which espoused an ideology similar to that of Marcus Garvey. Malcolm became a convert to the Muslim faith, and his life was completely turned around. He became an avid reader and educated himself thoroughly on black history and related subjects. When he was released from prison in 1952, he moved to Detroit to work with Elijah Muhammad to expand the movement in

---

[164] Alex Haley, *The Autobiography of Malcolm X: As Told to Alex Haley* (New York: Ballantine Books, 1964).

both membership and geographical reach. His efforts on behalf of the Nation of Islam were spectacularly successful, and as a reward, Elijah Muhammad made him second in command in the organization.

Malcolm was tall, sinewy, handsome, and a charismatic speaker. He was extremely intelligent and observant and had the deep understanding of true human nature that comes from many years of life on the streets of a big city as a con man, pimp, and small-scale drug dealer. His unflinching intellectual honesty made him break with the NOI and Elijah Muhammad after discovering the hypocrisy of his mentor and idol and having noticed on a trip to Mecca that true Muslims came in every variety of skin, hair, and eye color and had no racial prejudices. After breaking with the Black Muslims, Malcolm X started his own nonreligious organization, the Organization for Afro-American Unity (OAAU).

His activities as a Black Muslim inevitably involved him in the civil rights movement. But he did not subscribe to the completely nonviolent philosophy of Martin Luther King Jr. Malcolm X's influence in the movement kept growing until his death in 1965. He inspired the "black power" movement and laid the psychological foundation for the "black is beautiful" and "black pride" ethos of the '60s and early '70s. After his death, the Black Panther Party (BPP), established by Huey Newton and Bobby Seale in 1966, incorporated many of Malcolm's ideas into their ideology. By rejecting white leadership in their organization and advocating aggressive self-defense in case of physical attack, SNCC under Stokely Carmichael and CORE under Floyd McKissick likewise showed the influence Malcolm had among many black leaders, even after his death. Because of Malcolm's philosophical differences with Dr. King, the two never established a close, cooperative relationship. Malcolm had less trust in the goodwill of the white establishment than did Dr. King, and he took a more aggressive stand, emphasizing black self-reliance and self-defense.

Figure 39. Malcolm X speaking at a Harlem civil rights meeting, May 14, 1963.

Some news media feeding on sensationalism unfairly depicted Malcolm X as a dangerous, aggressive, and violent black racist. This image could be maintained because, under pressure, Malcolm often came across as defiant, utterly committed, and unyielding, and those who dared debate him came away dazed and humiliated by Malcolm's command of historical facts and his quick and witty, yet cutting, retorts. As a result, his standing among whites was never high, and American history books do not picture him as someone on the level of Dr. King. But the very characteristics that scared whites gave Malcolm high status among many impatient young blacks.

Chapter 4. The Days of Hardest Trials and Greatest Victories

The 1963 Birmingham riots

As 1963 began with the installation of George Wallace as governor of Alabama, things did not look hopeful for the civil rights movement. To maintain the momentum of the movement, and to prevent it from being taken over by impatient radicals and black racists, Dr. King needed a victory.

In Birmingham, Alabama, the previous six years had seen eighteen unsolved cases of bombings of the homes of blacks, earning Birmingham the nickname "Bombingham." On June 29, 1958, a bomb went off at Bethel Baptist Church at 3233 29th Ave. North. The same church had been bombed earlier, on Christmas Day of 1956, and would be bombed again on December 14, 1962. Fortunately, no one was killed in these attacks, but neither was anyone arrested for any of them. The pastor at Bethel Baptist Church was the Reverend Fred Shuttlesworth, one of the local leaders of the civil rights movement. In 1961, Birmingham had also been the scene of brutal beatings of Freedom Riders, as noted earlier, but no one had been arrested for those crimes, either. Rev. Shuttlesworth invited King to Birmingham to see if they could achieve anything in this big city where racial tensions ran high.

King's organization, the SCLC, staged a sit-in on April 3, 1963, but it drew little attention. On April 6, 1963, forty-five participants of a protest demonstration were arrested, but demonstrations continued the next day, leading to more arrests. A Birmingham judge ordered King and 132 other named civil rights activists not to organize any further demonstrations. The order, of course, worked to King's advantage. On April 12, 1963, King and other demonstrators marched again and were arrested—this time generating headlines in many papers across the nation.

King was placed in solitary confinement to prevent him from communicating with other leaders or speaking to the press. He did, however, receive a copy of the *Birmingham News*, in which a statement by local white ministers referred to him as a troublemaker. In response, writing in the margin of the newspaper and on a scrap of paper given to him by a janitor, King composed his famous "Letter from Birmingham Jail," dated April 16, 1963.[165] It became a classic, phrased in King's calm but compelling and well-reasoned style, and it had a historical impact that the *Birmingham News* would never approach. It contained, among many other things, the following acidic remark:

> While confined here in the Birmingham City Jail, I came across your recent statement calling our present activities "unwise and untimely"... Frankly, I have never yet engaged in a direct action movement that was "well timed," according to the timetable of those who have not suffered unduly from the disease of segregation. For years now I have heard the word "Wait!" It rings in the ear of every Negro with piercing familiarity. This "wait" has almost always meant "never."

---

[165] https://web.cn.edu/kwheeler/documents/Letter_Birmingham_Jail.pdf

King was released on April 20, 1963, but the demonstrations were to continue. Like the plans for the Freedom Riders in Jackson, the plans for Birmingham now were to fill the jails. On May 2, 1963, a children's march began, soon achieving exactly what King had hoped. Three hours after the beginning of the march, 959 children packed the city's jails.

The next day, May 3, 1963, more than a thousand additional black children stayed out of school and gathered in Kelly Ingram Park to participate in yet another march. Enraged, and having realized that he was being outwitted, Birmingham Public Safety Commissioner Bull Connor ordered an attack by police dogs and water cannons on the children as they marched. Television cameras and the cameras of newspaper reporters captured the chaotic scenes and broadcast the unforgettable images worldwide. The water cannons were powerful enough to rip the bark off trees, and shocked TV viewers saw children hammered by the powerful jets.

Figure 40. Police dogs attacking a demonstrator in Birmingham, May 3, 1963.

The reaction by demonstrators was one of outrage, and in Birmingham, the demonstrations only grew, threatening to deteriorate into a huge riot. The jails were already full, and police were at a loss about what to do in those circumstances. Downtown businesses, fearing costly damage to their facilities if the situation spun entirely out of control, then announced that they agreed to integrate their facilities as well as hire more blacks. This announcement, made over the objection of city officials, served as a capitulation flag, and the demonstrations were called off. At last, another dramatic, significant, high-profile victory had been achieved. The civil rights movement had momentum once again.

That momentum was needed because, just like the black civil rights leaders, the Southern segregationists were in no mood to abandon their cause. After the Birmingham campaign, where blacks had been physically roughed up but had scored a significant victory, militant voices were growing in strength on both sides.

Figure 41. Fire hoses battering young demonstrators, Birmingham, May 3, 1963.

Governor George Wallace was determined to demonstrate that he would be able to resist further advances by the civil rights movement. In his inaugural speech in January 1963, the newly elected governor had defiantly railed against the federal government and promised white Alabamans;

> "Today I have stood, where once Jefferson Davis [the president of the Confederacy] stood and took an oath to my people. It is very appropriate then that from this Cradle of the Confederacy, this very Heart of the Great Anglo-Saxon Southland, that today we sound the drum for freedom as have our generations of forebears before us done, time and time again through history. Let us rise to the call of freedom-loving blood that is in us and send our answer to the tyranny that clanks its chains upon the South. In the name of the greatest people that have ever trod this earth, I draw the line in the dust and toss the gauntlet before the feet of tyranny... and I say... segregation today... segregation tomorrow... segregation forever!"

Claiming states' rights authority and acting according to the 1956 Alabama legislative step to nullify the 1954 Supreme Court order to desegregate schools, he had vowed to personally "stand in the schoolhouse door" to block the integration of public schools.

George Wallace is forced to yield at the University of Alabama

An opportunity to fulfill that promise soon presented itself. The University of Alabama at Tuscaloosa had received hundreds of applications from prospective black students since the 1954 *Brown v. Board of Education* ruling but had rejected them all. In early June 1963, a federal court ordered the university to enroll three black applicants. Wallace seized the moment.

On June 11, when two of the three students were about to enter the school building, Wallace stood in the doorway, blocking the way. But the Kennedy administration, knowing of Wallace's plan to demonstrate his determination to maintain segregation, had dispatched Deputy Attorney General Nicholas Katzenbach to the school to remind Wallace of a federal court order issued earlier that forbade the governor from blocking the enrollment of the black students. Wallace ignored Katzenbach and the federal marshals who had accompanied him and instead read a lengthy proclamation, condemning any interference by the federal government as illegal under the US Constitution.

Figure 42. Governor Wallace (*left*) confronts Deputy Attorney General Katzenbach
(*right*) at the University of Alabama at Tuscaloosa, June 11, 1963.

Under the previously issued court order, the federal marshals had the authority to arrest Wallace and forcibly remove him from the door. However, such an action would have been extremely provocative. Most white Alabamans felt that Wallace was morally right in rejecting federal interference in this case, and a majority probably believed he had the constitutional right to do so under the states' rights doctrine.

Katzenbach then called President Kennedy, who immediately federalized the Alabama National Guard, an action the legality of which was undisputed. Arriving on the scene, General Henry Graham of the National Guard then commanded Wallace to step aside, saying, "Sir, it is my sad duty to ask you to step aside under the orders of the President of the United States." Wallace at first refused to move and continued to declare his proclamation. But he had no legal authority to disobey the federal order and eventually moved, allowing the two black applicants to enter and register as students.

The confrontation in Tuscaloosa had the potential to touch off violent public disturbances, and the news media—including TV stations—were there in force to cover it. The confrontation showed the nation that the situation in the South remained explosive and that Southerners were determined to insist that the states' rights issue was a valid constitutional argument that would, in the end, save the system of segregation. Coming soon after their defeat in Birmingham, segregationists were infuriated rather than dispirited by the very public defeat of their governor by federal power.

Martin Luther King Jr. was now a household name—not just in the United States but in the whole Western world. The black civil rights movement had caught the attention of everyone, and the news coverage made his nonviolent protest movement a much-admired and heroic story. King knew how to take advantage of the very favorable and voluminous coverage he received, and he criticized President Kennedy's cautious approach to the civil rights issue as tokenism. The pressure got results. On June 11, 1963, Kennedy addressed the nation on television, announcing that the government would begin a push to enforce the laws that had already been passed to dismantle segregation and to ensure that blacks would enjoy equal rights everywhere.

The South responds with violence

The response in the South was an increase in violent attacks on civil rights demonstrators and organizers. Just hours after Kennedy promised increased support by his administration for civil rights law enforcement, the prominent NAACP activist Medgar Evers was shot dead in the driveway of his home in Mississippi. A little more than a week later, Byron De La Beckwith, a member of the KKK and the WCC, was arrested for the murder. Twice, an all-white jury deadlocked in the case, and Beckwith was let go. At his second trial, the jury saw former governor Ross Barnett shaking hands with Beckwith. (In 1967 Beckwith ran an unsuccessful campaign for election as Mississippi lieutenant governor on the slogan "He's a straight shooter.")

After being named as the first field representative of the NAACP in Mississippi in 1954, Evers had pursued an investigation of the murder of Emmett Till but had not been able to gain enough evidence against the men accused of killing Till to warrant a new trial. Now his own murder, like that of Till in 1955, seemed destined to go unpunished.[166]

Figure 43. Medgar Evers, Mississippi NAACP official, assassinated June 12, 1963

The murder and the failure to convict anyone for it created an uproar. Evers was a World War II veteran who had been in campaigns in Europe in 1943–45 and was well-known and highly respected in the civil rights movement in Mississippi. His home had been previously firebombed on May 28, 1963, and on June 7, someone had tried to run him down with a car.

The civil rights cause had by now drawn the attention of most Americans, and it found increasing support in the white population outside the South. The black leadership saw that the time was ripe for a

---

[166] Beckwith was forced to stand trial for a third time in 1994 after the newspaper The Clarion-Ledger of Jackson published evidence that the then defunct pro-segregation Mississippi Sovereignty Commission, a state agency, had helped screen potential jurors at his earlier trials. At those trials, two policemen had sworn that around the time of the murder they had seen Beckwith in Greenwood, Mississippi, about ninety miles from the scene of the shooting. (He was not immune to prosecution since his previous trials had ended with hung juries, not an acquittal.)

Throughout the trial, Beckwith wore a Confederate flag on his lapel. He appeared shocked and dazed when the jury, consisting of eight blacks and four whites, returned a guilty verdict on February 5, 1994. He was sentenced to life in prison and died there on January 21, 2001.

major demonstration of unity and purpose by the various black organizations. Planning was soon underway for a massive demonstration in Washington later in the summer, with attempts to draw public support from many prominent whites.

The 1963 march on Washington

In 1941, black activists had planned a march on Washington as a protest against discrimination in jobs in the defense industry. Negotiations between President Roosevelt and the planner of the protest, A. Philip Randolph, eventually resulted in the demonstration being called off in exchange for concrete federal action. In June 1941, Roosevelt issued Executive Order 8802, forbidding racial discrimination by federal contractors. A commission was established to investigate claims of discrimination and to initiate necessary action to remedy such situations. As a result, two million blacks were employed in defense work by 1944. The victory was only temporary, however. With the war safely won, the government terminated the operations of the commission in 1946. Black unemployment shot up, further aggravated by the return from military service of millions of young white men who were eager to find civilian jobs.

The situation during 1941 had been very tense, with the nation on the brink of war. It had been imperative to avoid strikes and other interruptions in the production of war matériel. In 1963, serious domestic unrest and violence threatened, and black leaders believed that if they issued demands for action, the government, to avoid possibly bloody disturbances, might respond positively. This time, the march was to press the demands for federal action to outlaw racial discrimination in all areas of public life.

The march, which took place on August 28, 1963, was a spectacular success in terms of support and publicity. The primary driving force and planner behind it was again A. Philip Randolph, this time with his close associate Bayard Rustin, and they managed to bring together in a show of unity several black civil rights organizations that had previously been working with different agendas, philosophies, and tactics. "The Big Six" were there: A. Philip Randolph of the Brotherhood of Sleeping Car Porters, James Farmer of the Congress of Racial Equality (CORE), Martin Luther King Jr. of the Southern Christian Leadership Conference (SCLC), John Lewis of the Student Nonviolent Coordinating Committee (SNCC), Roy Wilkins of the National Association for the Advancement of Colored People (NAACP), and Whitney Young Jr. of the Urban League. The march drew supporters to Washington from all over the country, arriving in private cars, by train, and by bus. The crowd on the Mall was estimated at two hundred and fifty thousand people.

The highlights of the gathering were the speeches by several of the black leaders. The speech by John Lewis was the most aggressive. Lewis had toned down his criticism of the Kennedy government that had been part of his original speech, but he still issued a strong challenge:

> My friends, let us not forget that we are involved in a serious social revolution. By and large, politicians who build their careers on immoral compromise and allow themselves an open forum of political, economic and social exploitation dominate American politics...

There are exceptions, of course. We salute those. But what political leader can stand up and say, "My party is a party of principles?" For the party of Kennedy is also the party of [Mississippi Senator] Eastland. The party of Javits is also the party of Goldwater. Where is our party? Where is the political party that will make it unnecessary to march on Washington?...

We are tired. We are tired of being beat by policemen. We are tired of seeing our people locked up in jail over and over again, and then you holler "Be patient." How long can we be patient? We want our freedom, and we want it now.[167]

Figure 44. John Lewis at an SNCC meeting in April 1964.

---

[167] BillMoyers.com, https://billmoyers.com/content/two-versions-of-john-lewis-speech/

The speech by Martin Luther King Jr. was the one that would become the most famous. It is remembered as the "I Have a Dream" speech and is widely considered one of the best and most influential political speeches in American history; many of its phrases have become known and admired the world over:

> I have a dream that one day this nation will rise up and live out the true meaning of its creed: "We hold these truths to be self-evident, that all men are created equal." I have a dream that one day on the red hills of Georgia, the sons of former slaves and the sons of former slave owners will be able to sit down together at the table of brotherhood... I have a dream, that one day, even the state of Mississippi, a state sweltering with the heat of injustice, sweltering with the heat of oppression, will be transformed into an oasis of freedom and justice... I have a dream, that my four little children will one day live in a nation where they will not be judged by the color of their skin but by the content of their character. I have a dream today...
>
> I have a dream that one day down in Alabama, with its vicious racists, with its governor having his lips dripping with the words of "interposition" and "nullification," one day right there in Alabama little black boys and black girls will be able to join hands with little white boys and white girls as sisters and brothers. I have a dream today...
>
> And when this happens, and when we allow freedom to ring, when we let it ring from every village and every hamlet, from every state and every city, we will be able to speed up that day when all of God's children, black men and white men, Jews and Gentiles, Protestants and Catholics, will be able to join hands and sing in the words of the old Negro spiritual: "Free at last! Free at last! Thank God Almighty, we are free at last!"[168]

The demonstration was broadcast on live television nationwide and was also viewed by untold millions all over the world. Dr. King's speech solidified his reputation as a leader of historic status and was instrumental in the Nobel Prize committee's decision to award him the Nobel Peace Prize on October 14, 1964.

In Alabama, the speeches were met with derision and anger by the white population. Dr. King had specifically singled out their new governor, George Wallace, for criticism. Following the violent riots and demonstrations in Birmingham in April and May, stores in downtown Birmingham had been desegregated, dealing a stinging first defeat to the segregationists in the city. On June 11, 1963, Governor Wallace had been forced to allow two black students to enroll at the University of Alabama at Tuscaloosa. In early September, schools in Birmingham had been ordered by a federal court to integrate without further delay.

---

[168] Full text available at https://www.archives.gov/files/press/exhibits/dream-speech.pdf

Figure 45. Dr. Martin Luther King Jr., delivering his "I Have a Dream" speech, Washington, DC, August 28, 1963.

The 1963 Birmingham church bombing

Many Klansmen would not accept these defeats without retaliating. The most famous of the KKK's bombing attacks followed on September 15, 1963. Four young black girls, three aged fourteen and one aged eleven, died in a blast at the 16th Street Baptist Church in Birmingham. Twenty-two people were injured. The church had been the gathering point for the participants in the earlier demonstrations and a center for the organization and education of black activists.

Near the church, groups of white people began taunting the survivors. Johnny Robinson, a black 16-year-old, threw rocks at a gang of white teenagers laughing at the mourners. As Robinson then fled to the alley beside the 16th Street Baptist Church, a car blocked his path, and James Parker, a white police officer, sitting in the back seat of the car, shot Robinson dead with a shotgun.

A few hours later, 13-year old Virgil Lamar Ware was killed by two 16-year-old white teenagers Michael Farley and Larry Joe Simms, who shot Ware after they heard he was out throwing rocks at their friends.

Neither Jack Parker, Michael Farley, or Larry Joe Simms served a day in prison.[169]

Figure 46. The four girls killed in the 1963 church bombing in Birmingham.

The names of the four girls in Figure 33 were, clockwise from top left: Denise McNair, Addie Mae Collins, Cynthia Wesley, and Carole Robertson.

Despite the extensive publicity generated by the bombing, no witnesses came forward, and no one was arrested for the attack. Continued FBI investigations produced the names of four suspects in 1965—all KKK members. A fifth man was rumored to have been involved, but his identity was never established. Owing to the lack of witness testimony and physical evidence, no charges were filed against any of the men for the bombing.

---

[169] https://www.al.com/spotnews/2013/09/virgil_ware_and_johnny_robinso.html

Figure 47. Damage inside the Birmingham church where the bombing victims died.

Figure 48. Damage to windows and cars at the 1963 Birmingham church bombing.

The assassination of John Kennedy

Even more shocking violence would soon follow after the Birmingham church bombing. On November 22, 1963, at 12:30 p.m., President John F. Kennedy was shot and killed. The assassination took place at Dealey Plaza in Dallas, Texas, while the president and his wife, Jacqueline, were riding in an open car through the city. Also in the car, and wounded in the assassination, was Governor John Connally of Texas. The assassin fired a total of three shots by a high-powered rifle, two of which hit the president—one in the back and one in the head.

Only seventy minutes after the shooting, a suspect by the name of Lee Harvey Oswald, who had received rifle training as a marksman, was in custody. Before his arrest (in a movie theater), he had also shot and killed a police officer who had attempted to apprehend him. There could be little doubt that Oswald was the assassin, but he was never put on trial. Just two days later, while in police custody, he was, in turn, shot and killed by an obscure Dallas nightclub owner named Jack Ruby. Ruby's stated motive for killing Oswald sounded strange, and the full circumstances of his involvement in the case have never been explained to everyone's satisfaction. Ruby died not long after his arrest as the result of a rapidly spreading cancer that some suspected was actually another assassination. Rumor had it that people with unknown connections to the assassination of the president wanted to prevent him from revealing certain facts.

News of the Kennedy assassination stunned the nation and shocked the entire world. At first, it was unclear whether Vice President Lyndon Johnson, who had been riding in another car behind that of the president, had also been shot. Wild speculation immediately broke out regarding the motive for the shooting and who might be responsible. Fears rose that the assassination was just the first act in a planned attack by the Soviet Union. Some assumed that a fanatical racist was the gunman, angry at Kennedy's support of the black civil rights movement.

Figure 49. Lee Harvey Oswald shot by Jack Ruby, Dallas, November 24, 1963

A high-level commission, named after the Chief Justice of the Supreme Court, Earl Warren, was charged with investigating the case. After a lengthy investigation, it concluded that only Oswald had been involved. Conspiracy theories of many kinds proliferated for years after the event, and high-profile official investigations of the event by several additional agencies reached somewhat different conclusions. Today, the prevailing opinion is that Oswald was the only gunman and that no other people were involved in the planning or execution of the crime.[170] [171]

The death of President Kennedy elevated Vice President Lyndon Johnson to the presidency. Kennedy had selected his vice-presidential candidate in the 1960 election out of strictly pragmatic political reasons. Lyndon Baines Johnson was a Texas senator of somewhat rustic habits and was looked upon by Kennedy and the liberal Democratic elite as a crude cowboy type. However, Johnson being a Texan counted for much in the South and had probably been a deciding factor in the very tight 1960 election. Now the nation had to swallow hard to accept this unsophisticated Southerner as a replacement for the stylish, brilliant, and handsome Kennedy.

Blacks, in particular, were filled with misgivings at hearing the Texas twang of his speech. Kennedy had been less forceful in his support of the civil rights movement than many blacks had hoped and believed he would be, but Johnson did not inspire much hope, either. A Southerner in the White House! It was not a happy prospect for those in the civil rights movement. Fortunately, Johnson would soon prove to be a stronger supporter of the civil rights movement than Kennedy had ever been.

Legislation to strengthen the rights of blacks in the South had been proposed several times in the late 1950s and early 1960s but had met determined resistance by segregationists in Congress, and no significant progress had been made. However, in June of 1963, President Kennedy, shaken by the strength of Southern resistance to racial integration, had proposed by far the most comprehensive civil rights legislation to date, saying the United States "will not be fully free until all of its citizens are free." The president of the nation had publicly committed his administration to the cause. His assassination muted the optimism that civil rights activists had felt at his words.

Allaying the misgivings of many civil rights activists at the prospects of a Texan as the new President, Lyndon Johnson immediately declared his support for the cause. In his first State of the Union address, Johnson exhorted the lawmakers:

"Let this session of Congress be known as the session which did more for civil rights than the last hundred sessions combined."

Intense efforts began in Congress to hammer out meaningful and comprehensive legislation. The proposed bill managed to pass in the House of Representatives but was at first blocked in the Senate. Southern senators adamantly objected to what they declared was an unconstitutional encroachment by the federal government on the rights of states to formulate their own laws. They staged the longest filibuster

---

[170] In 1979, the United States House Select Committee on Assassinations agreed with the original Warren Commission conclusion that Lee Harvey Oswald had been the assassin, but that there was a "high probability" that two shooters were involved, and that a conspiracy to kill the president was probable. However, it gave no names of additional suspects and recommended no further investigations.

[171] The 1991 Oliver Stone movie *JFK* is a fascinating exploration of one of the many conspiracy theories that sprang up after the assassination.

in history, seventy-five days of continuous, mostly irrelevant talk, to try to make the proponents of the bill give up. Senator Robert Bird of West Virginia spoke for over fourteen consecutive hours. But in negotiations behind the scene, proponents of the bill managed to obtain the required two-thirds majority of senators to put a stop to the filibuster. The Civil Rights Act of 1964 then passed by a vote of seventy-three to twenty-seven and was signed by President Johnson on July 2, 1964.

The Act bans segregation and discrimination based on race in almost all public places and circumstances. It also makes it unlawful for employers and labor unions to discriminate on the base of race, gender, religion, or national origin. Martin Luther King hailed the passage of the law as a "second emancipation." Although the bill was very significant given the political situation in the nation at the time, it fell well short of what black civil rights leaders thought was necessary. Its most significant flaw was that it did not specifically address voting rights. The bill probably would have failed in Congress if it had included meaningful voting-rights guarantees.

The murder of Chaney, Goodman, and Schwerner

During the "Freedom Summer" of 1964, a black voter registration drive continued in Mississippi as a high-priority effort. It was an attack on segregation in the most hard-core segregationist state in the union. It had a large black population, and the memories of Reconstruction made the white population fiercely opposed to voting rights for blacks. Already in 1946, the US Supreme Court had declared that Mississippi could not bar blacks from voting, but the governor, Theodore Bilbo, defiantly declared in response: "I call for every red-blooded white man to use any means to keep the nigger away from the polls. If you don't understand what that means, you are just plain dumb."[172]

Stokely Carmichael and SNCC were heavily involved and worked with many courageous locals to sign up black voters. To get around the complete rejection by the regular Mississippi Democratic Party organization, the activists formally organized a rival party that they called the Mississippi Freedom Democratic Party (MFDP). The MFDP succeeded in registering a significant number of blacks, but the group also had some white Mississippians as members as well as candidates for office of both races. It conducted classes on how to vote and how to campaign, how to sign up volunteers for the registration effort, and how to be a candidate in an election.

The Mississippi voter registration drive and its associated activities attracted hundreds of white volunteers, most of whom were male college students from big-name universities in the North and Midwest. They were the subjects of particularly intense hatred and contempt by Southern whites. Among them were Michael Schwerner and Andrew Goodman. Like other volunteers, they had been thoroughly briefed on the dangers of their work before they went down to Mississippi. They knew they were risking their lives and were instructed to call the volunteer center—not the police—if they were in danger.

---

[172] Philip Dray: *At the Hands of Persons Unknown: The Lynching of Black America.* (New York: Random House, 2002) p. 418.

In late June 1964, the volunteer center reported them and a local black civil rights worker named James Earl Chaney as missing following their arrest and subsequent release by police near Philadelphia, Mississippi. An alarm immediately went out to the FBI, and the FBI informed President Johnson of the disappearance. The disappearance was very ominous, and it made the national news. Less than a month earlier, Schwerner had been declared a target for elimination by members of the local KKK because of his work for CORE. On June 16, Klansmen had raided the black Mount Zion church in Longdale, Mississippi, and beaten church members during their search for Schwerner. Later in the evening, the Klansmen returned and burned the church to the ground. Schwerner had escaped that time since he happened to have been in Ohio, training more volunteers.

Figure 50. James Chaney, Andrew Goodman, and Michael Schwerner.

The search for the three men after they went missing was initially unsuccessful. The FBI then intensified the search, adding to the effort 150 more FBI agents from New Orleans and hundreds of military personnel from Meridian Naval Air Station. On the CBS newscast broadcast on June 25, 1964, Walter Cronkite called the disappearances "the focus of the whole country's concern."

Mississippi officials played down the events. Neshoba County Sheriff Lawrence Rainey gave his opinion that "they're just hiding and trying to cause a lot of bad publicity for this part of the state." Governor Paul Johnson of Mississippi also dismissed concerns, saying that the civil rights workers "could be in Cuba," alluding to the widespread belief among segregationists that a communist conspiracy was behind the civil rights movement.

Finally, on August 4, investigators announced that they had found the bodies of the three missing civil rights workers. The FBI, acting on tips from informants within the Klan, located them buried underneath a newly constructed earthen dam. Schwerner and Goodman had each been shot once in the heart; Chaney, a black man, had been severely beaten, castrated, and shot three times.

The identities of the perpetrators of the killings of Chaney, Goodman, and Schwerner soon became known to the investigators, but hard evidence was difficult to come by. Not until late November 1964 was the FBI able to formally accuse twenty-one Mississippi men of involvement in the murders. The accusations fell flat. Mississippi officials refused to file state murder charges against any of them.

Figure 51. The bodies of civil rights workers Chaney, Goodman, and Schwerner were found on August 4, 1964.

Malcolm X saw the failure of the initial prosecution on the charges of murder as further proof—if any was needed—that the white power structure was not willing to protect black lives, and that blacks would have to protect themselves.

A protracted legal struggle then began, where the federal prosecutors, unable to bring charges of murder, a state crime, instead brought charges of deprivation of civil rights, a federal crime. The long process leading to a guilty verdict even in the federal civil rights case put the racist corruption of the Mississippi legal system on full display and eventually produced only meager results. Not until October 1967 was a guilty verdict achieved, and only against seven of the twenty-one accused. None served more than six years in jail for the murder of the three civil rights workers. Three men were let go when the jury deadlocked, 11 to 1 in favor of conviction. The rest were found not guilty.

While looking for the bodies of Chaney, Goodman, and Schwerner, searchers also discovered the bodies of Henry Hezekiah Dee and Charles Eddie Moore, as well as five unidentified Mississippi blacks.[173] On September 10, the body of fourteen-year-old Herbert Oarsby was found floating in a river in Canton, Mississippi. These bodies were all of black men who had disappeared without it creating much stir outside of the local communities. No arrests were made in their murders. The previous disappearances and murders of so many black Mississippians had not drawn national attention, but with two Northern whites being the victims, the national media provided full coverage of the disappearance and, and hundreds of FBI agents and military personnel became involved in the search for them.

President Johnson and liberal Democrats took advantage of the uproar over the disappearance and probable murder of the three civil rights workers in the efforts to have Congress pass the Civil Rights Act of 1964.

Reopening the 1964 murder cases

In 2005, a new trial in the case of Chaney, Goodman, and Schwerner achieved the conviction of one of the accused men, Edgar Ray "Preacher" Killen. On June 21 of that year, exactly 41 years after the murder, he was found guilty and sentenced to three times twenty years in prison. He appealed the conviction, but the Mississippi Supreme Court upheld the verdict on January 12, 2007, ensuring that Killen would end his life in prison.

No suspects were at the time named in the murder of the other men whose bodies were found in the search for Chaney, Goodman, and Schwerner. More than forty years later, as the result of evidence uncovered during a documentary project by the Canadian Broadcasting Corporation in 2007, Mississippi state and federal officials reopened the case of Henry Dee and Charles Moore, leading to the conviction of kidnapping and murder of James Ford Seale. Seale received a prison sentence of three life terms. Mississippi authorities could not explain why the case had been considered "cold" for four decades.

---

[173] The Civil Rights Cold Case Project: Henry Dee and Charles Moore case, http://coldcases.org/cases/henry-dee-and-charles-moore-case

Chapter 5. Political Controversy and Major Legislative Victories

The Republican presidential election campaign of 1964

In the election year of 1964, the civil rights crisis and the problems in Vietnam were the two most contentious and emotional issues facing voters. The public was deeply split on the issue of civil rights, which dominated the angry debates and arguments during both the primary and general campaigns. The Vietnam situation was rapidly becoming another concern in informed political circles and played a significant role in the campaign rhetoric of both political parties.

At a stormy National Republican Convention in July 1964, the Republicans nominated Senator Barry Goldwater to be the next president. Emotions ran hot on the convention floor, where two very different candidates were on offer: the liberal Republican Nelson Rockefeller of New York versus the archconservative Barry Goldwater of Arizona. Goldwater's win weakened the Republicans in the Northeast, where his radical conservatism and aggressive stand on the Vietnam War issue had little support. However, his victory brought a flood of Southern conservatives into the Republican fold. It began the swing of the South from being a bastion of the conservative "Dixiecrat" wing of the Democratic Party to becoming the solid center of a very conservative Republican Party. The switch in party label did not represent a change in ideology in the South but was the beginnings of the transformation of the Republican party that would eventually result in it being the party of Donald Trump.

Goldwater was Jewish—a fact that somewhat surprisingly seemed to matter less to Southerners than his conservatism and his hawkish and aggressive stand toward Vietnam. Goldwater favored an all-out, full-force assault on Vietnam to evict the communists not only from South Vietnam but also from North Vietnam. He had initially been critical of the decision to involve America in the war, but once the nation had committed itself to it, Goldwater argued, it had to follow through and win. This stand was very popular in the highly patriotic and anticommunist population of the South.

In the South of the 1960s, the issues of segregation determined the outcome of every election, and the rise of the Republican Party in the South was in large measure a desertion from a Democratic Party that had become far too liberal for the South. What clinched the victory for Goldwater was his strong support of states' rights. The Republicans were quick to appeal to the South on the grounds of their now being the conservative party and being opposed to strong control by the federal government over individual states. Goldwater was not personally prejudiced against blacks but voted against passage of the 1964 Civil Rights Act as being an unconstitutional dictate by the federal government. "Democrats for Goldwater" offices opened across the South, urging Southerners to register as Republicans, or, where crossover voting was permitted, to remain Democrats but vote for Goldwater in the general election. In his acceptance speech, Goldwater declared that while the Democrats described him as an extremist, "extremism in defense of freedom is no vice."[174] That spirit permeated the white South, encouraging extralegal means and brutality in the suppression of black protests.

Figure 52. Barry Goldwater, campaigning in the South, 1964. (Note the "Democrats for Goldwater" sign.)

The 1964 Democratic National Convention in Atlantic City

If the Republican National Convention (RNC) in July had been stormy, the Democratic National Convention (DNC) a month later in Atlantic City, New Jersey, was nothing if not chaotic. All the major networks covered the convention, and the dramatic proceedings drew a big viewership. The Mississippi Freedom Democratic Party (MFDP), mentioned earlier, sent a delegation of sixty-eight representatives to the convention and mounted a stiff challenge to the seating at the convention of the Mississippi representatives

---

[174] Barry Goldwater's 1964 speech at the 28th Republican National Convention, at the Cow Palace, Daly City, California, on July 13 to July 16, 1964.
https://www.washingtonpost.com/wp-srv/politics/daily/may98/goldwaterspeech.htm

of the regular Democratic Party. The MFDP challengers claimed that the regular party had illegally excluded blacks from voting and from presenting black candidates as representatives. The MFDP, in contrast, had met all formal rules of the Democratic Party, represented the voters of all races in the state, and contained an integrated set of representatives.

The MFDP delegates had been elected by a much smaller total number of votes than the ones cast for the representatives of the regular Mississippi delegation. Even so, objectively, the MFDP had a strong case, and attendees at the convention were sharply divided on the issue. The MFDP received support from all over the country. Supporters held a continuous vigil outside the convention hall to lobby for the MFDP's recognition and seating, with people taking turns to rest and sleep in nearby churches. Several prominent Democratic Party organizations, including the Americans for Democratic Action (ADA) and the United Auto Workers (UAW), supported the challenge. The compelling testimony and speeches on the convention floor by both the MFDP delegate Fannie Lou Hamer and Joseph Rauh, the lawyer for the MFDP, convinced many that the only morally right choice was seating the mostly black MFDP delegation instead of the regular, all-white Democratic Party representatives.

Fannie Lou Hamer, the daughter of a Mississippi sharecropper, experienced all the humiliation and violence of being poor and black in Mississippi. But she was not broken by it. She was fiery, full of spirit, and a very engaging and inspiring speaker. Some of her most famous quotes include "I'm sick and tired of being sick and tired!" and "You can pray until you faint, but unless you get up and try to *do* something, God is not going to put it in your lap."

The Democratic Party leadership, including the president himself, feared that seating the MFDP delegates instead of the regular Mississippi delegates would cause Democrats to lose all the support they had traditionally enjoyed among Southern voters and might cost Johnson the presidency in the general election.

The Democratic Party leadership proposed a compromise. The party would seat the all-white delegation if the members pledged to adhere to the Democratic Party platform, which included implementing the recently signed Civil Rights Act. The offer was expected to assure the MFDP delegates that their goals would have the full backing of the federal government if Johnson remained in the White House. Also, two members of the MFDP would be seated as at-large delegates, not as regular Mississippi delegates. At first, negotiators for both delegations reluctantly accepted the compromise.

The proposal did not go over well with the regular delegates from Mississippi, all but three of whom refused to sign an agreement that would, in effect, put their signatures on the Civil Rights Act. They walked out, angrily and visibly demonstrating their refusal. Members of the MFDP delegation then quickly took their empty seats. For several hours, convention security tried to remove MFDP delegates from the seats by force, but the MFDP received help from delegates from other states, who blocked the guards from reaching the MFDP members. When the MFDP delegation returned the next day, intending to stage a sit-in at the convention, security personnel had removed the chairs. MFDP delegates then occupied the space anyway and sang freedom songs.

....I don't want you to say, 'Honey, I'm behind you.' Well, MOVE. I don't want you back there. Because you could be 200 miles behind. I want you say, 'I'm with you'. And we'll go up this freedom road together.
-Fannie Lou Hamer

Figure 53. Fanny Lou Hamer, a powerful and inspiring speaker, 1964.

The disappointment of the MFDP at the convention was as deep as the anger of the regular Mississippi delegation. Johnson appeared to have lost both the white and the black votes in the South, and the remaining hard feelings among factions of the Democratic Party proved difficult to soothe. Fortunately for Johnson, Americans tend to rally around their leader when the country is at war. The votes from delegates in Mississippi were not needed. He was accepted with acclamation as the Democratic candidate for the presidency. Johnson selected as his vice president Hubert Humphrey, a veteran liberal senator from Minnesota.

Johnson was a good politician, and he used the issue of the conflict in Vietnam masterfully. The nation was reluctantly at war—split on whether American involvement was morally justified. Many felt that the war should be taken care of quickly and decisively and, for that reason, agreed with Goldwater. America should show the communists that America had drawn a line in the sand and would meet continued aggression with overwhelming force. But Goldwater had overplayed his hand. His initial opposition to American involvement in Vietnam was difficult to reconcile with his later very aggressive tone. In his presidential campaign, he emphasized that America should escalate its involvement sharply by bombing and invading North Vietnam to bring about a quick victory.

Johnson was able to depict Goldwater as an extremist—a dangerous warmonger who threatened to pull America into a wider war in Asia, perhaps involving China, which might feel threatened by a powerful and active American military presence on its border.

Since 1960, China had developed tense relations with the Soviet Union, and the two neighbors had fought a few military battles in their disputed border territories. In contrast, following the Cuban missile crisis, relations between the Soviet Union and the United States had become less confrontational. Mao Tse Tung, later known as Mao Zedong, the leader of China, did not trust Moscow to come to China's aid in case of an American attack. Both Mao and President Johnson had to take into account the odds that the Soviet Union might prefer to sit back and enjoy the spectacle of its two enemies fighting each other. To the Chinese leadership, an American invasion of North Vietnam thus seemed possible and would constitute a potential threat to China. President Johnson had to consider the possibility that if America invaded and occupied North Vietnam, then China might be tempted to draw large forces to its border with Vietnam. China might even launch a preemptive strike, using its vast advantage in manpower and the far simpler logistics involved in maintaining an offensive to push the American forces back. It had done so in Korea in 1950 and had saved the North Korean regime. "A vote for Goldwater is a vote for a big war," the Johnson campaign kept saying, and this fear contributed significantly to Johnson's overwhelming victory in the November election.

Not all Americans considered Vietnam to be the most critical issue of the day: Goldwater won the South, where the majority of voters saw racial integration at home as a more serious threat than a war in far-off Asia. In the South, Johnson's victory produced both desperation and gallows humor. Quipped one Southerner following the escalation of the war after the election: "Johnson was right. He said that if I voted for Goldwater, America would get involved in a big and bloody war."

Stung by the failure of the MFDP to get seated at the Democratic National Convention and feeling betrayed by the Johnson administration, black activists became more receptive to the message by Black Muslims and others that they should not appeal to the white man for favors and justice. Malcolm X taught that blacks must insist on their dignity and self-respect. One seldom obtains power by begging for it—power has to be taken by power. That message resonated with many blacks, who had endured slights, insults, and humiliations their entire lives. To an increasing number of blacks, especially outside the South, always responding to physical and verbal abuse by whites with nonviolence felt akin to begging. Integration per se began to seem less important than the right to live in freedom and with equal rights, whether within an integrated society or just among other blacks. Blacks in the urban North were far more willing to abandon nonviolence as a tactic than were the Southern blacks. The idea of a separate black nation carved out from within the borders of the United States gained popularity. A new slogan began to be heard: "What time is it? It's NATION time!"

The Gulf of Tonkin incident

The Johnson administration had, for a while, been searching for a way to obtain public support for a larger military presence to aid the South Vietnamese military. The present US "advisory" role, aided by covert military action and large-scale economic and weapons support, was clearly insufficient to prop up the unpopular Saigon government. But the general public did not become aware of the seriousness of the Vietnam situation until after the North Vietnamese attack on the destroyer *Maddox* in the waters off North Vietnam, said to have occurred on August 4, 1964. Later congressional investigations made it clear that the attack was used as a hyped-up pretext to justify, in the eyes of the American public, an open declaration of war and a much-increased military effort in Vietnam.

The attack on the *Maddox* took place on August 2, 1964. It was not reported until two days later when the ship allegedly suffered a second attack. (Later investigations have established that the second attack never happened.) According to the report made on August 4, three North Vietnamese torpedo boats attacked the *Maddox* while it and another similar vessel, the USS *Turner*, were on an alleged "signals intelligence" mission in the Gulf of Tonkin outside North Vietnam. Their presence in or near North Vietnamese waters was, in fact, intended to provoke a North Vietnamese attack.

Earlier, the United States had covertly set ashore a team of agents in North Vietnam, where they were promptly captured. The United States had also secretly participated in attacks by South Vietnamese speedboats on facilities on two islands claimed by North Vietnam, and two CIA-sponsored aircraft had bombed areas just north of the border between the two Vietnams. The North Vietnamese military was, therefore, on high alert, suspecting that further attacks would be forthcoming. The appearance of American destroyers in North Vietnamese territorial waters set off an alarm, and the North Vietnamese sent three torpedo boats to investigate.

In the early afternoon on August 2, 1964, USS *Maddox* (DD-731) detected the three North Vietnamese torpedo boats approaching at high speed. According to an internal National Security Agency (NSA) historical study, the *Maddox* then fired three rounds from its cannons to ward off the North Vietnamese boats. The North Vietnamese launched two torpedoes, none of which hit the *Maddox*. A single round of 14.5 mm machine-gun fire hit the *Maddox*'s superstructure, but no further damage or injuries occurred. The North Vietnamese boats then retreated, chased off by four American F-8 Crusader jets launched from the aircraft carrier USS *Ticonderoga*, which was not far away. The jets reported sinking one of the torpedo boats and heavily damaging another.

Figure 54. The USS Maddox.

President Johnson eagerly seized on the incident, which became known as the Gulf of Tonkin incident. On August 4, 1964, shortly before midnight Washington time, he interrupted national television broadcasts to announce that the North Vietnamese had attacked an American warship. Johnson described the attack almost as a second Pearl Harbor—as a major, unprovoked, and unacceptable attack on an American navy ship by the North Vietnamese. He declared that a forceful American response was necessary and issued this promise: "The determination of all Americans to carry out our full commitment to the people and the government of South Vietnam will be redoubled by this outrage."[175]

The news of the Gulf of Tonkin incident shook the nation. America was now officially at war, attacked by a communist power. Earlier the same day, FBI agents had found the bodies of the three murdered civil rights workers in Mississippi, but the Gulf of Tonkin incident wiped that off the front pages of the newspapers.

For the moment, the Gulf of Tonkin incident increased popular support for Johnson, who was now officially a wartime president. Many who felt that America had been too feeble in its response to communist aggression in Vietnam now believed that Johnson had put his foot down and was ready for the resolute action the country needed. The more cynical observers suspected that Johnson's aggressive response was not dictated so much by military consideration of the situation in Vietnam as by domestic politics in the context

---

[175] https://usa.usembassy.de/etexts/speeches/rhetoric/lbjgulf.htm

of the presidential election, which was only three months away. Because of his support for the civil rights cause, Johnson had become very unpopular in the South. But the South was where the calls for strong action in Vietnam were the loudest. It would support a wartime president for patriotic reasons.

The build-up to the Selma to Montgomery march

Black civil rights activists had taken great pride in the recent liberation of African nations from colonial rule, and some high-profile people had moved to Africa to escape oppression and humiliation in America. Now the African heritage of black Americans became a matter of pride for many, and the pride was mutual. Malcolm X and Muhammad Ali discovered during their independent trips to Africa in 1964 that in every country they visited, they were well-known and greeted as great heroes.

As 1965 began, there was a defiant, angry determination among blacks to obtain full voting rights and to elect black candidates to political offices in the South. They had not succeeded in replacing the all-white Mississippi delegation at the Democratic National Convention the previous August, but they were determined that things were going to be different the next time. Martin Luther King Jr. observed that blacks were no longer intimidated by threats, bullying, and violence by the KKK. In 1964 alone, thirty-seven black churches had been bombed or set on fire in Mississippi, but that had not broken the will of their congregations. A new spirit stirred in the black community—one of steely determination and confidence in ultimate victory. At last, blacks across the South now believed that they would indeed triumph, that their centuries of oppression, deprivation, and subservience would come to an end and that in the future, their children would live as free and respected members of society. They now felt as if they indeed had something to live for—and, if necessary, to die for.

Dallas County in the western part of Alabama was notorious for its strict and violent enforcement of segregation laws. The passage of the Civil Rights Act the previous July had changed nothing in this mostly rural, central part of the state. The SCLC and other black organizations had long kept an eye on the situation in the county and decided that it was a perfect target for expanding the voting rights effort in Mississippi into Alabama, where Governor George Wallace still maintained that he would preserve segregation and fight any attempts by an overbearing federal government to encroach on the freedoms inherent in states' rights.

The voter registration efforts by local blacks in Dallas County had a long and violent history, but by the end of 1964, despite substantial help from the SCLC and SNCC, these efforts had produced no significant results. Less than one percent of the black population who were of voting age had managed to get registered. On October 14, 1964, Dr. King was awarded the Nobel Peace Prize, giving him immense prestige as a leader and as a human being. In January 1965, he spoke with President Johnson on the telephone about his plans to make a major effort in Alabama to secure voting rights for its black population. Johnson was receptive to the idea, and on February 9, Dr. King informed the president that the city of Selma would be the immediate target.

America's domestic problems with segregation and discrimination had severely damaged its image abroad as the land of freedom, democracy, and equality. Johnson and the liberal leadership of the Democratic Party believed sincerely in the end goal of equal rights for all citizens and full integration of blacks into mainstream society. It was now politically necessary, both domestically and internationally, for Johnson to show that he was fully backing Dr. King in trying to overcome these problems. Following Goldwater's capture of a majority of white Southern votes, the Democrats would need a significant new black vote in the South if they hoped to bring the region back into the Democratic fold. They wanted to reach that goal as quickly as possible, but they also saw the difficulties and dangers they might encounter on the road there.

They supported Dr. King not merely because they agreed with him on the goal but also because Johnson needed the nonviolent approach of Dr. King to succeed. That would reduce the appeal of aggressive antiwhite groups such as the Black Muslims and perhaps alleviate some of the fear and anger of white Southern voters. Johnson understood that his own popularity also hung in the balance. Significant opposition to the war in Vietnam already existed, and that was likely to increase and to become directed toward him and his Democratic administration if the war dragged on inconclusively. He did not need additional big problems on the civil rights front. In his inaugural speech on January 20, 1965, Johnson did not mention the issue of voting rights at all—a remarkable omission that most voting-rights activists took notice of.

Many prominent civil rights leaders (black and white) responded to Dr. King's invitation to come to Selma and take part in the demonstrations there for voting rights for blacks. The publicity also drew hardline segregationists to Selma, ready to demonstrate that they were not going to meekly tolerate the aggressive behavior of troublemaking blacks. On January 18, a member of the neo-Nazi National States' Rights Party (NSRP) kicked Dr. King and knocked him to the ground. The attack drew a response from Malcolm X via an open telegram to George Lincoln Rockwell, the leader of the American Nazi Party, which was affiliated with the NSRP. In the telegram, Malcolm X stated, "If your present agitation against our people there in Alabama causes physical harm... you and your KKK friends will be met with maximum physical retaliation from those of us who... believe in asserting our right to self-defense—by any means necessary." Malcolm's expression "by any means necessary" became famous, and its connotation of invincibility added to Malcolm's prestige among blacks and struck fear in many whites.

His words were not an empty threat. Malcolm X could by now count large numbers of members all across the country in his newly chartered Organization for Afro-American Unity (OAAU) and could easily mobilize very motivated forces for physical confrontations anywhere and at any time. Malcolm spoke to three thousand students at the Tuskegee Institute, which was not far from Selma, and was invited by some of the listeners to address a mass meeting in Selma on February 4, 1965, to kick off the day's protest demonstration.

SCLC staff initially wanted to block his talk, fearing that the discipline of nonviolence would break down following a fiery speech by Malcolm X. But they could sense that refusing to let Malcolm speak would possibly encourage even more blacks to espouse Malcolm's positions. During his address, Malcolm X said that in his opinion, an overly meek attitude was a hindrance to black liberation. Dr. King took the statement as a personal attack on him, but Malcolm said he meant to aid Dr. King's effort. He was warning white people that if nonviolent tactics did not succeed, then blacks would be forced to try other approaches. He promised to start recruiting in Alabama for his own organization.

Many blacks were beginning to agree with Malcolm. People had the right to defend themselves and to stand up for themselves when bullied and abused. One CORE member said, "Martin [Luther King Jr.] and those white friends of his keep telling us to turn the other cheek. Malcolm tells me to kick ass if they hit me. I think I'm getting ready to go with Malcolm on that."

Malcolm X did not personally take part in the demonstrations and marches that followed, nor did official representatives of his organization. Dr. King and most of the other leaders must have drawn a great sigh of relief. The risk of bloody street fights between whites and blacks, with numerous people dead and wounded on both sides, was for the moment averted.

On February 21, 1965, Malcolm X was assassinated. The initial reaction of those who heard the news was to assume that some white person had done it and to fear more racial violence. As details began to emerge, it became clear that he had been shot by several black gunmen at a meeting of Malcolm's OAAU. The motive for the shooting was the split between Malcolm and the NOI, the group still led by Elijah Muhammad. Elijah Muhammad adamantly denied ordering Malcolm killed, but the assassination was not wholly unexpected. Malcolm had recently received a rash of death threats, clearly from supporters of Elijah Muhammad, and several confrontations had occurred between NOI men and OAAU men, seemingly involving an attempted assassination of Malcolm. His home in New York had been firebombed, and Malcolm himself was in no doubt that a Black Muslim had thrown the bomb.

Many people received the news of Malcolm's assassination with relief, especially once it became clear that enmity among Black Muslims, and not whites, had precipitated the attack. In the news media, however, the event was completely overshadowed by what was happening in Selma at the same time. By the end of February, more than three thousand demonstrators had already been arrested and at least temporarily put in jail. Many were roughed up, kicked, and verbally abused in the process. On February 18, 1965 (three days before Malcolm X's assassination), Alabama state trooper James Bonard Fowler, without provocation, had shot a black deacon named Jimmie Lee Jackson. When Jackson died on February 26, feelings ran very high in the black community, and many wanted to retaliate. The SCLC then called for a dramatic, massive demonstration—a march from Selma to the Alabama state capitol of Montgomery to talk to Governor Wallace personally. The idea was put forth as a way to focus on a high-profile but nonviolent goal and to prevent the hot anger caused by Jackson's death from sparking a riot.

Bloody Sunday

A march by close to six hundred marchers began in Selma on Sunday, March 7, but did not get very far. The day before, Governor Wallace had said, "There will be no march between Selma and Montgomery." He had given the order to Alabama Highway Patrol Chief Col. Al Lingo, to "use whatever measures are necessary to prevent a march." As the marchers crossed the Edmund Pettus Bridge, they encountered a massive roadblock in the form of helmeted state troopers and a large county posse deputized by Sheriff Jim Clark.

After a fruitless attempt by Rev. Hosea Williams to negotiate with the commanding officer, the troopers attacked the demonstrators with their nightsticks, knocking many down and continuing to beat them. Mounted troopers rode their horses into the crowd, knocking more people down and leaving many lying wounded and bleeding in the street. One of the leading organizers of the march, Amelia Boynton, was beaten unconscious, and a picture of her lying in the road in the melee of the Edmund Pettus Bridge appeared on newspaper front pages all over the world.

Figure 55. Bloody Sunday—the assault on demonstrators in Selma, Alabama, March 7, 1965.

In all, seventeen marchers were beaten so severely that they had to be hospitalized, while fifty others were treated for lesser injuries. Many more suffered bruises and abrasions from being hit or pushed and falling to the ground but did not require medical care. The day became known as Bloody Sunday.

Aware of the worldwide impact the televised event would have, President Johnson immediately issued a statement in which he deplored "the brutality with which a number of Negro citizens were treated..." The event further angered most blacks and made them question the nonviolent principle, which had recently failed to yield results in the South. Even the NAACP, the nation's oldest civil rights organization, issued a statement that suggested that the patience of black Americans was running out:

> If Federal troops are not made available to protect the rights of Negroes, then the American people are faced with terrible alternatives. Like the citizens of Nazi-occupied France, Negroes must either submit to the heels of their oppressors, or they must organize underground to protect themselves from the oppression of Governor Wallace and his storm troopers.[176]

---

[176] Statement issued by the Executive Committee of the NAACP on March 8, 1965

The violence with which the demonstration had been beaten back no longer scared blacks as much as it infuriated them and hardened their resolve. Tempers were now so hot that the demonstrators defiantly made a decision to march again just two days later, on March 9, 1965. A call went out for support from clergy and concerned citizens from all over the country. Hundreds responded and traveled to Selma to join in the second attempt to march. Dr. King had been out of town to raise money on March 7, but he decided to lead the demonstration personally on March 9.

The decision to march all the way to Montgomery on March 7 had been taken too hastily. There had been insufficient preparation for such a long march. SCLC and SNCC leaders were aware of that, and secret negotiations between SCLC and Selma authorities worked out an agreement where a short, symbolic march would take place on March 9. President Johnson was kept closely informed of what was happening and sent Assistant Attorney General John Doar and Florida Governor LeRoy Collins to Selma to speak with King and others. Collins helped negotiate the agreement with the Selma authorities that would allow the march to take place without interference from Sheriff Jim Clark or the Alabama state troopers, provided that the march followed a particular route that would keep it within the Selma city limits. The marchers had to turn around at the end of the Edmund Pettus Bridge, where the bloody confrontation had taken place two days earlier. There would be no march to Montgomery.

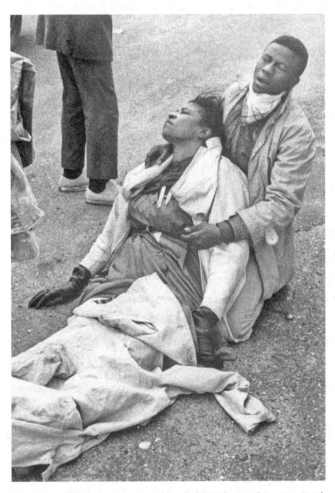

Figure 56. Amelia Boynton, beaten unconscious at the Edmund Pettus Bridge, March 7, 1965.

Amelia Boynton could easily have died that day but kept on going for another fifty years, dying on August 26, 2015, age 104.

Turn-around Tuesday

On the morning of March 9, an assembly of about twenty-five hundred people gathered and began the march under Dr. King's leadership. In addition to prominent black leaders from several civil rights organizations, the crowd contained many Northern white church leaders, who had arrived in Selma to demonstrate solidarity with the cause of equal rights for black citizens. The march took place without violence. There had not been time to inform all participants of the short route and turnaround on the bridge, however, and many were disappointed—especially those who had come from a considerable distance to take part. The day became known as "Turnaround Tuesday." Dr. King promised those who had taken part in this limited march that the goal was still to continue to Montgomery, and that this would soon take place.

In the evening of March 9, 1965, three white ministers from the Unitarian Church were severely beaten by members of the KKK. One of the ministers, James Reeb, died of his injuries. Reeb's death prompted headlines and caused outrage across the nation. Tens of thousands of vigils were held to mourn his death. President Johnson called Reeb's parents to personally express his condolences and would later mention Reeb's death when he delivered the draft of the Voting Rights Act to Congress. Many blacks noted with some cynicism and bitterness the great attention that Reeb's death received: the unprovoked shooting of the black deacon Jimmie Lee Jackson less than two weeks earlier had not produced similar coverage. In many people, this reinforced the conviction that the recently slain Malcolm X had spoken the truth: the white establishment was not genuinely concerned about the lives of blacks. Stokely Carmichael of SNCC commented that "the movement itself is playing into the hands of racism because what you want as a nation is to be upset when anybody is killed [but] for it to be recognized, a white person must be killed—Well, what are you saying?"[177]

The "turnaround" agreement negotiated with Selma officials damaged King's credibility among the more aggressive black organizations. Criticism of him became more frequent and pronounced. The demands that a march all the way to Montgomery take place grew more insistent. To many, it seemed self-evident that they would have to confront Governor Wallace directly. Impatient with Dr. King, students at the Tuskegee Institute decided to start a march of their own to Montgomery to deliver a petition to the governor. James Forman, SNCC leader, quickly said that he and many of SNCC staff would join such a march.

Blacks across the country followed the events in Selma with intense interest. There was a general sense that the civil rights movement was at a crucial point, where only rapid, substantial progress would prevent large-scale violence. Leading black organizations like SNCC and CORE organized protests in more than eighty cities, and representatives met with President Johnson at the White House. On March 12, 1965,

---

[177] Stokely Carmichael, as quoted in "Teaching for Change; Building Social Justice Starting in the Classroom." http://www.teachingforchange.org/selma-bios

Johnson had a contentious meeting with civil rights advocates that included the very aggressive H. Rap Brown. The civil rights activists demanded that federal troops be sent in to protect demonstrators in Alabama and wanted to know why Johnson had not yet sent a voting rights bill to Congress.

Figure 57. "Turnaround Tuesday," Selma, March 9, 1965.

In a press interview about these meetings, Johnson tried to assure the nation that he was not going to be "blackjacked" by disorderly pressure groups, but the very next day he met personally with Governor George Wallace to argue that the Alabama National Guard must be used to protect demonstrators from mob violence. The implication, of course, was that if Governor Wallace did not want to protect the marchers, then Johnson would federalize the National Guard, as Kennedy had done in 1963 to force Wallace to back down on the issue of school segregation. Wallace preferred to be forced by federal power rather than voluntarily give in to black demands.

Johnson also began work on the final draft of the Voting Rights Act. On March 15, in a historic TV broadcast that was carried live nationwide, he described the content of the new bill and demanded that Congress pass it once he submitted it, which would be shortly. In his speech, he took a firm stand in favor of the civil rights movement. He called Selma "a turning point in man's unending search for freedom," suggesting that the march would turn out to be similar in importance and decisiveness to the Battle of Appomattox, the April 1865 battle almost exactly a century earlier that had led to the surrender of the Confederacy and ended the Civil War. What especially made viewers sit up and catch their breath was when Johnson said, his face hard with determination and emotion, "And we shall overcome!" It represented a long-in-coming but irrevocable commitment by the federal government to the cause of equal rights. The Voting Rights Act of 1965 was formally introduced in Congress two days later, on March 17.

The die was cast. Johnson had unequivocally taken sides in the tense situation. There could be no more half measures, no more careful political give-and-takes, procrastination, or compromises on the part of the federal government. The full prestige of Johnson and his administration was on the line. There could be no doubt that, if necessary, federal military force would swiftly be employed to enforce federal law. By likening Selma to Appomattox, Johnson put those in the South who called for open rebellion against the federal government on notice that they faced inevitable and costly defeat.

On March 15 and 16, SNCC led demonstrations in the city of Montgomery, with participants numbering in the hundreds. A posse on horseback commanded by the Montgomery County Sheriff dispersed the demonstrators, whipping them and driving them back. Some demonstrators responded by throwing bricks and bottles; afterward, a furious James Forman drew enthusiastic response at a mass meeting when he declared, "If we can't sit at the table of democracy, we'll knock the fucking legs off."[178]

The march to Montgomery and the murder of Viola Liuzzo

There was now no turning back on the part of the civil rights activists gathered in Selma. The eyes of the entire nation were on Selma, and the march to Montgomery had to take place. Johnson knew that Governor Wallace was not going to ensure the safety of the marchers but would prefer to use the National Guard to stop the march and arrest demonstrators. That was likely to cause a violent reaction among black activists—perhaps across the entire nation. The scale of the violence might be great; the situation was unpredictable. It was necessary to play it very safe and to have more than enough federal armed forces in place to suppress any attempt to attack the marchers. On March 20, Johnson federalized the Alabama National Guard, and one thousand military policemen and two thousand regular army troops were ordered to Selma to protect and escort the marchers.

On Sunday, March 21, about eight thousand demonstrators gathered at Brown Chapel AME Church in Selma to set out for Montgomery. Additional enthusiastic participants kept joining the march along the way, so that on Thursday, March 25, 1965, by the time they reached the steps of the state capitol building in Montgomery, they numbered some twenty-five thousand. The thousands of military guards had kept the march safe all along the way.

On the steps of the capitol building, King gave his emotional speech titled "How Long? Not Long."[179] A large and excited crowd listened and cheered, giddy with the feeling of being on the threshold of success:

> The end we seek is a society at peace with itself, a society that can live with its conscience...
> I know you are asking today, 'How long will it take?' I come to say to you this afternoon,

[178] Clayborne Carson, *In Struggle: SNCC and the Black Awakening of the 1960s* (Cambridge, MA, Harvard University Press, 1995) p. 160
[179] Stanford University, the Martin Luther King, Jr. Research and Education Institute, https://kinginstitute.stanford.edu/our-god-marching

however difficult the moment, however frustrating the hour, it will not be long.... How long? Not long, because "no lie can live forever."

"How long? Not long!" Now with a strong federal commitment to enforce the Civil Rights Act and the Voting Rights Act, Dr. King's optimism may have seemed justified. But laws are one thing; the actual circumstances of daily life are quite another. The right to be treated as an equal does not instantly make one an equal when one has not been treated as such for a very long time. Across the nation, blacks suffered the effects of centuries of oppression, discrimination, and prejudice that had stamped them as inferior in too many ways. Dr. King's struggle was by no means over.

After giving his speech, Dr. King attempted to present Governor Wallace with a petition, but he and other marchers were refused entrance to the capitol building by a line of state troopers who blocked their path. They told King that the governor was not in the capitol building. Determined to deliver the petition anyway, King and his fellow marchers made it clear that they were going to remain on the steps of the building until the governor received the petition. After a while, one of the governor's secretaries appeared and took the petition, presumably to give it to Wallace.

That was sufficient to consider the long march a success. The throng of marchers began to dissipate and head home. Many had joined the march from points along the road and needed rides from Montgomery back toward Selma. A white housewife and mother of five named Viola Liuzzo, who had come down from Detroit to join the march, was driving back and forth between Montgomery and Selma to transport march participants when she was shot dead in Selma by KKK members in a passing car.

The FBI had planted an informant in the Klan who happened to be in the car from which the fatal shot was fired. That led to the quick apprehension of two shooters, who were arrested the next morning. The informant, Gary Rowe, obtained immunity for his testimony, but even his eyewitness testimony and admission that he had been in the car with the shooters did not suffice to convict the other three Klan members—not in Alabama, with an all-white jury.

The tactics of the defense were to smear Mrs. Liuzzo's reputation and to paint a horrifying picture of integration and its advocates. The strategy played expertly on the fears and sexual fantasies of Southern segregationists. Liuzzo was said to have been mentally unstable and to have come to Selma primarily to have sex with young black civil rights activists. The tactic worked well, as it almost always did. Under the circumstances, the all-white jury was unwilling to punish the killers. They found the Klansmen innocent of the murder charges. Neither the killer of Jimmie Lee Jackson, (Alabama state trooper James Bonard Fowler), nor those who had beaten Rev. Reeb to death, nor those who killed Viola Liuzzo (Collie Wilkins, FBI informant Gary Rowe, William Eaton, and Eugene Thomas), could be convicted in an Alabama state court.

But the Klansmen involved in the shooting of Liuzzo also faced federal charges—and in the federal court, the verdicts were different. Gary Rowe, the FBI informant, was not indicted, but the other three were found guilty of depriving Liuzzo of her civil rights and were sentenced to the maximum of ten years in prison. It was a landmark in Southern legal history.[180]

---

[180] Forty-two years later, in 2007, Fowler was charged with the murder of Jackson; he pleaded guilty to manslaughter in 2010.

The events in Selma and the march to Montgomery had an enormous impact on public opinion in the United States. It was no longer possible for the average citizen to remain oblivious to the injustices and violent oppression suffered by one-tenth of America's population. The news media coverage of the civil rights movement was intense, and the shocking scenes of peaceful demonstrators being brutally beaten by helmeted, club-wielding state troopers were seen on televisions worldwide. The events contributed to the successful introduction and passage in Congress of the Voting Rights Act, signed by President Johnson in August 1965. The Act provided for enforcement of the fourteenth and fifteenth amendments to the Constitution, amendments that the Southern states had opposed when they were proposed during Reconstruction and had refused to obey since then.

Segregationists did not have a change of heart. They were, if anything, hardened in their convictions about the evils of integration and the moral depravity of those who advocated and worked toward that goal. In Congress, the new Republican congressman from Alabama, William L. Dickinson, spoke on March 30, 1965, expressing the conviction of many Southerners that the civil rights movement was rife with drug and alcohol abuse and sexual promiscuity among the marchers. Religious leaders who participated in the marches denied those charges, and journalists who covered the marches saw no evidence to support them.

President Johnson had to perform a tricky balancing act. He had to prevent further deterioration of the racial situation and was acutely aware of the anti-Washington feelings of most white Southerners. He did not want to be too heavy-handed in the enforcement of the new federal civil rights laws, which Southerners viewed as being communist-inspired, freedom-robbing, pro-black laws. The enforcement of those laws thus proceeded only gradually, which angered black activists. The segregationists, for their part, were angered that any enforcement was taking place at all.

Chapter 6. Frustration Turns Violent

The Watts riot of 1965

With the passage of landmark civil rights legislation, the attention of blacks outside the South became focused more on local conditions, marked by high unemployment, ghettoization in deteriorating inner-city neighborhoods, and discrimination in the treatment of blacks by the police. On August 11, 1965, a scuffle between a white policeman and a black motorist in the Watts section of Los Angeles grew into a major riot that lasted for six days, leaving massive property damage, thirty-four blacks dead, more than one thousand people injured, and more than forty million dollars in property damage. More than thirty thousand people are estimated to have taken an active part in the rioting. The Los Angeles police required the aid of four thousand California National Guard troops to quell the riot.

Figure 58. The aftermath of the Watts riot, Los Angeles, August 1965.

The riot shook the nation and raised racial tensions and fears even higher. Television news broadcasts showed what looked like war zones, with smoke billowing from burning buildings and cars, soldiers firing their rifles at shadowy figures in windows, and people being slammed into cars and buildings and onto the ground by police as more than thirty-four hundred people were arrested.

The administrations of major urban areas across the country realized that what had triggered the Watts riot could easily happen in their cities too. At the bottom of what had happened was the frustration and hopelessness of living in the rundown, grimy, rat- and roach-infested centers of most major American cities where public services were inadequate, crime, drug addiction, and unemployment were high; and oppressive, bullying police behavior was to be expected. It was depressing to feel trapped in this environment and to see the contrast between the inner cities and the mostly white suburbs, where beautiful private homes nestled among green lawns along clean, tree-lined streets. The stark contrasts had a long history.

In the first half of the twentieth century, millions of blacks fled the South to escape the hardships and humiliations of its Jim Crow society. The major cities of the North seemed to promise job opportunities in their industrial factories and greater personal freedom in society. But most blacks found that they were victims of exploitation and segregation there, too. Discriminatory practices proliferated, spreading beyond the South to the big cities in the North. Blacks were less the victims of bullying and violence than in the South, but they were sharply segregated into poor, dilapidated areas of the cities and often swindled out of their meager savings by ruthless real estate agents and landlords. No matter what his financial situation, education, or job was, a black person found it virtually impossible to find a place to live in the better, more desirable areas of the cities. Banks would not make mortgage loans to blacks, and real estate agents would not show houses or apartments in "white areas" to black customers.

Real estate agencies increasingly employed "redlining" and "blockbusting" to transform the aging, central areas of major cities into overcrowded, decaying, poorly maintained, vermin-infested, and crime-ridden black ghettos. "Redlining" was the term used by real estate companies to mark on maps the part of a city where blacks were allowed to rent or buy residences. The limits of the "black areas" were marked on maps in red, either by drawing lines around them or otherwise clearly marking where real estate companies and banks could make it possible for blacks to reside. Houses in those areas were usually sold at low prices and with small down payment requirements that made it possible for poor blacks to buy them. But the houses were sold "on contract," like cars, which meant that the buyers did not get ownership of the property until the mortgages were fully paid off. Still, the buyers were fully responsible for all maintenance and repairs and lost both the down payment and all eventual equity in the house if they did not make the mortgage payments on time.

In many cases, the properties were in such poor conditions that it proved impossible for the residents to both meet the cost of the constant, necessary maintenance and repairs and to make the mortgage payments. The real estate company then simply evicted the residents, retaining its full ownership of the property. They perhaps made a few perfunctory repairs to be able to sell it again to another black customer, and so on in a constant, merry-go-round of deals. Thus many black families newly arrived from the South with high hopes and some very modest life savings lost both their money, their property, and their hope of a better life. The practice was highly profitable for many real estate agents but devastating to both the black ghettos as such and their residents. In his book, *We Were Eight Years in Power* Ta-Nehisi Coates provides a well-researched, eloquent, and perceptive analysis of the custom.[181]

"Blockbusting" was the tactic used to scare white property owners into selling their homes cheaply to real estate speculators. Speculators warned that blacks were moving into the neighborhood and were causing

---

[181] Ta-Nehisi Coates, *We Were Eight Years in Power: An American Tragedy* (New York; One World, an imprint of Random House, 2017)

a drop in property values. The owners ought to sell before that happened, and they would find themselves surrounded by noisy, dirty blacks! The properties were acquired at depressed prices and then sold at inflated prices to blacks.

Rental fees were held low by the renters being responsible for the costs of all utilities, maintenance, and repairs, which often became more than the monthly rental cost. Few of the older apartment buildings in the center of the cities had air conditioning, and the temperature there in the summer could be insufferable. In the winter, many renters sacrificed comfortable warmth to afford electricity or gas bills.

"White flight" from the inner cities in combination with a steady stream of whites from farms to the cities produced an unprecedented boom of residential construction in the suburbs, where blacks were barred by the redlining practice from obtaining homes. The segregation of housing became even more total in the cities of the North than it was in the rural South. In addition to a racial divide, the suburbs illustrated an economic divide in America, with the ghettoized black population generally far below the white suburbanites in income and wealth. Crime being the product of poverty, frustration, and hopelessness, the black ghettos came to have an alien image of violence, drug addiction, and prostitution, feeding and strengthening white fears and prejudices. In contrast, in the eyes of the growing numbers of white TV viewers, the image of the "real" America, white America, was the beautiful suburban home with a neat lawn surrounded by a white picket fence.

Martin Luther King in Chicago

The practice of redlining was well-known to Martin Luther King Jr. After the string of successes in the South, he sought to broaden his efforts into the many black centers in the urban North and Midwest. He had visited Chicago several times and spoken to large rallies in 1964 and in the summer of 1965. There, he had noted with dismay the city's de facto segregation of housing and schools. He decided to redirect his efforts toward the deplorable conditions in many of the nation's largest cities, and Chicago was a prime example of what was wrong. In the fall of 1965, King responded to requests from local civil rights forces and committed the SCLC to join the fight to desegregate Chicago's public schools. It was to be a joint effort between the SCLC and the local Coordinating Council of Community Organizations (CCCO), which had already organized a few demonstrations and protest marches in the city.

On January 7, 1966, King announced a program that would be called the Chicago Freedom Movement, and which was to focus on both school and housing segregation. He moved into an apartment in the slums of Chicago's West Side and began planning and organizing for marches and demonstrations. Chicago had broad, large-scale, and deep-seated problems, and it was evident that the work there would require substantial time and effort. To effect de facto school desegregation, one had to solve the problem of the very thorough housing segregation that compartmentalized the city into black and white areas. Black areas were almost all riddled with problems of various kinds that resulted from neglect by the white power structure of the city. Although segregation was theoretically not allowed by law in Chicago, it did exist in practice, and racial prejudice was in many parts of the city as strong and prevalent as it was in the South.

In addition to the Chicago Freedom Movement, the SCLC also launched Operation Breadbasket, headed by Jesse Jackson. This operation was focused on the discriminatory hiring practices of companies in the Chicago area. The two efforts had begun to pick up momentum when a march encountered a violent response in the white area of Cicero on Chicago's southwest side. Jeering whites threw rocks, bottles, and firecrackers at the demonstrators and held up signs that said, "Keep Chicago's white areas white." At another demonstration in Marquette Park, led by Dr. Martin Luther King, a rock hit Dr. King in the head and knocked him to the ground. Another thirty people were injured.

Negotiations took place between city officials, the SCLC, and the CCCO throughout the summer. However, the problems in Chicago and other major cities were so broad that they were difficult to deal with comprehensively. In August, Dr. King and Chicago Mayor Richard Daley reached an agreement on some of the issues. Dr. King hailed the agreement as very significant, but not much of practical consequence resulted from it. Attempts to iron out the problems in Los Angeles following the Watts riot the year before had stumbled and come to a halt because promises made by city officials were never kept. Similarly, the limited agreements reached in Chicago produced few actual results.

James Meredith is shot during the March Against Fear

While Chicago was the main focus of the SCLC in the spring and summer of 1966, marches and violence continued in the South. In 1962, as mentioned earlier, James Meredith had gained registration at Mississippi State University only after Governor Barnett of Mississippi had lost control over the situation to a federalized National Guard and faced arrest for contempt of court and heavy fines for refusing to let Meredith register. In the summer of 1966, despite the continuous hostility from white students, Meredith graduated from the university. He then announced that he planned a 220-mile "March Against Fear" from Memphis, Tennessee, to Jackson, Mississippi. He invited other individual blacks to join him but rejected help from civil rights organizations. Soon after setting out from Memphis on June 6, he was shot at and suffered multiple shotgun pellet wounds, but they were not life-threatening injuries.

The shooting created national headlines. While Meredith was recuperating in a hospital, leaders of many civil rights organizations vowed to complete the march in Meredith's name. The new governor of Mississippi, Paul Johnson, agreed to let the march go forward—and by the time it reached Jackson on June 26, 1966, having picked up supporters along the way, its ranks had swelled to fifteen thousand. Having by then largely recovered from his wounds, Meredith was able to rejoin the march before it reached Jackson. The news media, sensing the strong possibility of dramatic developments, kept the march in the news—but heavy protection by the National Guard kept the marchers safe. The march was a great success: it encouraged about four thousand blacks to register to vote along the way and became a catalyst for increased voter-registration drives.

Stokely Carmichael and the push for "black power"

Next to Martin Luther King Jr. and Malcolm X, Stokely Carmichael became the most influential of the leaders in the black civil rights movement. Born June 29, 1941, in Port of Spain, Trinidad, he and his mother immigrated to the US in 1952 and settled in New York City, where Stokely attended high school. He was a bright student and was accepted at Howard University in Washington, DC in 1960. He joined the Student Nonviolent Coordinating Committee (SNCC), and in 1961 he was one of the Freedom Riders to travel through the South to challenge the segregation laws. During his arrest in Jackson, Mississippi and incarceration at the notorious Parchman Farm penitentiary he became a leading figure among the black prisoners because of his wit, speaking ability, and inexhaustible energy. He became a driving force behind the voting registration drive in the South and the chairman of SNCC in 1966.

Carmichael coined the phrase "black power," which would become a rallying cry for almost all the militant black civil rights organizations in the late 1960s. Often portrayed by whites as a strident, anti-white radical, Stokely Carmichael was in private a soft-spoken, considerate man with a great deal of humor. His youth and idealism probably contributed to his growing disillusionment with his adopted country. True black equality and respect in society appeared to be beyond reach even as the legal barriers to it were gradually erased.

By 1966, Stokely Carmichael had taken over leadership of SNCC from John Lewis, and his stand had taken a turn toward advocacy of black power. By the phrase "black power," Carmichael meant that American blacks needed to feel a sense of unity and pride and take greater initiative in and responsibility for the struggle to secure their rights. But it was a phrase that many whites felt sounded too much like a mirror image of white racism. Carmichael participated in the March Against Fear and afterward explained the phrase in a speech for the first time: "It is a call for black people in this country to unite, to recognize their heritage, to build a sense of community. It is a call for black people to define their goals, to lead their own organizations." [182]

To some degree, the formulation of his speech echoed Malcolm X, who thoroughly distrusted white participation in organizations whose aim it was to achieve equal rights for minorities in American society. Other black leaders were also becoming less enthusiastic about integration with and support by whites. James Farmer of CORE had become somewhat disillusioned with nonviolent tactics, and when Floyd McKissick replaced him in January 1966 as the head of CORE, white members were no longer welcome. Racial polarization increased rather than decreased.

---

[182] Ahmed Shawki, *Black Liberation and Socialism* (Chicago, IL: Haymarket Books, 2005) p. 193

Figure 59. Stokely Carmichael speaks at the University of California, Berkeley, 1966.

Frustrated with the situation in the United States, Carmichael moved to Guinea, West Africa in 1969 and took the name Kwame Ture. He died there on November 15, 1998.

Black frustration flares up in urban riots

In poor rural areas of the Deep South in the early 1960s, few blacks belonged to civil rights organizations. They were very well-aware of the injustices and hardships associated with living in a segregated society, but as a consequence of being born into such a society for many generations, they had become, to some degree, accustomed to their plight. It could also be dangerous to be a member of an organization that advocated for equal rights for blacks. Drawing white attention as a "troublemaker" could invite threats and physical harm. Blacks had traditionally sought consolation in their strong religious beliefs, which gave them hope of divine intervention, or at least relief in a better afterlife. Until the civil rights movement began to achieve some traction in the early 1960s, few Southern blacks envisioned ever successfully making a change in society themselves.

A comparable situation existed among black inhabitants of the centers of the larger cities outside the South. They lacked, as Stokely Carmichael observed, a sense of belonging to overall society, or any hope and vision for the future of their earthly lives. Scraping by and somehow making do tended to be the prevailing ambition. By the mid-1960s, however, both the newscasts of the dramatic events in the South and the teachings of Malcolm X were beginning to have an impact.

The United States had little de jure segregation outside the South. The passage of the Civil Rights Act and the Voting Rights Act made little difference to the plight of inner-city blacks, who suffered from de facto discrimination and segregation and the attendant evils of poverty, unemployment, poor schools, subpar housing, and almost nonexistent social services—all of which were aggravated by high crime rates and unfair and humiliating treatment by both police and the criminal justice system. Martin Luther King Jr. spoke eloquently about his dream of a future society where black and white children would walk hand in hand, but the experiences of inner-city blacks did not make them very receptive to such sentiments. They had diminishing hope in a system where de facto segregation kept increasing, and politicians had nothing to gain by appealing to those who neither voted nor contributed money to their campaigns.

Beginning to understand their collective suffering as the result of willful neglect and rejection by whites—something that would always be present—blacks were increasingly in favor of getting the white power structure off their backs altogether and seeking an all-black environment where they could fend for themselves. Black power advocates and black nationalists spoke in ways that inner-city residents could relate to.

The rioting in Watts in 1965 was only the first in a devastating series of riots in major cities over the following three years. The highly publicized and eventful struggle for civil rights in the South and the progress that had been achieved—at least on paper—contrasted sharply with the static situation in the inner cities of the North. Problems there went largely ignored by both the media and the city administrations. Demands for changes were usually rejected with some insulting rationalizations, showing that the improvement of conditions in the inner cities was low on the list of priorities. Promises made—if any—were not kept. The level of anger and frustration among the people of these decaying black ghettos kept increasing. Black power, revolt, and a separate black nation began to seem like the only real solutions.

The "Motor City" of Detroit was one such city. Home of the mighty, world-leading American automobile industry, Detroit looked outwardly like the archetypal model of American success. The Motown record company, dominating the hit lists in most of the nation, was a black entrepreneurial success. But this glitzy surface hid a swamp of poverty, unemployment, and despair. The black population of the inner city had grown for decades through the arrival of large numbers of young people from the South, drawn by hopes of well-paying jobs in the auto industry and of an escape from the humiliating and oppressive conditions they faced back home. Many saw their hopes realized. The work on the production lines was monotonous and unfulfilling, but the auto industry workers were unionized, and their pay and working conditions were good.

While the auto industry was at first able to absorb a high number of the poorly educated, unskilled arrivals from the South, the number of job applicants eventually exceeded the number of jobs available. Lacking air conditioning in their sweltering apartments, thousands of strong, testosterone-charged but unemployed and bored young men hung out on street corners on hot summer evenings. Feeling ignored, bullied, and disrespected by the white authorities, powerless and doomed to a bleak future. Perhaps in some cases, their despair was not justified, and in some cases, it may have been exaggerated—but the fact was that in most cases, those feelings were justified. It was also true, as most blacks believed, that the ultimate cause of their misery was white racism in various degrees and forms. The segregation they faced in the North was just as apparent as what they had experienced in the South. Rosa Parks had moved from Montgomery to

Detroit in 1957, and in 1964, she told an interviewer, "I don't feel a great deal of difference here, personally. Housing segregation is just as bad, and it seems more noticeable in the larger cities."[183]

On the hot evening of August 9, 1966, the first rumblings of what would eventually happen in Detroit could be heard from the Kercheval district at the intersection of Kercheval and Pennsylvania Streets. An argument between teenagers and police who were trying to disperse the crowd led to a standoff, with the policemen radioing for backup. The teenagers, full of hatred for the police, were intentionally provoking a physical confrontation that they hoped would grow into a riot—or a rebellion, as they saw it.

It just so happened that a large number of police units were only blocks away because of an antiwar demonstration downtown. A specially trained force called the Tactical Mobile Unit (TMU) was on hand to handle this predominantly white demonstration. The TMU had been instructed not to react with violent force to insults and other provocations from the crowd. The TMU was, however, riot-equipped, heavily armed, and provided with armored vehicles, and as such, had been calculated to be sufficiently intimidating to forestall an attack. The TMU was ordered to proceed up along Kercheval Street and soon paraded through the intersection with Pennsylvania Street, where a crowd of hundreds had now gathered. Soon the street was curb-to- curb with police and TMU troopers.

Confronted by an overwhelming force, the crowd remained orderly, except for a few badly made and poorly thrown Molotov cocktails. A few store windows were broken, but looting was minimal. One observer, aware that the intent of the confrontation had been to start a large-scale disturbance, commented, "Hell, they did a much better job in Watts. They can't seem to get this riot off the ground."[184] Frustrated, a member of the crowd threatened that the next night, they would have assembled a larger force, presumably also armed. The black ghettos had plenty of firearms. "It'll be just like Vietnam!" one angry teenager shouted.[185]

The next evening, city administrators were not going to take any chances. Detroit city police and the TMU swept up and down Kercheval Street, with convoys of TMU vehicles showing shotguns and rifles, with bayonets affixed, protruding from the windows. The display of force was sufficient. Again, the outbreak of large-scale violence was avoided, undoubtedly in no small way because of the training the TMU troops had received.

It rained the following evening, cooling off both the city itself and the tempers of the crowd. For the time being, a riot had been avoided—but nothing had been resolved. It would only be a matter of time before the inevitable explosion would come.

Meanwhile, the racial tensions in the South showed no signs of abating. In Alabama, where term limitation rules prevented George Wallace from seeking re-election as governor, he got around that obstacle by running his wife as the candidate, and she won the 1966 election handily. In Georgia, a restaurant owner by the name of Lester Maddox gained a lot of publicity and admiration by wielding an ax handle to chase out some blacks who had attempted to be served in his establishment. His image as a staunch defender of segregation propelled him to be elected governor of his state.

---

[183] Susan Youngblood Ashmore and Lisa Lindquist Dorr, eds., *Alabama Women: Their Lives and Times,* (Athens, GA: The University of Georgia Press, 2017) p. 297

[184] http://www.detroits-great-rebellion.com/Kercheval---1966.html

[185] Ibid.

The white Southern power structure and groups like the KKK continued their intransigence and intimidation tactics in resisting black voter registration. That, plus the weak response by the federal government to the procrastination in implementing the Civil Rights Act, the Voting Rights Act, and the school desegregation order of 1954, led many blacks to agree with Malcolm X that white Americans could not be trusted to have the best interests of black citizens at heart.

Dr. King had received the prestigious Nobel Peace Prize in 1964 for his policy of nonviolence, but his successes following the Selma march had been few. He was beginning to lose the trust of the black community. Several black leaders were beginning to speak of black power and of rejecting integration as a goal. The NAACP, the oldest major civil rights organization in the country, historically had a large white membership but was now playing an ever-smaller role in the overall movement. The leadership was shifting to SNCC, which since 1966 had been led by Stokely Carmichael, and to CORE, which under the leadership of Floyd McKissick became wholly dedicated to black power. CORE's membership became almost exclusively black. Both Carmichael and McKissick held that physical self-defense was fully compatible with the principle of nonviolence as long as one was not striking the first blow. In this, they followed the teachings of Malcolm X, whose influence on the self-image of black Americans remained very strong, and whose distrust of white institutions seemed well justified.

Carmichael clarified his position and spoke for an increasing segment of the black population when he stated, referring to the governor of Mississippi and the sheriff who had led the violence in Selma, respectively:

> When we went to Mississippi, we did not go to sit next to Ross Barnett; we did not go
> to sit next to Jim Clark; we went to get them out of our way... we were never fighting for
> the right to integrate, we were fighting against white supremacy.[186]

Carmichael's support for black power and all-black organizations did not signal that he had become an anti-white racist. Under his leadership, SNCC worked closely with Students for a Democratic Society (SDS), which was almost all white, and he urged the SDS to focus on militant antidraft resistance and opposition to the Vietnam War.

Julian Bond is elected to the Georgia legislature

In Georgia, in 1965 and 1966, SNCC organized a black voter-registration drive to help the campaign of SNCC member Julian Bond for a seat in an Atlanta district in the Georgia State Legislature. Carmichael was initially opposed to an initiative by the local Atlanta leader of the campaign to expel white members from SNCC—but in the end, he agreed. He was persuaded that whites had enough work ahead of them to organize and help poor and disenfranchised whites, of which there were large numbers. SNCC should take responsibility

---

[186] Catherine Ellis and Stephen Drury Smith, eds., *Say It Plain: A Century of Great African American Speeches* (New York: The New Press, 2005), p. 58.

for the task of helping blacks. Both SNCC and CORE had then come down on the side of the rejection of integration as a goal and favored the use of all-black organizations to further the goals of black citizens.

Figure 60. SNCC member and Georgia legislator Julian Bond, 1967.

Julian Bond won the election, but the Georgia legislators at first refused to seat him, using as an excuse his support for SNCC's official stand opposing America's involvement in Vietnam. There can be little doubt that the real reason was that Bond was black. Bond sued in a state court but lost. On appeal, the US Supreme Court ruled 9 to 0 that Bond must be seated. On January 9, 1967, a mere twenty-six years old, Julian Bond took his seat in the legislature. Many blacks were triumphant. This victory by an all-black SNCC effort demonstrated that black power was a viable idea.

The FBI responds to the rise of the Black Panther Party

Starting in California, the Black Panther Party emerged in 1966 as the most militant and politically radical organization to advocate black power. Its leader and co-founder (with Bobby Seale) was Huey Newton, who soon established the party as a nation-wide movement. By 1970, the party had offices in sixty-eight major cities and thousands of dedicated, highly motivated members. Some scholars have credited the Black Panther Party with being the most influential black organization of the late 1960s.

Figure 61. Huey Newton, co-founder (with Bobby Seale) of the Black Panther Party, 1967.

The Black Panthers organized armed patrols to monitor the activities and brutal behavior of police forces in predominantly black areas. In 1969, the group broadened its operations to include social services—most notably to provide free nutritious breakfasts for children in black ghettos, and quality, low-cost health care. The group's political program was to use radical socialism and communism to distribute the abundant goods of a very rich segment of American society to the poor and powerless.

Alarmed at the Black Panther Party's growth and communist political orientation, FBI director J. Edgar Hoover on June 15, 1969, called the Black Panthers "the greatest threat to the internal security of the country."[187] The FBI utilized an extensive covert organization called COINTELPRO, short for COunter INTELligence PROgram, to counteract the group's growth and influence. Created by FBI in 1956, allegedly in the security interest of the nation, the program used both legal and illegal means toward that end,

---

[187] http://www.pbs.org/hueypnewton/people/people_hoover.html

including secret surveillance, infiltration, slander, perjury, and police harassment of members. The arrest and prosecution of leading Black Panther party members on false and trumped-up charges were intended to weaken party leadership and to discredit the party as being a criminal organization.

To further its goal to weaken, discredit and destroy the Black Panther Party, COINTELPRO incited violent gang wars between powerful street gangs and the Panthers. Among the means employed was a persistent program of false letters purporting to be from the Panthers and various street gangs, containing threats, false accusations of treachery and dissent, and incendiary ridicule. The program appears to have had as an important goal the murder of Black Panther members, including Huey Newton.[188] It was bloodily successful and reaped its ultimate prize on August 22, 1989, when Huey Newton was shot dead in West Oakland, California, by Tyrone Robinson, a member of the gang Black Guerrilla Family.[189]

COINTELPRO did not target the Black Panthers exclusively; the program also included surveillance and "dirty tricks" directed toward SCLC, SNCC, CORE, and the NOI. Leaders placed under surveillance included Martin Luther King Jr., Stokely Carmichael, H. Rap Brown, and Elijah Muhammad.

Hoover personally did not like the civil rights movement and wanted Dr. King to modify his policies and tone down his rhetoric. Rumors of marital infidelity on the part of Dr. King were spread and exploited as a part of the FBI's "dirty tricks" campaign against many black civil rights and left-wing movements in the 1950s and 1960s. A particularly noteworthy case was a letter sent by the FBI to Dr. King before his acceptance of the Nobel Peace Prize in 1964. It pretends to be written by a former admirer and supporter of Dr. King who has become disillusioned with him because of his alleged multiple extramarital affairs. It is written on cheap paper on a bad typewriter and contains several typing errors and other problems that were intended to show that the writer was a black person of limited means. It contains accusations of hypocrisy and rampant sexual misconduct. The final part of it is seems to suggest that Dr. King should commit suicide.

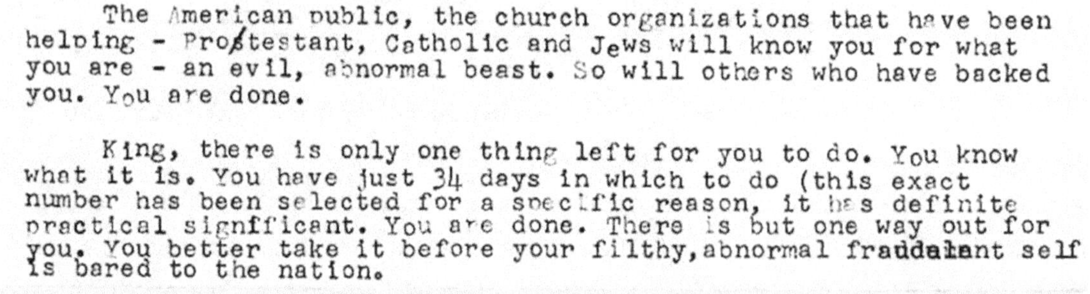

```
      The American public, the church organizations that have been
helping - Protestant, Catholic and Jews will know you for what
you are - an evil, abnormal beast. So will others who have backed
you. You are done.

      King, there is only one thing left for you to do. You know
what it is. You have just 34 days in which to do (this exact
number has been selected for a specific reason, it has definite
practical significant. You are done. There is but one way out for
you. You better take it before your filthy,abnormal fraudulent self
is bared to the nation.
```

Figure 62. The FBI to MLK "suicide letter."

---

[188]

[189] http://assatashakur.com/cointelpro-blackpanthers.htm

Chapter 7. The Civil Rights Movement Broadens

The splits in society widen and deepen

The split in the ranks of the black civil rights movement and the radicalization of segments of it mirrored a similar political and ideological division of the white population. Many young Americans were becoming frustrated and disillusioned with American society and its political system, which they perceived as being misguided, ineffective, and corrupt. They expressed some of this discontent by turning to activist, left-wing political movements like the SDS. Others decided to go the other way, to drop out, to become hippies, or to withdraw from mainstream society altogether and join nonpolitical, idealistic, and utopian communes. Still others, particularly in the South and Midwest, were deeply conservative and proudly nationalistic and supported America's involvement in Vietnam. For them, military service was an honorable duty, requiring toughness and courage. They believed that the American military was the best the world had ever seen, and it was the ambition of many to be a part of it. Being a combat veteran was glorious and glamorous, and conservatives tended to honor vets as true heroes—proud, red-blooded, macho American men. Those who supported the American involvement in Vietnam tended to be conservative on both moral and political issues, leading them to be very critical of black civil rights efforts and even to be outright racists.

While many of the military volunteers were conservative, strongly nationalistic, prone to violence, and racist, the draftees tended to be less so. Many white draftees had a bonding experience with their black compatriots in the hell of the Vietnam War that left lifelong impressions and made them strongly supportive of demands by blacks for full equality in American society.

San Francisco (and to a lesser extent Greenwich Village in New York City) became the center of the substantial hippie culture that developed in the latter half of the 1960s. The Haight-Ashbury section of San Francisco became almost wholly taken over by this culture, which reached its peak there in 1967. Haight-Ashbury came to be more than a name of a section of San Francisco—it came to signify an attitude, a morality, and a value system that shocked, intrigued, and titillated many people. It combined what seemed like a deeply spiritual and religious emphasis on love, peacefulness, communal sharing, and the rejection of materialism with extremely liberal attitudes regarding sex and drug use.

In the following years, the news media helped expose the entire nation to some of the hippie philosophy. The exposure influenced even the more conservative sectors of society. Many hardened their attitudes of hatred and contempt for what they saw as slothful, irresponsible, and morally corrupt dregs of society, but others, who had previously without much reflection adhered to the political, ethical, and moral beliefs which they had absorbed from their parents, became more willing to question traditional customs and values rooted in a worldview and a frontier society that no longer existed.

In recent decades it has become fashionable to see the hippie culture as a temporary, negative aberration with few redeeming and lasting effects, but its ethos of broad tolerance and rejection of violence and racism was, to some degree, an icebreaker that facilitated progress on many social issues. Furthermore, hippies were not as homogenous a group as the superficial or hostile observer might believe.

They were, of course, mostly young people who dressed in colorful garb, wore long hair, and shared an attitude of rejection of the traditional conformist ethos of their parents. Most hippies rejected consumerist values and felt contempt for the business world as well as for the government and its policies. But some were interested in politics and strongly opposed the Vietnam War, while others—sometimes called flower children—wanted to create an alternate, peaceful society that would focus on art or spiritual and meditative practices. The modern concern with ecology and environmental protection had a forerunner and perhaps an inspiration in the love of nature expressed by some of the hippies. Some of the hippies were united mainly by their love of the music of the era, often also by their heavy use of various drugs.

The California surfing culture was also an offshoot of the hippie movement and spread around the world, making beaches in Hawaii and Australia famous. With a slight stretch of the boundaries one can also include the biker gangs, especially the chopper biker fad portrayed in the very popular movie *Easy Rider*.

The "Summer of Love"

The summer of 1967 became known as the Summer of Love, during which as many as a hundred thousand people converged in Haight-Ashbury. Hippie gatherings occurred in many other places in the United States, Canada, and Europe, but San Francisco was the most well-known location for the hippie subculture.

The first big communal happening of the hippie scene took place at the "Human Be-In" in Golden Gate Park on January 14, 1967. It attracted a hippie crowd estimated at thirty thousand people. James Rado and Gerome Ragni, the creators of the groundbreaking musical *Hair*, attended the event. Rado was frank about the deep and inspiring impression the event made on him and credited the Be-In as the foundation of the musical, which went on to set records and gather awards for many years. He remembered later:

> There was so much excitement in the streets and the parks and the hippie areas, and we thought if we could transmit this excitement to the stage, it would be wonderful... We hung out with them and went to their Be-Ins [and] let our hair grow. It was very important historically, and if we hadn't written it, there'd not be any examples. You could read about it and see film clips, but you'd never experience it. We thought, "This is happening in the streets," and we wanted to bring it to the stage.[190]

While not at all racist in its philosophy and values, the hippie movement was almost entirely a white youth phenomenon. Wearing one's hair very long and dressing in torn clothes created a look that to some looked Jesus-like but to others was the epitome of sloth. Other stereotypical hippie characteristics included sexual wantonness and heavy drug use, adding to the conviction of many conservative and religious Americans that the hippies were lazy, irresponsible bums, and godless communists.

---

[190] https://worldofwonder.net/onthisday-1967-musical-hair-opens-off-broadway/

Figure 63. Hippie gathering during the Summer of Love, San Francisco, 1967.

Among most hippies, marijuana was the drug of choice. The more extreme hippies, popularly known as flower children, withdrew into a cocoon of utopian convictions and drugs of various kinds and refused to interact with mainstream society. They aspired to be fully self-sufficient, growing their own food and making their own clothes, and by using free sharing and barter instead of money. The favorite drugs among the flower children were hallucinatory, or psychedelic, drugs—LSD and peyote. It was at the 1967 Human Be-In that the most famous advocate of LSD use, Timothy Leary, first publicly used the phrase "Turn on, tune in, drop out!" The psychedelic art style of strange and colorful cartoonlike flowers that were often painted on Volkswagen buses was probably inspired by drug-induced hallucinations.

The "Be-In" label was, of course, a takeoff of the term "sit-in," which was the expression first used in the desegregation of restaurants a few years earlier. The term hints at the all-embracing attitude of community and the broad tolerance of individual differences that were the hallmarks of hippie ideology. The Human Be-In was followed by the Summer of Love in Haight-Ashbury and the areas surrounding San Francisco in what has been termed a "social experiment." The Summer of Love was a gathering of many budding social movements like gender equality, and it broke many conventions—especially in the area of sex and communal living—yet produced no significant violence or angry arguments between participants.

Similar but smaller gatherings of hippies occurred in many places during the summer of 1967. The intense media coverage of the events, which were all considered to be part of the Summer of Love, made sure that the hippie as a cultural phenomenon became a familiar piece of the colorful cultural jumble that was America in the late 1960s. The hippie image became perhaps the most beloved icon of America among the world's youth.

In the South, the hippie movement became another symbol of the perceived decadence, godlessness, and immorality that threatened young Americans—and with them the future of the nation—and indeed the entire white race. Fundamentalist preachers denounced them in passionate sermons, and KKK spokesmen declared them to be vile, race-mixing communists who were the agents of Jews. Anti-hippie demonstrations flared up in many places.

Music remained a leading feature of American white culture in the late 1960s. The music most popular among young whites was still labeled rock and roll but became dominated by groups in the British Invasion category, like the Beatles, the Who, Herman's Hermits, Dusty Springfield, and the Dave Clark Five. Their music had the enthusiasm of rock and roll, but melodically they were not based primarily on the American blues and gospel traditions. The British band that maintained the closest connection to the roots of rock and roll was the Rolling Stones.

American bands of the era patterned their music mostly on the style of the leading British bands, but some also incorporated elements of American country music—thereby keeping alive the musical style of rockabilly that must be given a lot of credit for the rock and roll revolution of the mid to late 1950s. Rockabilly's happy ebullience was also present in the early hits of The Beach Boys, who began their recording career in California in 1961. By the mid-1960s, they had reached a popularity that rivaled those of the British bands. The list of hits of the era contained a wide variety of music styles: along with the many songs by British groups, one saw songs by the duo Simon and Garfunkel, the groups the Fifth Dimension, the Supremes, and the Mamas and the Papas, and even by Staff Sergeant Barry Sadler who performed "The Ballad of the Green Berets." The white youth usually favored white performers, but many black performers also reached the *Billboard* Top 40 list, scoring heavily among white as well as black fans.

The Detroit-based Motown record label was created by Barry Gordy, the great-grandson of a Georgia slave owner, James Gordy, and his female slave. (James Gordy would have another famous offspring. His son by his white wife was the grandfather of President Jimmy Carter.) Motown, started as Tamla Records in 1959, was incorporated as Motown Record Corporation on April 14, 1960. It became the most profitable black-owned business in American history.

Motown's main competitor in the 1960s was Stax Records, a Memphis-based company owned by the white siblings and business partners Jim Stewart and Estelle Axton. (STewart/AXton.) While Motown developed a varied, often pop-flavored repertoire, Stax became the favorite label for those who favored a rawer, more Southern blues-oriented sound. Among its most popular artists were Otis Redding, Sam & Dave, Isaac Hayes, and the Staple Singers.

Though they were predominantly white, the speech, dress, and musical tastes of hippies incorporated influences from black society. Artists like Jimi Hendrix had more white fans than black ones, and the "Motown sound" of the Four Tops and the Temptations mingled easily with the Mamas and the Papas.

The flower children were the extreme edge of the hippie culture: they were overwhelmingly white, strongly pacifist, and enjoyed pseudo-religious experiences through psychedelic drugs and transcendental meditation. They tended to gravitate toward Far Eastern philosophies and musical styles. The Maharishi Mahesh Yogi, an Indian "wise man" who was a guru to the Beatles, the Beach Boys, and others, became famous as the foremost practitioner and teacher of transcendental meditation, which eventually became a fad in mainstream American society. Helped by his association with George Harrison of the Beatles, the Indian sitar player Ravi Shankar became a familiar name within flower children circles. His music soon achieved wider recognition, and in 1967, he won a Grammy Award for Best Chamber Music Performance for his recording of "West Meets East." American bands popular among hippies and flower children tended to have strange names, like Strawberry Alarm Clock and Jefferson Airplane, reflecting a dreamy, reality-rejecting ethos. The Jefferson Airplane album *Surrealistic Pillow* is widely considered to be an essential example of the psychedelic rock favored by hippies and flower children.

The black youth of the era contributed more to a split in musical tastes than did their white counterparts. Few white artists found favor with the black audience. The black stars on Motown and related labels, such as The Four Tops, the Temptations, Marvin Gaye, The Supremes, Smokey Robinson, and Stevie Wonder were popular in the black as well as white audience. Favored mostly by black listeners were the Stax recording stars and other artists with a very definite black soul sound such as James Brown, Wilson Pickett, Gladys Knight, and Aretha Franklin. The "soul" era of "black is beautiful" was dawning.

The women's liberation movement gains momentum

The liberalization of sexual attitudes that occurred in the 1960s had the effect that American women began to rebel against the narrow role that society had assigned to them since the end of World War II. Women, many of whom had held important jobs themselves during the war, were no longer content to be confined to the new suburban house, where they were expected only to produce, raise, and feed the children while keeping the house clean. The 1950s image of the perfect wife was the passive, content, and subordinated woman living in the comfort and security of a marriage to a successful man. Prior to her marriage, she was expected to remain a virgin. It was an image projected to the world as the typical American female, and it was assumed to be the dream of every woman in the world.

The sexual revolution of the 1960s resulted in a general liberalization of attitudes regarding human sexuality, which was a dramatic break from the guilt, shame, ignorance, and fear that had characterized the Victorian era. A precursor of the 1960s had occurred during the Jazz Age of the 1920s, when young women felt free to dress more provocatively, dance the Charleston, and smoke cigarettes in public. In the 1960s, this liberal trend came into full bloom, helped by the acceptance and popularity of rock and roll, the Pill, and the beginnings of a strong movement for equal rights for blacks, women, and homosexuals.

In the area of politics, progressive idealism and the sense of being oppressed drove the black civil rights movement. The spirit was catching on among other groups, the largest of which was, of course, women. In 1962, Helen Gurley Brown published a book titled *Sex and the Single Girl*,[191] which provided advice for young women. The advice was very frank and open about sexual matters and supported the idea that women should be free to enjoy sexual relations without guilt or shame. It became an instant bestseller and was of

---

[191] Helen Gurley Brown, *Sex and the Single Girl: The Unmarried Woman's Guide to Men* (New York: Barricade Books, 2003).

considerable influence on the young women of the time. Brown received a flood of fan mail asking her for advice about behavior, sex, health, and beauty.

In 1965, Brown became the chief editor of *Cosmopolitan* magazine. She completely restyled it as a magazine for modern, single career women. From the beginning of her time as chief editor, the magazine focused on sex, beauty, and glamour. Its message was that women should be strong and independent and should seek and enjoy sex without shame or inhibitions. The very first issue of the magazine under Brown's editorship featured an article on the Pill. The magazine, featuring beautiful, glamorous, and scantily clad young women on its covers, soared in popularity and has become the most popular women's magazine in the nation.

Betty Friedan's 1963 book, *The Feminine Mystique*,[192] was the first shot in the women's liberation movement, which would join the forefront of the overall struggle for liberalization and equal rights that would convulse the nation for more than a decade. In protest against the sexist stereotyping of women and the barriers to equal rights and pay they faced, women organized bra-burning demonstrations, shocking most of their contemporaries.

"The Problem That Has No Name," the title of the first chapter of her book, became a well-known phrase and expressed the feelings of millions of married women:

> The problem lay buried, unspoken, for many years in the minds of American women. It was a strange stirring, a sense of dissatisfaction, a yearning that women suffered in the middle of the twentieth century in the United States. Each suburban wife struggled with it alone. As she made the beds, shopped for groceries, matched slipcover materials, ate peanut butter sandwiches with her children, chauffeured Cub Scouts and Brownies, lay beside her husband at night—she was afraid to ask even of herself the silent question: "Is this all?"[193]

The women's liberation movement was a rejection of that role—a protest against being objectified as creatures who existed primarily for the titillation, convenience, and pleasure of men. Women began to seek respect and equal opportunity on the same level as men. Women should have the same chance as men to have challenging careers, should get equal pay for equal work, should be able to live lives on their own without being attached to a man, and should have the same right and freedom as men to seek pleasure in temporary relationships or to find a life partner—when and if they felt ready to have one. They felt that, like men, they should be valued for what they could contribute to the world—not merely for what they could provide for a husband.

The Feminine Mystique became a clarion call for millions of American women who had more or less silently experienced a simmering sense of dissatisfaction and frustration with the role that society had assigned them—that of homemakers and child bearers without much recognition or authority outside the walls of

---

[192] Betty Friedan, *The Feminine Mystique: 50 Years* (New York: W. W. Norton & Co.,2013).
[193] Ibid., beginning of chapter 1.

their homes. They were expected to be good wives in the sense of being content and obedient attachments to husbands, who were the breadwinning, career-oriented, and hardworking masters of their households and competitors with others in the larger world. Until women achieved that highly sought position of being a wife, many men viewed them primarily as sex objects whose value was determined by how sexually attractive they were.

The women's liberation movement, while initially overshadowed by the black civil rights movement, was inspired and empowered by it, and the movement continued to be effective in addressing the concerns of women well beyond the fading away of the black civil rights movement. It attracted many high-profile, glamorous women—many of whom, ironically, could credit their physical appearance with much of their popularity. Perhaps the foremost of these was Gloria Marie Steinem, born March 25, 1934. She was a columnist for *New York* magazine and became nationally recognized as a leader and spokeswoman for the feminist movement in the late 1960s and early 1970s.

In 1969, she published an article titled "After Black Power, Women's Liberation,"[194] which helped establish her as a nationally known and admired feminist leader. Together with Dorothy Pitman Hughes, she founded the feminist magazine *Ms.* in 1971. The magazine became a big success and a leading voice in the advocacy of full equality for women in society.

Figure 64. Gloria Steinem at the typewriter.

---

[194] Gloria Steinem, *"After Black Power, Women's Liberation,"* *New York Magazine*, April 7, 1969, p. 8

Native American, Chicano, and Puerto Rican groups enter the fray

Other groups also began to demand their rights more forcefully. In California, fruit and vegetable harvesting was wholly dependent on migrant farmworkers of Mexican and other Latino backgrounds, groups who had long been exploited by their employers. They were paid meager wages, worked very long hours, and were treated with arrogance and disrespect. Under the leadership of Cesar Estrada Chavez and Dolores Huerta, the National Farm Workers Association was formed in 1962 to create an organization able to advocate for the powerless workers. The organization was later renamed United Farm Workers (UFW) and became an effective voice for the improvement in wages and working conditions for farm workers. Cesar Chavez used strikes, marches, and highly publicized personal fasting to draw attention to his cause. He became one of the leading figures in the workers' rights movement in the 1960s and 1970s and has been the recipient of numerous awards. Born in Yuma, Arizona, in 1927, he died in 1993 of natural causes.

His humble yet forceful appeals for justice gained him the support of the liberal political establishment and the black civil rights organizations. In 1969, Chavez led a march to the Mexican border to protest against the use of strikebreakers and poorly paid undocumented immigrants to defeat his movement. It generated good publicity, with Democratic Senator Walter Mondale and black civil rights leader Ralph Abernathy joining the march.

The UFW activities worked hand-in-hand with "Il Movimento," the broader movement by "Chicanos," Americans of Mexican ancestry, to get the respect and civil rights to which they are entitled. The movement for respect and rights for Chicanos had gained momentum since the end of World War II with the formation of the American G. I. Forum (AGIF) and other organizations. In a significant ruling in 1954 in the *Hernandez v. Texas* case, the Supreme Court decided that Mexican-Americans and other groups that had historically suffered discrimination because of their ancestry were entitled to equal protection under the Fourteenth Amendment of the U.S. Constitution.

Chicanos experienced the same problems of racism, discrimination, ghettoization, poverty, and police brutality that bedeviled black Americans. They felt that white society did not accepted them as "real" Americans. They suffered from negative stereotyping that depicted them as less intelligent and responsible than whites. In 1968, thousands of Latino students in schools in East Los Angeles took part in a series of demonstrations against the poor conditions of their schools. The classrooms were overcrowded, with as many as 40 students per classroom; the attitudes of the teachers were demeaning, and the study material had little relevance to the lives and history of the Latino community.

A militant Chicano organization named the Brown Berets took its cues from the Black Panthers movement. In 1969, in association with the activist Latino students in Los Angeles Schools, they organized the National Chicano Moratorium Committee (NCMC). It soon received support from other groups, including Puerto Rican and American Indian activists. On August 29, 1970, there were mass demonstrations for recognition, rights, and respect in a dozen major cities, many of them attracting more than a thousand participants. The largest one took place in Los Angeles, with as many as 30,000 participants. Violent confrontations with Los Angeles police left four dead, scored of injured, and more than 150 demonstrators arrested.

The Mexican American Legal Defense and Educational Fund (MALDEF), founded in 1968, has become the preeminent Chicano organization. Modeled after the NAACP Legal Defense and Educational Fund, it has active programs in political advocacy and the training of local leaders.

The calls for Puerto Rican independence or statehood also grew louder in the 1960s. They had a long history. Puerto Rico was acquired by the U.S. in 1899 as a result of the American victory in the Spanish-American War but was never given statehood status, mostly because of its Spanish-speaking, mixed-race population. Puerto Ricans were granted citizenship in 1917, but the territory was not granted statehood and had no voting members of Congress. The issue continued to be debated both in Puerto Rico and in the states. In 1940, the Democratic party platform in the presidential election called for procedures that would lead to statehood for Puerto Rico, Alaska, and Hawaii, but the American entry into World War II put the issue on the back burner.

After the war, statehood for Puerto Rico became an important issue again. Puerto Rican advocates of independence were increasingly vocal and strident in their demands when they became organized in 1956 as The Pro-Independence University Federation of Puerto Rico, in Spanish Federacion Universitaria Pro Indepencia, or FUPI. Although they were always a minority, the American government identified FUPI and other independence movements as particularly dangerous movements. Puerto Ricans were now citizens of the United States, therefore, advocating independence amounted to sedition.

Like the Black Panthers, the Puerto Rican nationalists were victims of police harassment, provocations, and assassinations.[195] Undercover operations by the CIA, FBI, and COINTELPRO tracked, counteracted, and sabotaged their efforts. The American government placed about seventy-five thousand individuals in Puerto Rico and the mainland under surveillance and kept files on their activities. Those files listed about fifteen thousand individuals as political subversives.

Native Americans, for many generations victims of the most outrageous treatment by both individual whites and civilian and military government forces, also became a part of the widespread, broad-spectrum rebellion against established norms and authorities that was the hallmark of the "60s." In 1968, Dennis Banks, Clyde Bellecourt, Eddie Benton Banai and George Mitchell established the American Indian Movement (AIM), the original purpose of which was to help American Indians in urban ghettos where they had ended up after having been displaced by government programs that made it impossible to live a life of dignity and comfort on Indian reservations. They were later joined by Russell Means, an Oglala Lakota native political activist, writer, and musician who became the most effective spokesman for the group. The goals of AIM broadened to encompass a range of issues, including economic independence, preservation of traditional culture, and protection of legal rights. Perhaps most important was the establishment of autonomy over tribal areas and the reacquisition of tribal lands that AIM claimed had been illegally seized by whites.

On November 20, 1969, 90 Native Americans occupied the bleak, abandoned island of Alcatraz in the San Francisco Bay, once used by the notorious Alcatraz prison. The purpose was to draw the nation's attention to the plight of the original inhabitants of the North American continent. For nineteen months,

---

[195] See the 1978 ambush at Cerro Maravilla in Puerto Rico, leading to the death of Carlos Soto-Arrivi and Arnaldo Rosado-Torres.

they held out, claiming the barren rock "in the name of all Indians." With bitter irony, they proclaimed it more than suitable for an Indian reservation, in that:

> It is isolated from modern facilities, and without adequate means of transportation.
> It has no fresh running water.
> It has inadequate sanitation facilities.
> There are no oil or mineral rights.
> There is no industry and so unemployment is very great.
> There are no health-care facilities.
> The soil is rocky and non-productive, and the land does not support game.
> There are no educational facilities.
> The population has always exceeded the land base.
> The population has always been held as prisoners and kept dependent upon others.

The occupiers' list of demands included the return of Alcatraz to the American Indians and sufficient funding to build, maintain, and operate an Indian cultural complex and a university. There was no meaningful response by the government, which was increasingly preoccupied with the Vietnam War and the growing protest movement against it.

On July 4, 1971, members of AIM and the group United Native Americans (UNA) occupied Mount Rushmore, which was located on land that was considered sacred to Native Americans local to the area. In an interview with CBS News, Lehman Brightman, a founder of the UNA, explained the purpose of the occupation:

> Well, first I should say, the Federal Government said this land would belong to us as long as the grass grows and the water flows and the sun shines. Then six years later, they sent General Custer to this area on an exhibition, and they discovered gold here in the Black Hills. Then they turned around and took this land from us. We're sick and tired of sitting back and turning the other cheek and bending over to get those other two kicked. You're going to see some wide-awake, educated Indians. We got some new Indians coming up, new warriors. And this is a breeding ground, right here. You are going to see a spark.

In November 1972, a group of about five hundred Native Americans occupied for a week the office of the Bureau of Indian Affairs in Washington, D.C. They wanted to highlight the long record of treaties negotiated between the federal government and Native American chiefs, treaties that were subsequently all broken and violated by white settlers and various government agencies. The group delivered a twenty-point position statement, containing the following items:

1. Restoration of treaty making (ended by Congress in 1871).
2. Establishment of a treaty commission to make new treaties (with sovereign Native Nations).

3. Indian leaders to be permitted to address Congress.
4. Review of treaty commitments and violations.
5. Unratified treaties to go heard by the Senate for action.
6. All Indians to be governed by treaty relations.
7. Relief for Native Nations for treaty rights violations.
8. Recognition of the right of Indians to interpret treaties.
9. Joint Congressional Committee to be formed on reconstruction of Indian relations.
10. Restoration of 110 million acres (450,000 km²) of land taken away from Native Nations by the United States.
11. Restoration of terminated rights.
12. Repeal of state jurisdiction on Native Nations.
13. Federal protection for offenses against Indians.
14. Abolition of the Bureau of Indian Affairs.
15. Creation of a new office of Federal Indian Relations.
16. New office to remedy breakdown in the constitutionally prescribed relationships between the United States and Native Nations.
17. Native Nations to be immune to commerce regulation, taxes, trade restrictions of states.
18. Indian religious freedom and cultural integrity protected.
19. Establishment of national Indian voting with local options; free national Indian organizations from governmental controls
20. Reclaim and affirm health, housing, employment, economic development, and education for all Indian people.

In 1973, AIM organized the occupation of a site at Wounded Knee, South Dakota. Wounded Knee was the site of a December 29, 1890 massacre of between 250 and 300 Native American men, women, and children by cavalry troops of the U.S. Army. Some women and children, seeking shelter in a nearby ravine, were blown to bits by four rapid-fire cannons, each firing fifty two-pound shells a minute. Others fleeing the slaughter were cut down by pursuing mounted troops. The massacre left no survivors. The corpses were piled into a mass grave the following spring when the thawed ground made digging the large trench easier.

The AIM group, counting some 200 members, occupying the site on February 27, 1973, was immediately surrounded by federal marshals, demanding that they surrender and leave. A siege ensued, where negotiations were interspersed with some shots fired back and forth. The stand-off lasted until May 8 and caused the death of two of the occupiers. A federal marshal was seriously injured.

Their demands have since been partially met. President Nixon was sympathetic to some of the demands, and more progress could possibly have been achieved if he had not been wrapped up in the Watergate scandal and forced to resign on August 9, 1974.

The Gay Liberation movement steps out of the closet

The women's liberation movement was a very large and important aspect of the general liberalization of attitudes that marked "the 60s," but it never elicited the same broad, fevered, and violent response as did the black struggle for equality. Another sex-related movement—namely, the struggle for acceptance and equal rights by gay men and women—triggered a more visceral reaction. Most devout Christians believed that "gay" sex was not only sick and disgusting but a mortal sin. God had utterly destroyed Sodom and Gomorrah in a rain of fire and brimstone because of its practice there.

In the United States in the 1950s, homosexual relations between men were criminal offenses. It was understood, but seldom openly acknowledged, that a community of gay men existed in every city of any size. Every city of any size had bars and other public meeting places that were frequented almost entirely by gay men. The police occasionally raided these places and roughed up and arrested their patrons if they fought back, but prosecution on charges of homosexuality remained rare. Women were not perceived to be as sexually motivated and aggressive as men, and lesbian feelings were thought to be quite unusual. Where they were known, lesbians were regarded with contempt, but their relationships were not illegal. Lesbians had an image as "butch," hard and masculine in attitude and behavior.

Under J. Edgar Hoover, the FBI became obsessed with the "problem" of male homosexuality. Hoover himself was a closet homosexual who was terrified of the feelings that he could not accept in himself. He was determined to find and fire every federal employee who was known as or strongly suspected of being gay. Hoover used as his rationale that a gay man would be very fearful of being exposed as such a monster—thus, if the communists knew of his weakness, he would be a useful target for communist blackmailers. The communists might then be able to extract information from their target that could be valuable in their espionage system.

Earlier, in 1948, the famous Kinsey Report had documented, using massive amounts of statistics, that an unexpectedly high percentage of American adults engaged in what most people considered sinful sexual behavior. The Kinsey Report consists of two volumes. The first, *Sexual Behavior in the Human Male*, was published in 1948, followed in 1953 by *Sexual Behavior in the Human Female*. They are massive tomes of more than eight hundred pages each, with data extensively tabulated in forms that allow for making easy comparisons across different segments of the population. The Kinsey Report found that homosexual and bisexual feelings and acts were far more common than expected: between 5 and 10 percent of the population experienced sexual attraction to someone of the same sex and were sexually excited by pictures or thoughts of homosexual acts.

The contents of the Kinsey Report created a minor but shocked sensation when it was published, but like those of Myrdal's *An American Dilemma*, its findings were quickly suppressed and forgotten and did not affect the legal status of homosexuals. The American Psychiatric Association's *Diagnostic and Statistical Manual of Mental Disorders* classified homosexual desires as a serious mental disorder. Legally, the act was a criminal offense.

The fear of communism helped increase public awareness of homosexuality. Government agencies began to consider it a threat to national security. If one were known or even suspected of being homosexual, the result was usually social ostracism at best or job loss and even confinement in an insane asylum. In December 1950, a US Senate subcommittee issued a report, entitled *Employment of Homosexuals and Other Sex Perverts in Government*. The report concluded that "those who engage in acts of homosexuality and other perverted sex activities are unsuitable for employment in the Federal Government."

Investigations by the FBI between 1947 to 1961 resulted in more than five thousand federal civil servants losing their jobs because of admitted or merely suspected homosexuality. Thousands more were investigated and harassed. Thousands of applicants were rejected for federal employment for the same reason. The fear of homosexuality spread to state and municipal agencies, where thousands more were fired. Much of the private industry followed the same practice, also firing thousands of employees.[196]

With the breakthrough of rock and roll in the 1950s, the young generation of fans came to accept and enjoy the often sexually suggestive lyrics of the rebellious new music. The very spirit of the times and the freedom young people found with the availability of cars provided both the ambition and the opportunity to explore sexual matters more openly than had been the case with their elders. The embarrassment, fear, guilt, and shame previously associated with these matters began to recede.

With the loosening of rigid sexual taboos, some progress was also made on the demands by homosexuals of both sexes for acceptance of their sexual orientation. In 1962, Illinois became the first state in the nation to decriminalize homosexual acts in private between two consenting adults. Most of the nation, particularly the states of the Bible Belt, comprising the deeply religious, conservative areas of the Deep South and the Southwest, lagged far behind. In the fundamentalist Christian faith, homosexuality was a grievous sin.

As part of the liberal mindset of the hippie culture, the city of San Francisco, and in particular the district of Haight-Ashbury, also became known for its tolerance of homosexuality, which turned that area into a magnet for gays from all parts of the nation. Similarly, the Greenwich Village neighborhood of New York City had long been popular among gays. A bar named the Stonewall Inn was known for having a gay clientele and had, from time to time, been the target of police raids. On June 28, 1969, a violent confrontation between police and gay rights activists began outside the bar.

Over the following several days, it grew into a full-scale riot. The event produced feelings of solidarity among homosexuals across the nation and was the impetus for the foundation of several organizations for advancing the rights of homosexuals, bisexuals, and transsexuals across the nation. Acceptance has been slow in coming. Not until 1973 did the American Psychiatric Association remove homosexuality from its official list of mental disorders. Homosexual couples gradually found acceptance in the general population, but it would take more than another generation for homosexuals to get full legal recognition of their relationships as marriages.

---

[196] University of California at Los Angeles Law School: The Williams Institute
https://williamsinstitute.law.ucla.edu/wp-content/uploads/5_History.pdf, pages 5-2, 5-3, 5-4.

Figure 65. The Stonewall riot in New York City, June 28, 1969

Somewhat ironically, blacks have been more reluctant than whites to recognize homosexual relations as legitimate. Part of the explanation is that blacks, even as they moved to the North in greater numbers after World War I, retained the deep, fundamentalist religiosity with which they had been imbued in the South. Those beliefs included a very strict and conservative pattern of role assignments for men and women. For the same reason, the women's rights movement also made slower progress among blacks than among whites.

Martin Luther King Jr., for example, expressed little concern about the discrimination suffered by women and gays. It was more troubling to him that when racial segregation and discrimination were declared illegal, the continued injustices suffered by blacks were no longer a high-priority issue for white supporters. Many whites—particularly the young—were becoming focused on the Vietnam War. The war was a threat to these young whites personally, as the draft put them at risk of being sent to Vietnam.

The laws against interracial intimacy and marriage are overturned

Fundamentalist Christians in the Bible Belt placed interracial sex and homosexuality in the same category of depraved, perverse lechery. That attitude conflicted with the anti-discrimination laws of 1964, which appeared to grant legality, at least in theory, to interracial marriage, if not yet as clearly to homosexual marriage. It still took until 1967 for the last formal legal underpinning of racial segregation to be eliminated.

On June 12, 1967, the Supreme Court unanimously declared unconstitutional the laws in twenty-four states that made it illegal for members of different races to marry each other. The victory was won only after a long, multiyear court battle. The case was brought against the state of Virginia on behalf of a mixed-race couple, fittingly named Loving.

Richard Loving, who was white, and his black wife Mildred were both born and raised in Virginia but married in Washington, DC, where such a marriage was legal. After returning to Virginia, they were arrested by a local sheriff and two of his deputies who burst into the Loving's home in the middle of the night while the couple was sleeping. The two were both put in jail for breaking the law against race-mixing. Their eventual victory in the courts allowed them to live together for the first time in several years.[197] Ironically, the political and racial situation in the South was such that many politicians there did not dare take the initiative to remove the segregation laws from the state lawbooks even after the 1967 Supreme Court decision concerning interracial marriage. Sixteen Southern states kept the ban on such marriages for years, even though the laws were unenforceable. The last state to eliminate the law was Alabama, and that did not occur until the year 2000.

Figure 66. Mildred and Richard Loving, 1967.

---

[197] Phyl Newbeck, Virginia Hasn't Always Been for Lovers; Interracial Marriage Bans and the Case of Richard and Mildred Loving (Southern Illinois University, 2004)

Atheists score a court victory

Most Americans viewed atheists as dangerous and loathsome individuals. Lacking a belief in God, they were expected to have no moral compass, no conscience, no fear of divine retribution for evil deeds. Naturally, they were drawn to ideologies like communism and would have no scruples about perverse sexual activities such as interracial or homosexual relations. In the 1950s, only a few adult Americans in a thousand doubted the existence of God, and to be a respectable member of society, one had to be a member of a church. Public distrust was not the only reason atheists were discouraged from seeking public employment or running for office. In many states, atheists were barred by law from working in many occupations, especially in government and in professions involving law, where one might be required to take an oath affirming a belief in God.

In 1961, a case known as *Torcaso v. Watkins*, bearing on the freedom of religion, reached the Supreme Court of the United States. A person by the name of Roy R. Torcaso had applied for a job as a notary public in Montgomery County, Maryland. State law required him to declare a belief in God to be officially sworn in, but Torcaso refused to do so and was therefore declared ineligible to hold the position. He sued and lost in Maryland court with the justification that Torcaso was not compelled to seek the position, which required a belief in God. Therefore, his freedom of religion was not violated.

The case came to the attention of the American Civil Liberties Union, which, together with the American Jewish Congress, brought the case to the Supreme Court. The court unanimously ruled in Torcaso's favor in June 1961. The court held that the Maryland requirement of a belief in God to hold public office "unconstitutionally invades [Mr. Torcaso's] freedom of belief and religion guaranteed by the First Amendment and protected by the Fourteenth Amendment from infringement by the States."

The ruling narrowly applied to the Maryland statute, but it was a foregone conclusion that suits brought in other states would also declare similar laws unconstitutional. Roy Torcaso was sworn in as notary public in a ceremony where he swore to uphold the laws of Maryland and the Federal Constitution. There was no mention of any belief in God. Torcaso's victory in that case did not prevent him from losing a second case, where he challenged the exclusion of atheists from performing marriage ceremonies.

Though they are not enforceable, there are still laws today (2019) on the books of seven states limiting the rights of those who do not believe in God:

Arkansas, Article 19, Section 1:
No person who denies the being of a God shall hold any office in the civil departments of this State, nor be competent to testify as a witness in any Court.

Maryland, Article 37:
That no religious test ought ever to be required as a qualification for any office of profit or trust in this State, *other than a declaration of belief in the existence of God;* nor shall the Legislature prescribe any other oath of office than the oath prescribed by this Constitution.

Mississippi, Article 14, Section 265:

No person who denies the existence of a Supreme Being shall hold any office in this state.

North Carolina, Article 6, Section 8

The following persons shall be disqualified for office: Any person who shall deny the being of Almighty God.

South Carolina, Article 17, Section 4:

No person who denies the existence of a Supreme Being shall hold any office under this Constitution.

Tennessee, Article 9, Section 2:

No person who denies the being of God, or a future state of rewards and punishments, shall hold any office in the civil department of this state.

Texas, Article 1, Section 4:

No religious test shall ever be required as a qualification to any office, or public trust, in this State; nor shall any one be excluded from holding office on account of his religious sentiments, *provided he acknowledge the existence of a Supreme Being.*

Religiosity is presently fading at a rapid rate in the United States. In October 2019, a Pew Research Center study showed that twenty-six percent of American adults declared themselves "religiously unaffiliated," up from seventeen percent just ten years earlier. The decline is particularly marked among the young. Among "millennials," those born between 1981 and 1996, there was a decline of sixteen percent in those who called themselves "Christians," and an increase of thirteen percent in the group calling themselves "unaffiliated." It is evident that discrimination based on religion is no longer a serious problem. With the diminution of the power of religious dogma has come a healthier attitude toward sex and a lessening of racial prejudice.

Martin Luther King speaks out against the Vietnam War

Eventually, Dr. King began to realize that not only did the war hinder continued progress on civil rights domestically, but also that it was a morally objectionable evil in itself. By 1967, he had become a passionate opponent of the war in Vietnam. The war drained economic resources and demanded the sacrifice of the lives of many young Americans—predominantly poor and in the majority white. He began to speak out ever-more forcefully against the war. On April 4, 1967, exactly one year before his assassination, he delivered a passionate speech at Riverside Church in New York City in which he said:

Perhaps the more tragic recognition of reality took place when it became clear to me that the war was doing far more than devastating the hopes of the poor at home. It was sending their sons and their brothers and their husbands to fight and to die in extraordinarily high proportions relative to the rest of the population. We were taking the black young men who had been crippled by our society and sending them eight thousand miles away to guarantee liberties in Southeast Asia which they had not found in southwest Georgia and East Harlem. So we have been repeatedly faced with the cruel irony of watching Negro and white boys on TV screens as they kill and die together for a nation that has been unable to seat them together in the same schools. So we watch them in brutal solidarity burning the huts of a poor village, but we realize that they would never live on the same block in Detroit. I could not be silent in the face of such cruel manipulation of the poor.[198]

His stand on this issue put him in direct opposition to the government of President Lyndon B. Johnson. Johnson had forced through Congress the crucially important bills of 1964 and 1965 that made discrimination on the basis of race illegal in public life, but he was now pursuing a costly, hopeless war with steadily diminishing political support at home, and he was no longer as concerned with the demands of black civil rights leaders. Dr. King found himself marginalized by the political establishment, and he was also beginning to lose the faith of the black community. The circumstances of life in inner-city ghettos were miserable and were not easily addressed by the kind of nonviolent resistance that was the tactic used by Martin Luther King and the SCLC.

The 1967 Newark and Detroit riots

The smoldering discontent in black inner-city neighborhoods burst into open flame again in Newark, New Jersey, on July 12, 1967. The majority of the city's population was black, but its political and economic power structure contained few blacks. As in most other cities, the police force was overwhelmingly white, and blacks perceived the police as being a harassing and bullying presence rather than a protective one. Black youths were routinely stopped and questioned without reasonable cause, treated with disrespect and brutality, and often beaten severely or shot if they in any way disputed with the officer or resisted arrest.

The violence on July 12 was triggered by a simple traffic stop, where a police cruiser stopped, and the officers beat a black cab driver for improperly passing them. The beating was severe enough that the cab driver had to be hospitalized. A rumor started that he had been killed. Some violence broke out in which several black men were shot dead by the police.

The New Jersey governor called in the National Guard to restore peace, and a couple of calmer days followed. However, ultimately, members of the National Guard triggered the worst of the disturbance. On the evening of July 15, they—for reasons unclear—fired an intense fusillade of bullets into the window of a second-floor apartment, killing the resident, Rebecca Brown.

---

[198] Ahmed Shawki, *Black Liberalism and Socialism* (Chicago, IL: Haymarket Books, 2005), pp. 202, 203.

In the ensuing days of rage, burning, and looting, twenty-four blacks, a police officer, and a firefighter were killed, more than eight hundred people were injured, and about fifteen hundred people were arrested. Property damage was estimated at more than $10 million. The rioting spilled over into Plainfield, New Jersey, about eighteen miles away, but the scale of the disturbance there was much smaller.

Disorder erupted again in Detroit about a week later, on July 23, 1967, and evolved into one of the deadliest and most destructive riots in American history. Before it was all over five days later, the rioting had claimed forty-three dead, more than eleven hundred injured, more than seventy-two hundred arrests, and at least two thousand buildings destroyed. Monetary estimates of the damage ranged between $40 and $80 million.

The Detroit police at first underestimated the size of the disturbance and found themselves unequal to the task of controlling the crowd of looters breaking into stores along Twelfth Street, smashing and carrying away goods with little regard for the police force that was present. A witness describing the scene reported that a "carnival atmosphere" prevailed, rather than that of an angry mob.

The rioting continued on July 24, and the Detroit police received reinforcements from the Michigan State Police and the Wayne County Sheriff's Department. The reinforcements proved inadequate. A partisan argument between George Romney, the Republican governor of Michigan, and President Johnson caused a delay in the deployment of federal troops, but on July 25, Johnson authorized the use of the US Army 82nd and 101st Airborne Divisions to reinforce the eight thousand Michigan Army National Guard troops who were also deployed to restore order.

The Detroit police, 93 percent of whom were white, engaged in well-documented, widespread, and grave misconduct during the rioting. Mugshots showed that detainees suffered many of their injuries after they had been arrested and detained. Three black men were shot dead in cold blood in a motel after police had searched their room and found no weapons. The book *Violence in the Model City* provides nauseating, graphic descriptions of violent, humiliating, and abusive behavior of the police in the arrests and detention of black rioters.[199] Men were treated with the utmost brutal contempt, beaten bloody, viciously kicked, and compared to monkeys. During searches for weapons, women were roughly manhandled, stripped, fondled, and subjected to verbal abuse and lewd comments by police officers while others took pictures.

At the height of the rioting and in response to fears that a general uprising of the entire black population of the city might occur, tanks and machine guns were brought in. Television news showed them deployed in smoke-engulfed streets, littered with looting debris and lined with destroyed and burning buildings and patrolled and swept by troops in full battle gear. It looked very much like a war zone.

In the wake of the riot, the government created the National Advisory Commission on Civil Disorders, also known as the Kerner Commission, to investigate the riot's causes and to recommend steps to correct the problems that had given rise to such events. The Kerner Report, released in February 1968, found that the causes were manifold and wide-ranging but that white racism was behind many of the conditions that contributed to the outbreak of riots. Detroit was in many ways doing better in hiring and promoting blacks

---

[199] Sidney Fine, *Violence in the Model City: The Cavanagh Administration, Race Relations, and the Detroit Riot of 1967* (Ann Arbor, MI: The University of Michigan Press, 1989) pp 240 – 243. (See https://archive.org/details/violenceinmodelc0000fine)

than most other cities, but the racist attitude of its police force was one outstanding shortcoming. Regarding the Detroit police department, which was 93 percent white, the Kerner Commission found that 45 percent of the police force who worked in black neighborhoods had very strong anti-black feelings, and an additional 34 percent were classified as prejudiced.

The commission's report contained scathing criticism of both federal and state authorities for the conditions of housing and health-care services in black areas. Overall, the report provided very little good news and painted the future as grim. The most famous of the conclusions of the Kerner Commission was the following sentence: "Our nation is moving toward two societies, one black, one white—separate and unequal."[200]

Figure 67. The Detroit riots of July 23–24, 1967.

[200] *The Kerner Report: The National Advisory Commission on Civil Disorders* (Princetown, NJ: Princeton University Press, 1968) p. 1

Martin Luther King broadens his views

The black civil rights movement had achieved some decisive legislative victories in 1964 and 1965, but those victories had not substantially improved the lives of blacks in big-city ghettos. Martin Luther King Jr. began to realize that the oppression of blacks was a part of a wider, systemic problem in American society that also held many whites down in hopeless despair because of poverty and a lack of education. He began to address himself to the issue of the economic inequality and powerlessness of millions of Americans, regardless of race. In May 1967, he spoke at a meeting of SCLC leadership and made it clear that his organization needed to take a new approach. His words hint at a radicalization of the group's demands in which the SCLC would focus on the entire structure of American society—not just the injustices blacks experienced:

> I think it is necessary for us to realize that we have moved from the era of civil rights to the era of human rights... When we see that there must be a radical redistribution of economic and political power, then we see that for the last twelve years we have been in a reform movement... That after Selma and the Voting Rights Bill, we moved into a new era, which must be an era of revolution... In short, we have moved into an era where we are called upon to raise certain basic questions about the whole society.[201]

In August of 1967, he again stressed that the struggle was no longer black against white but that there was an urgent need to set aside racial and other differences and to unite in the struggle that was about the common problem:

> One unfortunate thing about [the slogan] Black Power is that it gives priority to race precisely at a time when the impact of automation and other forces have made the economic question fundamental for blacks and whites alike. In this context a slogan "Power for Poor People" would be much more appropriate than the slogan "Black Power."[202]

One can see in the last days of his life that he had broadened his view to encompass the entire world. He was envisioning a worldwide movement that would, like the vision of the Marxists, unite poor and exploited people everywhere to achieve a radical transformation of society. In his last Sunday sermon, he said:

> "There can be no gainsaying of the fact that a great revolution is taking place in the world today... There is a human rights revolution, with the freedom explosion that is taking place all over the world...[203]"

---

[201] https://www.poorpeoplescampaign.org/history/
[202] KAIROS: The Center for Religions, Rights, and Social Justice
https://kairoscenter.org/poor-peoples-campaign-concept-paper/ (Quotation in "The Legacy of MLK's Poor People's Campaign" section.)
[203] Ibid. (Quotation in "Addendum: The 1967–68 Poor People's Campaign)

In the summer of 1967, he began to contemplate another March on Washington—another mass demonstration like the one that had been so successful in 1963. This time it was to be called a Poor People's March—a demonstration for a transformation of the entire economy to fulfill the promises of the American Constitution to create a society with justice and freedom for all. In 1964, President Johnson had declared an official War on Poverty, but its practical results were insignificant. Dr. King and many others realized that no war on poverty could be won without making fundamental changes in the economic system of the nation. In December 1967, King announced plans for another march in the nation's capital to demand such changes:

> We are coming to Washington in a poor people's campaign. Yes, we are going to bring the tired, the poor, the huddled masses... We are coming to demand that the government address itself to the problem of poverty. We read one day: We hold these truths to be self-evident, that all men are created equal, that they are endowed by their creator with certain inalienable rights. That among these are life, liberty, and the pursuit of happiness. But if a man doesn't have a job or an income, he has neither life nor liberty nor the possibility for the pursuit of happiness. He merely exists... We are coming to ask America to be true to the huge promissory note that it signed years ago. And we are coming to engage in dramatic nonviolent action, to call attention to the gulf between promise and fulfillment; to make the invisible visible.

The Poor People's Campaign planned to put forward a petition to the government to pass an "economic bill of rights" that would in an effective way tackle the problem of widespread poverty in the midst of plenty in the nation. This demonstration was not to be just a one-day affair—it would include the setting up of a shantytown of tents on the National Mall between the Lincoln Memorial and the Washington Monument. The tents were to be occupied by fifteen hundred to three thousand campaign participants. Other participants would be housed in private homes and other facilities in the Washington area. The purpose was to keep the demonstration in the news for an extended length of time to make sure that its presence in the nation's capital and its purpose would be noted and discussed by a large percentage of the American population.

The timing of the demonstration was calculated to have the maximum political effect: it would begin on April 22, 1968, and thus would occur in the middle of the primary political campaign of 1968, which was already shaping up to be extremely heated, with civil rights, poverty, and the Vietnam War all being explosive and divisive issues. Dr. King hoped that the daily news of the demonstration would force the various political candidates to take public stands on these issues during their campaigns.

Chapter 8. "Hell No, We Won't Go!"

The protests against the Vietnam war take center stage

In 1968, war-related economic and political problems were beginning to overshadow even the costly riots and the profound domestic social problems that the Johnson administration faced. The opposition to the Vietnam War was becoming extremely vocal and active, breaking apart the Democratic Party and causing millions to lose faith in the entire political system. Johnson had won the 1964 presidential election in a landslide of unprecedented size and had begun his presidency with massive popular support behind his historic landmark legislative victories in Congress. But gradually, anti–Vietnam War sentiments began to undermine his image as a champion of civil rights and social reform. His image was transformed into that of a brutal, amoral warlord, responsible for the death of innumerable defenseless innocents in a campaign of high explosives and firebombs dropped from giant bombers high in the sky. Protest marchers chanted and carried placards in the streets, asking, "LBJ, LBJ, how many kids have you killed today?"

The opposition to the war among young Americans was not expressed only as public protest and demonstrations. A draft system was in effect, and between September 1965 and January 1966, one hundred seventy thousand Americans between the ages of eighteen and twenty-six were drafted. The majority served willingly, others less so, but they decided that a refusal to serve would simply be too costly. Among the one hundred eighty thousand men and women who volunteered for service without being drafted, many volunteered because doing so would give them the best chances of joining a branch of the service that would be relatively safe, such as the coast guard.

For many blacks and poor, uneducated whites, volunteering for military service offered the best chances to obtain an education, secure employment, and perhaps to earn some respect. But for most young whites from more affluent backgrounds, seeking a deferment was the preferred way out. Deferment could in practice be indefinite: if a man reached the age of twenty-six, then his risk of being called up for combat duty was almost nil.

Being a student at a college or university was the most common justification for deferment. By January 1966, two million young Americans had obtained a college deferment. A college education was very expensive—thus, most of those who were granted deferment as students came from the upper economic levels of society. The result was that a disproportionate portion of American combat soldiers in Vietnam was either black or were whites from relatively poor backgrounds.

Some did refuse to be inducted into service after being drafted. Many antiwar demonstrations expressed this refusal. Angrily, the crowds shouted, "Hell no, we won't go!" Some participants emphasized their refusal by burning their draft cards. Refusal to serve could have severe legal consequences, and many fled the country—mainly to Canada—to avoid arrest. One very high-profile case of refusing to serve was that of world heavyweight boxing champion Muhammad Ali, who had become a devout Muslim and a follower of Elijah Muhammad. He declared that he had "no quarrel with the Viet Cong... no Viet Cong called me a nigger."[204] In 1967, he was sentenced to five years in prison, but he was released on appeal after obtaining a religion-based waiver from service. The rest of his sentence was left standing, however: his heavyweight boxing crown was declared forfeited, and he was banned from boxing for three years.

Nobel Peace Prize laureate Martin Luther King Jr. lent his status to the antiwar movement. In his April 4, 1967 speech at Riverside Church in New York, he said:

> Somehow this madness must cease. We must stop now. I speak as a child of God and brother to the suffering poor of Vietnam. I speak for those whose land is being laid waste, whose homes are being destroyed, whose culture is being subverted. I speak for the poor of America who are paying a double price of smashed hopes at home and death and corruption in Vietnam. I speak as a citizen of the world, for the world, as it stands aghast at the path we have taken. I speak as an American to the leaders of my own nation. The great initiative in this war is ours. The initiative to stop must be ours.[205]

To the Johnson administration, the outspoken opposition to the war by a leader with the international prestige and domestic following of Dr. King was a stinging political blow. Many other influential voices joined his in opposition to American policies. Daily television newscasts by reporters on the ground made it evident that the military dictator in Saigon did not have the support of the South Vietnamese people, and the graphic video pieces caused shock and dismay among many Americans who had hitherto not formed a definite opinion on the issue of the war. The nation saw Buddhist monks setting themselves on fire in protest of the war, gruesome scenes of burning villages, and American soldiers with life-threatening wounds being evacuated by helicopters amid hails of flying bullets and exploding artillery shells.

During the 1968 campaign for the presidency, the war and the social unrest it caused were the dominating and most contentious issues. Johnson did not want to add fuel to the fire of antiwar sentiments by raising taxes to pay for the war or his social programs, and the result was budget deficits not seen since World War II. These became an easy target for Republican campaigning.

The timing of events in 1968, both foreign and domestic, could not have been worse for the Democrats. On January 30, the North Vietnamese forces launched what became known as the "Tet Offensive," so named after the Vietnamese New Year holiday of that date. Earlier, American military leaders had assured the Johnson administration that the tide of the war had turned and the North Vietnamese and their South Vietnamese allies, "Viet Cong," were exhausted and had no more offensive capability. The Tet Offensive came as a complete surprise and was a massive, coordinated attack on more than 100 cities and military outposts in South Vietnam. It managed to overrun several important cities, notably the old Vietnamese capital of Hue. After fierce fighting, the Tet offensive was a failure from a purely military perspective but was a stunning political success, proving that the US government was not in control of the situation in Vietnam and had not understood the strength and capabilities of the North Vietnamese and the Viet Cong.

---

[204] Jonathan Eig, Ali: *A Life* (New York: Houghton Mifflin Harcourt Publishing Company, 2017), p. 214.
[205] http://www.informationclearinghouse.info/article2564.htm (Section "This madness must cease") The reader is recommended to read the entire speech.

The credibility of the American government and its policies in Vietnam took a huge blow. Opposition to the Johnson administration shot up as the failure of its intelligence operations and its foreign policy became obvious.

Figure 68. Buddhist monk setting himself on fire to protest the Vietnam War, 1963.

The election campaigns heat up

The Republican strategy for the upcoming elections would focus on winning the support of conservatives with promises to roll back some of Johnson's so-called socialist programs, such as his Great Society suite of programs, and to lower taxes. Still, the Republicans hoped that by further shutting off tax revenues, they could demonstrate to the American people that Johnson's ambitious social projects were unaffordable. Capitalizing on the widespread disapproval of the Johnson government's conduct of the war in Vietnam, the Republicans also implied that if a Republican president were elected, he would bring the war to a rapid conclusion. Exactly how was not specified, but many Americans felt that the nation had become bogged down in Vietnam, and a new approach was needed. Ending the costly war would also end a spiraling increase of the budget deficit—an issue Republicans were traditionally concerned about.

The first primary election of 1968, that of New Hampshire, which was held the second week of March, showed how deeply unpopular the war was becoming. A senator from Minnesota, Eugene "Gene" McCarthy, who was previously unknown nationally, came close to winning the Democratic primary on the strength of his opposition to the war. McCarthy, a soft-spoken but engaging speaker, attracted a large youthful following that the press had dubbed the "Children's Crusade." His campaign motto — "Come Clean with Gene!"—

alluded to the moral morass that he and his supporters felt America was sinking into through its actions in Vietnam.

The results shook up both the electorate and the leadership of the Democratic Party. Seldom had a sitting president been challenged so strongly from within his own party. McCarthy showed himself to be an unexpectedly strong vote-getter. However, only four days after the New Hampshire primary, an even bigger threat to the renomination of Lyndon Johnson as the Democratic candidate in the presidential election appeared when Robert Kennedy announced his candidacy. Kennedy was John F. Kennedy's brother and the attorney general in the Kennedy administration. He said that he entered the contest not to compete with McCarthy but to be "in harmony with McCarthy" regarding the Vietnam War. His motivation for joining the race may have been his surprise at the strength of the antiwar vote as well as his conviction that he would be a stronger candidate than McCarthy for that cause.

The Johnson administration realized that the war threatened not only to cost the Democrats the election in the fall but also to wreck the entire democratic process in the election year. Also, it was doing enormous damage to America's image in the world. The world did not see America's military machine in Vietnam as a tool for protecting freedom and democracy. It saw it as a brutal and unwarranted invasion of a nation torn by civil war, where America had taken the side of a dictator and a regime that were simply vestiges of French colonial rule holding on to power by force against a popularly supported national unification movement. Johnson tried hard to achieve an end to the hostilities via negotiations to enable the withdrawal of American forces, but the North Vietnamese would not agree to the proposed basis for negotiations. Their unwavering goal was to reunite North and South Vietnam as agreed on with the French in the Geneva accord of 1954.

Frustrated and heartbroken by what was happening to the nation and his vision of the Great Society, Johnson took an unprecedented and astonishing step: he announced that he was not going to seek the re-nomination as president. Instead, he was going to devote all his time to try to achieve peace—both domestically and in Vietnam.

On March 31, 1968, he scheduled a major television appearance in prime time to brief the nation on his plans. With a stony face, but with a voice that betrayed great anguish, he spoke about the situation domestically and in Vietnam:

> With America's sons in the fields far away, with America's future under challenge right here at home, with our hopes and the world's hopes for peace in the balance every day, I do not believe that I should devote an hour or a day of my time to any personal partisan causes or to any duties other than the awesome duties of this office—the presidency of your country.
>
> Accordingly, I shall not seek, and I will not accept, the nomination of my party for another term as your president.[206]

---

[206] Text:https://www.presidency.ucsb.edu/documents/the-presidents-address-the-nation-announcing-steps-limit-the-war-vietnam-and-reporting-his

The shock to the nation was immense. Many were jubilant, seeing the move as a victory for their antiwar, anti-Johnson campaigns. Others were frightened; it seemed as if the captain was abandoning the ship in the middle of the storm. Was the situation so hopeless? What would happen next? Still others were curious about what the immediate political ramifications were: What was Johnson going to leave to others to handle for the remainder of his term? Would a shake-up in administration personnel occur, or would any special office be created?

On April 2, 1968, Wisconsin held its primary, which was won by Eugene McCarthy—underscoring the fact that the war was destroying the Johnson presidency. The contest of the primaries on the Democratic side became one between McCarthy and Kennedy, who were both strongly opposed to the war. Only fourteen states held primaries, however. In the rest of the states, the Democratic Party machine piled up electoral votes for Vice President Hubert Humphrey, who did not enter any primaries and could hardly come out in opposition to the policies of his own president. A Gallup poll on June 1 revealed that nationwide, Humphrey was the favorite choice of Democratic Party officials.

Chapter 9. The Cities Explode in Riots, and the Nation Elects a Law-and-Order President

The cities erupt in fiery chaos when MLK is assassinated

The inhabitants of the centers of most large cities did not have to read the Kerner Report to see the problems it identified. Despite the report's grave warnings, little was being done to improve conditions in the inner cities. "White flight" from the cities to the suburbs was already a fact, and the riots created new fears and resentments that only accelerated the trend. The inner cities saw poverty and unemployment increase once investments there started to look like losing propositions, and white businesses began to move away. Whatever government programs were implemented to improve the inner-city environments were seldom able to counteract this trend. De facto segregation increased rather than decreased almost everywhere. In many cities, only a spark was needed to cause an explosion of the frustrations, hopelessness, and anger of black residents. Right in the middle of the presidential campaign, such a spark was struck.

Not much more than a month after the release of the Kerner Report, the nation was shaken by the most widespread and destructive rioting in its history. It was the greatest outbreak of violence in the nation since the Civil War. The initial spark was the assassination of Martin Luther King Jr. on April 4, 1968, at the Lorraine Hotel in Memphis, Tennessee. King was in Memphis in support of striking black sanitation workers, who were paid significantly less than the already poorly paid white workers. The day before, April 3, he had delivered his "Mountaintop" speech, a highly emotional speech delivered in his inimitable, deliberate but intense style, where he predicted his own death but spoke of his jubilant conviction that his cause would succeed:

And then I got to Memphis. And some began to say the threats... or talk about the threats that were out [there]. What would happen to me from some of our sick white brothers?

Well, I don't know what will happen now. We've got some difficult days ahead. But it doesn't matter with me now. Because I've been to the mountaintop... And I don't mind... Like anybody, I would like to live a long life. Longevity has its place. But I'm not concerned about that now. *I just want to do God's will.* And He's allowed me to go up to the mountain. And I've looked over. And I've *seen* the promised land... I may not get there with you. But I want you to know tonight, that we, as a people, will get to the promised land!... And so I'm happy, tonight. I'm not worried about *anything.* I'm not fearing *any* man. *My eyes have seen the glory of the coming of the Lord!*[207]

---

[207] The full text of the "Mountain Top" speech is available at
http://www.americanrhetoric.com/speeches/mlkivebeentothemountaintop.htm

A suspect was quickly named in the shooting: James Earl Ray, a fugitive from the Missouri State Penitentiary who had stayed at a rooming house across the street from the Lorraine Hotel and had fired from the window of his room. An intense manhunt began, and on June 8, Ray was caught at Heathrow Airport in London and extradited to the United States. It seemed rather peculiar that he had made it to London. How did he, a fugitive, obtain a passport, and where did he get the money to travel? How did he expect to support himself in England? Conspiracy theories immediately sprang up about him being hired and supported by others, but Ray always claimed to have acted totally on his own.[208] He pleaded guilty on March 10, 1969 and was sentenced to ninety-nine years in the Tennessee State Penitentiary, where he died on April 23, 1998, at the age of seventy.

When the news about King's assassination broke, full-scale rioting broke out in more than one hundred cities. In many of these places, the local police forces were quickly overwhelmed, and both National Guard troops and federal forces were called in. In Washington, President Johnson called in more than thirteen thousand federal troops, making it the largest occupation of any city by federal troops since the Civil War. Marines armed with machine guns guarded the Capitol building, and army troops from the Third Infantry surrounded the White House.

The worst-hit cities were Baltimore, Washington, Chicago, and (again) Detroit. In these cities, the rioting started in the evening of the assassination or the evening after. The inner cities were devastated, and thousands of buildings were destroyed. Thanks to new training and orders to the military forces, the number of deaths were limited. In Baltimore, the rioting saw fifty-four hundred arrests but only six deaths. On the other hand, cleanup and reconstruction took a long time in most cities, and some of the hardest-hit areas would remain economically unproductive for decades. In Washington, the U Street corridor would remain partly ruined until the 1990s.

In Baltimore, Governor Spiro Agnew took a hard line toward the black community, which in Maryland contained a substantial middle class and many professionals. In a televised speech, the Republican governor spoke to black leaders, urging them to control "your people," as if blacks were not "his" people. Blacks, hearing the expressions "you people" and "your people," needed to hear no more to understand the governor. His already poor rating among blacks dipped even further, but many conservative and frightened whites saw him as a courageous and straight-talking leader who put the blame for the out-of-control situation where it belonged. His reputation spread among conservative Republicans and caught the attention of Richard Nixon, who was campaigning for election as president. Some historians credit Agnew's speech with gaining him the vice presidency.

Not all the riots were motivated entirely by the assassination of Dr. King. Anger over local conditions also triggered some of the riots, and outbreaks occurred over a period of almost two months following the assassination.

---

[208] In December 1978, the House Select Committee on Assassinations determined that Ray was the killer. However, it concluded that there likely had been a conspiracy to kill King, most probably involving Ray's brothers John and Jerry. A later investigation by the U.S. Department of Justice concluded in June 2000 that there was no evidence for new theories of a wider plot to kill Dr. King, possibly involving J. Edgar Hoover and the FBI.

Figure 69. Baltimore in flames in the wake of Martin Luther King Jr.'s assassination, April 5, 1968.

Figure 70. Soldiers and firefighters in the aftermath of rioting in Washington, DC, April 1968.

Figure 71. Burning buildings on Chicago's West Side, April 5, 1968.

The assassination of Robert Kennedy

The results of the spring primary elections gave some reason for hope for the black population. The leading Democratic candidates were adamantly opposed to the war in Vietnam as well as being strongly in favor of more decisive action domestically to improve the living conditions of black citizens. The voter turnout in the Democratic primaries appeared to signal a possible Democratic victory in the November general election. On May 28, McCarthy won the important Oregon primary, and on June 4, Robert Kennedy came back with a narrow win in California of 46 versus 42 percent. But the hopes of a Democratic victory in November were soon shattered. Celebrating his victory at the Ambassador Hotel in Los Angeles, Robert Kennedy was fatally wounded by a shot from a pistol fired by Sirhan Sirhan, a young Palestinian immigrant who hated Kennedy because of Kennedy's record of support of Israel. As in the case of the assassination of his older brother, John Kennedy, the circumstances of Robert Kennedy's death have been the subject of some dispute, and even Robert's son, Robert F. Kennedy Jr, has expressed doubts that Sirhan was the only person involved, and perhaps not the actual shooter.[209]

---

[209] https://www.washingtonpost.com/news/retropolis/wp/2018/05/26/who-killed-bobby-kennedy-his-son-rfk-jr-doesnt-believe-it-was-sirhan-sirhan/

The death of Robert Kennedy threw the Democratic Party into renewed turmoil. Disgusted and frightened by what had happened, McCarthy withdrew his candidacy, leaving his supporters stunned and eventually flocking to another antiwar candidate, George McGovern. Many of Kennedy's supporters attempted to draft Kennedy' younger brother, Edward "Teddy" Kennedy, but Edward did not want to enter the political fray so soon after his brother's death. That left the antiwar campaign almost leaderless at the top political levels since the primary season was over, and the relatively unknown McGovern had neither the time nor the money to run a viable campaign.

Many people feared a renewed outbreak of city riots since Robert Kennedy had been strongly in favor of enforcing the Civil Rights Act and the Voting Rights Act and was the overwhelming favorite among black voters. Those riots did not materialize, but antiwar sentiments were reaching a fever pitch on college campuses and produced a constant drumbeat of demonstrations and angry speeches.

The Poor People's Campaign

The long-planned Poor People's Campaign added to the political problems piling up for the Democrats. The War on Poverty that Johnson had launched with great fanfare in 1964 had produced some major legislation, including (from 1964) the Economic Opportunity Act and the Food Stamp Act and (from 1965) the Elementary and Secondary Education Act and the Social Security Act. In the annual State of the Union speech on January 8, 1964, Johnson had stated that "our aim is not only to relieve the symptom of poverty, but to cure it and, above all, to prevent it."[210]

Such an ambitious goal was reminiscent of John F. Kennedy's inspiring promise to land a man on the moon by the end of the decade. By 1968, despite all the troubles the United States was experiencing both domestically and in the war in Vietnam, the moon-landing program appeared to be on schedule. The War on Poverty was equally ambitious in its scope. It was launched with the intention of winning it, but this "war" would obviously be costly. The programs launched as part of the war became the targets of intense opposition by the Republicans, who described them as socialist and said that they would be responsible for creating a permanent parasitic welfare class of lazy, irresponsible people and would benefit primarily blacks.

Not surprisingly, the effects of these programs did not immediately meet the high expectations of the impoverished citizens. Frustration grew and made a Poor People's Campaign inevitable. Even after its foremost advocate, Martin Luther King Jr., was assassinated, and all major cities were rocked by devastating riots, preparations for the second March on Washington got underway—albeit later than initially planned.

In terms of demographics, the march was a success. From across the nation, it drew white, black, Latino, and Native American participants who, for the first time, identified themselves as belonging to the same "tribe"—namely, poor people. A ramshackle shantytown named Resurrection City was hastily constructed on the National Mall in Washington in accordance with the plans laid in December 1967. It was built using unpainted plywood sheets and tents, and for six weeks in May and June of 1968, it became

---

[210] http://www.presidency.ucsb.edu/ws/?pid=26787 (Quotation from Section III of the speech)

the home for about three thousand people. Others found temporary living quarters in schools, churches, and rooms provided by sympathetic private citizens.

The weather became a stress factor. It was hot and rainy, making the grounds of the Mall a mucky mess and the poorly constructed housing facilities uncomfortable and a health hazard. Sanitary facilities were primitive and insufficient, and providing food and drink for the inhabitants of this eyesore on the Mall was reportedly costing the arrangers $27,000 a week. Money was running low, and Congress failed to respond to the leaders of the Poor People's Campaign about their demands. Campaign leadership made repeated efforts to meet with congressional representatives, with no success. The circumstances of the event were beginning to cause frustration and demoralization among the participants.

Figure 72. The Resurrection City shantytown during the Poor People's
Campaign, National Mall, Washington, DC, June 1968.

Following King's assassination on April 4, 1968, Ralph Abernathy had taken the leadership role of the Poor People's Campaign. On June 19, he led a "Solidarity Day" rally to emphasize the common cause of all the various groups of participants. The march was the only event worthy of being called a success. It drew a crowd of between fifty and one hundred thousand people, although many of those in attendance might have come out of curiosity rather than any sympathy with the cause. The Poor People's Campaign failed to produce the hoped-for progress on economic and political issues.

On June 24, more than a thousand police officers were sent into the camp to clear it and to remove the remaining inhabitants. Two hundred and eighty-eight people were arrested, including Abernathy. Some of the police reported being hit with rocks, which caused one hundred more police to be sent in wearing riot gear and responding with tear gas. To forestall a wider disturbance, the mayor of Washington then declared a state of emergency in the city and ordered four hundred and fifty National Guard troops to begin patrolling the city at night.

Figure 73. Cleanup on the Mall after Resurrection City, June 1968.

The end of Resurrection City created angry feelings on all sides and an unsightly mess on the Mall. The campaign made an overall bad impression on most of the American public, as it ended in disorder and violence and with no significant positive results. Fearing that a major riot could break out in the context of the Poor People's Campaign, Johnson ordered twenty thousand army soldiers to be prepared for a full-scale occupation of Washington if demonstrators attempted to seize important buildings.

Conservative Americans flock to Richard Nixon

An increasing number of white citizens were enraged by the constant demonstrations, riots, and social disorder, and they demanded more forceful measures from government authorities to arrest troublemakers and restore order. Many of those who wanted more forceful measures were middle-class manual laborers. They became stereotyped as construction workers wearing protective headgear, and therefore became known as "hard hats." Many were members of organized labor and thus were traditionally Democratic voters. They were also traditionally profoundly patriotic and nationalistic and deeply resented the accusations of antiwar groups and black activists that there was something fundamentally wrong with American society. Their motto was "America! Love it or leave it!" The motto proclaimed their proud allegiance to everything that in their minds America stood for and alluded to the lack of patriotism and courage of the draft resisters who were escaping to Canada and Europe to avoid the draft. It also implied "Good riddance!" Hard hats were beginning to turn to the Republican Party, whose leading candidate for nomination as the Republican presidential candidate was Richard Nixon.

Richard Milhous Nixon was a well-known figure in American politics. He had been President Eisenhower's vice president for eight years and had narrowly lost the presidential election in 1960 to John F. Kennedy. He campaigned as a champion of law and order who would restore peace domestically and somehow bring the conflict in Vietnam to an honorable end. Nixon took advantage of the disaffection in the traditionally Democratic ranks and asked Congress not to give in to the demands that black leaders had made.

His message found a great reception not only in the South but also among conservatives and hard hats. In the view of most white Southerners, as well as many white factory workers in the large cities of the North and West, the civil rights marches and demonstrations, and the riots in the cities, were nothing but black and "commie" leftist troublemaking. To these voters, Nixon's campaign motto of "law and order" meant a clampdown on rampant disorder and rebelliousness. Nixon took advantage of these circumstances without acknowledging any racial connotations.

At the Republican National Convention in Miami Beach, Florida, held in early August 1968, Nixon won the nomination as the Republican presidential candidate on the first ballot. Due to the headline-grabbing sensations coming in a steady stream from the war, riots, assassinations, and the Democratic Party's troubles, the Republicans had escaped scrutiny and scandal during the primary elections. In contrast to the cacophony of shrill accusations and arguments flying between feuding factions of the Democratic Party, the Republicans appeared calm, confident, and united in their ideology, which was cautiously conservative and emphasized the restoration of domestic order.

At the Republican National Convention, Nixon announced that he had selected Spiro Agnew, the Maryland governor, as his running mate. Conservatives in both parties—especially whites in the South—had an image of Agnew as a tough law-and-order man due to his strong condemnation of black leadership during the rioting in Baltimore. At the time, the choice of Agnew seemed like a brilliant move. It was part of what became known as Nixon's "Southern strategy."

Four years earlier, a political landslide had transformed the South from a solid bastion of the Democratic Party into a region captured by the Republicans. The reason had been the federal government's strong support for the black civil rights movement during the Kennedy and Johnson administrations, which contrasted sharply with Goldwater's support for states' rights and advocacy of a forceful offensive in Vietnam. Goldwater's supporters wanted a quick victory, followed by a return home of American forces. Nixon solidified the Republicans' grip on the South by his choice of vice president and his promises to somehow achieve peace in Vietnam.

Nixon had lost the 1960 presidential election to John F. Kennedy by the narrowest of margins. Many attributed his loss to his physical appearance during the televised debate with Kennedy. It was the first televised debate between two candidates for the presidency, and Nixon's handlers showed that they were inexperienced and did not understand the nature of the medium of television. On the TV screen at home, the debate became a beauty contest: TV cameras showed close-up shots of the debaters' faces as they listened to the arguments made by the opponent, and viewers could study both the body language and the eyes of the speaker as he made his point. The spoken words became little more than the background to the fascinating visuals. In the heat and brilliance of the television studio, the handsome, glamorous Kennedy came across as calm and confident, while Nixon was visibly perspiring and looked unshaven, pale, and flustered.

By 1968, the handlers had learned this lesson well. Television coverage of the 1968 Republican National Convention showed Nixon smiling confidently, and his policies spoke to that segment of the American people who just wanted things to calm down and go back to normal: the so-called silent majority. Such normalcy meant different things to different people but promised a restoration of peace, orderliness, and respect for traditional American values and customs.

The 1968 Democratic National Convention becomes a political disaster

The contrast to the Democratic National Convention, which took place in Chicago from August 26 to 29, could not have been greater. Mayor Richard Daley and the Chicago Democratic Party machine did not tolerate dissent and disorder, and together they ruled the city with an iron hand. Daley had handed Martin Luther King Jr. his first significant defeat while Dr. King was attempting to break down the strongly segregated pattern of housing and employment in the city. Now, only months after the devastating riot that had caused so much material and political damage to the city following King's assassination, the mayor was firmly determined to keep both the convention and the city orderly and peaceful. As mayor, he wanted to show the strength, competence, and discipline of his city administration—and as a Democrat, he planned to dismiss the Republicans' charges that the Democrats had become the party of radical left-wing splinter groups who were unable to keep peace even among themselves, much less in the nation and the world at large.

Daley knew that protests and demonstrations were inevitable. Radical groups of various types had announced that they would be in the city and would make their voices heard. The antiwar organizations were diverse, and some had conflicting agendas. Some groups actively supported McCarthy or Robert Kennedy for president, while others supported neither. At a conference of antiwar groups at Lake Villa, Illinois, on March 23, 1968, plans were worked out for coordinated demonstrations.

Not all antiwar groups were part of this effort at coordination. A group called Youth International Party (YIP) wanted to have a separate "Youth Festival" in Chicago during the convention. They became known as yippies to distinguish them from the far less politically focused hippies. The leaders of YIP included Abbie Hoffman and Jerry Rubin, both of whom would shortly achieve notoriety, and they were hoping to achieve a gathering of as many as one hundred thousand people.

YIP attempted to obtain a permit from the city of Chicago for this gathering, but Mayor Daley, realizing that a crowd of young activists that size would be uncontrollable, turned down the application. News of the planned festival had already spread among the YIP ranks, however, and a large number of yippies arrived in Chicago anyway.

Daley was perfectly aware of the sharp differences among the official Democratic delegates to the convention and the intense feelings among the supporters of the various presidential candidates. The potential for trouble was unquestionably there inside the convention itself, and he did not want a repeat of the scandalous and divisive chaos of the previous Democratic National Convention in 1964, which had seen the party passionately divided on the issue of whether to seat the all-white delegation of the regular Mississippi Democrats or the mixed white and black delegation of the Mississippi Freedom Democratic Party, the MFDP. Daley had limited authority to control what went on inside the convention hall, but he did have full authority to police the streets of his city, and he wanted to prepare for all eventualities.

It was obvious that the convention would become the target of protests and demonstrations outside, and Daley gave orders to his very loyal police force of almost twelve thousand officers that they must quell any and all disorderly behavior by demonstrators. They must take rapid, forceful action to suppress any disturbance before things got out of hand. To make sure he had enough forces at his disposal, Daley obtained the support of seventy-five hundred army troops and an equal number of members of the Illinois National Guard, plus one thousand men from the Secret Service. In total, he was in command of a force numbering twenty-eight thousand.

Daley's tactics backfired disastrously. On the Sunday before the official start of the convention, violent confrontations between police and protesters took place in Lincoln Park, close to the Amphitheater building where the convention was held. To evict the protesters from the park, police in gas masks moved in, throwing tear-gas grenades at the crowd and assaulting them in force with billy clubs. Many reporters were there to record what was happening, and the police saw them as enemies. Seventeen reporters were attacked but were able to get good video as well as still photos of the police assault. The results were broadcast and printed by all major national newspapers and television stations. The behavior of the police seemed shockingly brutal and undisciplined, causing the media to refer to the event as a "police riot."

President Johnson had decided not to attend the convention, fearing that his presence there would raise the risk of out-of-control antiwar demonstrations. Vice President Hubert Humphrey arrived with enough delegates assigned by party officials in nonprimary states to clinch the nomination on the first ballot, but he could not be sure of having sewn up the nomination because many of his delegates were being challenged by others in their states. The mood on the floor of the convention was ugly, because Humphrey, being the sitting vice president, was closely tied to the war policies of the president.

Senator Inouye of Hawaii gave the keynote address speech, and it was not the usual cheery party pep talk. Instead, the senator spoke of a grim list of serious problems the nation faced both domestically and abroad. It was a relevant introduction to what would follow, which was a debate on the party "plank"—the policy statement that the Democrats would advocate in the general election.

Figure 74. The media-dubbed "police riot" at the Democratic Party convention in Chicago, 1968.

The organizers of the convention knew that the most contentious debate would concern the "peace" plank—the policies recommended by peace activists within the party. The format of the debate was structured to minimize the risk of openly hostile arguments. Each side had only one hour to present its case before the convention would take a vote. In an attempt to minimize TV viewership of what could still become an embarrassing display of party disunity, the debate was initially slotted for late in the evening, past prime time. The antiwar delegates strenuously protested this timing, so the debate was rescheduled to take place in the afternoon the following day.

The presentation of the two contrasting policy proposals and the subsequent voting went peacefully. The Humphrey delegates were in the majority, and the voting came out in favor of the policies with which Humphrey was associated. The delegates from California and New York, favoring the peace proposal, then rose in protest and began singing in unison the hymn made famous by the black civil rights movement, "We Shall Overcome." They began marching around the convention floor and were soon joined by other delegations. In their hunt for scoops and sensations, television camera crews eagerly followed every sign of disorder and angry argument and broadcast them to the nation.

While decorum was breaking down inside the convention hall, violent clashes between demonstrators and police continued outside. Outraged at the brutality of the police, Connecticut Senator Abraham Ribicoff, who entered the name of George McGovern as the Democratic candidate for president, added a spur-of-the-moment statement to his speech: "With George McGovern as president of the United States, we wouldn't have Gestapo tactics in the streets of Chicago!" That infuriated Mayor Daley, who was already upset at the breakdown of his carefully laid plans for keeping order. Daley shook his fist at Ribicoff and shouted an invective that started with an F but could not be heard clearly by reporters over the noise in the room. Daley, who was of Irish extraction, later claimed to have said "Faker," which was supposedly a serious insult in the world of Irish politics.

The violence reached a peak on Wednesday, August 28, with what would become known as the "Battle of Michigan Avenue." A protest march was blocked by a massed force of police, who beat everyone within reach with their billy clubs. Many of them, including innocent bystanders and reporters, were sufficiently injured to require medical help. Medical personnel who happened to be at the scene were also beaten when they attempted to provide service.

Figure 75. The "Battle of Michigan Avenue," Chicago, August 28, 1968.

Further violence erupted on the final day of the convention. Protest marchers tried twice to reach the convention but were beaten back by police. A barricade was put up around the building to prevent protest marchers from reaching the convention building and perhaps entering it and creating chaos on the convention floor. Formal, official credentials were required to be allowed through the checkpoints.

Despite all the disorder and acrimony in the convention, the Democratic Party managed to elect Hubert Humphrey as its presidential candidate and Edmund Muskie, who had placed Humphrey's name in nomination, as his vice-presidential candidate. At that point, the top priority of the party was to win the upcoming general election, so George McGovern, the antiwar candidate, toned down his attacks on the policies of Lyndon Johnson.

The Democratic National Convention and the angry confrontations both inside and outside the convention building did nothing to convince voters that the Democrats were capable of handling the challenges facing the nation. What transpired severely damaged the reputation of Mayor Daley. A subsequent study of the violence during the demonstrations placed most of the blame for what had happened on the police, and thus also on Mayor Daley, who was in command.[211] In its summary, the study report stated that police violence was "unrestrained and indiscriminate." Daley, angered at this indictment of his city's administration, made public his disagreement with the report and gave a pay rise to the entire police department.

The scandal of the 1968 Democratic National Convention did not end with the convention itself. Highly publicized trials of some of the leaders of the demonstrations continued to keep the media spotlight on the events following the convention and to keep the feelings of the members of antiwar organizations inflamed. Among eight indicted demonstrators were some of the most well-known young political activists in the nation, including John Froines, Lee Weiner, Rennie Davis of the SDS, the head of the SDS Tom Hayden, Jerry Rubin and Abbie Hoffman of YIP; David Dellinger, chairman of the National Mobilization Committee to End the War in Vietnam; and Bobby Seale, one of the founders of the Black Panthers and the only black member of the group. They were at first tried together, but because of Seale's repeated angry outbursts in court and his arguments with the judge, he was separated from the other seven and tried separately. The remaining seven would achieve notoriety as the "Chicago Seven."

The proceedings in the trial were full of drama and dragged on and on. A jury verdict was not returned until February 18, 1970. Bobby Seale had earlier been sentenced to four years in prison for contempt of court. Rennie Davis, David Dellinger, Tom Hayden, Abbie Hoffman, and Jerry Rubin were convicted of having crossed state lines with the intent to incite a riot and were given five years in prison each, while the remaining two were acquitted. It is noteworthy that none of the defendants were convicted of having committed any crime during the demonstrations and marches. Their defense lawyers, William Kunstler and Leonard Weinglass, were also convicted of contempt of court. Kunstler, during a heated exchange with the judge, had said that the trial was nothing but a "legal lynching" and held the judge responsible for what was going on. All convictions of the Chicago Seven but not that of Bobby Seale, the original eighth defendant, were overturned on appeal in 1972.

The 1968 general election becomes a blow to the civil rights movement

With both the Republican and Democratic National Conventions over, the general election campaign took off. The Republicans appeared to be ahead following the embarrassing spectacle the Democrats had created. Humphrey was at a disadvantage because of his connection to the Vietnam War, which a minority of the American people now felt the Johnson administration had handled well.

But Nixon was not able to entirely erase the poor impression he had made in his debate against Kennedy eight years earlier. His campaign lost significant momentum when Johnson announced that he was going to

---

[211] Daniel Walker, director of the Chicago Study Team, *Rights in Conflict: The violent confrontation of demonstrators and police in the parks and streets of Chicago during the week of the Democratic National Convention of 1968*, submitted to the National Commission on the Causes and Prevention of Violence, December 1, 1968.

halt the bombing in Vietnam because negotiations and a peace deal were becoming possible. The race for the presidency looked like it might be a close one.

The closeness of the contest provided an opportunity for Alabama governor George Wallace to jump into it as a third-party candidate. Wallace had no illusions that he could win the presidency. However, he was still a hero in most of the South and believed he could win enough states there to prevent either of the two leading candidates from obtaining sufficient electoral votes of his own to become president. Wallace could become a "kingmaker," negotiating with the two others to swing his electoral votes to whomever would promise the most to him in terms of political concessions along the lines that Wallace wanted.

As his vice-presidential candidate, Wallace selected Curtis LeMay, an air force general with a very aggressive stance regarding what America should do in Vietnam. LeMay thought a few atom bombs might bring a quick end to the war. His philosophy was simple: "If you kill enough of them, they'll stop fighting." He advocated "bombing them back into the stone age." Such talk horrified most of the nation, but that did not worry Wallace. It sounded good to Southern conservatives—almost like something Goldwater might have said four years earlier when his tough talk on Vietnam had helped him win the South. A win in a few Southern states might be all that Wallace needed to block either Humphrey or Nixon from outright victory.

Wallace, who was a gifted orator with a humorous, blunt, and feisty style, coined many memorable expressions and phrases. He was what he claimed to be, a man of the people—a no-nonsense, plainspoken man with nothing but contempt for "pointy-head liberals" who were so removed from the practical aspects of everyday life that they "couldn't even park a bicycle." Wallace was a populist demagogue and an opponent of big federal government and spending. Although he was in favor of heavy bombing of North Vietnam, he was opposed to big new military programs to modernize military equipment. Regarding the aging fleet of B-52 bombers used in Vietnam, he saw no need to develop more modern planes. He asked, "Why does the Air Force need expensive new bombers? Have the people we've been bombing over the years been complaining?"

He accused the white liberal establishment in Washington of being hypocritical on the race issue. As the nation's capital was becoming mostly black, whites were moving to the suburbs, as they were doing in other large cities. Wallace scoffed, "They are building a bridge over the Potomac for all the white liberals who are fleeing to Virginia." (The Washington suburbs in northern Virginia were almost all white, and de facto segregation in housing persisted.)

He was talking tough about political demonstrators who disturbed the daily lives of ordinary people. He promised, "If a demonstrator ever lays down in front of my car, it'll be the last car he ever lays down in front of."

By using such language, he was stealing some of Nixon's thunder on the issue of law and order. It brought him a lot of support from many working-class people in the North and Midwest in addition to his solid Southern base. Racism was by no means dead in those areas, but the anti-American and strongly leftist language of antiwar protesters was an even stronger factor in turning the "average Joe" against the protesters and demanding that stronger efforts be made to punish troublemakers.

Wallace's entry into the campaign made the election results difficult to predict. It was anyone's guess as to how much support he would siphon away from the two main candidates, and which of them would be hurt the most. Reflecting back after the election, *Time* magazine noted that the chances of the Democrats winning had been slim: "In August, the party that nominated Humphrey at Chicago was a shambles. The old Democratic coalition was disintegrating, with untold numbers of blue-collar workers responding to Wallace's blandishments, Negroes threatening to sit out the election, liberals disaffected over the Vietnam War, the South lost. The war chest was almost empty, and the party's machinery, neglected by Lyndon Johnson, creaked in disrepair."[212]

Wallace was not the only candidate who would draw Democratic voters away from Humphrey. Comedian Dick Gregory was a heroic figure to many blacks because of his participation in various demonstrations, and his cutting wit and logic sliced to pieces the policies of the white power structures. He was a write-in candidate for the presidency. A white comedian, Pat Paulsen, was another write-in candidate. He was immensely popular among white students for his droll but devastating satirical comments on Johnson's war policies. He was a frequent guest on the top-rated TV comedy show *The Smothers Brothers Show*. The YIP offered yet another write-in candidate—one that was wholly imaginary—named "Pigasus." The yippies wanted to make a political statement that "one pig is as good as any other." Numerous new small parties also offered candidates, but they had an insignificant impact.

Wallace's overall impact was probably greatest on the Republican side. But he failed in his goal to deny the outright win to either the Democratic or the Republican Party. Nixon received 43.4 percent of the popular vote, while Humphrey received 42.7 percent. Wallace's American Independent Party pulled a respectable 13.5 percent of the vote nationwide and won five Southern states. But the American voting system is not a direct system where the person receiving the majority of the popular vote is the winner. Each state is contested individually for a set of electoral voters, with the number of such voters determined by the size of the state's population. What counts is the total number of electoral votes, not the popular vote, and Nixon won 301 electoral votes versus Humphrey's 191 and Wallace's 46. No other candidates won any state or any electoral votes. Nixon, therefore, had more than 50 percent of the electoral vote, making him the outright winner with no need for support by electoral votes for Wallace.

The outcome was a disappointment for Wallace, but it still allowed him to show that he was a force to be reckoned with nationally, not just in the South. Having received so many votes in the North and Midwest further enhanced his standing in the South. But his selection of Curtis LeMay as his running mate cost him the vote of many people outside the South who could not see someone as warlike as LeMay being "a heartbeat away from the presidency." A more moderate running mate would have increased Wallace's vote count in the rest of the country. Whether he could then have denied Nixon an outright victory is still doubtful.

Divided opinions on the meaning of the 1968 elections

Some historians, mainly those of the conservative political persuasion, argue that the election of Richard Nixon was a significant political event that broke a steady trend that had begun during the Depression with the election of Franklin D. Roosevelt in 1932. In this view, FDR's New Deal had set America on a leftist path

---

[212] "The Loser. A Near Run Thing", *Time* Magazine, November 15, 1968, Article p. 1

that culminated with Johnson's plans for the Great Society. The trend had greatly expanded the power of the federal government and its influence on the lives of all Americans. That era included only one Republican administration—that of Dwight Eisenhower—and even the Eisenhower administration had used federal power in 1957 to enforce the 1954 Supreme Court order to abolish school segregation. At the time, the Supreme Court was heavily weighted in a liberal direction, since so many of the judges had been appointed and confirmed by the Roosevelt administration.

The 1968 election, according to the above view, represented a reaction against the liberal trend. In the view of conservatives, Nixon's election was the result of the reaction of the people against the loss of individual freedom they had experienced due to the expanded power of the federal government. As previously mentioned, in his inaugural speech in 1963 as the governor of Alabama, George Wallace had stated, "I draw the line in the dust and toss the gauntlet before the feet of tyranny, and I say, segregation now, segregation tomorrow and segregation forever."[213] He was referring to the federal court's orders to abolish segregation despite the strong opposition of Alabama voters. Now Nixon's Southern strategy and his campaign theme of law and order hinted at a more conservative states' rights–oriented political philosophy.

Such an interpretation of the 1968 election results does not recognize the disintegration of the broad Democratic coalition built by FDR during the Depression, including organized labor, poor rural Southerners and Midwesterners, and liberal, college-educated Americans. The disintegration of the coalition was not a wholesale swing from the left toward the right by the American voters. It was caused in part by the loss of the already conservative South to the Republicans over the issue of desegregation, and in part by the strong opposition to the Vietnam War among the young. A third factor was the successful appeal by both Wallace and Nixon to patriotism, and anger over the disorder, destruction, and "moral decay" caused by demonstrations, riots, and hippies.

Wallace based his campaign on fears of racial integration and not fundamentally on opposition to the trend of modern democratic socialism that was visible in almost all industrial Western nations by this point. Southerners resented federal power primarily because it threatened to demolish the walls of segregation. In other words, Nixon's victory was not predominantly a backlash against "socialism" and "liberalism." Instead, it was a rejection of Hubert Humphrey, tainted by his identification with the administration of Lyndon Johnson, just as the 2016 election of Donald Trump was in large part a rejection of Hillary Clinton as a person, and for many whites in the South, due to simmering anger over having had eight years of a black president. In 1968, many young Americans were frustrated by the failure of the nation to fulfill the promises of its egalitarian constitutional precepts and were opposed to its involvement in a distant war. Many other previously Democratic voters, who were upset by the government's failure to halt the breakdown of order in society, voted for Nixon in the belief that he would bring what he promised: law and order, and respect for authority and traditional morality.

Historians and party politicians will probably always debate the reasons behind Nixon's victory. The results for the nation were, in any case, not what Nixon had promised. Antiwar demonstrations continued to

---

[213] National Public Radio Special Series, Radio Diaries. Heard on *All Things Considered* https://www.npr.org/2013/01/14/169080969/segregation-forever-a-fiery-pledge-forgiven-but-not-forgotten

rock the nation. On April 5, 1969, an estimated one hundred thousand people marched in New York City to demand an end to the war. Similar demonstrations were held in San Francisco, Los Angeles, Washington, and other cities. In October, more than two million people nationwide participated in Vietnam moratorium protests, and in November 1969, a demonstration in Washington drew more than half a million participants, while more than one hundred fifty thousand took part in demonstrations in San Francisco.

The Nixon administration encouraged the FBI to continue its attempts to discredit and split radical political movements via undercover activities carried on by COINTELPRO, the FBI's "dirty tricks" organization mentioned earlier. High-priority targets were organizations like the SDS and the Black Panther Party. The orders for COINTELPRO were stated in a directive from J. Edgar Hoover in 1969 to FBI field offices to "exploit all avenues of creating dissension within the ranks of the BPP" and to "submit imaginative and hard-hitting counterintelligence measures aimed at crippling the BPP."[214] To that end, the FBI worked with the Los Angeles police to harass and intimidate Black Panther Party members. False arrests and warrantless searches were conducted—and in the process, several members of the party were killed by the police. Through planted evidence and the start of incendiary rumors, the FBI spread dissension and distrust within organizations and instigated power struggles between them. In 1969, at the University of California, Los Angeles (UCLA), two Black Panther leaders, "Bunchy" Carter and John Huggins, were shot by a member of a rival black organization. Congressional hearings in 1975 revealed that COINTELPRO agents had deliberately provoked division and enmity between the two groups by sending death threats and humiliating cartoons to each group, made to look as if they had come from the other group. The intention was to incite deadly violence and division.

Attempts to end the war fail; young people lose faith in America

Toward the end of the Johnson administration, the bombing of North Vietnam was halted for a while in the hope that doing so would encourage negotiations, and the buildup of American troops stopped at somewhat over half a million soldiers. But attempts to negotiate a cease-fire and withdrawal of American forces went nowhere, and the domestic cost of the war was steadily becoming more obvious and painful by the day. Tens of thousands of young Americans returned in black rubber body bags, additional tens of thousands would be forever crippled, and further tens of thousands suffered from psychological damage that produced panic-inducing flashbacks, depression, feelings of guilt, domestic violence, and divorces. Protests against the war roiled the nation's colleges and universities.

Meanwhile, the hippie culture was slowly morphing from a carefree, drop-out-and-light-up scene to a "hard rock" culture, harder-edged and characterized by music that howled and screamed with anger. Popular bands had names like Megadeth and Motörhead, whose album covers featured skulls and monstrous, threatening creatures—all symbols of death, terror, and destruction. The last spectacular explosion of the

---

[214] Memorandum from FBI Headquarters to Baltimore Field Office (and 13 other field offices), 11/25/68.
   See https://sites.google.com/site/cointelprodocs/the-fbi-s-covert-action-program-to-destroy-the-black-panther-party, note #13 in Section 1. "The Effort to Promote Violence Between the Black Panther Party and the United Slaves (US)"

more traditional hippie culture was the Woodstock Music & Art Fair—commonly called Woodstock—in the town of Bethel, New York, from August 15 to 18, 1969. It was billed as "An Aquarian Exposition: 3 Days of Peace & Music." The term "Aquarian" referred to the age of Aquarius, the astrological name for the present age of the world, and was used in the title of "The Age of Aquarius," a song from the rock opera *Hair*. The age of Aquarius is said to be the age of love, camaraderie, unity, and integrity – exactly the opposite of what was happening in American society at the time.

Woodstock saw a gathering of about four hundred thousand young people and spilled over into a fourth day. It was an experience that no one attending would ever forget. Thirty-two musical acts highlighted the festival, which was characterized by an abundance of drugs, sex, and a feeling of communal love and happiness. Performers included, among others, Ravi Shankar, Arlo Guthrie, Joan Baez, Santana, the Grateful Dead, Creedence Clearwater Revival, Janis Joplin, Sly and the Family Stone, the Who, Jefferson Airplane, Crosby, Stills & Nash, and Jimi Hendrix—who performed a unique, improvised, tortured rendition of "The Star-Spangled Banner." Hendrix's rendition became a fittingly torn closing song for the '60s.

Figure 76. A crowd of hundreds of thousands at Woodstock, Bethel, New York, August 1969.

Chapter 10. Crash and Burn: The '60s Revolution Dies in Bitter Disillusionment

The Vietnam War becomes an ugly horror instead of a noble cause

The following years produced an even greater and angrier polarization of the public. Constant unrest on campuses in California motivated Governor Ronald Reagan to shut down the state's colleges and universities for the first time in California's history. The news from Vietnam was invariably bad, with American casualties mounting and the cost of the war being a significant drain on the economy. The Tet offensive by the North Vietnamese had made it obvious that the war was not being won, and news reports brought ghastly pictures of death and destruction. The American public was beginning to understand that the South Vietnamese government was utterly dependent on American military might to keep itself in power. It did not have the allegiance of the majority of the people.

It was apparent that massive numbers of Vietnamese civilians – men, women, old people, and children – were killed by American bombs. Napalm was a particularly terrifying weapon, causing severe and extremely painful burn injuries and destruction of villages by fire. American news organizations showed the indiscriminate killing of innocent Vietnamese by bombs and so-called "seek–and–destroy" raids by American foot soldiers. One picture became publicized across the world and showed children running screaming from an area that had been attacked by napalm bombs. It brought home to many Americans the moral morass that the war had become and helped turn the public negative against American involvement (Figure 77).

One of the seek–and–destroy raids achieved worldwide notoriety when it became known. On March 16, 1968, an American patrol led by Lieutenant William "Rusty" Calley massacred an entire village, named My Lai, leaving up to five hundred dead of all ages, male and female. An unknown number of individuals managed to escape, many of whom were probably injured. There had been no armed resistance. Many of the bodies showed a large number of bullet holes, indicating that they had been shot multiple times at close range. The incident became known to the public in November 1969 (Figure 78).

Lieutenant Calley was the only one to be convicted in the case. In 1971, he was convicted of twenty-two counts of murder. He was sentenced to life in prison by a military court but served only three years under house arrest after President Nixon intervened and reduced his sentence.[215]

---

[215] http://www.nbcnews.com/id/32514139/ns/us_news-military/t/calley-apologizes-role-my-lai-massacre/#.W_gR3eIo_AQ

Figure 77. Vietnamese children fleeing from a napalm attack

Figure 78. Some of the victims at My Lai, March 16, 1968

For months in late 1969 and early 1970, the Nixon administration had conducted a secret bombing campaign in Cambodia, aimed at disrupting communist supply lines into South Vietnam. The campaign proved fruitless. On April 30, 1970, Nixon announced that American and South Vietnamese ground forces had invaded Cambodia to achieve the same purpose. The announcement immediately ignited angry protests, and many people felt that Nixon had expanded the war further and had gone back on his campaign promise to reduce American involvement. The international reaction was also sharply negative. The American involvement in Vietnam was beginning to look like the greatest foreign policy blunder in the nation's history.

Further left-wing radicalization of white youth

The apparent intensification rather than de-escalation of the war further radicalized already radical antiwar groups. The SDS was now split into two factions. The less radical faction of the student organization remained committed to nonviolent but massive demonstrations and civil disobedience, while the more radical breakaway group embraced violence as a justified tactic in a struggle to eventually overthrow the American government and establish a new revolutionary society based on communist principles. Their perspective on world history over the preceding three decades convinced them that "the winds of history" included the destruction of imperialism and the advance of communism all across the world, leading to the rise of free nations of all races—and, finally, world peace. Nations such as the United States would be swallowed up in this irresistible historical tsunami of radical change, and it was only a matter of time before its war-based economy and plutocratic political system would be overthrown and a revolutionary communist regime would be established, just like in Cuba. Members of the group firmly believed they were on the right side of history.

At an SDS convention in Chicago on June 18, 1969, the breakaway group issued a position paper titled "You Don't Need a Weatherman to Know Which Way the Wind Blows."[216] The group took the title from a song by Bob Dylan that contained the same words. The group, therefore, became known as Weatherman (or Weathermen, later as the Weather Underground).

The Weatherman position paper called for a "white fighting force" that would ally itself with the Black Liberation Army (BLA) and other radical left-wing groups. The goal of their efforts would be to cause "the destruction of US imperialism and achieve a classless world: world communism."

The group was fully committed to communist ideology and racial equality in the United States and around the world. Its membership was overwhelmingly white, but many members had earlier been activists in the black civil rights struggle. The group was strongly supportive of the black power movement and the Black Panther Party, which, like Weatherman, adhered to a communist political ideology.

Because of their open advocacy of communism and violent action, the Weatherman group immediately became a target of high-priority FBI attempts to arrest and prosecute its members. The FBI forced many

---

[216] Full text of the twenty-eight-page typewritten position paper available at https://archive.org/details/YouDontNeedA WeathermanToKnowWhichWayTheWindBlows_925

members to "go underground" and hide by adopting false identities and conducting only covert activities. The group then became known as the Weather Underground Organization (WUO). Its most prominent female member, Bernardine Dohrn, was placed on the FBI's Ten Most Wanted Fugitives list. The FBI repeatedly attempted to tie members of the WUO to several bombings that had caused death and injuries, but eventually, those particular cases turned out to be the work of the BLA, although the BLA and the WUO were close allies.

The WUO was responsible for a number of bombings over the next several years. They issued warnings in advance—and, fortunately, the explosions killed no one in those incidents. But on March 6, 1970, an accidental explosion in a Greenwich Village townhouse occupied by members of the group killed four of its members and caused extensive damage to the building.

The WUO openly took responsibility for its bombings and stated what had motivated each incident. In May 1970, the WUO issued a declaration of war against the US government in response to the death of Black Panther leaders Fred Hampton and Mark Clark in a police raid the previous December. During that raid, four others had been wounded by the hailstorm of more than one hundred bullets that the police had fired. The police claimed that they had fired only in self-defense, even though a later investigation showed that the Panthers had been sleeping when the raid began and had not resisted arrest, except for one Panther who had fired a single shot. It was not clear who had fired the very first shot.

On June 9, 1970, the WUO exploded ten sticks of dynamite at the headquarters of the New York City Police Department "in outraged response to the assassination of the Soledad Brother George Jackson." (The Soledad Brothers will be discussed shortly.) In a statement following a March 1, 1971, bombing at the US Capitol building in Washington, the WUO explained that it was "in protest of the US invasion of Laos." A bombing at the Pentagon on May 19, 1972, was "in retaliation against the US bombing of Hanoi." On January 29, 1975, a bomb was set off at the US Department of State building "in response to the escalation in Vietnam."

Weatherman and the Weather Underground Organization never had large active memberships; estimates range widely from a few dozen to a couple of thousand. The split with the larger SDS organization in 1969 led to the disintegration of the SDS, which at its peak in the late 1960s had more than one hundred thousand members. Within a few years, both the WUO and the SDS had lost almost all their influence on the youth of the United States. But the protests against the Vietnam War nevertheless continued and grew in strength.

Figure 79. Weatherman antiwar march, 1969.

National guard troops shoot and kill demonstrating students

From the very start, in an attempt to reign in domestic disorder, the Nixon administration had taken an aggressive stand against protest demonstrations. The individual state governments mostly followed suit.

On May 4, 1970, four unarmed students were shot dead and nine others wounded when Ohio National Guard troops opened fire on campus demonstrators at Kent State University. The victims were white, and the incident created a furor when leading newspapers and magazines published dramatic pictures of the victims lying on the ground. Outraged, four million students at four hundred and fifty universities and colleges declared a strike to protest the Cambodian invasion and the use of lethal armed force to achieve the suppression of free speech.

Less than two weeks later, on May 15, 1970, a similar incident occurred at Jackson State College in Jackson, Mississippi, where two students were shot dead and twelve others wounded. The college was predominantly black, and all the dead and wounded students were black. A later FBI investigation revealed that about four hundred bullets or pieces of buckshot had been fired into Alexander Hall, a dormitory for women. Windows on three floors were shot out, and the building was left pockmarked by bullets. A spokesman for the police claimed that they had been fired upon by a sniper somewhere in the dorm, but the investigation found "insufficient support" for that allegation. Compared to the nationwide uproar caused by the killing of white students at Kent State, the incident received very little publicity, and few whites took notice.

Figure 80. Ohio National Guardsmen firing at Kent State University students, May 4, 1970

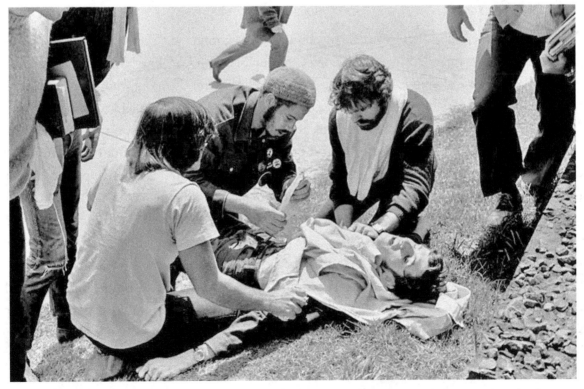

Figure 81. Wounded student at Kent State University, where four students were shot dead

Figure 82. Firearm damage, Alexander Hall, Jackson State College, May 15, 1970.

Nor had the earlier lethal incident at Orangeburg, South Carolina, on February 8, 1968, drawn much national attention at the time. During that incident, a group of South Carolina Highway Patrol officers had fired wildly into a crowd of about one hundred and fifty black demonstrators who were protesting racial discrimination at a local bowling alley. The police gunfire resulted in three dead and twenty-eight wounded.

The conservative reaction against the chaos and disorder of the constant war protests and the left-wing, anti-American rhetoric of the war protesters put Richard Nixon in the White House. Ironically, this conservative backlash also expressed itself in protest demonstrations—protest against the protest. The antiwar sentiment and the disorder it had brought also sparked demonstrations by conservative war supporters. On April 4, a march in Washington organized by the right-wing fundamentalist preacher Carl McIntire drew fifty thousand participants. On May 20, a large prowar demonstration with somewhere between sixty thousand and one hundred and fifty thousand participants took place on Wall Street in New York City. But President Nixon's failure to extract America from Vietnam continued to produce massive and loud antiwar demonstrations. On April 24, 1971, a demonstration of about two hundred thousand people on the National Mall in Washington called for an end to the war. In San Francisco, a crowd of more than one hundred and fifty thousand made the same demand.

Nixon shows his authoritarian character

Nixon then showed that he intended to make good on his campaign promise to restore order. Two days later, a massed force of five thousand police and twelve thousand troops foiled related attempts in Washington to shut down the government. Another attempt to do so from May third through the fifth resulted in another failure and 12,614 arrests. It was the highest number of arrests in American history in connection with a single event.

Nixon was a very complex individual who was far more progressive in his political activities than his many detractors tend to acknowledge. He achieved a much-improved school integration of the South. In 1968, 70 percent of black children had attended black-only schools, but by the end of 1970, that figure had been reduced to 18 percent. He took significant steps to reduce gender inequality in the workplace and increased the number of female appointees in his administration. Nixon also gave strong support to the Clean Air Act of 1970. To enforce the act, he created two new agencies, the Department of Natural Resources and the Environmental Protection Agency. In negotiations with the Soviet Union, his administration achieved the first Strategic Arms Limitation Treaty (SALT), thereby reducing the likelihood that the Soviet Union would opt for a first-strike nuclear attack. Perhaps his most surprising move took place in the middle of his efforts to scale down the Vietnam War. Always an ardent and outspoken anti-communist, Nixon surprised everybody by going on an official visit to communist China in February 1972. The visit achieved notably better and closer relations with China.

Nixon's constructive policies vis-à-vis the Soviet Union and China contrasted with the actions of his administration against Chile, where a Marxist named Salvadore Allende had been fairly and democratically elected as the nation's president. Using bribery, various economic measures, and an array of undercover operatives to undermine the Allende regime, the Nixon administration was able to trigger a military coup in 1973 that overthrew and killed Allende. A military dictator, Augusto Pinochet, took power and began a reign of terror that included thousands of "disappearances" and mass arrests of suspected and actual Allende supporters. The coup caused a mass flight of thousands of the best and brightest people of the nation to safety in Europe.

Nixon had tragic character flaws as a person. Extremely intelligent and capable, he still seems to have been deeply insecure and always felt that he was disliked and unfairly attacked. His personality included some degree of paranoia and a predisposition to let the ends justify the means. He was aware of the activities of the COINTELPRO group under J. Edgar Hoover and had no problem with the illegal means the group used to achieve its ends. That was, after all, the standard operating practice of intelligence-gathering organizations on all sides during the Cold War.

J. Edgar Hoover was still sure that communists were busily fomenting disunity and disorder in American society via the black civil rights movement and the antiwar protests, which, as noted earlier, was not a totally unfounded assumption. In the mid to late 1960s, the left wing of the American political spectrum was very clearly identified with both movements. The line between communist sympathy and left-wing liberalism was blurry, and some political opposition groups embraced ideas borrowed from Karl Marx. Some radical organizations like the Black Panther Party and the Weather Underground Organization openly advocated communist ideas.

FBI's COINTELPRO operations heavily targeted all activist organizations. FBI informants infiltrated all the leading civil rights organizations and political opposition groups, and surreptitiously investigated all their leaders. As briefly mentioned earlier, the FBI used various dirty tricks in many cases, which included secret wiretapping and making false anonymous accusations against people within an organization to sow distrust and to cause internal fighting. To cause disruption of organizations and smearing of their reputations as being criminal and violent, the FBI continued to provoke violence against the police by using the harsh and humiliating treatment of suspects during warrantless and unfounded searches and arrests. As planned, the tactic often caused an escalation of violence, to the point where the police could claim that lethal force had been justified in overcoming resistance.

Often, the arrest and prosecution of members of radical opposition groups like the SDS and YIP were politically motivated. The list of people involved on the defending side in such trials sometimes reads like an extract from a *Who's Who* of the American left-wing political and legal establishments. A good example, mentioned earlier, is the trial of Bobby Seale and the Chicago Seven following the disturbances at the Democratic National Convention in 1968.

Law enforcement agencies were overwhelmingly white and were commonly infected with racist prejudice. Blacks and other minorities were disproportionately targeted by law enforcement. They were more often arrested and convicted in courts, and once convicted, they were given harsher sentences than whites for the same crimes. Once in prison, they were more often placed in the highest-security sections or solitary confinement and were usually treated in more humiliating and brutal ways than whites.[217]

The Angela Davis case

The radical political opposition groups had many members who began their political activities in the civil rights movement during the early 1960s. Although most political radicals were white, they were acutely aware of the injustices that blacks suffered within the criminal justice system. The famed Soledad Brothers case in 1970 and the related story of Angela Davis present a good illustration of the bias in the system.

Angela Davis was born in Birmingham, Alabama, on January 26, 1944. As a black child, she was quite aware from an early age of the racial polarization and discrimination that existed in American society. She was personally acquainted with one of the four young girls who had been killed in the bombing of the 16th Street Baptist Church in 1963. Her mother was a leading organizer of the Southern Negro Youth Congress, an organization closely tied to the American Communist Party. In contrast to the vast majority of Southern blacks, Angela Davis thus had been familiar with communist ideology since early childhood.

---

[217] In his book *Race to Incarcerate: The Sentencing Project*, (New York, The New Press, 1999) Mark Mauer of *The Sentencing Project* presents a wealth of data and reasons how and why great disparities exist in the arrest, conviction, sentencing, and incarceration statistics of black citizens versus white ones.

With sponsorship by the American Friends Service Committee, a Quaker organization, Davis enrolled at Elisabeth Irwin High School in New York City, where she was recruited by and joined a communist youth group called Advance. She later graduated magna cum laude from Brandeis University in 1965, after which she spent several years studying in Frankfurt, Paris, and San Diego. Her outstanding academic credentials landed her a position as an assistant professor in the philosophy department of the prestigious University of California, Los Angeles.

By that time, Davis had joined the Black Panther Party because of its communist ideology and activist agenda to serve the black community. At UCLA, she quickly became known as a very outspoken advocate of communism, black power, and radical feminism.

Figure 83. Angela Davis, an advocate of communism, black power, and radical feminism, 1972.

Her outspoken radicalism brought her to the attention of California Governor Ronald Reagan, who urged the board of regents of the University of California to fire her. She temporarily lost her job until a judge ordered her reinstated, saying that the university could not fire her on the grounds of her being a member of the Communist Party. Then, the regents fired her again for using "inflammatory language" in four separate speeches. The speeches attacked the university for alleged responsibility for the death of demonstrators and used the word "pigs" to describe the police.

Davis's association with the Communist Party and the Black Panther Party made her a high-profile subject in the FBI hunt for purported subversives. In 1970, J. Edgar Hoover finally found legal grounds to move against her when he found a link between her and two men, George Jackson and his brother, seventeen-year-old Jonathan Jackson.

George Jackson, Fleeta Drumgo, and John Clutchette were three prison inmates who became known as the "Soledad Brothers" because they were imprisoned in California's Soledad prison. They were not brothers in a biological sense, but at the time, the term "brother" referred to any black man, and "sister" to any black woman, at least as long as they were sympathetic to the cause of black unity and black power.

George Jackson became interested in politics while in prison and wrote many letters to friends and supporters. These would later be edited and compiled into two books, *Soledad Brother*[218] and *Blood in My Eye*[219]. They became big sellers that brought him a great deal of attention, not only in the United States but also from leftist intellectuals in Western Europe.

The three Soledad Brothers were charged with the January 16, 1970, death of a white prison guard named John Vincent Mills. On February 14 of that year, they were indicted on the charge of murder. The case against them was weak and drew great interest from activists from the left wing of the American political spectrum. The case was made a showcase by the left-wing groups and the press, bringing into the open the brutal treatment and conditions the inmates experienced at Soledad, according to the letters and notes written by George Jackson, and stressing the racism of the law enforcement and court systems. Concerned observers feared that the three would be convicted not because of the weight of the evidence against them but because of prejudicial biases in the justice system. A defense committee was formed to facilitate publicity regarding the unjustness of the case and to assist in the financing of legal aid for the three.

The Soledad Brothers Defense Committee attracted a spectacular collection of high-powered people and celebrities including Julian Bond, Marlon Brando, Noam Chomsky, Jane Fonda, Allen Ginsberg, Tom Hayden, the lawyer William Kunstler, Nobel Prize laureate Linus Pauling, the singer Pete Seeger, Dr. Benjamin Spock, and many others. Also among them was Angela Davis, who was not yet as widely known by the American public as many others on the committee.

On March 27, 1972, two of the three Soledad Brothers were declared not guilty by a San Francisco jury. If the regular legal process had been allowed to run its course, all three probably would have been acquitted. But for George Jackson, it did not end well. In a strange and deadly incident just days before the start of his trial in 1970, Jackson allegedly obtained a gun and started a deadly riot at San Quentin prison, where he was shot dead by a guard. A .38 caliber revolver was allegedly found in his hand—a revolver registered to Angela Davis. It may have been smuggled into the prison to Jackson by one of his attorneys, Stephen Bingham, but for what reason is a mystery. For Jackson to start the riot and use the gun was clearly tantamount to suicide.

---

[218] George L. Jackson, *Soledad Brother; The Prison Letters of George Jackson* (Chicago: Lawrence Hill Books, an imprint of Chicago Review Press, 1994)
[219] George L. Jackson, *Blood In My Eye* (Baltimore, MD: Black Classic Press, 1990)

Bingham fled the country following the incident but has always denied having provided the gun to Jackson. After returning to the United States and being arrested in 1986, he was tried but acquitted of the charges for lack of evidence of having done so. How and why Jackson obtained the gun was never established. Not all were convinced that he had indeed obtained or had fired the gun; many believed that whoever shot him placed it in his hand after he had been shot and killed. Conspiracy theories flourished, including one that the killing of Jackson was part of a plot by the FBI to get rid of this dangerous and influential Marxist revolutionary and, at the same time, get Angela Davis.

Angela Davis was not suspected of having smuggled the gun to Jackson or of having persuaded him to start the riot. But the fact that the gun found with Jackson was registered to Davis made her complicit, according to California law, to the killing of three prison guards and two prisoners. She would soon get into more trouble. On August 7, 1970, while the trial of the two remaining Soledad Brothers was going on, Jonathan Jackson, George's brother, burst into a different courtroom in Marin County, heavily armed. He provided arms to two black defendants in the courtroom, and together they took the judge, the prosecutor, and several female jurors hostage. The intent was to set free the two Soledad Brothers who were on trial. As they fled the court building in a car, the police started shooting at the vehicle. Jonathan Jackson, the two defendants, and the judge were killed, and the prosecutor and one of the jurors were injured in the hail of bullets. The judge was not killed by police bullets but by a sawed-off shotgun fired by someone in the car.

Investigation of the weapons Jonathan Jackson had obtained showed that they had been purchased two days earlier by Angela Davis. How they ended up in the hands of Jonathan Jackson has never been established. Davis denied having given them to Jackson but could not explain why she had bought them, or who might have taken them. She was charged with aggravated kidnapping and first-degree murder in the death of Judge Harold Haley.

The FBI issued a warrant for her arrest on August 14. Four days later, with Davis still not captured, J. Edgar Hoover made Angela Davis the third woman to ever appear on the Ten Most Wanted Fugitives list, where Bernardine Dohrn of the WUO soon followed her.

FBI agents found and arrested Davis in New York City on October 13, 1970. The arrest occasioned a message from President Nixon to Hoover and the FBI, congratulating them on the "capture of the dangerous terrorist, Angela Davis."

Davis declared herself innocent of all charges against her. The many strange and unexplained circumstances and events connected with the Soledad Brothers case, that of Jonathan Jackson, and the connections of those cases to Davis gave rise to a number of conspiracy theories regarding the possible involvement of undercover FBI agents. Her trial became another high-profile event and generated a huge groundswell of support from a broad spectrum of progressive organizations in both the United States and abroad. By February of 1971, more than two hundred committees had been formed in the United States and sixty-seven in foreign countries to free Davis. In 1972, an all-white jury found her not guilty on all counts. The strange circumstances of the case never received a satisfactory explanation.

The Attica prison uprising

The tensions and controversies associated with the Soledad Brothers case led to unrest and disturbances in other prisons, the largest and most famous of which was the rebellion at Attica Correctional Facility in Attica, New York. On September 9, 1971, about a thousand of the mostly black and Latino Attica inmates seized control of the prison and took forty-two of its all-white staff members hostage. It was not a riot but an organized uprising that took hostages to prevent correctional officers from immediately using deadly force to wrest back control. Leaders elected from among the prisoners maintained order. Four days of negotiations followed with the prison officials and representatives of New York Governor Nelson Rockefeller. The prisoners demanded improved prison conditions, better food, and more humane treatment of the inmates. The hostages were kept safe and treated well while negotiations were being held.

Many highly respected public figures and reporters were on site to observe what was happening and to provide help in negotiations and maintaining order. They included, among others, *New York Times* editor Tom Wicker, James Ingram of the *Michigan Chronicle*, New York State Senator John Dunne, New York State Representative Arthur Eve, the lawyer William Kunstler, and Minister Louis Farrakhan of the Nation of Islam.

After four days of inconclusive negotiations, Governor Rockefeller ordered the police to reestablish control of the prison by armed force. The police then released massive amounts of tear gas against the inmates and their hostages—and for two minutes, the police fired nonstop into the cloud of gas, most of the time unable to see whom they were shooting. By the time the order came to cease fire, thirty-three of the inmates and ten of the hostages were dead; nine of the ten hostages had been killed by "friendly fire" from state troopers and soldiers, not by the prisoners. Another eighty individuals were wounded.

Figure 84. Casualties collected following the Attica prison riot, September 1971.

None of the attacking police or military personnel suffered injuries. A commission that was later formed to investigate what had happened wrote in its report: "With the exception of Indian massacres in the late nineteenth century, the State Police assault which ended the four-day prison uprising was the bloodiest one-day encounter between Americans since the Civil War."[220]

The seasoned *New York Times* newsman Tom Wicker, who had been instrumental in the negotiations with the leaders of the uprising, emerged from the scene thoroughly shaken by the indiscriminate mass shooting and the subsequent brutal punishment of the surviving inmates by prison guards. His book *A Time to Die: The Attica Prison Revolt*[221] provides a harrowing account of the events at Attica by a neutral observer who was also an important participant.

The Pentagon Papers reveal administration lies and deceptions

Nixon wanted to expand the intelligence-gathering abilities of his administration even further and to use undercover special-agent groups to collect information on his political adversaries. To that end, he asked White House aide Tom Huston to develop a plan for the composition and activities of such groups. The plan, worked out in close cooperation with Hoover's assistant, William Sullivan, was submitted to Nixon in July 1970. It included items such as burglaries, illegal surveillance, and opening the private mail of American citizens. The plan also proposed special camps where the FBI could hold people who had been arrested for antiwar protests or allegedly subversive political activities for lengthy periods of time without trial. The plan became known as the Huston Plan. Nixon ratified the plan in mid-July and sent it out to the FBI, the CIA, the NSA, and the Defense Intelligence Agency (DIA).

Hoover had some reservations about the plan. Together with Attorney General John Mitchell, he was able to make Nixon cancel it. The Nixon administration abandoned the plan as a package but still implemented many of its provisions. They expanded the use of student informants on college campuses, conducted domestic burglaries, opened private mail, and forwarded any information they gathered to the CIA. They used the Internal Revenue Service (IRS) to subject political-opposition members to particularly intense scrutiny and harassment by asking endless questions about their tax returns. Other activities included using anonymous sources to spread false and damaging information about political opponents.

Nixon and his administration had learned from the debacle at the Democratic National Convention in Chicago in 1968. There, the televised spectacle of police attacks on demonstrators had created sympathy for the demonstrators because of the excessive and indiscriminate brutality of the police. Under Nixon, the police and military forces employed to prevent the anti-war demonstrations from turning into riots displayed calm, professional behavior, which was the result of much-improved training and leadership.

While the size of the demonstrations and their associated violence were reduced, opposition to the war nevertheless kept increasing. In 1971, the *New York Times* published the "Pentagon Papers," a top-secret

---

[220] Attica: The Official Report of the *New York State Special Commission on Attica* (New York: Bantam Books, 1972), p. xi. See also Shaun L. Gabbidon and Helen Taylor Greene, *Race and Crime* (Thousand Oaks, CA: SAGE Publications, 2005), p. 234.

[221] Tom Wicker, *A Time to Die: The Attica Prison Revolt* (Chicago: Haymarket Books, 2011).

study officially titled "United States–Vietnam Relations, 1945–1967: A Study Prepared by the Department of Defense." The study was commissioned in 1967 by Robert McNamara, the Secretary of Defense of the Johnson administration.

The report was leaked to the *New York Times* by Daniel Ellsberg, one of its authors. Ellsberg had become increasingly disillusioned with the war and his decision to let the American public know the truth about it dated to 1969. But releasing classified information to the public was an act that risked incurring severe criminal penalties. He was unable to find anyone to publish the classified content until the *New York Times* was willing to take the risk. The study revealed the truth about America's involvement in Vietnam and gave a discouraging assessment of the nature and prospects for success of the war effort. The publication of the first part of the document was a sensation. The government sued the paper, which then complied with the order to cease and desist from publishing any more of the document.

Learning of the agreement by the *New York Times* to comply with the federal order, Ben Bradlee, the chief editor of the *Washington Post,* declared himself willing, against the advice of the paper's lawyers, to publish the rest of the material. The *Washington Post* managed to obtain a copy of the full report and published a portion of it in its morning issue on Friday, June 18, 1971. In the afternoon, Mr. Bradlee received a phone call from US Attorney General William Rehnquist (later to become Chief Justice of the Supreme Court) demanding that the *Washington Post* stop publication of the material. Bradlee refused, and the government brought a suit against the paper.

The case of the *New York Times* and the *Washington Post* vs. the government was an extremely important and urgent one and quickly found its way to the Supreme Court. On June 30, 1971, less than three weeks after the first publication of parts of the Pentagon Papers by the *New York Times*, the court announced a decision in favor of the newspapers. The resolution of the case was decisive victory for freedom of the press and free speech but enraged President Nixon.

The government also brought a suit of espionage against Ellsberg, who could have received as much as one hundred and fifteen years in jail if the government had been completely successful in its prosecution. But the case was bungled: the court discovered that to stop further leaks and to prepare lawsuits against leakers, Nixon administration officials had assembled a special task force, named "the plumbers." The group had burglarized the office of Ellsberg's psychiatrist to obtain compromising data on Ellsberg. The trial lasted four months and resulted in Ellsberg being declared innocent of all charges because the evidence against him was obtained illegally.

Meanwhile, daily news reports contributed to the conviction on the part of an increasing number of citizens that the war was a mistake and could not be won. Many still believed America *could* win the war but would not, because the administration would not, for a variety of reasons, commit the necessary economic and military resources. America seemed to be inexorably sliding toward voluntary defeat. The morale of the troops was deteriorating, as there seemed to be nothing worth fighting for in Vietnam—or dying for. With increasing frequency, reports trickled out about individual soldiers or entire units refusing to obey orders, and there were rumors of cases where officers were killed by their own men. There was even a word for it: "fragging," for killing by a fragmentation hand grenade.

The mood of the entire nation turned very sour, and the Nixon administration, realizing that it must extract America from the war, stopped trying to win it and instead sought ways to achieve an honorable end that would not be too humiliating for the nation.

Troop buildup stopped and attempts to negotiate an end to the war intensified. The North Vietnamese were well aware of the deteriorating domestic support for the war in the United States and had no doubt that they would achieve an easy victory in the south of Vietnam if American support for the Saigon government were withdrawn. They had a winning hand at the negotiating table and saw that time was on their side. Negotiations were making no progress. To put more pressure on Hanoi, Nixon decided in May to further escalate the bombing of North Vietnam and to mine the harbor of its capital, Hanoi. The escalated military measures produced another wave of protest both domestically and internationally, but the negotiations remained fruitless.

The Watergate case, Nixon's resignation and the end of the war

In 1972, another election year, Nixon felt intense pressure to end the war, or at least to show some significant progress toward that goal by the time of the election in November. The Democratic Party had not yet restored internal peace and harmony following its chaotic 1964 and 1968 national conventions and had nominated a weak candidate, George McGovern, whose left-leaning political positions and strong opposition to the war were too radical for many moderate, patriotic Americans. Nixon still wanted to know more about the Democratic Party's plans for the fall election, and one of the special groups created as a result of the Huston Plan was authorized to break into the offices of the Democratic National Committee in the Watergate office complex in Washington, where they were to gather whatever information they could from the files they found there.

The first burglary took place in May 1972. A group affiliated with the CIA stole some secret information and attempted to wiretap two telephones. The wiretaps failed to work correctly, so a second burglary to fix the problem and search for more documents to copy took place on June 17. An alert security guard, Frank Wills, discovered the break-in and called the police, leading to the arrest of five men.

Based on material they had in their possession, the men appeared to be connected with the CIA and to have some ties to the White House. The president gave a televised speech in August in which he declared that no one in or connected to the White House staff was involved in or knew of the burglary beforehand. The public, unwilling to think that the president would knowingly be involved with what Nixon called "a third-rate burglary," believed him. His standings in political polls did not change appreciably, and they showed him ahead of his Democratic challenger.

Nixon may have been more concerned about the effect of George Wallace, who had once again entered the race. In the primaries, Wallace had received almost one-quarter of all votes cast. But on May 15, 1972, while campaigning in the Washington suburb of Laurel, Maryland, Wallace was shot by an apparently deranged young white man, Arthur Bremer. He survived but was permanently paralyzed and had to withdraw from the campaign.

Meanwhile, McGovern had to dismiss his vice presidential running mate, Thomas Eagleton, because it had come to light that Eagleton had received electric shock therapy for depression and that a recurrence of depression was a possibility. A desperate scramble began to find a replacement, but six prominent Democrats declined his offer of a vice presidential spot on the ticket. Finally, a relatively unknown Democrat, Sargent Shriver, accepted the offer. By that time, McGovern's standings in the polls had dipped to 24 percent. The result was that Nixon won the presidential election by a margin surpassed only by Johnson eight years earlier. As the case had been in 1968, his margin was wide enough to overcome the support Wallace had received before he dropped out of the race after his shooting.

Nixon was still in trouble because of an investigation of the Watergate burglary pursued with great skill and determination by two *Washington Post* reporters, Bob Woodward and Carl Bernstein. The scandal resulting from their investigation gave rise to the most extensive television coverage of congressional hearings in history. Gradually, more and more members of Nixon's closest confidants and subordinates were revealed to have taken part in illegal activities and an extensive effort to obstruct justice. The noose was tightening around the top levels of the Nixon administration, and Nixon resorted to more and more desperate measures to defend himself. He fired the special prosecutor who had been conducting the congressional inquiries, as well as many of his own top aides.

In the middle of the Watergate investigations, Vice President Agnew was charged with bribery, conspiracy, and tax fraud related to his involvement with a Maryland horse-racing track. The evidence was too strong for Agnew to fight, and he had to resign, becoming the only vice president to have been forced to do so because of criminal charges. Now it was Nixon's turn to quickly find another vice president. The final choice was Gerald Ford, a veteran congressman from Michigan. Ford was, in many ways, Nixon's complete opposite as a person. Polite, warmly personable, considerate, and thoroughly honest, Ford was, on the other hand, nowhere near the intellectual equal of Nixon. Ford had played football for the Michigan State University team when they had taken two successive national titles in 1932 and 1933, and Lyndon Johnson expressed the opinion that Ford had played too much football without a helmet.

The dramatic congressional Watergate inquiry stunned the nation's television viewers with the scale of criminal misconduct that the inquiry revealed to have taken place at the highest levels of the government. As a result of the investigations, forty top-level administration officials, including Attorney General John Mitchell, were indicted on criminal charges, and most of the highest-level people from the White House staff and the Committee to Re-Elect the President (popularly known as CREEP) were given jail sentences. On August 8, 1974, Richard Nixon resigned—the first president in American history to do so. Advisers had told him that Congress would most certainly impeach him if he did not.

With the resignation of the president, Vice President Ford was now in command and was sworn in the next day, August 9, 1974. He thus became the first American president ever to have been elected to neither the vice-presidential nor the presidential office. He appointed as his vice president Nelson Rockefeller, a former governor of New York. As a result, neither the president nor the vice president was ever elected to a national office. It seemed symbolic of what had happened to American democracy.

After some difficult and protracted negotiations, President Ford managed in 1975 to bring the Vietnam War to an end. The end was a humiliating defeat, with American television news showing tragic scenes of desperate South Vietnamese clamoring to be taken by helicopters from the American embassy building in Saigon as North Vietnamese forces entered the city. With that, an era came to an end in America. The nation emerged scarred, humbled, and full of sharp and bitter political divisions. Confidence in its government institutions was at an all-time low. But the United States had, to a considerable degree, shaken off the poisonous delusion of racism. That is not to say that its historical effects had disappeared.

Playboy Magazine and the moral rebellion of "the '60s"

Up until the 1960s, the image of the black rapist continued to be the most powerful image to be employed by obsessed segregationists. That image was what fundamentalist preachers at KKK rallies inevitably spoke of—or, at least, alluded to. But segregationists have always preferred to use a different, more reasonable-sounding argument in conversations with those who want to abandon segregation. They insist that blacks are inferior to whites in character and intellectual capacity and that the mingling of the races would have catastrophic effects for the future of the white race and the American nation — indeed, for all of human civilization. They often call attention to this alleged long-term genetic danger in their attempts to justify the strict segregation and control of blacks.

As history shows, humans do not naturally have loyalty to their race as the dominant instinct. As a defense mechanism against the temptation to do the forbidden, we might create artificial barriers in the form of laws or physical separation from what produces the temptation. Such barriers often have the intended effect but are seldom infallible, and they extract a price in the form of obsession with the maintenance of the barrier and hypersensitivity to the source of the temptation.

However, the emotions produced by our procreative instinct usually win over those associated with our tribal instinct. In a choice between the two alternatives, most emotionally healthy people of both sexes would choose to have offspring with someone from another "tribe" rather than swearing off all sexual relations and having no children at all. That makes evolutionary sense because sexual abstinence is guaranteed to terminate our genetic line, while mixing with another tribe will allow the line to continue. Involuntary abstinence can be the result of being outcompeted in sexual attractiveness; thus one can expect that whites who harbor fears in that regard will be prone to be hostile to blacks.

As one of many results of the '60s, the United States has seen dramatic changes in beliefs, attitudes, and feelings about race. Most young people today have a much more relaxed and liberal attitude toward sex than did adults in the 1950s. In part because of this change in attitude, few white youths today experience nervous tension, anxiety, fear, and hatred when they encounter people of African ethnicity. The rate of mixed-race pairings and marriages has seen a steady upward trend, and mixed couples now seldom risk disapproving stares or violence when they are in public. This new atmosphere, however, has also made it difficult for today's young people to fathom the intense emotions that the very idea of interracial intimacy could cause only a few generations ago.

The moral attitudes of Americans were beginning to become more open and tolerant in the post-WWII era, possibly because of the overseas experiences of more than seven million young men and women in the war and its aftermath. Playboy magazine began appearing on the newsstands in December 1953, featuring the "ultimate sex symbol," Marilyn Monroe, on its cover. At first, to meet public standards of decency, the magazines were often hidden or covered on the shelves, but most men knew how to get them by asking for them.

Playboy became a huge commercial success, achieving a circulation of more than seven million copies with its November 1972 edition. One-quarter of American college men were then buying or subscribing to the magazine each month. College men might have been the demographic segment most attuned to the *Playboy* worldview, but the magazine was read (or at least perused) by millions more, and it achieved a wide readership all across the Western world. The magazine remained focused primarily on the visual presentation of young and beautiful nude or semi-nude women but did not shy away from controversial subjects in the political arena—it featured articles by leading intellectuals, politicians, and artists.

The sophisticated content helped *Playboy* rise above the reputation for smut and pornography the magazine had initially received. *Playboy* became accepted as a hip and trendsetting magazine that people did not have to be ashamed of reading. It did not itself create any new political movements but helped publicize the opinions of most of the important figures of its day. In so doing, *Playboy* must be credited with supporting and strengthening the liberal and antiwar trends of the 1960s.

Hugh Hefner, the owner of *Playboy* magazine, became one of the most envied men in America. Hefner projected an image of having easy access to any number of the most beautiful women in the world. For women, becoming a *Playboy* centerfold was to achieve official recognition as being outstandingly beautiful and desirable.

The magazine still took until March 1965 to feature a black woman, Jennifer Jackson, as its centerfold. The era of the '60s was then at its peak, and the picture of a black woman in *Playboy* did not create much of a stir. (Jennifer Jackson was relatively light-skinned and had rather European-looking facial features. It would not be until October 1971 that a black woman, Darine Stern, was on the cover of Playboy.)

Figure 85. Hugh Hefner and *Playboy* bunnies, 1966

Figure 86. Jennifer Jackson, the first black *Playboy* centerfold

Only a few months later, in its August issue, the magazine featured its famous interview with KKK leader Robert Shelton of Alabama, where Shelton reaffirmed the KKK's beliefs that blacks are superior to whites in the areas of genital size, potency, strength of sex drive, and virility.[222] Extracts of the interview are shown at the beginning of this book. From a psychological point of view, it is significant that Shelton claims that there is an increase in both crime and sex during times of a full moon. He feels that crime and sex are somehow in the same category, and, like classic vampires and other evil creatures, the lustful impulses of blacks become activated by the full moon. It fits perfectly with the general air of superstition and erotophobia that characterize white American prejudice against the black stereotype.

By August of 1965, not many readers of *Playboy* were among those with racist or fundamentalist Christian beliefs, and few took Shelton seriously, especially since Shelton kept insisting that his Klan group did not believe in or engage in violence. The Shelton interview, despite Shelton's outrageous views, caused no great public outrage. The sensitivity to issues of race and sex had become much diminished, which *Playboy* magazine had helped to achieve. In 1994, Shelton acknowledged that the KKK had lost its influence. He said, "The Klan is my belief, my religion. But it won't work anymore. The Klan is gone. Forever."[223]

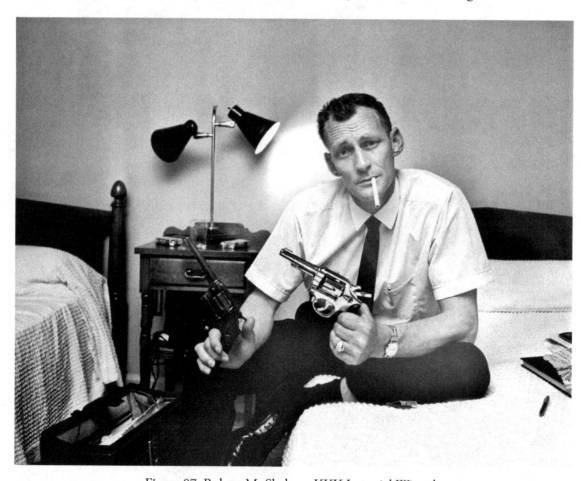

Figure 87. Robert M. Shelton, KKK Imperial Wizard.

---

[222] Statement in August 1965 *Playboy* interview with Robert Shelton
[223] Statement in 1994 Associated Press interview with Robert Shelton

Part Eight: The stubborn residue of racism in America

Facing our responsibility

Following the momentous *Brown v. Board of Education* decision in 1954, it has taken a long time for segregationist and racist feelings to fade away in the South. In 1985, members of the old White Citizens Council (WCC) met in Saint Louis to create a successor to their organization, which had seen its reputation sullied by its openly segregationist activities. To make its agenda less obvious, they removed the word "White" from its name and renamed it "Council of Conservative Citizens" (CCC). Until recently, it counted as its members and supporters many leading Southern congressional politicians such as Republican past Senate Majority Leader Trent Lott of Mississippi, North Carolina Senator Jesse Helms, and Georgia Congressman Bob Barr. As mentioned in Chapter 2, the WCC continued collaboration with the Ku Klux Klan and similar groups with white supremacist political agendas, and its successor, the CCC, carried on its mission. As stated in its newspaper, *Citizens Informer*, its "Statement of Principles" include the following:

> "We believe that the United States of America is a Christian country, that its people are a Christian people, and that its government and public leaders at all levels must reflect Christian beliefs and values... We also oppose all efforts to mix the races of mankind, to promote non-white races over the European-American people through so-called 'affirmative action' and similar measures, to destroy or denigrate the European-American heritage, including the heritage of the Southern people, and to force the integration of the races... We believe in states' rights, as guaranteed by the Ninth and Tenth Amendments to the Constitution; in the individual right to keep and bear arms, as guaranteed by the Second Amendment to the Constitution; and in all the rights and liberties guaranteed by the body of the Constitution and the Bill of Rights. We therefore oppose all efforts by the federal government to dictate to the states and local governments and communities,

and we oppose federal efforts to engineer or impose behavior and beliefs on citizens and communities."[224]

Racial prejudice and racially charged violence did not end altogether with the 1960s. A steady stream of violent incidents has occurred in America since that time. In many people of older generations, the prejudice has not so much disappeared as it has gone underground because law and customs have made outspoken racism less socially acceptable. The political slogan "Make America Great Again" has been heard by white supremacists as a call to return to a society controlled by whites, preferably including closing the borders to immigrants of non-European ethnicity and deporting all illegal immigrants. Blacks continue to be the victims of a disproportionate share of the violence—including brutality and lethal force by the police.

Unfortunately, world history has provided the American government many excuses to shunt aside issues of domestic economic and racial justice. External events that might affect national security or threaten America's commercial interests have been considered more urgent. To counter such threats, and to advance its own worldwide political and economic goals, America has come to rely to an excessive degree on military might. In the past seventy years, America has spent tens of trillions of dollars and tens of thousands of American lives on wars and interventions in other nations across the globe. Diplomacy, based on an understanding of the unique histories, values, self-images, and ambitions of foreign nations, has been devalued, leading to misunderstandings and costly mistakes in foreign policy. The focus on international military interventions has strained the economic resources of the nation and resulted in a huge national debt, ultimately payable by taxes on everyone.

Meanwhile, domestic problems have been allowed to fester and have made America a nearly dysfunctional, third-world-like flawed democracy.[225] Some of those trillions of dollars spent on killing people and blowing things up in other countries would have been better spent on healing domestic wounds and improving the quality of life for American citizens.

By many measures, America is now in decline, and that has not gone unnoticed on the world stage. It has become weakened by its misplaced priorities, immobilized by political gridlock in its administrative system, and corrupted by the power of money in the democratic processes of its society. It has become enthralled by a romantic chimera of self-sufficient individualism, tenacious hard work to be "the smith of one's own fate," and fierce competition.

It is a philosophy that is not compatible with the realities of the modern world, where progress for all is the result of consensus-building, cooperation, and government policies that favor the common good, not the ambitions of the individual. However, it is a notion that America cherishes as the essence of "the American way." In theory, it produces fame and fortune to all who can dedicate him- or herself to its tenets. It is the core of the belief that the United States is the number one "land of opportunity." In reality, socio-economic

---

[224] Citizens Informer, *Statements of Principles*, (2007) Published by The Council of Conservative Citizens. Its website has click-on links to extreme right-wing sites and articles with rabidly racist and conspiracy theory contents.

[225] The Economist 2019 whitepaper on its "Democracy Index" lists the United States as a "flawed democracy," occupying number 25 on its rankings of nations. The Economist is a left-leaning but highly regarded British publication with worldwide distribution.

mobility in America is now among the lowest of major industrialized economies.[226] A combination of inflation and tax cuts benefitting the wealthiest individuals and corporations has caused the nation to become ever more divided along economic lines where those among the wealthiest one percent of the population own more assets than the total wealth of the least wealthy fifty percent. The wealth differential between white and black families has increased rather than decreased.

America is still the largest economy in the world, but China, the most populous nation in the world, now challenges America for the lead. China, which only a few decades ago ranked as a backward, third-world nation, now graduates several times as many highly educated engineers each year as does the United States. In contrast to the United States, it has succeeded in almost eliminating poverty and hunger at home and is emerging as an economic and technological giant. [227]

Remaining racial injustice

Domestically, for many, the progress begun in the '60s has not yet come to full fruition. Males and females working the same job still experience a pay gap. Only in recent years has the institution of marriage become available to couples of the same sex. Today (2020), America is still struggling with the residue of racism. "Black Lives Matter" is a slogan that does not always reflect reality. Blacks are disproportionately the victims of police brutality and shootings and tend to receive more severe sentences than whites convicted of the same crimes. These practices have a long tradition, especially in the South. There, in the past, the killing of a black person hardly ever resulted even in the indictment of a white perpetrator.

In the South, in particular, the disrespect of black individuals and unwillingness to accord them the same rights as whites has remained a deeply ingrained societal custom. It goes back all the way to the era of slavery, when the slaves were by law declared the private property of their owners. In 1705, the Virginia General Assembly formally granted slave owners the absolute right over the lives and welfare of their slaves:

> All Negro, mulatto and Indian slaves within this dominion... shall be held to be real estate. And if any slave resists his master, or owner, or other person, by his or her order, correcting such slave and shall happen to be killed in such correction... the master, owner, and every other person so giving correction, shall be free and acquit of all punishment and accusation for the same, as if such incident had never happened.[228]

---

[226] A 2016 "State of the Union" study by the Stanford Center on Poverty and Inequality ranked the United States number sixteen of the twenty-four high- and medium-income nations studied concerning inter-generational economic mobility.

[227] The threshold of "poverty" is defined differently in different countries, and the median household income in China remains far below that in America. However, the standard of living has risen rapidly in China, and hunger has indeed been virtually eliminated.

[228] Darity Jr., William A. and Mullen, Kirsten A.. *From Here to Equality* (pp. 94-95). The University of North Carolina Press, 2020.

To illustrate how the lives of white persons have been valued higher than those of blacks, one can use, for example, the death-sentence statistics for murder.

On September 6, 1991, South Carolina executed Donald "Peewee" Gaskins for killing a fellow inmate at the prison where he was already serving multiple consecutive life sentences for killing several people. The case was unusual in that Gaskins was white and his victim black. It was the first time a white man had received a death sentence in South Carolina for killing a black person since 1880, during the tail end of Reconstruction.[229] During the same 1880–1991 period, hundreds of blacks were executed in South Carolina, by court order or by lynching, for killing white persons. Between 1976 and 1998, six white men were executed for killing one or more black persons, while 115 black men were executed for killing someone white.[230] For decades following the Civil War, death by lynching was almost inevitable for a black man accused of raping, or trying to rape, or thinking about trying to rape, a white woman, and not just in the South. Nationwide, in the first half of the twentieth century, in addition to those lynched without a trial, 405 black men were convicted in court and executed for rape. At the same time, there was not a single case in which a white man was executed for the rape of a black woman, even though the latter occurrence was far more common.[231]

Recently, the issue of police brutality and the use of lethal force by police against unarmed blacks have received especially widespread publicity. There has been a long row of young blacks who have been killed in their homes or in the streets without representing any threat to the policemen. They have been shot in the back while attempting to flee or choked to death while subdued by several police officers, or simply shot when police busted into their homes unannounced and started shooting the residents, allegedly because they were suspected of drug dealings. In most of these incidents, the black victims have not been suspected of a violent crime. The standard procedure for police in using their firearms is not to merely immobilize the target so that he or she can be apprehended. They make little attempt to properly arrest the black "suspects," take them in a police car to a police station, book them on whatever suspicion, and place them in jail where they could have access to a lawyer and a court procedure. Instead, the police are free to act as jury, judge, and executioners on the spot. They shoot to kill.

A thoroughgoing reform of the entire policing practices is urgently needed, including retraining of personnel at all levels. Instead of quickly upping the stakes in confrontations to the threat of lethal force, police should learn de-escalation techniques in conflict situations and avoid the use of intimidation tactics and humiliating behavior. Effective policies should be instituted to identify and fire individuals who habitually use overly forceful, confrontational, and disrespectful means to deal with suspects and offenders. They do not belong in the police force and clearly create more problems than they solve.

In many cases, the events have demonstrated a horrifying out-of-control killing frenzy by groups of policemen. Behaving as a bloodthirsty hunting pack, they have used massive firepower far beyond what

---

[229] David Cole, *No Equal Justice: Race and Class in the American Justice System* (New York: The New Press, 1999), p. 132.
[230] Ibid.
[231] Michael Radelet and Margaret Vandiver, "Race and Capital Punishment: An Overview of the Issues," *Crime and Social Justice* 25 (1986), p. 98, http://www.jstor.org/stable/29766297.

would have made the victim incapable of offering any resistance, in fact, far beyond what would have ensured his or her death.

A case that drew widespread attention and condemnation occurred in New York City in 1999. Amadou Diallo, 23 years old at the time, was a fully documented, legal immigrant from Guinea, West Africa, who had come to America to earn a computer science degree. Mistaken by four plainclothes police officers for a rape suspect, he was standing in the doorway of his home when the policemen opened fire, claiming, erroneously, that Amadou was brandishing a gun. Diallo was ripped to pieces in a hail of forty-one bullets by the four police officers, who were later acquitted in court of any wrongdoing. Obviously, Diallo was dead long before the last rounds were fired.

In East Cleveland, Ohio, in November 2012, a car driven by Timothy Russell was forced to stop by several police cars, following a 22-minute car chase. In the passenger seat was Russell's girlfriend, Malissa Williams. Thirteen of the police officers on the scene fired a total of 137 bullets into the car, with one of the officers jumping up on the hood of the vehicle, firing forty-nine bullets straight through the windshield into Russell and Williams. That required reloading his gun time after time to continue shooting long after the two were dead. A search of the car failed to produce the gun that the police claimed represented a risk to their lives. None of the police officers were found guilty of any wrongdoing.

Many incidents have received publicity recently (2020) because of video recorded on private cell phones. What finally created a massive public protest was the slow, public execution in Minneapolis of George Floyd, helplessly prone on the ground, offering no resistance. He was choked to death by a policeman keeping his knee pressed on Floyd's neck until Floyd was dead. The event was captured in video on a cell phone by a bystander. It showed the policeman, protected from intervention by the crowd by three other policemen, keeping his knee on George's neck for eight minutes and forty-five seconds. The anger created by police brutality and the all-too-obvious discrimination faced by black Americans has created a worldwide movement against racism and police brutality.

For many poor whites as well as black Americans, the possibilities of socio-economic advances can seem hopelessly remote. Then a combination of hopelessness and anti-black, anti-Jewish, and xenophobic prejudice contributes to the growth of violence-prone political extremism and racial hatred. Some develop a desperate desire to strike out, somehow, against whatever they think holds them back. Similarly, some in the black community, long accustomed to being frustrated in their hopes and dreams of a better life, simply give up on social integration and regular careers and become lawless predators.

Almost one hundred thousand people in the United States are hit by gunfire each year. According to the Center for Disease Control (CDC), an official US government agency, 116,414 nonfatal injuries, and 38,658 deaths occurred by firearms in 2016.[232] Over two years, the number of civilian deaths by gunfire in the United States significantly exceeded the death toll of ten years of American involvement in Vietnam. Blacks constitute about 13 percent of the population of the United States but about 55 percent of the victims of gun violence, while non-Hispanic whites are about 65 percent of the population—five times that of the

---

[232] Centers for Disease Control and Prevention, data for 2016,
   https://webappa.cdc.gov/sasweb/ncipc/mortrate.html

ANDERS EKLOF

black population—but only constitute about 25 percent of the victims, i.e., less than half as many as the black victims. A black person is roughly ten times more likely than a white person to be the victim of gunfire.

The advent of the Internet has led to the proliferation of easily accessible websites that promote white nationalism, rabid racial hatred, homophobia, and xenophobia. On those sites, the traditional racial prejudices, "states' rights" arguments, extreme right-wing ideology, uncompromising gun rights advocacy, and bizarre and scary conspiracy theories mix in an unholy witches brew that continues to poison American minds.

Mass murder by gunfire has become all too common in the nation, and it has increasingly taken on a racist slant. On June 17, 2017, a young white supremacist shot nine black worshipers to death in a church in Charleston, SC. On October 27, 2017, a young man entered a Jewish synagogue in Pittsburgh, PA, and shot to death eleven worshippers. On August 3, 2019, twenty-two people were killed and twenty-four injured in El Paso, TX, by a man who sought to kill as many Latinos as he could. The frequent mass shootings have intensified the efforts to come to grips with the problem of such shootings, but there has been little progress.

As in the 1950s, the problems and injustices in American society are again attracting international attention and are damaging the nation not just domestically but in the areas of international prestige and influence. In May of 2018, the Human Rights Council of the UN General Assembly released a report on poverty and human rights in the United States.[233] It is grim reading. The report documents the still existing racial discrimination and widespread poverty. It also notes the persistence of prejudice and unequal treatment of blacks in the justice system and the counterproductive policies of imprisoning people for not having the means to pay fines or debts. It highlights the extremes of economic inequality in the population. Regarding the economic policies announced by the Trump Republican administration, it states:

> The new policies: (a) provide unprecedentedly high tax breaks and financial windfalls to the very wealthy and the largest corporations; (b) pay for these partly by reducing welfare benefits for the poor; (c) undertake a radical programme of financial, environmental, health and safety deregulation that eliminates protections mainly benefiting the middle classes and the poor; (d)seek to add over 20 million poor and middle class persons to the ranks of those without health insurance; (e) restrict eligibility for many welfare benefits while increasing the obstacles required to be overcome by those eligible; (f) dramatically increase spending on defence, while rejecting requested improvements in key veterans' benefits; (g) do not provide adequate additional funding to address an opioid crisis that is decimating parts of the country; and (h) make no effort to tackle the structural racism that keeps a large percentage of non-Whites in poverty and near poverty.

While a snapshot of present-day America can look discouraging, a longer timeline still gives cause for optimism. Since the 1960s, racial and gender prejudices have decreased significantly in their pervasiveness across the nation. Among young Americans, racial prejudice has lost much of its emotional intensity as

---

[233] Available at http://undocs.org/en/a/hrc/38/33/add.1

296

social and professional contacts across racial lines have increased, and sexual attitudes have become more liberal. Compared to fifty years ago, America is a far better place now for racial minorities, women, and those with sexual preferences other than strictly "opposite sex, same race." America's young increasingly favor progressive policies that will aggressively attack the present injustices in the system.

Although much delayed compared to what has happened in Europe, the last few decades have seen a marked reduction in the percentage of Americans who consider themselves to be devoutly religious. Organized religion is losing its hold on the minds of most Americans, and nowhere is that more noticeable than among the young. The traditional, conservative, and fundamentalist churches have seen the most significant attrition, hit by the modern emphasis on scientific beliefs in schools. Racist and bigoted attitudes based on religious teachings now meet with social disapproval in most circles.

While some of the glitzy and TV-based charismatic megachurches have attracted many followers even among the young, the overall trend has been toward a diminution of the influence of fundamentalist, sexually repressed Christian teachings on the beliefs and mores of Americans. As a result, the nation has seen a steady reduction of racist prejudice and fear. There has been a substantial increase in the number of mixed-race marriages.

The recent rise of a strong, progressive movement in the Democratic party is a sign that America might still halt its decline and rescue its future. Women and ethnic minorities have made good progress in attaining elected positions at all levels of the political structure.

In recent years, progressive political movements everywhere have become increasingly concerned with severe threats on a global scale. Looming environmental and climate problems have global impacts, placing us all in grave danger, regardless of race, nationality, religion, or gender. The problems are going to have a negative effect on everyone, and adjustments and remedies are going to be difficult and costly. Perhaps our common peril can improve our sense of common interests and our willingness to place cooperation ahead of competition.

Reparations: A century and a half late, trillions of dollars short?

There is abundant evidence that the historical circumstance of slavery has left a very harmful legacy in the conditions of life in the American black population well past the end of slavery as such. Its immense, tragic consequences have become such an intrinsic part of American society that few Americans can see all its manifestations for what they are. Fewer still can envision a comprehensive, effective solution to all its various problems. To be able to envision such a solution, and realize the cost and time required to implement it, one must be thoroughly familiar with many issues, historical, psychological, political, and economical. It is beyond most individuals to have such a broad yet deep understanding. The preceding seven-part historical review gives but a hint at the extent of the problem and the complexity of its origins.

Many low-income Americans have no health insurance and are in poor health because they cannot afford to seek medical care. They suffer disproportionately from chronic ailments like hypertension, diabetes, and other health problems. It has been the case in most natural or humanmade disasters to strike America that low-income people have suffered the most from the consequences. They more commonly suffer severe symptoms and death from catching the present disastrous (2020) pandemic. They have also been struck harder by the record high unemployment that has followed the pandemic outbreak. Blacks and Latinos are more likely than whites to be among the lowest income group. They are the population segments that can least bear the loss of income, typically living paycheck-to-paycheck, with no significant savings to tie them over until they can find a new job – itself a low odds possibility in the near future.

In November 2017, the National Bureau of Economic Research published a study of household wealth trends in the United States, 1962 – 2016.[234] Its results were calculated using adjusted dollar figures normalized to 2016 values. The study showed that in 2016, the median income for white households was $60,000, while the median income for black ones was $35,000, a ratio of about 1.7. That ratio, while having improved somewhat since 1983, shows a still substantial gap in income between blacks and whites. The disparity is not mainly due to whites holding, relative to their population, more of the higher-paying occupations. According to the Bureau of Labor Statistics, "The earnings disparity across the major race and ethnicity groups for men holds for nearly all major occupational groups."[235]

The situation for blacks is, in reality, much worse than what the medium income figures might lead one to believe. The cost of living has increased faster than the inflation number used to translate all income numbers into 2016 dollars. An income of $35,000 per year per household does not permit saving and investing to increase the net worth of the household. White households, with a yearly income of $60,000, have done much better than black ones, as the "bottom line" figures of net household worth show.

In 1983, the median net worth for a white family was $105,300, while for a black household, it was $7,000, a ratio of about 15:1. In 2016, the median net worth of a white family had increased by about a third to $140,500, while that of a black family had *decreased* by over 50% to $3,400. The net worth ratio between white households and black ones almost tripled, from 15 to about 41. In other words, the financial situation for black households has become increasingly precarious. In 2016, thirty-seven percent of black households had a *negative* net value, i.e., their debts exceeded the total value of all their assets.

Poverty breeds crime, and vice versa. Those two are inseparably entwined in a vicious circle. It is no coincidence that people coming from poor backgrounds dominate America's prison population and that the black community is hit especially hard by the consequences. Broken families are the growing grounds for school truancy, drop-outs, psychological problems, and addictions of various kinds. Many of those young people see drug-dealing and other criminality as the only possible source of quick cash, which in turn leads to criminal records and incarceration and more broken families.

A 2016 study, published by The Sentencing Project and using data from the Bureau of Justice Statistics, presented some striking findings.[236] In state prisons, averaged across the nation, black youths are incarcerated, percentage-wise, at 5.1 times the rate of whites. In twelve states, blacks were over half the prison population.

Demographic trends will make those of European ancestry a minority in the United States by 2050. The prospect has produced a rising level of anxiety and racial tension among many conservative white Americans.

---

[234] Monthly Labor Review (MLR), November 2017, *"The unexplainable, growing black-white wage gap."*
[235] Bureau of Labor Statistics: *BLS Report #1082, October 2019, "Earnings"*
[236] The Sentencing Project: *Fact Sheet: Black Disparities in Youth Incarceration* 2015

With increasing frequency, one hears racial prejudice and xenophobia openly expressed. Reparations for slavery and its consequences is not an issue that presently has much support. However, the nation may, at last, be reaching a turning point. In recent years, the public, in particular the younger generation, has again awakened to the existence of systemic injustices and tensions in American society.

There are more poor whites than blacks in America because there are five times as many whites as blacks in the population. However, the poverty rate is much higher among blacks. That fact is a direct result of the conditions of slavery and oppressive discrimination in which blacks have been forced to live. It is an inexcusable injustice that screams for a redress. It will be a very difficult, time-consuming, and expensive task to correct the shameful situation and provide some compensation for past egregious wrongs. Still, the very honor of the nation demands that it be undertaken. It is more than a question of economics or political expediency; it is a question that tests the very soul of the nation. Its response will forever be a measure of its moral fiber and the degree of hypocrisy with which it proclaims its idealistic Constitution.

It is long overdue for America to deal with the issues of racial prejudice and injustice in a very fundamental and adequate way. In the past, many voices have risen to address the subject but to no effect. Every year since 1989, Representative John Conyers of Michigan (1929 – 2019) introduced House Resolution 40 (HR40), *The Commission to Study and Develop Reparations Proposals for African Americans Act,* which aims to find ways for America to remedy the injustices that have been the legacy of slavery.

The proposed Act is a modest one, seeking merely to establish a commission to *study* the issue and *recommend measures* to be taken to overcome the destructive effects that the legacy of slavery has had on the black populations. It recommends that the proposed commission performs the following tasks:

1. Identify, compile and synthesize the relevant corpus of evidentiary documentation of the institution of slavery which existed within the United States and the colonies that became the United States from 1619 through 1865. The Commission's documentation and examination shall include but not be limited to the facts related to—

   A) the capture and procurement of Africans;

   B) the transport of Africans to the United States and the colonies that became the United States for the purpose of enslavement, including their treatment during transport;

   C) the sale and acquisition of Africans as chattel property in interstate and intrastate commerce;

   D) the treatment of African slaves in the colonies and the United States, including the deprivation of their freedom, exploitation of their labor, and destruction of their culture, language, religion, and families; and

   E) the extensive denial of humanity, sexual abuse and the chattellization of persons.

2. The role which the Federal and State governments of the United States supported the institution of slavery in constitutional and statutory provisions, including the extent to which such governments prevented, opposed, or restricted efforts of formerly enslaved Africans and their descendants to repatriate to their homeland.

3. The Federal and State laws that discriminated against formerly enslaved Africans and their descendants who were deemed United States citizens from 1868 to the present.

4. The other forms of discrimination in the public and private sectors against freed African slaves and their descendants who were deemed United States citizens from 1868 to the present, including redlining, educational funding discrepancies, and predatory financial practices.

5. The lingering negative effects of the institution of slavery and the matters described in paragraphs (1), (2), (3), (4), (5), and (6) on living African-Americans and on society in the United States.

6. Recommend appropriate ways to educate the American public of the Commission's findings.

7. Recommend appropriate remedies in consideration of the Commission's findings on the matters described in paragraphs (1), (2), (3), (4), (5), and (6).

The House of Representatives has, in the past, largely ignored the proposal, but numerous Democratic members of Congress now (2020) support it. However, one must not underestimate the political difficulty in dealing with this emotionally charged issue. The extreme partisan divide in the nation will make it difficult to hammer out sufficiently radical legislation to achieve results. People of goodwill must somehow be found, willing to listen to arguments on all sides.

As suggested by the late Representative Conyers, a special commission must be appointed to study the appropriate methods and costs of "reparations." Such a commission must have members from all political parties and segments of society, with deep political and life experience assuring their credibility to speak on all subjects relevant to the problems of poverty and racism in America. Over the years, such a commission has been proposed in various forms by many prominent Americans, among them Randall Robinson[237] and Ta-Nehisi Coates[238].

"Doing the right thing"

The socio-economic problems in America affect especially the segments of the population who are the descendants of slaves. Radical reforms across all aspects of society will be necessary if one is to come to grips with the still lingering effects of slavery and anti-black prejudice in America. There can be no "quick fix." Only very large government programs can deal with the interconnected, deeply rooted and extensive problems and injustices that exist in American society. The remedies will be complex, time-consuming, expensive, and wide-ranging, and will unavoidably have a cost impact on the wealthier part of both the black and the white population. There can be no excuse for objecting to this task in the form of "I did not personally cause those problems; why should I be held responsible?" We must not see reparations as a "fine" paid by white society as a punishment for past wrongs. When an intolerable injustice exists, not to help solve the problem is a sin of omission. Helping to perpetuate the problem is a sin of commission.

---

[237] Randall Robinson: *The Debt: What America Owes to Blacks* (Penguin Putnam Inc., 375 Hudson Street, New York, NY 10014, 2001)

[238] *The Case for Reparations*, an essay (2014) in the collection of essays by Ta-Nehisi Coates: *We Were Eight Years in Power: An American Tragedy* (One World, an imprint of Random House, 1745 Broadway, New York, NY 10019, 2017)

ANTI-BLACK PREJUDICE IN AMERICA

Initiatives by private businesses to donate money to anti-racist causes and increase their hiring and promotion of black employees are per se helpful and commendable but are not addressing the fundamental problems. They merely will be skimming off the cream of the crop, so to speak, encouraging and enabling those who have already had some success to take further steps up the ladder. Those companies are using their promises as PR for the moment, but have neither the resources, the expertise, nor the short-term bottom line incentives to deal with the fundamental problems of failing schools, too-expensive higher education, broken families, poor health and expensive healthcare, drug addiction, high levels of criminality, dilapidated ghetto housing, feelings of outsider status and lack of respect by the white majority.

Increasing economic inequalities, a high poverty rate, and exorbitant costs of education and healthcare are problems that should not exist in a nation as rich and advanced as the United States, where the total wealth in private and public hands is more than sufficient to provide a good and secure life for everyone. A thorough overhaul of American society is necessary to make full and fair use of its abundant economic and human resources to the benefit of its entire population. Such an overhaul is what "reparations" must consist of to bring lasting justice, opportunity, and a bright future to the disadvantaged black population of America.

It would severely shortchange black Americans to limit reparations to some sort of overdue payment for unpaid slave labor, even though a fair accounting for centuries of slavery by millions of slaves would, with interest, amount to trillions of dollars. The oppression and discrimination suffered by blacks for a hundred years of Jim Crow cost the black population not just humiliation and violence, but additional hundreds of billions of dollars. The present substantial differences in average income and wealth among white families compared to black families is a direct result of historical circumstances and is a continuing wrong that must be corrected.

Following their release from slavery and the failed project of Reconstruction, blacks never had an opportunity to compete on fair terms with their former owners and their descendants. As Frederick Douglass observed in his 1875 essay "Celebrating the Past, Anticipating the Future:"

> The world has never seen any people turned loose to such destitution as were the four million slaves of the South... They were free without roofs to cover them, or bread to eat, or land to cultivate, and as a consequence died in such numbers as to awaken the hope of their enemies that they would soon disappear.[239]

About two decades later, the anti-lynching crusader Ida B. Wells made a similar observation:

> The Civil War of 1861–65 ended slavery. It left us free, but it also left us homeless, penniless, ignorant, nameless, and friendless... Russia's liberated serf was given three acres of land and agricultural implements with which to begin his career of liberty and independence. But to us, no foot of land nor implement was given. We were turned

---

[239] Darity Jr., William A. and Mullen, Kirsten A.. *From Here to Equality* (p. 7). The University of North Carolina Press, 2020.

loose to starvation, destitution and death. So desperate was our condition that some of our statesmen declared it useless to try to save us by legislation as we were doomed to extinction. —Ida B. Wells, "Class Legislation," 1893

(The promise made to blacks that each family would be given "forty acres of land and a mule" was reneged on by President Andrew Johnson.)

Reparations to those of African ancestry should not consist of simply handing out lots of money to individual blacks. Such a superficial measure would simply cause that money to quickly filter back into the present ruling system of powerful, mostly white individuals and corporations. Real, effective reparations must involve thorough systemic changes that benefit all those on the low end of the income and wealth ladder, regardless of ethnicity. However, efforts should be focused especially on those problems that predominantly plague blacks, like ghettoization in poorly maintained housing. They should include financial subsidies to make it possible for more black families to move to neighborhoods that are presently priced beyond what they can afford. It would also require improving physical maintenance and communal services in all areas currently suffering from poverty, neglect, and deterioration.

Poor primary education and a criminal record make it very difficult to get a job with adequate income to pull oneself up from this bad start in life. Parts of all segments of the American population experience the debilitating effects of poor primary education facilities, unaffordable higher education, inadequate and unaffordable health care, drug addiction, and a justice system that is unreasonably harsh in dealing with nonviolent crimes involving drugs. Those factors strike particularly hard against the black population and cause great harm to it.

To be effective, reparation programs must place high, long-duration priority on improving primary education in the inner-city districts. There, school buildings are in many cases in bad physical condition; teacher's aid equipment is much less extensive and sophisticated than in affluent suburban areas; the drop-out rate is high, and classroom discipline is poor. Local school districts where such problems are serious should give specialized, additional training to teachers willing to tackle the issues of poor discipline and bad student attitudes. There should be a significant salary premium to those who have the courage and sincere commitment to take on those difficult but essential tasks.

The number one factor that facilitates socio-economic advancement for an individual is higher education, the rise in the cost of which has far outstripped the growth of even white household income. It has made it ever more unlikely that someone born in unfortunate circumstances will achieve greater economic success than his or her parents. Higher education, therefore, must be made available at minimal cost to all who have the ambition and intellectual ability to benefit from it. More must be done to make clear to impoverished youth, especially inner-city blacks, that education, not sports or drug dealings, is a worthwhile effort and their tickets to better lives for themselves and their future children.

Low-cost, high-quality healthcare must be available to all who need it, including emphasizing prenatal healthcare for segments of the population presently having high levels of maternal and neonatal mortality in connection with childbirth. Problems of that type are particularly common in the black population. The ravages of the coronavirus pandemic have been particularly devastating in the black community from a health as well as an economic viewpoint. It has made abundantly clear that only a unified, national healthcare system, financed by federal taxes, can adequately and fairly deal with the healthcare for all citizens. Such a system has long been in successful operation in all modern, industrial nations except the United States. It has proved to cost the citizens less in taxes than the cost to the citizens in the American system, where a plethora of insurance corporations, high-priced lawyers, and high-profit drug manufacturers sponge off the vast river of dollars spent in America on healthcare.

Drug addiction should be treated as a healthcare issue and dealt with by medical services, not by law enforcement agencies. Legalizing the less addictive drugs like marijuana but regulating and taxing the sale of it will remove the financial incentive by criminals to traffic in it. That will reduce the crime rate and the number of incarcerated people, thereby reducing the cost of law enforcement and prisons and the number of broken families. It will bring down the horrendous death toll of street gang turf wars and provide additional tax revenue for local communities.

Index

16th Street Baptist Church 187
78 rpm records 136
101st Airborne Division 149, 243

A

Abernathy, Ralph 146, 164, 257
Acton, William 51
Agnew, Spiro 253, 259, 286
Alcatraz 233, 234
Alexander Graham Bell 97
Allport, Gordon 15
American Breeders Association (ABA). 96
American Psychiatric Association 236, 237
Americans for Democratic Action (ADA) 198
An American Dilemma 120, 121, 147
Andrew Johnson 25, 28, 31
Anniston 159
Anthony, Susan B. 84
Arkansas National Guard 148, 149, 150
Aryan 9
Ashmore, Harry 148
Assistant Attorney General John Doar 207
Attica 282, 283

B

Barnett, Ross 168, 169, 170, 216, 221
Battle Creek Sanitarium 78
Battle of Appomattox 209, 210
Battle of Michigan Avenue 263
Beckwith, Byron De La 182
behaviorism 2
Bernstein, Carl 286
Best, George 48
B. F. Skinner 2
Birmingham 159, 160, 161, 172, 178, 179, 180, 182, 186,
      187, 190, 278
Blackboard Jungle 136
blacklisting 134
Black Lives Matter 293
Black Moses 50
Black Muslims 174, 176, 200, 204, 205
Black Panther Party 176, 222, 223, 268, 272, 278, 279, 280
Black Panthers 223, 224, 264
Black Power 176, 217, 219, 221, 222, 231, 245, 272

black rapist 33
Black Rapist 60, 61, 69, 89, 112, 287
Bleser, Carol 53
Block busting 214
Blockbusting 214
Bloody Sunday 206
Bodin, Jean 47
Bombingham 178
Bond, Julian 221, 222, 280
Boom! Voices of the Sixties 130
Booth, John Wilkes 28
Boynton, Amelia 206
Bradlee, Ben 284
Branagan, Thomas 59
British Invasion 228
British West Indies 54
Brown, Helen Gurley 229
Brown, H. Rap 209, 224
Bryant, Roy 89, 141, 142
Byrd, Harry 139

C

Calhoun, Arthur W. 58
Calhoun, John C. 25
Cambodia 272
Candomblé 51
Caribbean islands 54
Carmichael, Stokely 176, 192, 208, 217, 218, 221, 224
carpetbaggers 30, 112
castrated 35, 36, 142
castration 33, 42
Chaney, James Earl 193
Chesnut, Mary Boykin 53
Chicago 136, 141, 174, 215, 216
Chicago Freedom Movement 215, 216
Chicago police riot 261
Chicago Seven 264, 278
Christian 22, 23, 43, 44, 50, 51, 73, 80, 87, 111, 164, 184,
      290, 297
CIA 134, 201, 283, 285
Circumcision 79
Civil Rights Act of 1964 168, 195, 196, 198, 203, 211, 218,
      221, 256
Civil Rights Movement 139, 225

Civil War 27, 32, 53, 60, 61, 62, 84, 111, 112, 128, 129, 146, 209, 252, 253, 283
Clark, Jim 205, 207
Clean Air Act of 1970. 277
COINTELPRO 223, 224, 268, 277, 278
Colfax, Louisiana 29
Colvin, Claudette 144
communism 134, 157, 166, 167, 223, 272, 279
communist 133, 134, 157, 159, 165, 193, 196, 202, 212, 223, 236, 272, 277, 278, 279
Communist Party 166, 280
Comstock, Anthony 80, 81, 82, 83
Confederacy 31, 128, 139, 146, 166
Confederate battle flag 163
Congress Of Racial Equality 158, 184
Connally, John 190
Connor, T. E. "Bull" 172
Connor, T. E. "Bull" 179
Coordinating Council of Community Organizations (CCCO) 215
CORE 159, 161, 162, 164, 168, 176, 184, 204, 208, 217, 221, 222, 224
Coweta County, Georgia 35
Craddock, Ida 82
CREEP 286
Crews, Tom 117
Cronkite, Walter 193
Cuban missile crisis 167, 172, 200
Cudjo Lewis (Oluale Kossula) 19

D

Dailey, Jane 142
Daley, Richard 216, 260, 261, 262, 263, 264
Davenport, Charles 95, 96, 97, 98, 99, 101, 102, 104, 105, 106
Davis, Angela 278, 279, 280, 281
Dealey Plaza in Dallas 190
Dellinger, David 264
Democratic National Convention 1964 197, 200, 203, 261
Democratic National Convention 1968 260, 263, 264, 278, 283
denial response 15
Department of Natural Resources 277
Dickinson, William L., Republican congressman from Alabama 212
Dohrn, Bernardine 273
Domino, Fats 136
Douglass, Frederick 25
Dred Scott v. Sanford 25
Dr. King 144, 145, 176, 177, 178, 186, 203, 204, 205, 207, 208, 211, 216, 221, 241, 242, 246, 248, 253, 260
Duffey, Eliza 51

E

Eagleton, Thomas 286
Edmund Pettus Bridge 205, 206, 207
Eisenhower 134, 140, 148, 149, 155, 158, 259, 267
Elijah Muhammad 174, 176, 205, 247
Ellsberg, Daniel 284
E. M. Harriman. 98
Emmett Till 142
Environmental Protection Agency 277
erotophobia 72, 73, 74, 80
Evers, Medgar 182, 183
Executive Order 9808, Establishing the President's Committee on Civil Rights 117, 122
extremism in defense of freedom is no vice. 197

F

Farmer, James 161, 164, 184, 217
Farrakhan, Louis 282
Faubus, Orville 147, 148, 153
FBI 134, 165, 188, 193, 202, 211, 223, 236, 268, 272, 274, 280, 281, 283
federalize 148, 209
federalized 150, 153, 170, 182, 210, 216
Fifteenth Amendment to the Constitution 31
Fifth Amendment to the Constitution 143
Five Civilized Tribes (Native Americans) 6
flower children 227, 228
Folsom, Jim 172
Ford, Gerald 286
Forman, James 208, 210
Fourteenth Amendment 30
Fourteenth and Fifteenth Amendments 31, 146
Fowler, James Bonard 205
Freed, Alan 137
Freedom Riders 158, 159, 160, 162, 178, 179
Freedom Rides 164, 165
Freedom Summer 192
Freud, Sigmund 1, 83
Friedan, Betty 230
Fuoss, Kirk W. 34

G

Gagarin, Yuri 157, 158
Galton, Francis 91, 92
Garrison, William Loyd 25
Gay Liberation 236
Genovese, Eugene D. 49, 64
Goldwater, Barry 196, 199, 200, 204, 259, 265
Goodman, Andrew 192
Governor J. Lindsay Almond of Virginia 153
Graetz, Robert 146
Graham, Henry 182
Graham, Sylvester 73, 74, 75, 77, 78, 83
Green, Ernest 153

Greenwich Village 225, 237, 273
Gregory, Dick 266
Griffith, D. W. 52, 112
Gulf of Tonkin 201, 202

H

Haight-Ashbury 225, 226, 227
Hale, Grace Elizabeth 35
Haley, Alex 175
Ham 48
Hamer, Fannie Lou 198
Hammond, James Henry 55
Hampton, Fred 273
Harriet Beecher Stowe 25
Hayden, Tom 264, 280
heaven 75
Hefner, Hugh 288, 289
Hemings, Sally 56, 57, 59
Herbert Spencer 92
Hitler, Adolf 104, 106, 107, 108
Hoffman, Abbie 260, 264
Holbert, Luther 40
Holmes, Oliver Wendell 104
Holocaust 42
Homosexuality 80
Hoover, J. Edgar 134, 165, 223, 236, 268, 277, 280, 281, 283
Hose, Sam 35, 142
How long? Not Long 210
Human Be-In 226
Humphrey, Hubert 199, 251, 261, 262, 263, 264, 265, 266
Hurston, Zora Neale 19
Huston Plan 283, 285
Huston, Tom 283

I

I Have a Dream 186
Illinois National Guard 261
indentured servants 18, 22, 23
indentured servitude 22

J

Jackson, George 273, 280, 281
Jackson, James Caleb 77
Jackson, Jennifer (First black Playboy centerfold) 288
Jackson, Jesse 216
Jackson, Jimmie Lee 205, 208, 211
Jackson, Jonathan 280, 281
Jackson State College 274
Jacobus 62, 63, 313
Jacolliot, Louis 62
Jamaica 54
James Rado and Gerome Ragni 226
Jamestown 18, 47
Jefferson, Thomas 47, 56, 57, 59

Jesus 13, 48, 226
Johnny Robinson 187
Johnson, Andrew 29, 30
Johnson, J. Monroe 163
Johnson, Lyndon 190, 191, 193, 195, 198, 199, 200, 201, 202, 203, 204, 206, 207, 208, 209, 210, 212, 242, 243, 246, 247, 248, 249, 250, 251, 253, 256, 258, 259, 261, 263, 264, 266, 267, 268, 286
Johnson, Paul 193, 216
Johnson, Sally 55
Jordan, Winthrop 47
Journal of Southern Religion 44

K

Katzenbach, Nicholas 181, 182
Kellogg, John 77, 78, 79
Kennedy, Edward \"Teddy\" 256
Kennedy, John F. 131, 157, 158, 161, 162, 164, 166, 168, 170, 172, 181, 182, 184, 190, 191, 209, 250, 256, 259, 260, 264
Kennedy, Robert 162, 164, 170, 250, 251, 255, 256, 260
Kent State University 132, 274
Kercheval 220
Kerner Commission 243, 244
Kerner Report 252
Keys, Sarah 163
King Cotton 59
King, Martin Luther, Jr. 135, 144, 154, 156, 161, 165, 176, 182, 184, 186, 203, 215, 217, 219, 224, 238, 242, 245, 248, 252, 256, 260
Kinsey, Alfred C. 87
Kinsey Report 87, 236
KKK 112, 154, 158, 159, 160, 163, 164, 187, 204, 208, 221, 287, 290
Knight, Richard Payne 11
Ku Klux Klan iii, 31, 32, 65, 85, 112, 153, 166, 182, 193, 203, 211, 228, 290
Kunstler, William 264, 280, 282

L

Laughlin, Harry 98, 99, 100, 101, 106, 108
Leary, Timothy 227
LeMay, Curtis 265, 266
Leo Africanus 47
Letter from Birmingham Jail 178
Lewis, John 184, 217
Lingo, Al 205
Little, Malcolm 175
Little Rock 147, 148, 149, 153, 155, 161, 162, 171
Little Rock Central High School 153
Litwack, Leon F. 39, 40, 41
Liuzzo, Viola 211
Long, Edward 54
Look magazine 89, 143
Lorraine Hotel 252

Loving, Richard and Mildred 239
LSD 132, 227

M

Maddox, destroyer 201
Maddox, Lester 220
Malcolm X 86, 87, 127, 174, 175, 176, 177, 194, 200, 203, 204, 205, 208, 217, 218, 221, 312
Mao Tse Tung 200
Mao Zedong (See Mao Tse Tung) 200
March Against Fear 216, 217
March on Washington 184, 246, 256
Marx, Karl 277
masturbation 72, 74, 75, 76, 79, 80, 87
Mathews, Donald G. 44
McCarthy, Eugene 249, 250, 251, 255, 256, 260
McCarthy, Joseph 82, 134, 167
McGovern, George 256, 262, 263, 285, 286
McKissick, Floyd 176, 217, 221
McNamara, Robert 284
Mehlinger, Kermit, M. D. 58
Melton, J. H. 167
Memphis, Tennessee 29
Mendel, Gregor 92
Meredith, James 168, 170, 171, 216
MFDP 192, 197, 198, 199, 200
Milam, J. W. 89, 141, 142
Mississippi Democratic Party 192
Mississippi Freedom Democratic Party 192, 197
Mississippi National Guard 170
Mitchell, John 283, 286
mixed-race children 22, 23
Monroe, Marilyn 288
Montgomery bus boycott 144, 146, 153, 159
Moore's Ford lynching 117
Motown 219, 228, 229
Mountaintop speech 252
Mount Rushmore 234
Muhammad Ali 203, 247
My Lai 270, 271
Myrdal 120

N

NAACP 42, 128, 144, 145, 147, 148, 154, 168, 182, 184, 206, 221
Nash, Diane 160
National States' Rights Party (NSRP) 204
Nation of Islam 174, 282
NBC Nightly News 131
Newark 242
New Jersey National Guard 242
Newton, Huey 176
Nixon, Richard 131, 253, 259, 260, 265, 266, 276, 281, 284, 286
Noah 48

Nobel peace prize 186
NOI 174, 175, 176, 205, 224
North Vietnamese 201, 202, 248, 250, 285, 287
Notes on the State of Virginia 47
nuclear war 167

O

OAAU 176, 204, 205
Ole Miss 168, 170, 171
Olmsted, Frederick L. 50
Operation Breadbasket 216
Orangeburg, South Carolina 276
Organization for Afro-American Unity 176, 204, 205
Orishas 51
Ostler, Jeffrey 6
Oswald, Lee Harvey 190, 191
Our Home on the Hillside 77

P

Parks, Rosa 144, 145, 219
Patterson, John 161, 162, 173
Paulsen, Pat 266
PBS 142
Peck, James 159
Pentagon Papers 283
Playboy iii, 288, 290
Plessy v. Ferguson 26
Poor People's Campaign 246, 256, 257, 258
Poor People's March 246
projection response 15
psychedelic art 132, 227

Q

Queen Victoria 73

R

Ralph Abernathy 161
Randolph, A. Philip 184
Rauh, Joseph 198
Ray, James Earl 253
Reagan, Ronald 270, 279
Reconstruction 30, 31, 32, 80, 111, 127, 146, 163
Redlining 214, 215, 300
Reeb, James 208
Rehnquist, William 284
Resurrection City 256, 258
Ribicoff, Abraham 262
Riverside Church in New York City 241
rockabilly 136
rock and roll 49, 130, 131, 135, 136, 137, 138, 139, 228, 229, 237
Rockefeller Foundation 99, 104, 106
Rockefeller, Nelson 196, 282, 286
Rockwell, George Lincoln 204

Rogers, William 148
Romney, George 243
Roosevelt, Franklin D. 85, 184, 266, 267
Rubin, Jerry 260, 264
Rush, Benjamin 47, 73
Rustin, Bayard 184

S

Sally Smith (Redoshi) 19
Sam Phillips' Sun Records 136
Samuel Johnson 25
San Francisco 225, 226, 227, 268, 276, 280
Sanger, Margaret 84, 95
Santeria 51
Schwerner, Michael 192, 193
SCLC 164, 168, 184, 203, 204, 205, 207, 215, 216, 224, 242, 245
Scopes, John Thomas 85
Scopes Monkey Trial 85
Scottsboro Boys 165
SDS 221, 225, 264, 268, 272, 273, 278
Seale, Bobby 176, 264, 278
segregation 1, 22, 31, 44, 49, 85, 89, 129, 133, 139, 140, 145, 146, 147, 153, 155, 158, 162, 163, 164, 166, 167, 178, 181, 182, 192, 196, 203, 209, 215, 218, 219, 220, 238, 239, 252, 265, 267, 287
Selma 203, 204, 205, 207, 208, 209, 210, 211, 212, 221, 245
Senator Inouye of Hawaii 261
sexual revolution 138, 229
Sharp, Harry Clay 101
Shelton, Robert iii, 65, 290

   SNCC 184
Student Nonviolent Coordinating Committee; SNCC 154
Students for a Democratic Society 221
Summer of Love 226, 227

T

Ta-Nehisi Coates 214
Tet Offensive 248
The Birth of a Nation 52, 112
The Confederate States of America 27
the Devil's mark 43
The Feminine Mystique 230
The lynching of Thomas Shipp and Abram Smith 36
The Trail of Tears 7
The United States 22, 23, 27, 32, 33, 46, 56, 59, 128, 134, 138, 143, 146, 148, 157, 158, 160, 164, 167, 175, 182, 200, 201, 212, 222, 256, 262, 272, 273, 281, 284, 285, 295, 314
the wholesale profligacy of the Old South 58
Thirteenth Amendment 30
Thurmond, Strom 164
Till, Emmett 89, 140, 141, 142, 144, 182
Tillman, Ben 33

Shepard Alan B. Jr. 158
Shriver, Sargent 286
Shuttlesworth, Fred 161, 178
Simms, William Gilmore 55
Simon Legree 25
Sirhan Sirhan 255
sit-in 154, 155, 168, 178, 198, 227
Slate Magazine 42
slavery 18, 22, 23, 24, 30, 46, 47, 48, 49, 50, 52, 54, 55, 56, 59, 60, 61, 77, 84, 85, 112, 117, 128
Smith, Henry 34, 35
Smith, Lillian 1, 58
SNCC 154, 159, 160, 162, 164, 168, 176, 184, 192, 203, 207, 208, 210, 217, 221, 222, 224
Sodom and Gomorrah 236
Soledad Brothers 278, 280, 281, 282
sour grapes response 15
South Africa 128
South Carolina 33, 53, 55, 71, 139, 163
Southern Belle 52
Southern Christian Leadership Conference 164, 178, 184
Southern strategy 267
Soviet Union 133, 134, 157, 158, 166, 167, 190, 200, 277
State National Guards 123
states rights 128
states' rights 140, 146, 147, 161, 163, 173, 182, 196, 203, 259, 267
Steinem, Gloria 231
Stephen Douglas 25
Stonewall Inn 237
Strategic Arms Limitation Treaty (SALT) 277
Student Nonviolent Coordinating Committee 217

Todd, John 77, 79
To Secure These Rights 122
Tubman, Harriet 50
Ture, Kwame (Stokely Carmichael) 218
Turnaround Tuesday 208

U

Uncle Tom's Cabin 25
Underground Railroad 50
United Auto Workers (UAW) 198
University of Alabama at Tuscaloosa 181, 186
USS Ticonderoga 201

V

venereal disease 85
Victorian 51, 62, 63, 73, 135, 138, 167, 229
Victorian age 72, 73
Viet Cong 247, 248
Vietnam 27, 132, 167, 196, 199, 200, 201, 202, 204, 220, 221, 222, 225, 226, 238, 241, 246, 247, 248, 249, 250, 255, 256, 259, 264, 265, 266, 267, 268, 272, 273, 276, 284, 285, 295

Vietnam War 27, 133, 167, 196, 221, 225, 226, 238, 246, 247, 250, 264, 266, 267, 273, 277, 286
vinyl 45 and 33 ⅓ rpm records 136
Virgil Lamar Ware 187
Voting Rights Act of 1965 208, 209, 211, 212, 218, 221, 256

W

Wallace, George 172, 173, 178, 180, 181, 182, 186, 203, 205, 206, 208, 209, 210, 211, 265, 266, 267, 285, 286
Walter White 32, 124, 125
Washington, Booker T. 125
Washington, DC 112, 257, 258, 265, 268, 273, 276, 277, 285
Washington, Jesse 35
Washington Post 284, 286
Watergate 285, 286
Watts 213, 216, 219, 220
Weatherman 272, 273
Weather Underground Organization 273, 278
W.E.B. Du Bois 125, 126
Weinglass, Leonard 264
Wells-Barnett, Ida 33, 34
What time is it? It's NATION time! 200

White Citizens' Councils 153
White, Ellen Harmon 76
White Lion 18
White, Walter 42
Wicker, Tom 282, 283
Wilkins, Roy 154, 184
Williams, Hosea 205
Williams, Robert 154
Wills, Frank 285
witch hunts 43, 134
Witch trial 43
Without Sanctuary 35, 39, 40, 41
Wood, Amy Louise 44
Woodstock 132, 269
Woodward, Bob 286
World War II 85, 87, 135, 155, 183, 229, 248
Wounded Knee 235
WUO 273

Y

YIP 260, 264, 266, 278
Young, Whitney Jr. 184

Bibliography

Acton, William. *The Functions and Disorders of the Reproductive Organs in Childhood, Youth, Adult Age and Advanced Life, Considered in Their Physiological, Social, and Moral Relations* (6th ed.). Philadelphia: Presley Blakiston, 1875.

Africanus, Leo. *The History and Description of Africa and of the Notable Things Therein Contained.* London: Hakluyt Society, 1896.

Allen, James, Hilton Als, John Lewis, and Leon F. Litwack. *Without Sanctuary: Lynching Photographs in America.* Santa Fe, NM: Twin Palms, 2000.

Allport, Gordon W. *The Nature of Prejudice.* London: Addison-Wesley Publishing Company, 1979.

Best, George. *A True Discourse of the Late Voyages of Discovery.* London: Henry Bynneman, 1578.

Black, Edwin. *War against the Weak: Eugenics and America's Campaign to Create a Master Race.* New York: Thunder's Mouth Press, 2003.

Bleser, Carol, ed. *Secret and Sacred: The Diaries of James Henry Hammond, a Southern Slaveholder.* New York: Oxford University Press, 1988.

Branagan, Thomas. *Serious Remonstrances, Addressed to the Citizens of the Northern States, and Their Representatives.* Philadelphia: Thomas T. Stiler, 1805.

Brokaw, Tom. *Boom! Voices of the Sixties: Personal Reflections on the '60s and Today.* New York: Random House, 2007.

Broun, Heywood, and Margaret Leech. *Anthony Comstock, Roundsman of the Lord.* New York: Literary Guild of America, 1927.

Brown, Helen Gurley. *Sex and the Single Girl: The Unmarried Woman's Guide to Men.* Fort Lee, NJ: Barricade Books, 2003.

Bullough, Vern L. and Bullough, Bonnie. *Human Sexuality: An Encyclopedia* New York: Routledge, 2013.

Calhoun, Arthur W. *A Social History of the American Family from Colonial Times to the Present.* Cleveland, OH: Arthur H. Clark Company, 1918.

Carter, Dan T. *The Politics of Rage; George Wallace, the Origins of the New Conservatism, and the Transformation of American Politics,* New York: Simon and Schuster, 1995.

Coates, Ta-Nehisi. *We Were Eight Years in Power,* New York: One World, an imprint of Penguin Random House LLC, 2017

Cole, David. *No Equal Justice.* New York: The New Press, 1999.

Darity, William A. and Mullen, A. Kirsten. *From Here to Equality; Reparations for Black Americans in the Twenty-first Century,* The University of North Carolina Press, Chapel Hill, NC, 2020.

D'Emilio, John, and Estelle B. Freedman. *Intimate Matters: A History of Sexuality in America.* New York: Harper and Row, 1988.

Davis, David B. *Slavery and Human Progress.* New York: Oxford University Press, 1984.

Davis, F. James. *Who is Black? One Nation's Definition* (Tenth Anniversary Edition), University Park, Pennsylvania: Pennsylvania State University Press, 1910.

Delumeau, Jean. *Sin and Fear: The Emergence of a Western Guilt Culture 13th–18th Centuries,* trans. Eric Nicholson. New York: St. Martin's Press, 1990.

Diamond, Jared. *Guns, Germs and Steel: The Fates of Human Societies.* New York: W. W. Norton, 1999.

Dollard, J. *Caste and Class in a Southern Town.* New York: Routledge, 1998.

Dray, Philip. *At the Hands of Persons Unknown.* New York: Random House, 2002.

Duffey, Eliza. *What Women Should Know.* New York: Arno Press, 1974. Originally published by J. M. Stoddart, 1873/1879.

Ellerbe, Helen. *The Dark Side of Christian History.* San Rafael, CA: Morningstar Books, 1996.

Ellis, Havelock. *Studies in the Psychology of Sex.* Philadelphia: Davis, 1910–1913.

Foner, Eric. *Reconstruction: America's Unfinished Revolution 1863–1877.* New York: Harper and Row, 1988.

Foner, Eric, and John A. Garraty, eds. *The Reader's Companion to American History* (article excerpts). New York: Houghton Mifflin, 1991.

Friedan, Betty. *The Feminine Mystique* (Fiftieth anniversary edition). New York: W. W. Norton & Co., 2010.

Fuoss, Kirk. "Lynching Performance: Theatres of Violence." *Text and Performance Quarterly* 19, no. 1 (1984): 1–37.

Gebhard, Paul, and Alan Johnson. *The Kinsey Data: Marginal Tabulations of the 1938–1963 Interviews Conducted by the Institute for Sex Research.* Bloomington: Indiana University Press, 1998.

Genovese, Eugene D. *Roll, Jordan, Roll: The World the Slaves Made.* New York: Vintage Books, 1976.

Graham, Sylvester. *A Lecture to Young Men.* Providence, RI: Weeden and Cory, 1834. Facsimile reprint edition: Arno Press, New York, 1974.

Hale, Grace E. *Making Whiteness: The Culture of Segregation in the South, 1890–1940.* New York: Pantheon Books, 1998.

Haley, Alex. *The Autobiography of Malcolm X: As Told to Alex Haley.* New York: Ballantine Books, 1989.

Harris, Trudier. *Exorcising Blackness: Historical and Literary Lynching and Burning Rituals.* Bloomington: Indiana University Press, 1984.

Hurston, Zora Neal. *Barracoon: The Story of the Last "Black Cargo."* HQ, an imprint of HarperCollins Publishers Ltd, 1 London Bridge Street, London SE1 9 GF, 2018

Jackson, George L. *Soledad Brother; The Prison Letters of George Jackson.* Chicago: Lawrence Hill Books., 1994.

Jackson, George L. *Blood in My Eye* Baltimore: Black Classic Press, 1990.

Jackson, James Caleb: *Hints on the Reproductive Organs* and *The Sexual Organism and Its Healthy Management* Boston: B. Leverett Emerson, 1862.

Jacobus (Jacolliot, Louis). *Untrodden Fields of Anthropology.* New York: Falstaff Press, 1898/1937.

Jacoway, Elizabeth. *Turn Away Thy Son: Little Rock, the Crisis that Shocked the Nation*. New York: Free Press, 2007.

Jordan, Winthrop D. *White over Black: American Attitudes toward the Negro, 1550–1812* (2nd edition). Chapel Hill, NC: Omohundro Institute of Early American History and Culture and the University of North Carolina Press, 1968.

Kellogg, John H., M. D. *Plain Facts for Old and Young Embracing the Natural History and Hygiene of Organic Life*. Burlington, IA: I. F. Segner, 1887.

Kendi, Ibram X.. *STAMPED FROM THE BEGINNING; The Definitive History of Racism in America*. Bold Type Books, New York,, NY, 2017

Kerner et al. *The Kerner Report: The National Advisory Commission on Civil Disorders*. Princeton, NJ: Princeton University Press, 1968.

Kinsey, Alfred, Wardell Pomeroy, and Clyde Martin. *Sexual Behavior in the Human Male*. Philadelphia: W. B. Saunders Company, 1948.

Kinsey, Alfred, Wardell Pomeroy, Clyde Martin, and Paul Gebhard. *Sexual Behavior in the Human Female*. Philadelphia: W. B. Saunders Company, 1953.

Knight, Richard P. *A Discourse on the Worship of Priapus* (1786), part of two-volume work also including *The Worship of the Generative Powers*. New York: Matrix House, 1966.

Lane, Charles. *The Day Freedom Died: The Colfax Massacre, the Supreme Court, and the Betrayal of the Reconstruction*. New York: Henry Holt and Company, 2008.

Lavoie, Jeffrey D. *Segregation and the Baptist Bible Fellowship*. Palo Alto, California: Academica Press, 2013.

Long, Edward. *The History of Jamaica, or General Survey of the Antient and Modern State of That Island*. London: T. Lowndes, 1774.

Malcomson, Scott L. *One Drop of Blood: The American Misadventure of Race*. New York: Farrar, Straus and Giroux, 2000.

Mathews, Donald G. "*The Southern Rite of Human Sacrifice, Part III: Sacrificing Christ/Sacrificing Black Men*" *Journal of Southern Religion*, Volume III, 2000

Maurer, Marc. *The Sentencing Project: Race to Incarcerate*. New York: The New Press, 1999.

Minz, Steven. *Moralists & Modernizers: America's Pre-Civil War Reformers*. Baltimore: The Johns Hopkins University Press, 1995.

Money, John. *The Destroying Angel*. Buffalo, NY, Prometheus Books, 1985.

Myrdal, Gunnar, with Richard Sterner and Arnold Rose. *An American Dilemma: The Negro Problem and Modern Democracy*. New York: Harper and Brothers, 1944.

Olmsted, Frederick Law. *A Journey in the Seaboard Slave States: With Remarks on Their Economy*. Reprint. New York: Cambridge University Press, 2009.

Pipes, Kasey S. *Ike's Final Battle: The Road to Little Rock and the Challenge of Equality*. Los Angeles: CA, World Ahead Publishing, 2007.

Pitch, Anthony S. *The Last Lynching: How a Gruesome Mass Murder Rocked a Small Georgia Town*. New York, NY: Skyhorse Publishing, 2016.

Radelet, Michael, and Vandiver, Margaret. *Race and Capital Punishment: An Overview of the Issues*. 1986
http://www.jstor.org/stable/29766297

Robbins, Rossell H. *The Encyclopedia of Witchcraft & Demonology*. New York: Bonanza Books, 1981.

Rushton, J. Philippe. *Race, Evolution and Behavior: A Life History Perspective*. Port Huron, MI: Charles Darwin Research Institute, 1994.

Russell, Jeffrey B. *Lucifer: The Devil in the Middle Ages*. Ithaca, NY: Cornell University Press, 1984.

Shawki, Ahmed. *Black Liberalism and Socialism*. Chicago: Haymarket Books, 2005.

Shufeldt, Robert W. *America's Greatest Problem: The Negro*. Philadelphia: Davis, 1915.

Smith, Lillian. *Killers of the Dream*. New York: W. W. Norton Company, 1994.

Thornely, Samuel, ed. The *Journal of Nicholas Cresswell, 1774–1777*. Carlisle, Massachusetts: Applewood Press, 1924.

Tissot, Samuel Auguste David. *A Treatise on the Diseases Produced by Onanism* New York: Collins and Hannay, 1832.

Wells-Barnett, Ida. *A Red Record: A Tabulated Statistics and Alleged Causes of Lynching in the United States, 1892–1894*. Salt Lake City, UT: Project Guttenberg, 1895.

West, Cornel. *Race Matters*. Boston: Beacon Press, 1993.

White, Walter. *Rope and Faggot: A Biography of Judge Lynch*. Notre Dame, IN: University of Notre Dame Press, 1992.

Wicker, Tom: *A Time to Die: The Attica Prison Revolt*. Chicago: Haymarket Books, 2011.

Wood, Amy L. *Lynching and Spectacle: Witnessing Racial Violence in America, 1890–1940*. Chapel Hill: NC, University of North Carolina Press, 2009.

CPSIA information can be obtained
at www.ICGtesting.com
Printed in the USA
BVHW012047160721
612125BV00003B/237

9 781737 537328